Marine Control Practice

Marine Engineering Series

Marine Auxiliary Machinery — 6th edition
David W. Smith, CEng, MIMarE

Pounder's Marine Diesel Engines — 6th edition
C. T. Wilbur, CEng, MIMarE and
D. A. Wight, BSc, CEng, MIMechE, FIMarE

Marine Electrical Practice — 5th edition
G. O. Watson, FIEE, FAIEE, FIMarE

Marine and Offshore Corrosion
K. A. Chandler, BSc, CEng, FIM, ARSM, FICorrT

Marine and Offshore Pumping and Piping Systems
J. Crawford, CEng, FIMarE

Marine Steam Boilers — 4th edition
J. H. Milton, CEng, FIMarE and
Roy M. Leach, CEng, MIMechE, FIMarE

Marine Steam Engines and Turbines — 4th edition
S. C. McBirnie, CEng, FIMechE

Merchant Ship Stability
Alan Lester, Extra Master, BA(Hons), MRINA, MNI

Marine Control Practice

D.A. Taylor
MSc, BSc, CEng, MIMarE, MRINA
Senior Lecturer in Marine Technology,
Hong Kong Polytechnic

BUTTERWORTHS
London—Boston—Durban—Singapore—Sydney—Toronto—Wellington

All rights reserved. No part of this publication may be reproduced or transmitted in any form or by any means, including photocopying and recording, without the written permission of the copyright holder, application for which should be addressed to the Publishers. Such written permission must also be obtained before any part of this publication is stored in a retrieval system of any nature.

This book is sold subject to the Standard Conditions of Sale of Net Books and may not be re-sold in the UK below the net price given by the Publishers in their current price list.

First published 1987

© Butterworth & Co (Publishers) Ltd, 1987

British Library Cataloguing in Publication Data

Taylor, D.A.
    Marine control practice.—(Marine
engineering series)
    1. Marine engineering
    I. Title   II. Series
    623.8'5   VM605

    ISBN 0–408–01313–3

Library of Congress Cataloging-in-Publication Data

Taylor, D. A., M.Sc.
    Marine control practice.

    (Marine engineering series)
    Includes index.
    1. Marine engines—Automatic control.   I. Title.
II. Series
VM731.T36   1987   623.85   86-31737
ISBN 0–408–01313–3

Phottypeset by Scribe Design, Gillingham, Kent
Printed in England by Anchor-Brendon Ltd, Tiptree, Essex

Preface

Any engineer who has ever glanced at a thermometer or a pressure gauge knows the value of instrumentation and ultimately the control of the parameters that influence machinery operation. This book progressively deals with instrumentation, control theory, control equipment and the control systems to be found on board ship. The final chapter examines microprocessors and computer control applications.

The text aims to cover the requirements for all the Certificates of Competency for Marine Engineers, including Extra First Class. Additional material and a deeper theoretical study is provided in areas where this is required for Higher Technical Certificates and Diplomas and Degree course syllabuses. The approach used is largely practical, dealing with actual equipment, its operation and maintenance. Where inevitably a mathematical approach is required this is combined with illustrations and examples to assist in understanding. Some advice on the use of this text for various courses is given at the end of Chapter 1.

While primarily aimed at the marine engineer it is hoped this book will also be of use to those involved in offshore engineering and any mechanical engineering field where the operating environment is severe.

Instrumentation and its associated control systems are increasing in use and application. The techniques used and the application of computerization are advancing the subject almost daily. The structured use of this text should enable the would-be, and the practising, marine engineer to understand what currently exists, and be prepared for what is to come.

D.A. Taylor

Contents

Acknowledgements

I would like to thank the many firms, organizations and individuals who have provided me with assistance and material during the writing of this book; in particular, my colleague Mr Tony Naylor, whose expert comments on the electronics material in Chapter 4 were most helpful.

To my many other colleagues and friends who have answered numerous queries and added their wealth of experience, I am most grateful.

The following firms have provided information on their products for which I thank them:

Advies-en Verkoopbureau voor
    Drijfwerkonderdelen bv
Alan Cobham Engineering Ltd
APV Hall International Ltd
ASEA Industries Ltd
Autronica A.S.
Babcock-Bristol Ltd
Bailey and Mackey Ltd
Bell and Howell
Benmar H & P Ltd
Bestobell Mobrey
Blakell (T.I.G.D.) Ltd
Blohm and Voss AG
Bowden Controls
Brown Brothers and Co. Ltd
Capper Neill Controls Ltd
CGEE Alsthom
Commercial Hydraulics Ltd
Commercial Shearing Inc.
Danfoss
Detector Electronics (U.K.) Ltd
Diamond Power Speciality Ltd
Draeger Manufacturing
Eagle Process Controls Ltd
EIL Analytical Instruments
Fiber-optic AG
Foster Wheeler Power Products Ltd
Foxboro Far East Pte. Ltd
Graviner Ltd

Hamworthy Engineering Ltd,
    Combustion Division
Hamworthy Engineering Ltd, Pumps and
    Compressors Division
Haven Automation Ltd
Haven Automation (H.K.) Ltd
Honeywell Controls Systems Ltd
Horiba Instruments Ltd
IMI Norgren Enots Ltd
ITT Conoflow VAF
Kent Industrial Measurements Ltd
Kent Meters Ltd
H. Maihak AG
Martonair Overseas Ltd
Moore Products Co. (U.K.) Ltd
MSW Control Instruments Ltd
Murray (Scientific Instruments) Ltd
National Semiconductor Corporation
Negretti and Zambra Ltd
Norcontrol
Normond Instruments Ltd
Perolin Marine
Regulateurs Europa Ltd
Reutlinger
G.L. Rexroth Ltd
Riley Corporation
Rotork Controls Ltd
Saab-Scania
Salen and Wincander (H.K.) Ltd

Saunders Valve Co. Ltd
Seetru Ltd
Siemens Ltd
Stal Refrigeration AB
Stal Laval Turbin AB
SMM Engineering Ltd
Taylor Instruments Ltd
George Taylor (Brass Founders) Ltd
Telegan Ltd

Telektron Ltd
Vibro-meter S.A.
Walton Engineering Co. Ltd
Westinghouse Brake and Signal Co. Ltd
Westinghouse Electric Corporation,
   Combustion Control Division
Whessoe Systems and Controls Ltd
Young and Cunningham Ltd

A special thank you goes to my wife, Jill, for her efforts on the word processor, which produced a readable manuscript from my untidy scribble.

1 Introduction

Marine engineers have always exercised control over the many items of machinery and equipment on board ship. Initially the controlling actions took place close to the equipment and were manual. Gradually, the use of remote operating devices led to controls being grouped at some convenient location. Automatic remote control ultimately followed with the location of equipment and the engineer in a machinery control room. The engineer's role then became more supervisory in nature, in that he monitored all the information provided and was often able to bring about corrective action without leaving the machinery control room. This monitoring role can now be undertaken by a computer-controlled system which will inform the engineer of any fault and detail the location. It therefore remains for the engineer to be available to remedy faults when they are brought to his notice by the monitoring system.

Condition monitoring systems are now available that can give considerable warning of impending problems or the need for maintenance. This, nevertheless, still means that the engineer must undertake the repairs and maintenance, although he is now usually able to plan and coordinate his activities to gain the maximum benefits from his skills. There is also the fact that automatic control systems, no matter what the degree of sophistication, do occasionally break down. Manual operation by a skilled engineer is the ultimate fail-safe. It is interesting to note that some of the latest microprocessor-based equipment is now able to monitor itself during operation and also transfer to a spare circuit incorporated within the unit should a failure occur. The modern marine engineer, therefore, must first be fully trained and conversant with all the machinery he is required to operate. Secondly, he must be aware of the instrumentation, control equipment and control systems used in conjunction with that machinery. It is to this second requirement that this book will address itself.

A ship is designed to be an efficient, economic, cargo carrier which travels the oceans of the world. Its cargo may be determined by the vessel design, its trade routes may be similarly restricted, but it must operate in an environment that is perhaps the most severe for any transport vehicle. Its operators must live on board for many weeks or months at a time with its equipment functioning all this time. Control systems have been developed to enable unattended operation of much of the machinery and equipment to ease the burden of the ship's staff and also reduce their numbers. Such methods of operation are, of course, carefully regulated by various authorities to ensure safe operation of the vessel. Each of these particular aspects will now be considered in further detail before examining the actual techniques employed in measurement, signal transmission and control.

SHIPS

The modern ship is a large complex vehicle which must be self-sustaining for long periods with a high degree of reliability. The marine engineer is responsible for the various systems which propel and operate the ship. To be precise, this means the machinery required for propulsion, steering, anchoring and ship securing, cargo handling, air conditioning, power generation and its distribution. All this equipment is, to varying degrees, automatically controlled. The particular type of vessel, e.g. oil tanker or refrigerated cargo vessel, may result in different systems. A marine engineer, however, is not confined to any one type of ship and must, therefore, be familiar with all kinds of systems on all types of ships.

The principal division usually used by marine engineers relates to the type of propulsion of the vessel. The broad classes are steam, slow speed diesel and medium speed diesel. Associated with each of these propulsion units will be appropriate auxiliaries essential to the total plant. A steam turbine vessel will have high pressure, high temperature, water tube boilers, a condenser, the various pumps and other items in the closed feed system and various steam driven auxiliaries. Slow and medium speed diesels vary little beyond the main propulsion units. Diesel driven alternators and electrically operated auxiliaries are usual, together with exhaust gas driven boilers. Sufficient steam is often obtained to operate a turbo alternator when at sea.

Three principal cargo carrying types of ship exist today, the general cargo vessel, the bulk carrier (liquid or solid) and the passenger vessel. The particular classification will bring with it appropriate systems for cargo handling and cargo conditioning. Cargo handling requirements would include pumping systems for bulk liquid carriers or hatch operating and cargo lifting equipment for general cargo carriers. Cargo conditioning would relate to air conditioning and refrigeration systems for perishable cargoes and sometimes even heating systems. The passenger ship would have a requirement for reduced ship motions, using stabilizers for passenger comfort. Many ferries are fitted with controllable pitch propellers for improved manoeuvrability although the use of this device has occasionally been extended to almost all types of vessel.

MANNING

The numbers of personnel in the various departments of a ship have all been drastically reduced in recent years. One engineer is now considered capable of standing watch alone. He is considerably assisted by the increased amount of automatically controlled equipment and systems and the remote operating features provided. Much of his supervisory work can be accomplished within the machinery control room although occasional visual checks are to be recommended. It has not so far been considered necessary to carry instrument or electronic engineering specialists on board ships. The marine engineer has been expected to operate, maintain and repair his control equipment. This has led to simplified repair-by-replacement of modules in control units or systems owing to the high level of knowledge and skill that would be required for an actual component replacement or repair. Whatever maintenance method is adopted the need for adequate supplies of appropriate spares is evident.

Specialized courses are now provided for marine engineers in order to update and further their knowledge of control systems and equipment. Marine Electronics Technicians courses are now provided by many marine colleges which will ultimately provide suitable personnel to maintain and service some of the specialized control equipment on board ship. It remains to be seen whether the marine engineer becomes more of a control equipment expert, at the expense of engineering knowledge, or whether a specialist control engineer is employed.

ENVIRONMENT

The marine environment and the ship's operating conditions present one of the most severe situations that any instrument or item of

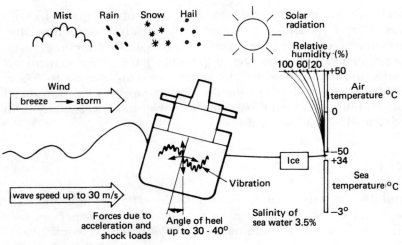

Figure 1.1 The marine environment

equipment must accept (see Figure 1.1). Equipment that has been operating satisfactorily ashore may immediately fail when used on board ship. The rules of the various classification societies attempt to ensure that equipment is suitable for its purpose. The national authorities, e.g. Department of Transport, UK, or US Coastguard, USA, produce regulations which are mandatory for equipment fitted on their vessels or vessels entering their ports. Consideration will now be given to the various aspects of the environment and the motion of the vessel.

Attitude and motion

A ship is free to move with six degrees of freedom—three linear and three rotational, see Figure 1.2. The linear motions are known as surge, sway and heave. The rotational motions are roll, pitch and

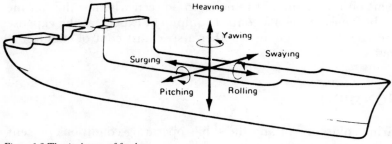

Figure 1.2 The six degrees of freedom

yaw. All six motions may be taking place in addition to the forward motion of the vessel. Marine equipment is required to function at an inclination of 22.5° to the vertical in any direction. While ships rarely reach this angle in normal operation it is possible that listing during cargo handling operations could be considerable. Any instrument, for example, must therefore function correctly, and within its specific accuracy limits, at this inclination. Dynamic forces resulting from the ship's motion must be damped out. Roll and pitch periods will vary for different sizes and loaded conditions of ships. The damping periods may be short, say a few seconds, or as long as 30 or more seconds. Acceleration forces in excess of $1\,g$ ($g = 9.81$ m/s^2) can occur and cause damage to floats, meter mechanisms and valves. Shock loads can occur due to slamming and so testing using pulses up to $15\,g$ has been considered. Equipment installed in tanks must withstand the surging effects of the liquids present. The cleaning systems employed in cargo oil tanks, i.e. crude oil washing using jets of hot liquid, also presents a special hazard for equipment in these areas.

Vibration

Vibration is always present to some degree in a ship's structure. It may be induced in the hull by waves or from the blades of the rotating propeller. Particular parts of the ship's structure may even resonate at or near propeller- or wave-induced frequencies. If equipment is located in such places it will constantly fail and the only solution may be to re-site it. Pumps, auxiliary engines, fans, etc. may create localized vibration problems resulting in malfunction or damage to adjacent equipment. Plugs and pin fitting devices should be secured in place otherwise they may float free at a particular frequency. The use of suitable vibration absorption pads may solve the problems for smaller items of equipment.

Moisture

Water in its various forms will adversely affect equipment, resulting in loss of insulation, oxidation, swelling, etc. Humidity tests are required on instruments which produce condensation at several different times. A salt-laden atmosphere may result in drops of moisture being deposited on instruments. Coating of electrical or electronic equipment may offer adequate protection or in some instances heating elements may be used to keep the equipment dry. Seals and gaskets which are used to exclude moisture must be suitable for their location and purpose. The need for dry air to operate pneumatic equipment is discussed in detail in a later chapter. Salt water can create electrolytic corrosion which may be severe depending upon the materials involved. This is in addition to the oxidation or rusting process that will occur because of the presence of moisture.

Temperature

The variation in temperature between the many compartments of a ship can be considerable. A liquefied gas cargo may be carried at $-161°$ Centigrade while an engine exhaust may register $400°$ Centigrade. Instruments may be located in a control room under almost ideal conditions or on an exposed deck subject to tropical or arctic temperatures. A maximum ambient temperature for internally installed equipment might be $55°$ Centigrade. An acceptable operating range for an exposed instrument may be $-25°$ to $+70°$ Centigrade. Instruments intended for extreme temperature duties will usually be tested for a number of hours at that temperature. Electronic components have operating temperature ranges of $-55°$ to about $+125°$ Centigrade.

Mains supply

A ship's electrical power supply can fluctuate both in terms of voltage and frequency. Transients may occur of considerable magnitude although short duration. The classification societies require certain specifications to be met but they do not cover all eventualities. Particularly sensitive electronic equipment may be adversely affected or damaged by large value, short duration current pulses. This topic is discussed in more detail in a later chapter.

Location

Two particular aspects of location are considered, namely the degree of exposure and hazardous areas. Equipment on the open deck must be watertight and also sufficiently strong to withstand pounding by waves. There is also the possibility of physical damage due to cargo working operations in the vicinity. Where instruments or equipment are located in hazardous areas they must be to the appropriate standards. Again classification society rules must be followed in this matter but often instruments must meet more stringent requirements than equipment such as motors.

TOTAL CONTROL

The steering gear was probably the first automatically controlled system on a ship. Control then spread to other individual systems and was then centralized in the machinery control room. The sophistication of modern control systems and the reliability of the equipment used has reached the point where the machinery space can remain unattended for considerable periods of time. In order to ensure the safety of the ship and its equipment during unattended machinery space (UMS) operation certain essential requirements must be met:

1. *Bridge control.* A control system to operate the main machinery must be provided on the bridge. Instrumentation providing certain basic information must also be provided.
2. *Machinery control room.* A centralized control room must be provided with the equipment to operate all main and auxiliary machinery easily accessible.
3. *Alarm and fire protection.* An alarm system is required which must be comprehensive in coverage of the equipment and able to provide warnings in the control room, the machinery space, the accommodation and on the bridge. A fire detection and alarm system which operates rapidly must also be provided throughout the machinery space, and a fire control point must be provided outside the machinery space with facilities for control of emergency equipment.
4. *Electrical power.* Automatic provision of electrical power to meet the varying load requirements. A means of providing emergency power and essential lighting must be provided. This is usually met by the automatic start-up of a standby generator.

Equipment operation from the machinery control room will be by a trained engineer. The various preparatory steps and logical timed sequence of events which an engineer will undertake cannot be expected to occur when equipment is operated from the bridge. Bridge control must therefore have appropriate circuits built into the system to provide the correct timing, logic and sequence. There must also be protection devices and safety interlocks built into the system.

The main propulsion engine is operated and its essential parameters are monitored from the bridge, see Figure 1.3. Where a controllable pitch propeller is fitted, this too is operated from the bridge and the steering gear always has been.

The automatic provision of electrical power to meet varying load demands can be achieved by performing the following functions automatically:

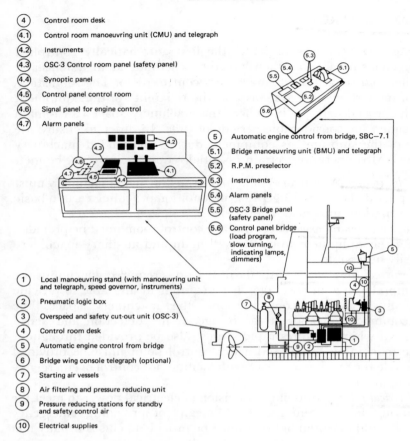

4 — Control room desk
4.1 — Control room manoeuvring unit (CMU) and telegraph
4.2 — Instruments
4.3 — OSC-3 Control room panel (safety panel)
4.4 — Synoptic panel
4.5 — Control panel control room
4.6 — Signal panel for engine control
4.7 — Alarm panels

5 — Automatic engine control from bridge, SBC–7.1
5.1 — Bridge manoeuvring unit (BMU) and telegraph
5.2 — R.P.M. preselector
5.3 — Instruments
5.4 — Alarm panels
5.5 — OSC-3 Bridge panel (safety panel)
5.6 — Control panel bridge (load program, slow turning, indicating lamps, dimmers)

1 — Local manoeuvring stand (with manoeuvring unit and telegraph, speed governor, instruments)
2 — Pneumatic logic box
3 — Overspeed and safety cut-out unit (OSC-3)
4 — Control room desk
5 — Automatic engine control from bridge
6 — Bridge wing console telegraph (optional)
7 — Starting air vessels
8 — Air filtering and pressure reducing unit
9 — Pressure reducing stations for standby and safety control air
10 — Electrical supplies

Figure 1.3 Bridge control system

1. Prime mover start-up.
2. Synchronizing of incoming machine with bus-bars.
3. Load sharing between alternators.
4. Safety and operational checks on power supply and equipment in operation.
5. Unloading, stopping and returning to standby of surplus machines.
6. Preferential tripping of non-essential loads under emergency conditions and their reinstating when acceptable.

The ultimate goal in the centralized control room concept is to perform and monitor every possible operation remotely from this location. This inevitably results in a vast amount of information reaching the control room, more than the engineer supervisor might reasonably be expected to observe continuously. It is therefore usual to incorporate data recording and alarm systems in control rooms. The alarm system enables the monitoring of certain measured variables over a set period and the readings obtained are compared with some reference or set value. Where a fault is located, i.e. a measured value outside the set value, audible and visual alarms are given and a printout of the fault and the time of occurrence is produced. Data recording or data logging is the production of measured variable information either automatically at set intervals or on demand.

CONTROL MEDIA

Control is accomplished by the use of a suitable medium for the transmission of signals and actuation of equipment. The earliest forms of control used mechanical linkages and these are still occasionally to be seen on some equipment. The three commonly used control media are compressed air, hydraulic oil and electricity. Fibre optics is a recently developed medium which is now finding favour in some applications. Each has its particular disadvantages and in a particular system more than one medium may be in use.

Compressed air

Compressed air has been widely adopted as a control medium for marine applications. It is, however, gradually being replaced as a transmission medium by solid state electronic equipment. Compressed air provides relatively cheap linear or semi-rotary actuators. It provides a reasonable power for a given size and the equipment used is simple and easy to understand and maintain. Air is light, clean, readily and freely available, almost unaffected by temperature change and presents no hazards if it leaks. Air can be stored in receivers to meet peak requirements or continue operation during compressor breakdowns. The compressors used are, however, expensive and must be supplied in duplicate. Filtration is a constant, expensive task since the air is not recycled. Where long piping runs are used this is expensive and any leaks are very difficult to trace. Power transmission using compressed air can be inefficient and slow and transient conditions can create problems. In the event of an air supply failure any fail-safe or maintaining of the current conditions may be difficult to arrange. Compressed air as a control medium is usually associated with operation by variation of pressure in the system. It can, however, also be used in logic devices as a fluidic medium and provide control in this manner.

Hydraulic oil

Hydraulic oil is normally used to provide high output powers using linear or semi-rotary actuators. It provides a fast, smooth, highly efficient operation and the actuator is self lubricating. Oil supply failure can be accepted since fail-safe or maintaining the current conditions is easily achieved. It may be possible in some systems to use the lubricating oil supply as the source of hydraulic oil; otherwise, expensive high pressure pumping plant is necessary. The oil is expensive, can be messy if leaks occur, and absolute cleanliness of the system is essential. The system performance can be affected by temperature changes which will alter the viscosity of the oil. Any system leaks may present a hazard to personnel and also a fire risk.

Electricity

Electricity is becoming the most widely used transmission medium. It is readily available, not normally contaminated, is carried in cables which are not easily damaged and does not leak in the sense that oil or air might. Signal transmission is rapid and distortion-free, the equipment used is becoming cheaper and cheaper and is extremely flexible in its design. Electricity is ideally suited for two-position or logic purposes, resulting in many applications for indicating, alarm and recording equipment and systems. Often the equipment is quite complex and in the event of failure is simply replaced by a new module. Neither large forces nor torques can be provided by electrical equipment. Actuators, where they are used, tend to be large, heavy and expensive and usually only provide rotary output. Supply failure can be difficult to guard against, mainly because of the need for almost instantaneous changeover with some electronic equipment. The use of electricity is not permitted in some areas of a ship where it is considered as a hazard.

Fibre optics

Fibre optics, the use of glass fibres to transmit control signals which exist as light, is a medium which is gaining popularity. Light from a solid state source, e.g. a diode or laser, is pulsed at high frequency using an electro-optical converter. The light signal is then fed into an optical fibre cable and travels along it. At the receiving end the light signal is converted back into an electrical signal, usually by a light-sensitive diode. Particular advantages include the absence of any interference from electrical or electromagnetic effects.

REGULATION AND CLASSIFICATION

Automatic control, whatever form it takes, is a concern of the regulatory authorities, e.g. Department of Transport in the UK, and the classification societies, e.g. Lloyd's, Bureau Veritas, etc. The International Maritime Organization (IMO), through its various conventions, imposes requirements which may affect control systems. These requirements are usually enforced by the national authority or by delegation to a classification society.

The major classification societies, for example, have requirements relating to visual inspection of equipment, its performance, a dry heat test, a humidity test and so on. These tests are largely to ensure that equipment can withstand the severe marine environment conditions which have been discussed earlier. Surveyors are usually in attendance during the building of a vessel and later for surveys at regular periods. Equipment and systems installed must meet the classification society's requirements as interpreted by the surveyor. Type approval is also granted to equipment that has been subjected to the various environmental tests under the supervision of classification society surveyors.

The regulatory authorities are particularly concerned with the safety aspects of control systems and, unlike the classification societies, their requirements are mandatory. An example of a Department of Transport (UK) requirement is that all alarms should automatically reset when the fault is rectified.

Perhaps the most comprehensive guide to equipment selection, installation and commissioning is the book *Recommended Code of Procedure for Marine Instrumentation and Control Equipment*, produced by the British Ship Research Association.

TERMINOLOGY

The subject of control engineering has its own specialist terms or jargon, which must be clearly understood. Most terms are explained as they are introduced and then occur again later in the text. To enable easy reference to definitions, a glossary of terms is provided as an appendix. Some of the definitions used here are taken from British Standards—in particular BS 1523:1967 *Glossary of Terms used in Automatic Controlling and Regulating Systems*, Part 1 and Section 5. They are reproduced by permission of the British Standards Institution, 2 Park Street, London W1Y 4AA, from whom copies of the complete standard may be obtained.

An understanding of computers and computing also requires a knowledge of a considerable number of specialist terms. These are provided as a separate glossary in the appendix. They are not, as yet, the subject of a British Standard and therefore the definitions given are simply based on current usage.

USE OF THE TEXT

This book contains a variety of material and covers a range of different courses. It is primarily intended for the marine engineer and his studies leading to the different Certificates of Competency.

The Class 4 Certificate is obtained by oral examination and is largely based on questions relating to ships that the candidate has sailed upon. A knowledge of Chapters 1, 2, 3 and some of the systems in Chapter 9 should be sufficient.

The Class 3 Certificate consists of written papers, and the Engineering Knowledge paper requires an understanding of the operation, testing and fault rectification of automatic control and alarm panels. Chapters 1, 2, 3 and parts of chapters 8 and 9 should be adequate.

The Class 2 certificate features at least one control question in the General Engineering Knowledge paper. It should be noted that an occasional question appears in the Motor or Steam Engineering Knowledge paper. The syllabus requires a knowledge of instrumentation, control systems, automation, unattended machinery space operation, and bridge control. Candidates for this examination should be familiar with the contents of Chapters 1, 2, 3, 6, 7, 8 and 9. The Electrotechnology syllabus requires a knowledge of electronics, some of which is covered in Chapter 4. Reference to recent examination papers should also be made, in order to note the areas which are of specific interest to the examiners and the level of knowledge required.

The Class 1 Certificate uses a similar examining technique to the Class 2 and the syllabus requirements are the same. Greater emphasis is usually placed on control systems, which are featured in Chapters 9 and 10. Occasionally questions refer to instrumentation and control equipment, therefore Chapters 1, 2, 3, 6, 7 and 8 must also be studied.

The Electrotechnology syllabus requires a knowledge of electronics, some of which is covered in Chapter 4. Again, it is important to examine recent examination papers and note the topics being covered.

The Extra First Class Certificate candidate will require knowledge of the complete text. The Theory of Machines and Electrotechnology papers both include automatic control and varying aspects of systems analysis in their syllabuses. Instrumentation is also a part of the Electrotechnology syllabus.

Engineer Cadets who are following courses leading to Higher Technician Diplomas and Certificates will find additional material is provided in this text for the deeper coverage required by their syllabuses.

Undergraduate Engineers should also find this text of value. The practical nature of much of the topic coverage will be of advantage once they are face to face with an actual system and its hardware.

2 Measurement and control

The concept of measurement, and what it represents, is first considered. A measuring system is necessary to obtain an actual measurement and the components of this system are examined. The performance of a measuring system is then reviewed with reference to both static and dynamic characteristics. Measurement is next considered as part of a control system, together with the other elements in the loop. The characteristics, response, controller action and stability in a control system are then described. This chapter provides a general introduction to topics which will be expanded upon later in the text.

MEASUREMENT

Information is the basis of all control. Instrumentation is the use of instruments to obtain this information. Measurement, a comparison with a basis or standard, is the key to satisfactory instrumentation. Accurate measurement of the various parameters in a control system is therefore the first requirement. This will necessitate a knowledge of the parameter to be measured, e.g. pressure, temperature, flow, and the standards used as a basis for the measurement. The functional elements which enable the measurement to be taken must be examined, i.e. the measurement system, and their actions understood. Then it will be necessary to determine how the actual measuring system performs as compared with an ideal measuring system. When all of these factors are established and in some way specified then suitable instruments can be selected for particular measuring duties. The actual measuring instrument may then act either as an indicating instrument or as a recording instrument. An indicating instrument will visually display the measured value but no record is kept, e.g. Bourdon-tube pressure gauge, voltmeter, liquid-in-glass thermometer. A recording instrument will provide some form of permanent record of measurements taken over a period of time.

Standards

Any reading given on a measuring instrument must be related to some accepted standard in order to be meaningful. All scales, graduations and markings are in some unit of measurement which can be related back to a standard of basis for the parameter under consideration.

A primary standard is the accepted basis for the particular parameter, for example, the unit of mass is the kilogramme and the primary standard is a metal cylinder maintained in the International Bureau of Weights and Measures at Sèvres, France. Duplicates of this primary standard are held in other countries under controlled conditions. Some standards are natural ones and can be accurately reproduced anywhere in the world. An example is the fundamental unit of length, the metre, which is equal to 1 650 763.73 wavelengths in vacuum of a particular radiation band emitted by the Krypton 86 atom.

Calibration

Where an instrument has its readings compared with some standard or known value, this is known as calibration. The actual process of calibration may be achieved by the use of a primary or secondary standard. It is usual for the primary standard to be used to calibrate a secondary or working standard. The working standard is then used for instrument calibration. The accuracy of the instrument can thus be traced back to the primary standard.

The measuring system

Any single item or number of items which provide a measurement can be considered as a measuring system. All such systems are made up of three basic functional elements—a transducer, a signal modifier or conditioner, and an indicator or recorder. These basic elements may in turn be further subdivided to identify all possible functions in the measuring system.

The transducer both detects and measures the particular variable (the measurand), and then may convert the signal received into a readily usable form. The usual forms of transducer output are either mechanical or electrical signals. Most transducers can be considered as made up of a sensing element and some form of conversion element. Consider, as an example, a diaphragm which senses a pressure change by deflecting and converting the pressure into a displacement. The sensor in a transducer usually extracts energy from the measured medium and thus changes it in some way. It is, therefore, virtually impossible to make a perfect measurement and this modifying or 'loading' effect, as it is called, must be minimized by careful design and installation of the transducer.

The signal modifier or conditioner will convert the transduced signal into a form suitable for transmission or to enable suitable recording or monitoring. This element may not be readily identifiable in some measuring systems or might be considered part of the transducer. Other measuring systems may require several modifications of the signal at different stages in the transmission, recording or monitoring. The modifying of the signal, as well as changing its physical form, may result in a numerical manipulation, e.g. it may be magnified by some ratio (amplified).

The indicator or recorder provides a visual display of the measurand. The recorder will, in addition, provide some record of the measurand on a chart or roll of paper as the measurand varies with time. Within the actual device there may be further signal modification in order to give the final presentation in some observable form.

The various functional elements so far described do not all necessarily have a physical element associated with them. One physical element may, for example, provide a signal which has been

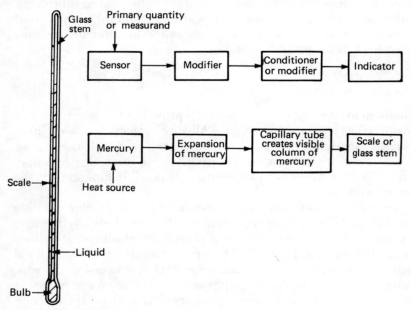

Figure 2.1 Temperature measuring system

sensed, modified and amplified. An example of a measuring system and its related elements is given in Figure 2.1.

The measuring system can also be classified by its mode of operation and measurement. The signals which provide the measuring information may be continuous or discrete in nature. A continuous signal can provide an infinite variety of values and is called an analogue signal. Discrete signals vary in steps and are thus limited in their possible values. When discrete signals are represented by a number, usually in the form of a code, they are called digital signals. A Bourdon-tube type of pressure gauge is an example of an analogue-type measuring instrument, while an engine revolution counter is a digital device. An increasing number of measuring systems are making use of digital signals because of the ease with which this information can be fed into computers and data-loggers. The existence and use of considerable amounts of analogue equipment does require the use of 'translators' which provide either analogue-to-digital or digital-to-analogue signal conversion. Two methods of measurement are also possible—null and deflection. A deflection device will have the measured quantity produce an effect which is physically detectable. Referring to the thermometer in Figure 2.1, the application of heat expands the mercury which rises up the capillary tube to enable a reading of the new level against the scale on the glass. A null-type device, however, will establish a zero deflection by creating an effect which nullifies or balances that of the measured quantity. A necessary requirement in such a device is some detector of imbalance and a means of restoring the balance which is accurately known in numerical terms. An example of such a device is a chemical balance which has a centrally pivoted beam with a pan hung from each end. The unknown mass is placed in one pan and known weights are added to the other until a needle at the pivot point (the detector of imbalance) is vertical.

SYSTEM PERFORMANCE

The selection of a particular instrument or measuring system will be based upon its suitability for the chosen task. Some measure of performance is therefore required in quantitative terms to enable comparisons to be made. An ideal measuring system would produce an output signal or value which had a linear relationship with the input or measurand. Also the output must faithfully follow the input during any variations that might occur. The indicated value for the instrument should always equal the measurand, i.e. there should be no errors present. No such ideal measuring system exists and it serves, therefore, only as a basis for comparison. The difference in value between the actual and the ideal is usually expressed in terms of errors. Other criteria in addition to simple numerical error are given when describing a system's performance and these are referred to as characteristics. These characteristics are generally divided into static and dynamic. Where the measured quantity is fairly constant, or varies only slowly, the measuring system can be adequately described by the use of static characteristics. Where a measurement of a rapidly changing quantity is required then the dynamic characteristics of the system are important. All measuring systems contain aspects of both types of performance characteristic and overall performance is then some combination of the two. It is mainly a matter of expediency to discuss certain aspects of measurement as static characteristics, e.g. accuracy and hysteresis, and others as dynamic, e.g. transient response and time constant.

Static characteristics

The various static characteristics of a measuring unit or system all result from a static calibration process. In this static calibration the main input is set to a number of different constant values while all other possible inputs are held constant. For instance, if pressure measurement is the main input, then temperature and any other variables are expected to remain constant or have a negligible effect. A number of different steady values of presure will then be used as inputs to the measuring system. The input to output relationship is obtained and is a static calibration obtained under the specified conditions.

Static sensitivity
As a result of the static calibration of a measuring system a calibration curve can be drawn. The slope or gradient of this line will be the static sensitivity. Where the curve is not linear the sensitivity will vary according to the input value. A correct measurement of sensitivity would give the relationship between the actual physical output, e.g. the angular deflection of the pointer, and the input; although often the scale reading provided is used. Where several elements in a system have static sensitivities and are connected in series then the static sensitivity of the system is the product of the individual values. This assumes that the loading effects between the elements are taken into account. Where the input and output to an element are in the same

physical form then the term 'gain' can be used. Other terms used with a similar meaning are 'magnification' and 'amplification'.

Linearity is a term associated with sensitivity and is a measure of the maximum deviation from a linear input/output relationship, usually expressed as a percentage of full scale.

Accuracy, precision and error

No measuring system is perfect and therefore no measurement is exactly correct. *Accuracy* therefore is an indication of the nearness with which the true value is measured.

The term *precision*, while associated with accuracy, does not mean the same thing. Where, for the same input, applied on a number of occasions, an instrument provides readings which are very close in value, it is said to have high precision. If however a zero error offset existed, i.e. for a zero of measured value the instrument gave a reading either above or below zero, then the instrument could not be said to be accurate, although of high precision. *Reproducibility* is a general term used with regard to precision and provides a measure of the closeness of readings given for a constant input. *Repeatability* refers to reproducibility when a constant input is repeatedly applied for short time intervals under fixed conditions. *Stability* concerns repeatability when the constant input is applied for a long time compared with the time required to take a reading under fixed conditions. *Constancy* refers to reproducibility when the constant input is provided continuously but the conditions during the measurement are permitted to vary within specified limits.

Errors exist in all measurement units or systems and are the difference between the indicated value and the true value, often expressed as a percentage of full scale deflection.

$$\text{Percentage error} = \frac{\text{Indicated value} - \text{True value}}{\text{Full scale deflection}} \times 100$$

Errors can be the result of incorrect observation, the incorrect position or graduation of a scale, an indication which is found to be incorrect following calibration, or a zero offset error. *Tolerance* is the term used for maximum possible error, in particular with regard to measurements of length. Where several devices are involved in a measuring system they will all introduce errors. It is unlikely that all errors would maximize or minimize together and therefore the system error cannot be determined precisely. The maximum possible error can be determined but the more likely or probable error may be significantly less.

Other terms

If an instrument's output readings were noted for an input increasing from zero to the maximum value and then back down to zero then they may appear as shown in Figure 2.2. If the instrument could read either side of zero and the exercise was continued in a negative sense back to the maximum value then the remainder of the graph could be drawn. This difference in reading for an input as a result of the direction of approach is known as *Hysteresis*. Hysteresis is a result of loading of the measuring instrument and subsequent less-than-complete unloading. The numerical value of hysteresis may be given in terms of output or input (see Figure 2.2) and is usually expressed as a percentage of full scale.

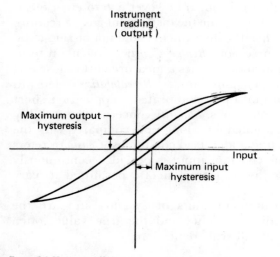

Figure 2.2 Hysteresis effect

Where the input to an instrument is slowly increased from zero, there will be a value below which no output change can be detected. This minimum value is known as the *threshold* of the instrument. The smallest change in input at any other point which can be definitely detected is known as the *resolution* of the instrument.

An instrument will be designed to measure an input variable between certain upper and lower limits. This extent of input values is known as the *span*. The difference between the upper and lower limits of the instrument's displayed measurements or output is called the *range*.

Dynamic characteristics

Where the measurement of a rapidly varying physical parameter is required the dynamic characteristics of the system are important. If a transducer is slow to respond to input signal changes then the measurement obtained may be inaccurate or perhaps useless. The dynamic characteristics of a system are determined by first obtaining a mathematical model. This is normally an ordinary linear differential equation with constant coefficients. Many systems which are different in nature will have mathematical equations of the same form or order. The mathematical model is then subjected to certain test inputs and the responses obtained are the dynamic characteristics. Typical test inputs are the step, ramp and sine wave and are shown in Figure 2.3.

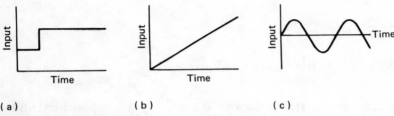

(a)   (b)   (c)

Figure 2.3 Dynamic test inputs: (a) step; (b) ramp; (c) sine wave

The step input is, in effect, a sudden or abrupt change of the input signal from one steady value to another. It is used to test the response of a system to sudden change. The result is a transient and then a steady-state response of the system.

The ramp input varies linearly with time and results in a response which shows the steady-state error in following the input.

The sine wave input shows how the system will respond to inputs of a cyclic nature as the frequency is varied. The frequency response of the system is the result. Frequency responses have considerable practical applications in the analysis and design of control systems.

No system will exactly follow a changing input and dynamic specifications are usually given as parameters related to the input applied. It should be noted that many systems, although different in their physical nature, will have identical forms of response since the systems dynamics are similar. It is usual, therefore, to make reference to the order of a system, using numbers from zero upwards. Systems of the same order will exhibit the same response to test inputs.

A zero-order measuring system has the output directly proportional to the input under all conditions, i.e. $\theta_o = K\theta_i$, where K is the static sensitivity, θ_o is the output variable and θ_i is the input variable. The output, therefore, exactly follows the input without distortion or delay. The zero-order measuring system therefore gives ideal dynamic performance. An example of a zero-order measuring system is the potentiometer, which provides an output voltage proportional to the displacement of the sliding contact, if the input is slow moving.

A first-order measuring system has its input and output related as follows:

$$a\frac{d\theta_o}{dt} + b\theta_o = c\theta_i$$

where a, b and c are constants. Expressed in a more usual or standard form, this becomes:

$$\tau\frac{d\theta_o}{dt} + \theta_o = K\theta_i$$

where $\tau = a/b$ = time constant, in seconds,
$K = c/b$ = constant.

The first-order system response to a step input is exponential and is shown in Figure 2.4(a). The dynamic error is the difference between the ideal and actual responses and this can be seen to decrease with time. One specification parameter used with the step input is the time constant, τ. This is the time taken to reach 63.2 per cent of the final value. This is a time, in seconds, which is independent of the size of the step change.

The system response to a ramp input will, after a short time, be a line parallel to the input, as shown in Figure 2.4(b). The steady-state error is now seen to be constant. The time lag is the time interval between equal values of input and output.

The frequency response is found by applying sine waves of known amplitude as the input and examining the output, as the frequency of the input wave is varied. A typical output response to a sine wave input is shown in Figure 2.4(c). It can be seen that the output lags behind the input and is reduced in amplitude. The ratio of output amplitude to input amplitude is known as the amplitude ratio. As the frequency is increased the output falls further behind and decreases in amplitude. Frequency is thus the independent variable, as opposed to time in the previous two responses.

An example of a first-order measuring system is a liquid-in-glass thermometer. The heat transfer through the sensing bulb to the liquid is described by a first-order differential equation.

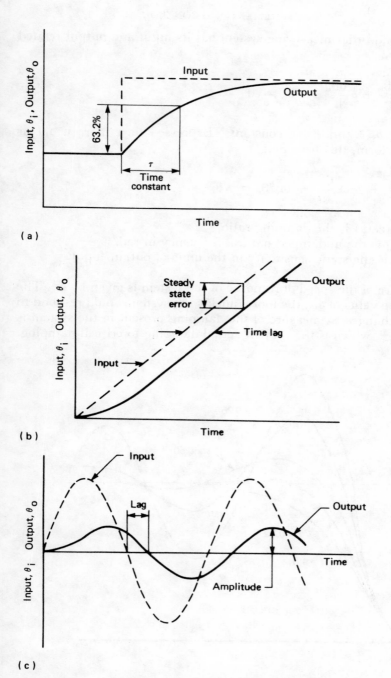

Figure 2.4 *First-order system responses: (a) step; (b) ramp; (c) frequency*

A second-order measuring system has its input and output related as follows:

$$a\frac{d^2\theta_o}{dt^2} + b\frac{d\theta_o}{dt} + c\,\theta_o = e\theta_i$$

where a, b, c and e are constants. Expressed in a more usual or standard form, this becomes:

$$\frac{d^2\theta_o}{dt^2} + 2\xi\omega_n\frac{d\theta_o}{dt} + \omega_n^2\theta_o = K\theta_i$$

where ξ (zeta) is the damping ratio,
ω_n is the undamped natural frequency in rad/s,
K is the static sensitivity in the units of output/input.

A measure of the speed of response of the system is given by ω_n. The higher the value of ω_n, the more quickly the system would respond to sudden changes. A measure of the damping present in the system is given by ξ, which is the ratio of actual damping to critical damping.

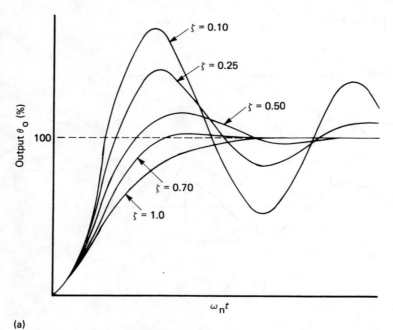

(a)

Figure 2.5 Second-order system responses: (a) step; (b) ramp; (c) frequency

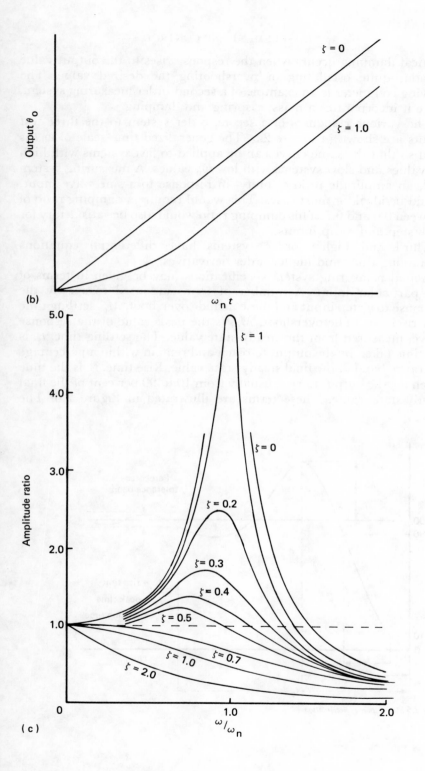

Critical damping occurs when the response rises to the output value without quite oscillating or overshooting the desired value. The moving coil meter is an example of a second-order measuring system, since it incorporates a mass, a spring and damping.

The various responses of a second-order system to the three test inputs are shown in Figure 2.5. The generalized time scale of $\omega_n t$ is used so that the same curve can be applied to fast systems with high ω_n values and slow systems with low ω_n values. A measuring system with an amplitude ratio of unity, in response to a sine wave input, would be ideal for most cases. This would require a damping ratio of between 0.6 and 0.7. This damping ratio would also be satisfactory for both step and ramp inputs.

Third and higher order systems have differential equations containing third and higher order derivatives.

Actual measuring system specifications may be given in terms of the particular input. A number of terms are used to specify the response to a step input and these include overshoot, M_p, settling time and rise time. The overshoot, M_p, is the peak value of the response curve, measured from the steady-state value. The settling time, t_s, is the time taken by the output to reach and remain within a percentage tolerance band of the final steady-state value. Rise time, t_r, is the time taken for the output to rise, usually from 10 to 90 per cent of the final steady-state value. These terms are illustrated in Figure 2.6. The

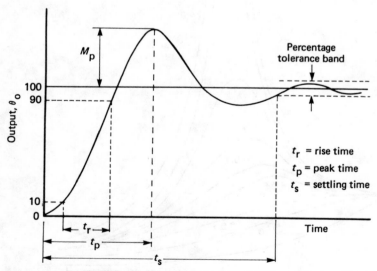

Figure 2.6 Step response specifications

steady-state error is used to specify the response to a ramp input, where

Steady-state error, $e_{ss} = 2\xi/\omega_n$

The frequency response specification is usually given in terms of bandwidth. This is defined as the range of frequencies between which the gain or amplitude ratio is constant to within $-3\,dB$ (i.e. a 30 per cent reduction in gain). Where a device operates from zero frequency upwards an operating range may be defined wherein the gain remains inside a certain tolerance band.

THE CONTROL LOOP

Measurement, in most applications, is part of a control system. The measuring system, comprising a transducer, a signal conditioner and a recording or display unit, will be formed into a loop by the addition of a control element. An engineer may, by his actions in operating valves, etc., act as the control element. This would be considered as manual control. Where it is achieved without human involvement it is referred to as automatic control. Where it is achieved from a distance, but by manual intervention, it is known as remote control. The applications for control are numerous and all involve the adjusting or varying of one or more parameters in a device or system. Most forms of control can be considered to act in a loop. The basic elements in a control loop are a detector or measuring element, a comparator and a regulator, all of which surround the process to form the loop. The representation for each of these items uses blocks which are suitably labelled as shown in Figure 2.7. The loop is considered closed if the elements are directly connected to one another and the control action

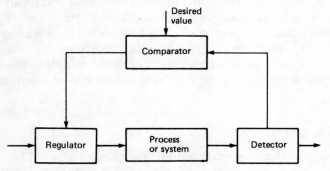

Figure 2.7 Basic elements in a control loop

takes place automatically. An open loop would exist where the output was not fed back into the system, or perhaps where a human operator performed some function to complete the loop.

In closed-loop control, therefore, the control action is dependent upon the output. A detecting or measuring element will obtain a signal related to this output which is fed back to the transmitter. From the transmitter the signal is then passed to a comparator. The comparator is supplied with some set or desired value of the controlled condition which is then compared with the measured value signal. Any deviation or difference between the two values will result in an output signal to the controller. The controller will then act according to the deviation and provide a signal to the correcting unit. The correcting unit will then increase or decrease its effect on the system to achieve the desired value of the system variable. This more involved control loop is shown in Figure 2.8.

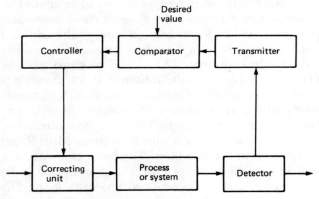

Figure 2.8 Actual elements in a control loop

In a mathematical analysis of the system, the equation or transfer function, which represents the relationship between output and input, for the element, would be shown in the block. The transmitter, controller and correcting unit are each supplied with an operating medium in order to function. This operating medium may be compressed air, hydraulic oil or electricity. For each medium there are various types of transmitting devices, controllers and regulating units in use.

Control loop characteristics

The movement or transfer of signals around the control loop will be subject to various time lags or delays. The action of the controller will also introduce a delay. In addition, the process being controlled may possess some self-regulating or inherent regulating ability. Some knowledge of these process and control system characteristics is therefore necessary in order to achieve the desired degree of control.

Inherent regulation is the ability of a process to reach some equilibrium state following a disturbance, without the application of any form of control. The more inherent regulation present in a system the easier it is to control. The *process reaction rate* is a measure of how quickly the controlled condition can be changed following a disturbance in the system. It is largely governed by the capacity and resistance of the process. A large capacity system would be affected or altered slowly. Resistance in a process control system is usually seen as an opposition to flow. A *distance-velocity* lag is a measure of the time between a process disturbance and its detection, as a result of the distance the disturbance must travel. A *transfer lag* results when energy is transferred through a resistance either to, or from, a process with a capacity. A *measurement lag* occurs between a disturbance occuring and a signal transmission relating to it being provided.

Control system response

In examining or analysing a process, various forms of test input or disturbance are applied and the system response can then be quantified. These test inputs are the same as those used for instruments, namely step, ramp and sinusoidal. The responses were discussed earlier.

Control systems are often referred to in terms of *capacity*. Capacity is the ratio of quantity to potential and exists in many forms, e.g. thermal capacity is given in terms of joules per degree C. Many simple processes deal with a single capacity, or simple control systems operate around a single capacity element. An example would be level control of a tank by varying the supply liquid to match changes in the discharge rate. A single capacity system is easy to control and will respond fairly quickly to load changes; unfortunately it rarely occurs in practice. A *resistance* is some form of opposition, usually to a flow. It is expressed as the potential change required to produce a unit change in flow, e.g. thermal resistance is given in units of degrees C per joule per second. Most control systems involve resistances and capacities in series. These introduce lags into the control system and affect its response to disturbances. The response of a multi-capacity system to a step input gives a very slow start, exactly the opposite effect to a single capacity system.

Controller action

The response of a process or a particular element in a control system will result from the various time and transmission lags that occur and also the nature of the correcting action brought about by the controller. There are various types of controller action, the choice of which will determine how well the control system operates.

Two-step or *on-off* control occurs when there are only extreme positions of the controller available, usually on or off. This type of control is usually only acceptable where a considerable deviation from the desired value is permissible. *Proportional control* action results when any change in controller output is proportional to the deviation between the desired and actual controlled parameter. This type of control will result in a sustained deviation or offset as a result of any load change in a process, i.e. close, but not exact, control about a desired value is possible. *Integral control* occurs when the output varies at a rate proportional to the deviation between the desired and actual controlled parameter. This type of action is used in addition to

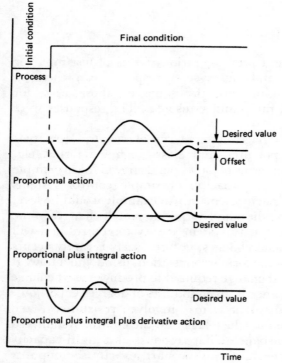

Figure 2.9 Controller action response

proportional in order to remove offset. *Derivative control* results when the output signal change is proportional to the rate of change of deviation. It is used in conjunction with proportional or proportional and integral actions to improve the response to small but sudden deviations. The number of terms of a controller refers to the various actions—proportional (P), integral (I), and derivative (D). A two-term controller may be P+I or P+D; a three-term controller is P+I+D. The various controller actions in response to a step change are shown in Figure 2.9. The improvement in control system response associated with the addition of integral and derivative action can readily be seen.

Stability

The dynamic response of a control system has been examined in terms of the parameters affecting it. The most important characteristic of this dynamic behaviour is absolute stability, i.e. whether a system is stable or unstable. A control system would be unstable if, after a disturbance, the output oscillated continuously or diverged without bounds. Other aspects of the system response which must be carefully considered are relative stability and steady-state error. When a control system suffers a disturbance it will, because of its system dynamics, react first with a transient response and then eventually a steady-state response. A relatively stable system exists when the magnitude and duration of transient oscillations are not excessive. Where the output of the system at steady-state does not exactly agree with the input, then a steady-state error is said to exist. This error is an indication of the accuracy of the control system.

Control system classification

Two basically different types of closed-loop control system exist and are classified as kinetic and process. These systems can, in addition, be continuous or discontinuous. *Kinetic control* employs servomechanisms or position controllers and results in control of motion parameters such as displacement, velocity and acceleration. The control system will act such that it will follow a continually changing desired value or input. It must be fast-acting, with very small time lags and response times, and will utilize electric or hydraulic actuation. *Process control* deals with parameters such as pressure, temperature, flow and level. The control system seeks to maintain some desired or set value of a parameter regardless of changes in external process conditions. These systems are usually slow-acting, with large time lags in the measuring system and process.

Discontinuous or on-off control is simple in operation but can only be used where changes in load are slow to occur and the process is very slow-acting therefore only needing occasional control action.

Continuous control is brought about by a controlling signal which is continuous and provides a smooth controlling action. It is used to obtain close control at, or near, the desired value.

3 Measuring instruments

The various instruments used for the measurement of different parameters and conditions are now considered. Where appropriate, the units of measurement are described and discussed. Often a particular instrument that measures one variable may be used to provide measurement of another, e.g. the measurement of differential pressure as a means of measuring liquid flow or liquid level. The most common parameters of pressure, temperature, level and flow are first described. Displacement, speed, vibration and torsion measurements then follow. General topics such as water purity, gas and oil analysis are then considered. Humidity, viscosity, photoelectric cells and fire detectors complete the instruments described. A final section deals with the testing and calibration of instruments using portable equipment.

PRESSURE MEASUREMENT

When a liquid or gas is in contact with a surface or boundary it exerts a force perpendicular to the surface. This force expressed in terms of a unit of area is known as pressure. The SI unit of pressure is the pascal (Pa), which is the specific name given to the derived unit of pressure, the newton per square metre (N/m^2). Other units commonly used for pressure measurement include the atmosphere (101.325 kPa) and the bar (100 kPa).

The measurement of pressure is always relative to some particular datum. Absolute pressure is a total measurement using zero pressure as datum. Gauge pressure is a measurement above the atmospheric pressure which is used as a datum. To express gauge pressure as an absolute value it is therefore necessary to add the atmospheric pressure. A differential pressure is the difference in pressure existing between two points.

Various methods of pressure measurement are used. These include the balancing of a column of liquid and the elastic deflection of various elements.

Manometers

All manometers balance the pressure to be measured against a column of liquid. The height of the column of liquid is then a measure of the applied pressure.

In its simplest form a U-tube is used, where one end is connected to the pressure source and the other is open to atmosphere. The liquid in the tube will be chosen according to the pressure range required, e.g. water for low pressures and mercury for high pressures. The excess of pressure above atmospheric will be shown as the difference in levels, see Figure 3.1(a). This instrument therefore measures gauge pressure. Where low pressure readings are required, such as for air pressures, an inclined manometer may be used, see Figure 3.1(b). The length of measuring scale, and hence the sensitivity, is considerably increased by this arrangement.

The mercury barometer is a straight tube type of manometer. A glass capillary tube is sealed at one end, filled with mercury, and then

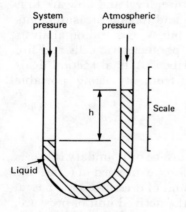

h = system pressure (gauge value)

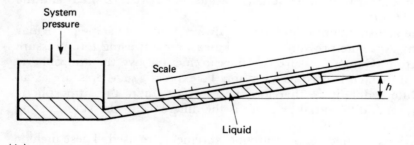

(b)

Figure 3.1 Manometers: (top) U-tube manometer; (bottom) inclined manometer

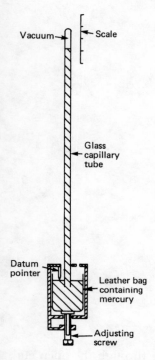

Figure 3.2 Mercury barometer

inverted in a small bath of mercury, see Figure 3.2. Almost vacuum conditions exist above the column of liquid, which is supported by atmospheric pressure acting on the mercury in the container. The mercury is actually contained in a leather bag which is surrounded by a bakelite casing. An adjusting screw is used to move the mercury bag such that the liquid surface just touches the datum pointer, i.e. zero on the instrument scale. The mercury level of the column is then read from the scale. An absolute reading of atmospheric pressure is obtained.

Bourdon-tube gauge

This is probably the most commonly used gauge pressure measuring instrument and it utilizes the elastic deflection of a metal tube. The applied pressure creates a force which elastically deflects the metal tube until an equilibrium condition exists between them. The displacement of the tube is then converted into a reading on a scale. An elliptical section tube is formed into a C-shape and sealed at one end, see Figure 3.3. The sealed end, which is free to move, has a linkage arrangement which will move a pointer over a scale. The

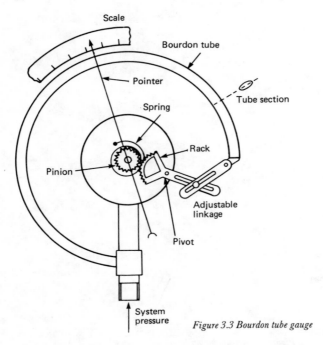

Figure 3.3 Bourdon tube gauge

applied pressure acts within the tube, entering through the open end which is fixed in place. The pressure acting within the tube causes it to change in cross-section and to attempt to straighten out. The resultant movement of the free end then registers as a needle movement over the scale. Other arrangements with the tube in a helical or spiral form are sometimes used with the operating principle being the same. While the datum or zero value is usually atmospheric to give gauge pressure readings, this gauge can be used to read vacuum pressure values, i.e. less then atmospheric. The needle-moving linkage is adjustable to enable calibration adjustments to be made as required.

Diaphragms and bellows gauges

A number of pressure measuring elements use the elastic properties of either a deflecting diaphragm or bellows.

The diaphragm in its simplest form is a thin flat plate of circular shape. The plate is held around its circumference and when a pressure difference occurs between the two sides the diaphragm will deflect. Only very small movements will give a linear relationship between pressure and deflection. The use of a corrugated diaphragm, however, will enable larger deflections which still provide a linear relationship to the applied pressure. A 'slack' diaphragm differential pressure gauge is shown in Figure 3.4. This arrangement provides a very flexible diaphragm for the measurement of low pressures up to about 10 kPa (0.1 bar).

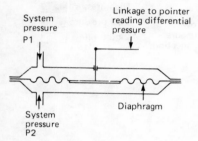

Figure 3.4 Diaphragm pressure gauge

A capsule is made up of two metallic diaphragms which are joined around their circumference. One pressure is applied to the outside of the capsule and another to the inside. The deflection of the capsule, if not excessive, will provide a linear relationship to the applied pressure. One particular application of a capsule is the aneroid barometer, see Figure 3.5. The capsule is almost completely evacuated and atmospheric pressure acts on the external surface. The capsule centre tends to collapse as atmospheric pressure increases or is lifted by the spring as atmospheric pressure falls. A series of linkages transfers the movement to a pointer moving over a scale.

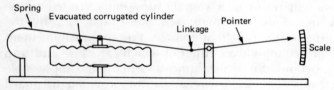

Figure 3.5 Aneroid barometer

A bellows is somewhat similar in shape and appearance to a capsule but is produced from a single thin metal cylinder. The walls are corrugated to permit reasonable deflection under the action of an applied pressure. Two bellows are used in the differential pressure measuring unit shown in Figure 3.6. The bellows are mounted either side of a central chamber and are connected by a spindle at their centre. Excess range or protection valves are mounted on the spindle to limit movement in either direction. Two collars on the spindle locate a follower arm which will transmit the spindle movement via a

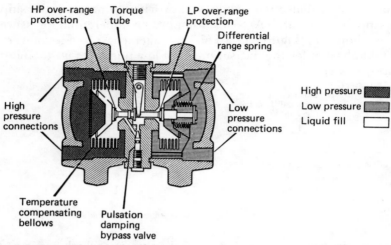

Figure 3.6 Differential pressure gauge

torque tube assembly. The complete internal volume betwen the bellows is filled with a constant viscosity, low freezing point liquid. An additional freely moving region of bellows at the high pressure end permits expansion and contraction of the liquid and thus provides temperature compensation. A spring acting on the low pressure bellows enables range adjustment. An adjustment orifice is often provided between the bellows to dampen out rapid fluctuations in liquid flow. The application of high and low pressures on their respective bellows will result in a spindle movement related to the differential pressure. This movement will be transferred by the follower through the torque tube to a pointer. The spindle movement is limited by the protection valves either of which can close and trap the liquid in each bellows. Since the liquid is virtually incompressible the bellows are supported and two valves are provided to guard against high or low pressures outside the normal range. The differential pressure unit, while measuring pressure difference can be utilized to measure flow and also liquid level.

Dynamic pressure measurement

Slowly changing pressures can be easily measured by the various devices already considered. A rapid variation of pressure will require a high-speed recording instrument as opposed to the normal 'static' gauges. The engine indicator will provide a diagram which represents either cylinder pressure against time (p-t diagram) or cylinder pressure against volume (p-v diagram). An engine indicator is shown in Figure 3.7. It consists of a small piston of known size which operates in a cylinder against a specially calibrated spring. A magnifying linkage transfers the piston movement to a drum on which is mounted a piece of paper or card. The drum oscillates under the pull of a cord. The cord is moved by a reciprocating mechanism which

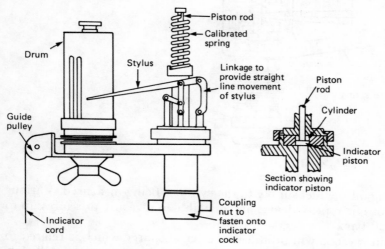

Figure 3.7 Engine indicator

is proportional to the engine piston movement in the cylinder. The stylus will draw out a p-v diagram which represents the gas pressure on the engine piston at different points of the stroke and the area of the diagram produced represents the power developed in the measured cylinder. A clearer indication of pressure changes in a cylinder can be obtained by an out-of-phase diagram, or draw card, where the indicator drum oscillates some 90° out of phase with the piston stroke. This device is particularly useful for comparing values between engine cylinders and bringing them into line, i.e. balancing.

The peak pressure indicator is used to measure the maximum compression or ignition pressures developed in high speed engines or the peak pressure in a hydraulic system. The unit is attached to an engine via the indicator cock. When the cock is opened the gas pressure acts on a piston which moves up and deflects a bar spring, see Figure 3.8. The bar spring deflection is indicated by a dial gauge which is graduated in bars. A special holding device in the dial gauge ensures that the actual peak pressure remains indicated until a higher pressure occurs. Maximum compression pressures can be measured

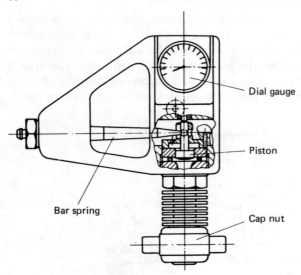

Figure 3.8 Peak pressure indicator

by cutting off the fuel supply to the cylinder being measured. Various designs of this type of device are available to measure pressures up to about 650 bar.

Certain crystals will produce an electric charge which is related to the pressure acting on them. This piezo-electric effect, as it is called, is found in quartz crystals and some synthetic materials such as barium titanate and lithium sulphate. The crystal is charged up, like a capacitor, as a result of the applied force. An actual sensor would be protected by a casing or sleeve which would also transmit the applied force. As with a capacitor, the crystal would be soon discharged when included in a measuring circuit. The device is therefore only useful for measuring dynamic or changing pressures. Sensors have been developed in the form of a washer which, when placed beneath a cylinder head bolt, can measure combustion pressures in an engine. When combined with a speed sensing signal the varying pressure measurement could be used to draw p-v diagrams for individual engine cylinders.

TEMPERATURE MEASUREMENT

Temperature is a reference to the 'hotness' or 'coldness' of a body. With SI units, the Kelvin scale is used where the unit of temperature is the kelvin (K). Two fixed points are assigned in this scale. Absolute zero, or 0 K, is the theoretical minimum temperature possible for any substance. The triple point of water is the second point and is fixed at 273.16 K. The triple point of water is where ice, water and water vapour are all in equilibrium and occurs at a pressure of one standard atmosphere. It can be reproduced with considerable accuracy using a triple-point cell. The International Practical Temperature Scale provides 11 fixed points on the Kelvin scale which can be reproduced accurately and enable calibration of instruments over a wide range of temperatures. Examples of these fixed points are the boiling point of water, 373.15 K, and the freezing point of silver, 1233.96 K. The Celcius scale is in normal use and uses 0°C as the temperature of melting ice and 100°C for the temperature of boiling water (each at normal atmospheric pressure). A comparison between scales indicates

$$X°C = (X + 273.15) \text{ K}$$

An approximation to 273 is made in most temperature conversion. A unit value, or the actual graduations on a scale, would be the same for each scale.

The second law of thermodynamics states that heat must flow from a hot body to a cold body. To measure temperature, therefore, an equilibrium must be set up between the sensor and the body. This is rarely achieved in practice and appropriate selection of the sensor must be made in order to obtain an acceptable measurement of temperature. Often the act of measurement, by inserting a sensor, will modify the condition that it is intended to measure. Heat is transferred from body to body by conduction, convection and radiation and due account of the prevailing conditions must be taken when selecting the measurement system. Finally, the transmission and indicating elements of the measuring system may be subject to temperature changes and some form of compensation will therefore be necessary.

Temperature measurement does not take place directly; some effect brought about by temperature changes is used. There are three broad classifications for the methods used: expansion, electrical and radiation.

Liquid-in-glass thermometer

Various liquids are used in this type of instrument depending on the temperature range required, e.g. mercury −35 to +500°C, alcohol −80 to +70°C. A bulb containing the liquid is used to sense the temperature change. An increase in temperature causes the expanding liquid to rise up a capillary tube in the narrow glass stem. The temperature reading is taken from a scale marked on the glass stem. High temperature measuring mercury liquid thermometers will have the space above the mercury filled with nitrogen under pressure. Most marine-use thermometers of this type will be enclosed within a metal guard with the bulb surrounded by a metal sheath.

Liquid-in-metal thermometer

A more robust instrument which can be read remotely has a metal bulb to contain the liquid. A flexible metal capillary tube joins the bulb to a Bourdon-tube gauge to provide a reading of temperature. The complete unit is filled with the liquid under pressure and expansion causes a movement which is indicated on the Bourdon gauge. The use of mercury provides a range from -39 to $+650°C$ and alcohol from -46 to $+150°C$. The Bourdon tube may be spiral or helical and with increasing temperature will tend to straighten. The free end movement is transmitted through linkages to a pointer moving over a scale.

Gas expansion and vapour pressure thermometers

Gas expansion thermometers and vapour pressure thermometers are identical in construction to liquid-in-metal thermometers, using a Bourdon tube to provide indication.

Gas expansion thermometers use an inert gas such as nitrogen or neon as the sensing and operating medium. A rise in temperature will cause expansion of the gas and an increase in pressure in the Bourdon tube. A short response time is obtained with a gas expansion thermometer, and the indicating scale is linear. The measuring range is from -130 to $+540°C$.

The vapour pressure thermometer has a bulb which is partially filled with a volatile liquid such as methyl chloride or diethyl ether. The remainder of the bulb, the capillary and the Bourdon tube are filled with the liquid vapour. A rise in temperature will cause some liquid to evaporate and an increase in pressure will occur in the Bourdon tube. A short response time is obtained with a vapour pressure thermometer, although the indicating scale is non-linear. The measuring range varies according to the liquid used, e.g. methyl chloride 0 to 50°C, diethyl ether 60 to 160°C.

Bimetallic strip thermometers

A bimetallic strip is made up of two different metals which are firmly bonded together. Typical metals used would be Invar (an iron-nickel alloy), which has a low coefficient of expansion, and either brass or nickel, which have high coefficients of expansion. When a temperature change occurs different amounts of expansion occur in the two metals causing a bending or twisting of the strip. A helical coil of bimetallic material with one end fixed is used in one form of thermometer, see Figure 3.9. The coiling or uncoiling of the helix as a

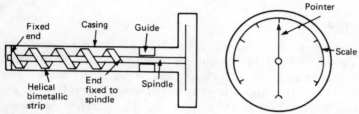

Figure 3.9 Bimetallic strip thermometer

result of temperature change will cause movement of a pointer fitted to the free end of the bimetallic strip. The choice of metals for the strip will decide the range, which can be from -30 to $+550°C$.

Resistance thermometer

The electrical resistance of a conductor, usually a metal, will change as its temperature changes. An increase in temperature will bring about a small increase in resistance, i.e. a small positive temperature coefficient. A coil of wire is usually used and is wound around a hollow ceramic former which acts as an insulator. A protective cement coating is applied to the wire and the complete assembly is housed in a metal sheath. Metals such as platinum or nickel are used, and copper wires connect the resistance wire to the terminals of the thermometer. A Wheatstone bridge may be used to measure the change of resistance and provide an indication of temperature. The measuring range is from about -200 to $+600°C$.

Thermistor

This type of resistance thermometer uses a semiconductor material. An increase in temperature acting on a thermistor will, however, bring about a large negative temperature coefficient. A thermistor is made up of finely divided copper to which is added cobalt, nickel and manganese oxides. The mixture is formed under pressure (sintered) into various shapes such as beads, or rods depending upon the application. They are usually glass coated or placed under a thin metal cap. The change in thermistor resistance as a result of temperature change is measured in an electric circuit. A range of measurement from −250 to +650°C is possible but a single thermistor would not be used over this range. The small size and high sensitivity are particular advantages of this device.

Thermocouple

The thermocouple uses two different metals or alloys jointed together to make a closed circuit. When the two junctions are at different temperatures an e.m.f. is generated and a current flows. The magnitude of the e.m.f. and the current flowing depend upon the temperature difference between the junctions. The arrangement used is shown in Figure 3.10, where extra wires or compensating leads are

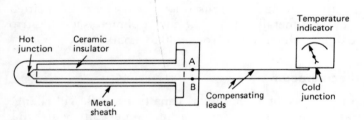

Figure 3.10 Thermocouple

introduced to complete the circuit and include the indicator. As long as the two ends A and B are at the same temperature the thermoelectric effect is not influenced. The choice of metals will determine the measuring range, e.g. Copper-Constantan −200 to +350°C, Platinum/Platinum and Rhodium 0 to +1500°C.

A thermopile is a number of thermocouples connected together in series or parallel. The series arrangement has all hot junctions at the same temperature and all cold junctions at the same temperature. A very sensitive measurement is therefore possible. The parallel arrangement has the hot junctions at different temperatures and the cold junctions all at the same temperature. An average reading is therefore obtained.

Radiation pyrometers

All bodies above 0 K, i.e. absolute zero, will emit electromagnetic radiation. The intensity of the radiation is a measure of the temperature of the body. The intensity ranges from the invisible infra-red rays to the visible light range and is measured using a radiation pyrometer. The temperature measuring range for radiation pyrometers is about 700 to 2000°C. A pyrometer is generally understood to be a high temperature measuring thermometer. The radiation emitted from the hot body is measured or detected in some way and the instrument is calibrated for black body conditions. Black body conditions are considered ideal for radiation measurement. The black body is a thermodynamic concept of a body, which need not be black, which absorbs all energy incident upon it and also is a good emitter of radiation. The emitted radiation should result only from the temperature of the body itself and not from any other reflected radiation. The nearest practical example is a furnace which is observed through a very small aperture and hence any radiation detected will be only from the furnace.

Two main types of radiation pyrometer are in general use, the infra-red pyrometer and the optical pyrometer. The infra-red pyrometer can theoretically measure temperatures from about 0 K up to 3300 K but would normally be used only for high temperature measurements, i.e. greater than 750 K. The optical pyrometer by measuring visible radiation is only able to measure temperatures greater than about 900 K. It is interesting to note that with these instruments the sensing device does not come into physical contact with the hot body.

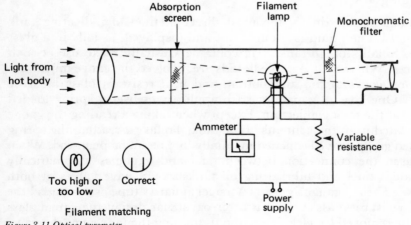

Figure 3.11 Optical pyrometer

The disappearing filament type of optical pyrometer is most common. The arrangement is shown in Figure 3.11. A heated filament lamp is positioned in the path of incoming light from the hot body. The current flowing through the filament is varied until the filament 'disappears'. The current through the lamp is thus a measure of the temperature of the hot body. The absorption screen is used to absorb some of the radiant energy from the source and thus extend the measuring range of the instrument. The monochromatic filter produces single colour, usually red, light to simplify filament matching.

The infra-red pyrometer uses a thermopile at the focus of the light rays instead of a filament lamp. There is no requirement for either screen or filter and the unit will produce a continuous reading of temperature.

LEVEL MEASUREMENT

There are two usual classifications for the methods of level measurement—direct and inferential. The use of the changing level of the liquid provides a measurement which is a direct method. Inferential or indirect methods employ another varying quantity such as air pressure, which changes with liquid level change, and this provides a measurement. Various pressure sensing devices including differential pressure cells can therefore be utilized in the measurement of liquid level.

Gauge glass

Without doubt, this is the most direct method of indicating tank contents. The liquid is brought out and displayed, usually in a glass tube. Small storage tanks and containers usually make use of such devices. Where inflammable liquids are involved the gauge must have shut-off cocks at top and bottom and heat resistant glass must be used. One type of gauge for such applications uses a spring loaded valve at the tank connection. Except when taking a reading the gauge is isolated from the contents of the tank. To take a reading the spring loaded gauge valve is opened manually by pressing a push-rod. When released the connection between tank and gauge is automatically resealed. Fuel and lubricating oil tanks would have valves at both ends of the gauge glass. A steel guard tube surrounds the heat-resistant glass tube. With this particular design the gauge glass can be removed for cleaning without draining the tank since the valve units remain closed. Also if the gauge glass was damaged no leakage would occur.

A remote water level indicating instrument often used for boilers is the Igema gauge. It is basically a U-tube manometer with the lower portion containing a red coloured liquid which does not mix with water and is much denser. The manometer leg above the gauge has a constant head of water provided by a condensing steam reservoir. A weir ensures the head of water is constant. The water level of the boiler acts on the other leg, see Figure 3.12. The gauge and liquid

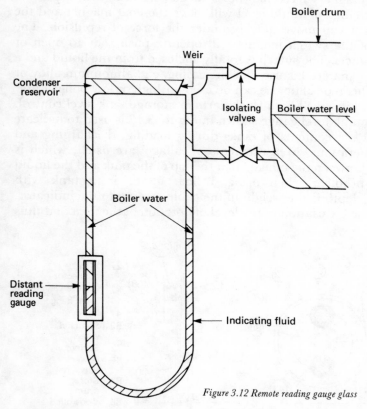

Figure 3.12 Remote reading gauge glass

interface are located at a point where equilibrium is established. If the boiler water level rises the indicating liquid will move around the U-tube and up the glass. Some water will then overflow from the condensing reservoir. If the boiler water level falls the indicating liquid will move down the gauge and around the U-tube. The condensing reservoir level will then fall but more steam will condense to fill it to the normal level.

Float operated

The float is usually a hollow ball or cylinder whose movement as the liquid surface rises or falls is transmitted to an indicator. For locally reading devices, a chain or wire usually provides the linkage to a pointer which moves over a scale of liquid level. A commonly used device of this type is the magnetic float switch. One permanent magnet forms part of the float assembly which rises and falls with changing liquid level. A second magnet is positioned within the switch body. Both magnets have like poles facing, i.e. they will repel one another. A change of liquid level will move the float magnet and the switch magnet will move quickly under the force of repulsion. The movement of the switch magnet will operate push rods to open or close the contacts. The switch is totally enclosed from the liquid and a non-magnetic material is used for the casing, e.g. aluminium alloy or gunmetal. This type of device can be used for high or low boiler water level control, bilge well high level alarm or storage tank level control.

The cargo tank level gauge shown in Figure 3.13 is used to indicate continuously the contents of tanks during loading, discharging and ballasting operations. Measurements of 'ullage' are usual, which is the distance between the ullage lip at the top of the tank and the liquid surface. A problem when using a float gauge in a tank with considerable depth is the weight of the cable leading to the indicator. This can cause a variation in the level of flotation of the float and thus

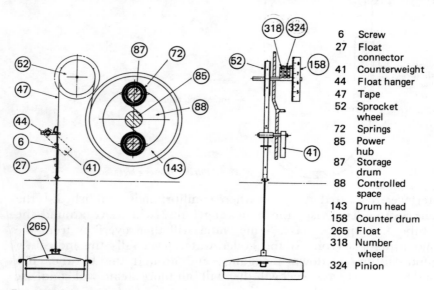

6	Screw
27	Float connector
41	Counterweight
44	Float hanger
47	Tape
52	Sprocket wheel
72	Springs
85	Power hub
87	Storage drum
88	Controlled space
143	Drum head
158	Counter drum
265	Float
318	Number wheel
324	Pinion

Figure 3.13 Cargo tank level gauge

inaccuracy of reading. In the device shown, a coiled spring is incorporated in the gaugehead which is forcibly unwound and then rewound in the reverse direction as the float descends into the tank with falling level. The float is connected by a stainless steel tape to the tape storage drum in the gaugehead. The spring is unwound by the rotation of this tape drum. An almost constant tension is thus maintained on the tape. The float weight is however greater than the pull of the springs on the tape. Thus the float may rise or fall freely with liquid level change. Float movement results in the tape passing over a sprocket wheel which turns a counter drum and then number wheels give a reading. When not in use the float can be wound up and secured beneath the gaugehead. The device can be modified by the addition of a transmitter which is linked to the sprocket wheel. Coarse and fine potentiometers provide electrical signals for remote readings in a cargo control room.

A displacer is similar in action to a float but its range of movement is much less and it does not remain on the liquid surface. Any change in liquid level will result in a change in the buoyancy force acting on the displacer. The movement is then transferred via a cable, linkage and torque tube to an indicator or control system.

Hydrostatic types

Hydrostatic pressure sensors can be used to measure liquid level indirectly in tanks. A pressure gauge located at the zero or empty level of a tank would read zero when the tank was empty. As the tank level increased a pressure reading would be given which could be displayed as liquid level or tank contents directly. A device which operates on the same principle but provides a remote reading uses a diaphragm sensor. Air or an inert gas is trapped in the tube leading to the pressure gauge. Liquid pressure on the diaphragm would be indicated on the gauge in appropriate units. Differential pressure cells may also be used for level measurement. Pressure tappings above and below the measuring range would be provided to either side of the cell to give a readout in appropriate units. Remote readings of boiler water level are possible using a condensing reservoir arrangement on the steam side as previously described.

Compressed air may be used as a transfer medium for the hydrostatic pressure exerted by a liquid in a tank. This pneumatic or 'pneumercator' gauge uses a mercury manometer in conjunction with a hemispherical bell and piping to measure tank level. The arrangement is shown in Figure 3.14. A hemispherical bell is fitted near the bottom of the tank and is connected by a small bore piping to

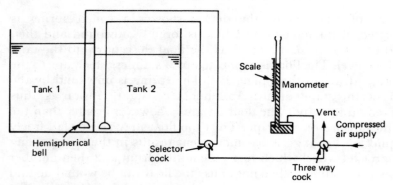

Figure 3.14 Pneumatic level measurement

the mercury manometer. A selector cock enables one manometer to be connected to a number of tanks, usually a pair. A three-way cock is fitted to enable air, gauge and vent positions. With the cock at the 'air' position, the system is filled with compressed air. The cock is then turned to 'gauge' when the tank contents will further pressurize the air in the system and a reading will be given on the manometer, which corresponds to the liquid level. The cock is turned to 'vent' after the reading has been taken.

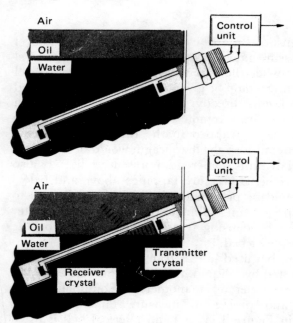

Figure 3.15 Oil/water interface detector

Interface detector

Oil/water interface detectors are a particular type of level sensor required in oil tanker slop tanks. The Marpol 73 and Tanker Safety and Pollution Prevention 1978 Conferences require that all tankers of 150 gross ton and above are fitted with slop tanks. Oil/water interface detectors are required in these slop tanks in order to avoid overloading the oil-in-water monitor which measures the oil content of discharged slop tank water. The sensor uses two piezo-electric crystals, one as transmitter and one as receiver, housed in a stainless steel enclosure. An electric output from the control unit is converted at the transmitter crystal to an ultrasonic beam. When the gap between transmitter and receiver is filled with a single liquid the ultrasonic beam will reach the receiver crystal. When an interface is present between the crystals, most of the beam is reflected and refracted, see Figure 3.15. The probe unit is angled at 10 degrees to give good reflective characteristics. A control unit will monitor the signals received and when an interface is detected will arrange for the oil to be discharged to an oily bilge tank.

FLOW MEASUREMENT

When measuring the flow of a fluid the various physical properties that must be considered are density, pressure, viscosity and velocity. Density and pressure are readily understood while viscosity, which is a resistance to flow, is of importance when dealing with oils. Velocity is important in flow measurement since it decides the behaviour of the fluid.

In smooth pipes when the velocity is low, and also when dealing with high viscosity liquids, the flow is usually streamline or laminar. This means that the particles of the fluid flow parallel to the pipe walls and the fastest moving particles are located at the centre. At high velocities the flow is turbulent and the fluid will have velocity components in various directions. A more even velocity will then exist throughout the fluid with various swirls and eddies present. The average velocity of a fluid stream will be given by the rate of flow in cubic metres per second divided by the area of the pipe in square metres. The nature of the flow can often be described by reference to a dimensionless index known as Reynolds number. A Reynolds number is given by the product of the average velocity, density and internal diameter of the pipe divided by the fluid viscosity. For any device there will be a value of Reynolds number above which the flow will change from laminar to turbulent. For circular pipes it is about 2000 and in most industrial applications flow is turbulent.

Bernoulli's theorem states that the total energy in each particle of fluid in motion remains constant provided there is no energy entering or leaving the system. This total energy is the sum of potential head, static pressure head and kinetic energy. If a horizontal length of pipe is considered then potential head will be constant. If a pressure reducing device is placed in a pipeline, by applying Bernoulli's theorem before and after the device, then,

$$\frac{V_1^{\,2}}{2} + \frac{P_1}{\varrho} = \frac{V_2^{\,2}}{2} + \frac{P_2}{\varrho}$$

Gravitational effects are constant and ϱ is the density of the fluid. Rearranging this equation gives the expression

$$V_2^{\,2} - V_1^{\,2} = \frac{2(P_1 - P_2)}{\varrho}$$

If V_1, the velocity upstream of the pressure reducing device, is considered small compared with the velocity at the device, V_2, then V_1 may be ignored. Hence,

$$\text{Velocity of fluid, } V_2 = \sqrt{[2(P_1 - P_2)]}$$
$$= K\sqrt{\text{Differential pressure}}$$

where K is a constant.

A number of flow measuring devices use this differential pressure relationship. It can be seen, however that the relationship is non-linear. Use is often made of 'square-root extractors' in order to obtain a linear signal where this is used for control purposes.

Flow measurement is usually one of two types, either a flow rate or a total flow. *Flow rate* is a measurement of the quantity of fluid which moves past a point per unit time. *Total flow* is the quantity of fluid which has passed a point in a specified period.

Flow rate measurement

Most flow rate measuring devices insert a restriction in the pipeline and obtain a measurement of differential pressure or orifice area. An electromagnetic flow meter will also be described which places no restriction in the pipeline.

Differential pressure meters

The flow rate in a pipe has been shown to be related to the pressure difference across a restriction placed in the pipe. When the fluid is forced through a restriction, i.e. a reduced area, the pressure slightly upstream is greater than the pressure just after the restriction. Tappings are taken from the pipe at suitable points and the differential pressure can be measured with a suitable device.

The simplest device in use is the orifice plate. In its most common form it is a thin metal plate with an axial hole. The hole edge is square facing the oncoming liquid and bevelled on the outlet side. The hole size is chosen to provide the necessary differential pressure at the maximum flow rate. The plate should be flat and smooth on the upstream side. A smooth flow of liquid into and away from the orifice plate, i.e. laminar flow, is essential. In order to achieve this it is usual to ensure that there are no bends or discontinuities for about 12 pipe diameters upstream and about half that downstream. Viscous fluids and those with solids or gases present may require different arrangements of orifice plate.

The liquid flow through an orifice continues to contract in area for a distance downstream. The minimum liquid area and minimum static pressure position is also the maximum velocity point and is known as the *vena contracta*. Its approximate location is half the pipe diameter downstream. The orifice plate is usually inserted between flanges in the pipeline and provision is made for pressure tapping on either side. Corner tappings are taken adjacent to the upstream and downstream faces of the plate. Flange tappings are taken at a distance of 25 mm either side of the plate. Pipe diameter and half-diameter tappings are taken at the said distances upstream and downstream of the plate respectively and are most accurate. Corner tappings or flange

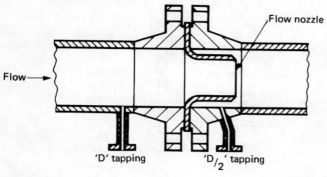

Figure 3.16 Flow nozzle

tappings are used where half-diameter tappings cannot be located because of thick flanges or small pipes.

Orifice plates may be manufactured from stainless steel, monel metal or rigid nylon. They do suffer erosion and scoring on the upstream face and the opening edge. They can, however, be easily replaced.

The flow nozzle is in many respects an improvement on the orifice

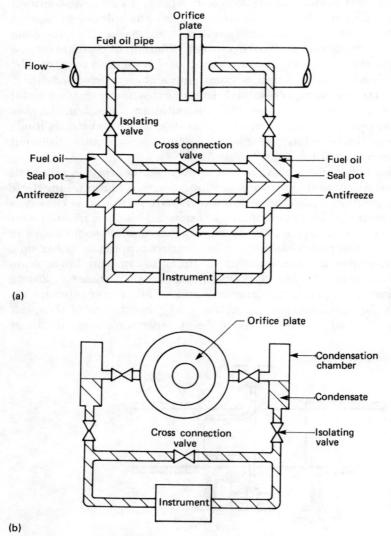

Figure 3.17 Seal pot and condensation chamber installation: (a) seal pot; (b) condensation chamber

plate, it consists of a smooth bell-mouthed convergent entry to a short cylindrical throat which projects downstream, see Figure 3.16. Corner tappings are used to obtain the differential pressure measurements. The flow nozzle enables a greater range of measurement for an equivalent differential head, requires less straight pipe upstream to ensure laminar flow, and suffers less from erosion and damage.

The venturi tube consists of a conical convergent entry tube, a cylindrical centre tube or throat and a conical divergent outlet. Pressure tappings are located half a pipe diameter upstream and in the cylindrical centre tube. The venturi is a further improvement on the flow nozzle in terms of erosion resistance and pressure recovery downstream. It is however more expensive, difficult to install and provides a degree of accuracy that is not normally required.

Special arrangements must be made when measuring the flow of high viscosity liquids or steam. If a high viscosity liquid, such as fuel oil, were to collect and cool in the dead-end pipe line leading to a measuring device it would coagulate within the instrument. A sealing chamber or pot must therefore be provided just below the tapping points, see Figure 3.17(a). The chamber has the viscous liquid in its upper half and a low viscosity non-mixing liquid, such as ethylene-glycol (antifreeze), in the lower half and the piping leading to the measuring unit. Steam flow measuring installations must be fitted with condensation chambers at the tapping points, see Figure 3.17(b). This ensures that the pipelines leading to the measuring element are always filled with liquid. Both tapping points must be at the same horizontal level and the measuring unit must always be located below the condensation chambers.

Variable area flowmeters
It was shown earlier that the increase in velocity of a fluid when passing through a constriction was equal to some constant multiplied by the square root of the differential pressure, i.e.

$$V_2 = K\sqrt{(P_1 - P_2)}$$

It can then be seen that

Volume flow rate, $Q = K_1 A \sqrt{h}$

where K_1 is a constant, A is the minimum cross-sectional area of the constriction and h is the pressure differential. The volume flow rate can, therefore, be measured by reference to the area of the constriction if the pressure differential is held constant. This is the principle of operation of variable area flowmeters.

The rotameter is one type of variable area flowmeter. A vertical tapered tube has the widest opening at the top, the fluid enters from the bottom and in moving through the tube displaces a float. This float is appropriately shaped for the liquid (or gas) whose flow rate is to be measured. The float moves freely in the tube and has slots cut into it so that it rotates as the liquid flows past. When the flow rate past the float increases, the float rises in the tube. This increases the annular area between the float and the tube sides and, in effect, maintains a constant pressure differential across the float. The displacement of the float is then a measure of the volume rate of flow. The reading is taken from graduations on the tube opposite a reading edge on the float. Metal tube rotameters may be used for high flow rates and high pressures. A magnetic follower may then be positioned on the outside of the tube to indicate the float position and give a reading of the volume rate of flow. This device can be installed immediately after valves and fittings in a pipeline, can handle viscous liquids if the correct shape of float is used, and provides a linear scale of readings.

Electromagnetic flowmeter

In this instrument a measuring tube of non-conducting material is fitted with two diametrically opposite electrodes. An electromagnet creates a magnetic field through the tube at right angles to the flow of liquid. The flowing liquid must be an electrical conductor. The movement of an electrical conductor (the liquid) through a magnetic field perpendicular to it results in the generation of a voltage. The generated voltage is in proportion to the strength of the magnetic field, the distance between the electrodes, both of which are held constant, and the velocity of the liquid. A linear read-out of flow rate is thus provided by the voltage generated. This device is particularly useful when measuring corrosive fluids or those with a high solids content.

Total flow measurement

Quantity flow meters usually take the form of positive displacement devices or a turbine. Both will permit the flow of a known quantity of liquid for each revolution.

Positive displacement meters

These devices will measure a flow quantity. The liquid is usually admitted to a chamber of known dimensions and the number of times it fills is counted. Various forms of this device are in use using rotating lobes, vanes, a nutating (moving about an axis) disc or a reciprocating piston. Construction of each is in many respects similar to a pump with the liquid pressure providing the drive and the impeller moving a counter. Positive displacement meters are extremely accurate, are unaffected by liquid pulsations and can handle liquids with high viscosities. Good upstream filtration is a requirement with these meters.

Turbine flowmeter

The total quantity of liquid passing a point can be measured using a small turbine. The turbine is mounted in the pipeline and is rotated by the passing liquid, see Figure 3.18. The helix angle of the blades

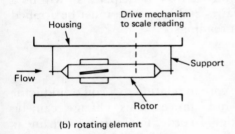

(b) rotating element

Figure 3.18 Turbine flowmeter

will determine a length of liquid that can pass through, and with the cross-sectional area known then the total quantity can be determined. A mechanical drive using a worm and pinion on the turbine shaft may be used to provide a quantity flow reading. Alternatively a magnetic pick-up assembly may be used. The blade tips are made of a magnetic material and a pick-up coil is used to sense voltage pulses created by the turbine rotation. A read-out in quantity flow is then given. Inlet conditions to the turbine must ensure that the water is not swirling. This may be achieved by having straight lengths of pipe some 10 pipe diameters upstream and five downstream.

DISPLACEMENT

The measurement of a small linear or angular distance is often required and a number of methods will now be described. These units all transduce, i.e. convert, the measurement of linear motion into an electrical signal. They may be used as independent units but are often to be found within a particular instrument that may utilize a linear motion for the measurement of pressure or temperature.

Variable resistance

A strain gauge consists of a length of fine wire whose resistance will change if it is displaced. Two gauges are usually placed in a measuring bridge, one active and a dummy which is not subject to a displacement. Any displacement of the active gauge will vary the current through the bridge circuit. The dummy gauge will compensate for any effects of temperature variation.

A potentiometer is a resistance element with some form of wiper arm which can move over its length. The wiper arm is moved by the displacement to be measured and this will divide the voltage which is applied to the resistance. The voltage across the wiper arm will be a measure of the displacement. A fairly stable voltage must be applied across the resistance for consistent readings.

Variable inductance

The movement of a ferromagnetic core in relation to a coil or inductor will bring about a change of inductance. This change can be measured by the use of an a.c. bridge. In order to obtain a more linear relationship, two inductors are often used. The displacement to be measured will move the ferromagnetic core or some part of the magnetic circuit. It is in fact the magnetic reluctance of the inductor which is varied and this is inversely related to the inductance.

Linear variable differential transformer

The operating principle of this device is the variation of reluctance in the magnetic path of a transformer which varies the e.m.f. induced in a secondary winding. The linear variable differential transformer consists of three coils wound on a cylindrical former. An iron core is able to move linearly within the cylindrical former and provides a path for the magnetic flux which passes between the coils. The three coils are a single primary and two secondaries. The secondary coils are connected in series but with their outputs in opposition. When the iron core is centrally positioned the supply to the primary will induce equal and opposite voltages in the two secondary coils. A meter connected across the secondary output would therefore give a null or zero reading. Movement of the core to the left or right will result in an output voltage which will be directly proportional to the movement.

Variable capacitance

Variable capacitance transducers can use a number of methods to measure displacement. The area of the plates or the permittivity between them is varied when measuring large displacements. The gap between the plates is varied when measuring small displacements.

SPEED

Most speed measurement with regard to rotating machinery is angular velocity, which is usually expressed in revolutions per minute. Tachometers provide a direct reading of angular velocity and are usually mechanical or electrical in operation.

Mechanical

The centrifugal tachometer is a portable device using the Watt governor principle. Two masses are fixed on leaf springs which are fastened to the driven shaft at one end and a sliding collar at the other, see Figure 3.19. The sliding collar, through a linkage mechanism, moves a pointer over a scale. As the driven shaft increases in speed the weights move out under centrifugal force, causing an axial movement

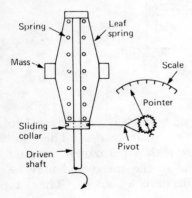

Figure 3.19 Mechanical tachometer

of the sliding collar. This in turn moves the pointer to give a reading of speed.

One type of vibrating read tachometer uses a set of thin reeds fixed at one end and each having a slightly different natural frequency of vibration. The reeds are arranged in ascending order of natural frequency. When the tachometer is placed in contact with a rotating machine the reed with the nearest natural frequency to that of the machine will vibrate the most. A scale is provided behind the reeds which indicates frequency and the corresponding speed. The length is changed by rotating a dial until maximum vibration occurs. The dial is then read and gives a frequency and corresponding speed value.

Electrical

The drag cup tachometer uses an aluminium cup which is rotated in a laminated iron electromagnet stator, see Figure 3.20. The stator has two separate windings at right angles to one another. An alternating current supply is provided to one winding and eddy currents are set up in the aluminium cup. This results in an induced e.m.f. in the other stator winding which is proportional to the speed of rotation. The output voltage is measured on a voltmeter calibrated to read in units of speed.

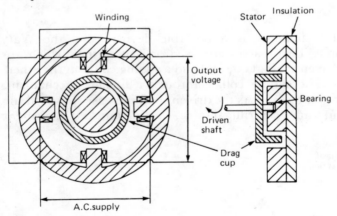

Figure 3.20 Drag cup tachometer

Tachogenerators provide a voltage value which is proportional to the speed and may be a.c. or d.c. instruments. The d.c. tachogenerator is a small d.c. generator with a permanent magnet field. The output voltage is proportional to the speed and may be measured on a voltmeter calibrated in units of speed. The a.c.

tachogenerator is a small brushless alternator with a rotating multi-pole magnet. The output voltage is again measured by a speed-displaying voltmeter although the varying frequency will affect the accuracy of this instrument.

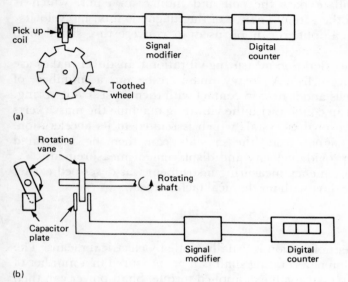

Figure 3.21 Pick-up tachometers: (a) inductive; (b) capacitive

Various pick-up devices can be used in conjunction with a digital counter to give a direct reading of speed. An inductive pick-up tachometer is shown in Figure 3.21(a). As the individual teeth pass the coil they induce an e.m.f. pulse which is appropriately modified and then fed to a digital counter. A capacitive-type pick-up tachometer is shown in Figure 3.21(b). As the rotating vane passes between the plates a capacitance change occurs which is detected and then fed to a digital counter.

VIBRATION

The measurement of vibration is largely for diagnostic purposes in order to detect problems with rotating machinery before damage occurs. Two different measurements are taken, the amplitude and the frequency. Amplitude may be taken as a measurement of displacement, velocity or acceleration and indicates the extent of the problem.

The frequency at which the maximum amplitude of vibration occurs may identify the source of the problem.

One type of velocity measuring vibration transducer utilizes a coil and a moving permanent magnet. Any vibration will cause the magnet to oscillate past the coil and induce an e.m.f. which is proportional to the rate of change of the magnetic flux, i.e. velocity. An integrating amplifier can be used to convert this signal into displacement.

One type of acceleration measuring vibration transducer makes use of piezo-electric cells. A heavy mass rests on a number of piezo-electric cells and is held in contact with them by a strong spring. With the sensor in contact with the vibrating machine the mass exerts a dynamic force on the crystals which is related to its acceleration. The electrical signal from the crystals can then be integrated successfully to provide velocity and displacement measurements.

One type of frequency measuring instrument was described earlier in the section dealing with mechanical tachometers.

TORSION

The measurement of torsion is usually made by electrical means. The twisting or torsion of a rotating shaft can be measured in a number of different ways to give a value of applied torque. Shaft power can then be calculated by multiplying the torque by the rotational speed of the shaft.

Strain gauge torsionmeter

With this device four strain gauges are mounted onto the shaft as shown in Figure 3.22. The twisting of the shaft as a result of an

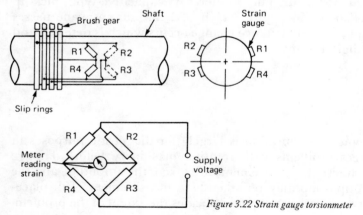

Figure 3.22 Strain gauge torsionmeter

applied torque results in a change in resistance of the strain gauge system or bridge. Brushes and slip rings are used to take off the electrical connections and complete the circuit as shown. More recently, use has been made of a frequency converter attached to the shaft to convert the resistance change to a frequency change. This frequency signal is then transmitted without contact to a receiver for decoding. When a torque is applied to the shaft, readings of strain and hence torque can be obtained.

Differential transformer torsionmeter

Two castings are used to provide a magnetic circuit with a variable air gap. The two are clamped to the shaft as shown in Figure 3.23 and joined to one another by thin steel strips. The joining strips will transmit tension but offer no resistance to rotational movement of the two castings with respect to one another. A differential transformer is

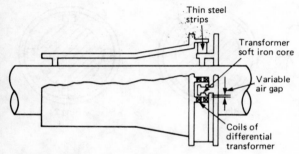

Figure 3.23 Differential transformer torsionmeter

fitted between the two castings, the two coils being wound on one casting and the thin iron core being part of the other. Another differential transformer is fitted in the indicating circuit, its air gap being adjusted by a micrometer screw. The primary coils of the two transformers are joined in series and energized by an a.c. supply. The secondary coils are connected so that the induced e.m.f.s are opposed, and when one transformer has an air gap different from the other there will be a net output e.m.f. which may cause a current to flow.

When a torque is applied to the shaft the air gap of the shaft transformer will change, resulting in a current flow. The indicator unit transformer air gap is then adjusted until no current flows. The air gaps in both transformers must now be exactly equal. The applied torque is directly proportional to the width of the air gap or the micrometer screw movement. Shaft power is found by multiplying the micrometer screw reading by the shaft speed and a constant for the meter.

Magnetic stress torsionmeter

Three rings are fitted around the shaft but not in contact with it, see Figure 3.24. The rings carry equal numbers of electromagnetic poles and the centre ring poles are advanced to a midway position between the other two. The centre ring is provided with an a.c. supply which sets up a magnetic field at 45° to the shaft axis. The coils in the outer

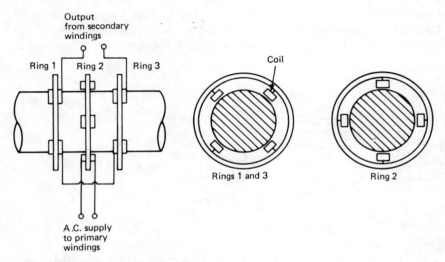

Figure 3.24 Magnetic stress torsionmeter

rings are connected in series and then the ring windings are formed in opposition to one another. The complete arrangement is therefore a transformer with the centre ring the primary, the outer rings the secondary and the shaft material completes the magnetic circuit.

With no torque applied to the shaft a symmetrical magnetic field exists and there is no current output from the transformer. When a torque is applied to the shaft the magnetic field becomes unsymmetrical and an e.m.f. is produced in the outer coils of the transformer. This e.m.f. is directly related to the torque in the shaft and, combined with a reading of speed, will give a value of shaft power.

WATER PURITY

Water purity may refer to the absence of dissolved salts, a measurement in terms of acidity or alkalinity, or the presence of oil in a sample. Various instruments which make these measurements, their operating principles and the need for the measurement, will now be described.

Salinity/conductivity

Water purity, in terms of the absence of salts, is a necessary requirement where it is to be used as boiler feed. Pure water has a high resistance to the flow of electricity, i.e. a low conductivity, so much so that it is considered non-conductive. Water containing dissolved salts, in particular sea water, has a high conductivity. A measurement of conductivity is therefore a measure of purity. A pair of electrodes of known area are placed in the sample solution at a known distance apart. The resistance between them is measured and expressed in conductivity units which are siemens. A siemen is a reciprocal ohm and represents the passage of one ampere at one volt potential through one cubic centimetre of the liquid. Where electrodes are smaller than one square centimetre and spaced closer or farther than one centimetre then a cell constant is used to correct the readings obtained. One common type of salinity indicator uses a small cell containing two platinum electrodes. The liquid sample passes through the cell and the current flow as a result of any conductance is measured. The reading given assumes all conductivity is due to sodium chloride which, although not strictly accurate, is acceptable for most practical purposes. Electrical conductivity rises with temperature and thus a temperature compensating resistor is incorporated in the measuring circuit. Other designs use two electrodes, either in a perforated probe which is inserted into a pipeline, or an insulated pipe section may have the electrodes inserted into the pipe walls on opposite sides.

The dionic water purity meter is somewhat similar in its operating principle. Conductivity is measured between two platinum wire ring electrodes and two gunmetal ring electrodes. The liquid flows through these rings which are separated by insulated lengths of tubing, see Figure 3.25. In effect measurements are made on two columns of liquid. A bimetallic strip operates a plunger which insulates the two columns and provides temperature compensation to 20°C. Specific conductivity in siemens/cm^3 is the conductance across a centimetre long column of mercury whose cross-sectional area is one square

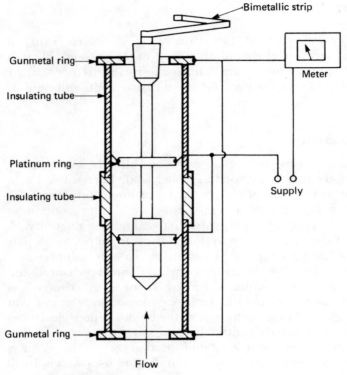

Figure 3.25 Dionic water purity meter

centimetre. A much smaller unit, the microsiemen/cm^3, when corrected to 20°C, is known as a dionic unit. Pure distilled water has a conductance of about 1 dionic unit while fresh water is about 500 dionic units. A de-gassifier should be fitted upstream of this unit to remove dissolved carbon dioxide since this will cause errors in measurement.

Acidity/alkalinity

Water, when acidic or alkaline, can cause corrosion. Boiler feed water when acidic or strongly alkaline will cause corrosion. It is usual to monitor and maintain boiler feed water slightly alkaline. A scale of measurement using pH values indicates the degree of acidity or alkalinity within a solution. A solution which is neutral is neither acidic nor alkaline. The pH scale is a measure of the concentration of hydrogen ions in a solution using numbers from 0 to 14. A strongly acidic solution has a pH of 0, a neutral solution a pH of 7 and a strongly alkaline (or basic) solution a pH of 14.

The measurement of pH, or hydrogen ion concentration in a solution, requires the use of two specially designed electrodes, see Figure 3.26(a). One electrode is used for measurement and is made up of a glass tube which contains a buffer solution of constant pH, e.g. potassium chloride, into which is inserted a silver chloride coated silver wire. The lower end of this glass tube has a thin walled special glass surface which acts as a membrane. The silver wire, which is in a

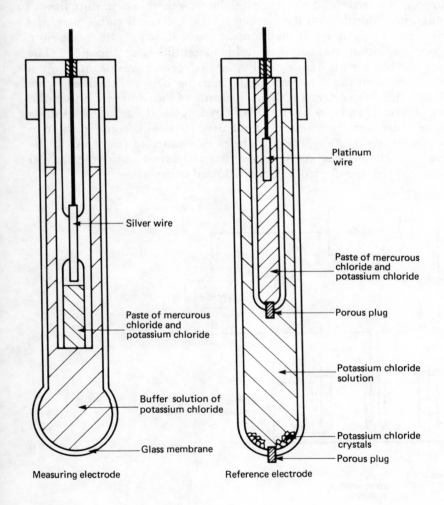

Measuring electrode

Reference electrode

Platinum wire

Silver wire

Paste of mercurous chloride and potassium chloride

Porous plug

Paste of mercurous chloride and potassium chloride

Potassium chloride solution

Buffer solution of potassium chloride

Glass membrane

Potassium chloride crystals

Porous plug

Figure 3.26 (a) pH measurement electrodes

solution of constant pH, is sensitive to changes in hydrogen ion concentration of the solution on the outer surface of the membrane. The reference electrode is used to enable a voltage measurement which is related to pH. A platinum electrode is located in a glass tube which contains a mercurous chloride and potassium chloride paste and has a porous plug at the bottom. This assembly is contained within another glass tube containing a potassium chloride solution and additional crystals, i.e. a saturated solution. This outer tube is also fitted with a porous plug at the bottom. The complete assembly is known as the reference electrode. As long as there is a minute flow of potassium chloride into the sample solution, a small stable potential will exist. The inner cell maintains a slight flow into the potassium chloride solution and another stable potential is set up here. The reference cell is thus unaffected by the hydrogen ion concentration of the sample solution. The potential occurring between the measuring cell and the reference cell is thus a measure of the sample solution pH. Temperature changes will affect hydrogen dissociation and a temperature compensating resistor is used to provide compensation in the circuit, see Figure 3.26(b). The performance of this unit can be adversely affected by dirty or distorted electrodes, poor electrical connections or the electrodes being allowed to dry out.

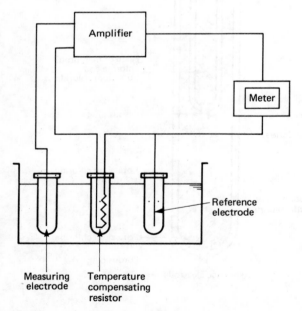

Figure 3.26 (b) pH measurement circuit

Oil content

The presence of oil in water is usually measured for discharging water, but this can also be applied to boiler condensate. Various methods of measurement are applied by different manufacturers.

The Bailey oil content monitor uses the principle of ultraviolet light fluorescence. This is the emission of light from a molecule that has absorbed light. During the short interval between absorption and emission, energy is lost and light of a longer wavelength is emitted. Oil fluoresces more readily than water and this provides the mean for its detection.

The measurement technique of the Oilcon monitoring unit is based on scattered light. Almost infra-red light is passed through a water sample at right angles to the flow. One silicon detector collects the straight-through light beam and acts as a zero setting. A second detector collects the light which has been scattered by the oil droplets in the water sample. Both light signals are used to compute an electrical output which is proportional to the oil concentration in the water sample. The complete unit is described in Chapter 9.

GAS ANALYSIS

Samples of the gas present in an atmosphere or the exhaust from a combustion process may be analysed to detect the presence of one or more specific gases. The oxygen content of an enclosed space may be measured prior to personnel entry in order to ensure the presence of a safe atmosphere. The measurement of oxygen or carbon dioxide in an exhaust gas can be used as an indicator of efficient combustion of fuel.

Oxygen analyser

The measurement of the oxygen content in an atmosphere is important to personnel, particularly when entering enclosed spaces. Also, inert gas systems use exhaust gases which must be monitored to ensure that their oxygen content is below 5 per cent. Use is also made of the measurement of oxygen in boiler exhausts as a means of ensuring efficient combustion. Various techniques have therefore been developed for this measurement, two of which will be described.

An electrochemical type of analyser is shown in Figure 3.27. The oxygen sensor is an yttria stabilized zirconia disc with platinum electrodes attached to the opposite faces of the disc. A heater is used to maintain the sensor at a fixed temperature of 800°C. Air is supplied to

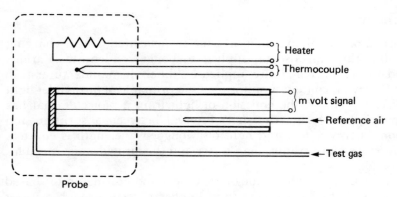

Figure 3.27 Electrochemical oxygen analyser

the inner or reference face of the disc and the flue gas to be measured is in contact with the outer face of the disc. A voltage is generated between the disc faces which is a function of the temperature and the ratio of oxygen partial pressures on each side. With all parameters except exhaust gas oxygen pressure being held constant, the output voltage is a measure of oxygen content in the exhaust gas. The output voltage increases logarithmically with increasing oxygen concentration, thus providing high sensitivity at low concentration values. The complete assembly of disc, heater, electrodes, etc. forms a probe which is located in the flue gas. Calibration of the unit can be checked by supplying a test gas of known oxygen content through a special pipe to the sensing disc. The output reading is unaffected by water or carbon dioxide present in the flue gases and is rapid in response.

The magneto-dynamic type of analyser uses the fact that oxygen is attracted by a magnetic field, i.e. it is paramagnetic. The measuring cell contains a quartz dumb-bell which is partially filled with nitrogen and suspended in a powerful magnetic field, as shown in Figure 3.28(a). A mirror is mounted in the centre of the cell and faces a window. An outside light source is focused on the mirror and the reflection strikes a pair of photocells. The cell is zeroed when no oxygen is present such that both photocells receive equal light. When an oxygen-containing sample enters the cell the dumb-bell will rotate because of oxygen's effect upon the magnetic field. A feedback circuit returns the dumb-bell to its original position and the current supplied is a measure of the oxygen content of the gas. This basic sensor can be used in portable and fixed measuring instruments. The sampling system for an inert gas main is shown in Figure 3.28(b). The probe at the tap-off point has an integral filter to remove dust. The gas then passes through a separator, a three-way valve and a flow valve. The

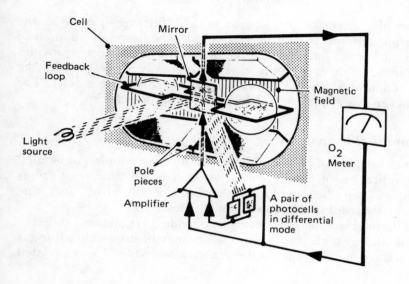

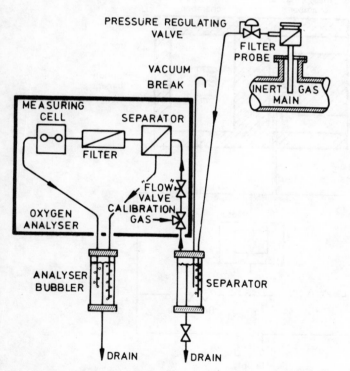

Figure 3.28 Magneto-dynamic oxygen analyser: (top) cell analyser; (bottom) sampling system

gas sample, after further separation and filtering, passes to the measuring cell and part of it is bypassed. The flow valve is used to obtain the correct flow through the measuring cell. A meter provides the reading of oxygen content. The three-way valve permits the introduction of a zeroing gas (nitrogen) and a span gas (air). The span gas gives a 21 per cent reading as a calibration check.

Carbon dioxide analyser

The measurement of carbon dioxide in a flue gas sample can be used as an indication of good combustion in a boiler furnace. Various techniques can be employed in this measurement and one continuously reading device will now be described.

The thermal conductivity of carbon dioxide is significantly different from all other gases (except steam) which may be present in a flue gas sample. Carbon dioxide has a thermal conductivity of 1 when related

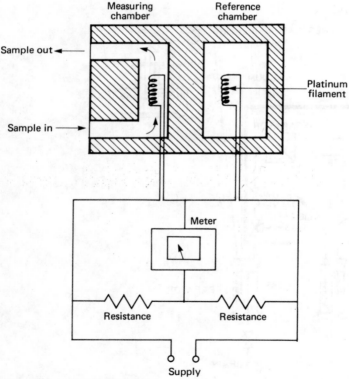

Figure 3.29 Carbon dioxide analyser

to carbon monoxide of 4, oxygen of 2, nitrogen of 2 and water (steam) of 1. The measurement obtained therefore relates to carbon dioxide as long as the gas sample was previously dried. Any, usually small, amounts of hydrogen or carbon monoxide will register as carbon dioxide unless they have been previously burnt off or otherwise removed. A hot wire thermal conductivity gas cell can be used for this measurement. It consists of two chambers, each containing a platinum wire filament. The measuring chamber has the dried filtered gas flowing through it and the other contains a dried filtered reference gas such as air. The reference chamber may be open to a steady flow of air or completely sealed. The two cells form resistance arms of a Wheatstone bridge as shown in Figure 3.29. The power supply applied will result in the filaments being heated. This heat then transfers to the walls of each chamber through the gas present. Both reference and measuring cells are identical in construction and form part of a single large block of metal. Any difference in the filament temperatures can only therefore be as a result of differences in thermal conductivity of their respective gases. The difference in filament temperatures will cause a difference in resistance and unbalance the Wheatstone bridge. The meter measuring imbalance will give a reading of carbon dioxide present in the flue gas.

HUMIDITY

This is the measurement of the amount of water vapour in a given volume of a gas. Most measurements relate to air. A given volume of air is able to hold a particular amount of water vapour. This amount varies with temperature such that the higher the temperature the more water the volume can hold. If the temperature of a volume of air was to fall such that the maximum amount of water was exceeded, then precipitation as condensation or mist would occur. The two terms to describe humidity are *absolute humidity* and *relative humidity*. Absolute humidity is the amount of water present in a given volume of air and is expressed, usually, in grams per cubic centimetre. Relative humidity is the more common measurement and is the ratio of the amount of water vapour present in a given volume of air to the maximum amount of water vapour that can be present before precipitation occurs. The measurement is usually given as a percentage. Dew point is the temperature at which water vapour in the atmosphere precipitates as drops of water or condensation on surfaces. Actual measurements of relative humidity can be obtained using either a psychrometer or a hygrometer.

The psychrometer uses two thermometers. The bulb of one (wet bulb thermometer) is kept moist by wrapping in a water-soaked material or wick which is fed from a small bath. The other (dry bulb thermometer) is exposed to the air. The wet bulb will always show a lower temperature because of the evaporation of water from the wick. The two temperature readings, when plotted on a psychrometric chart, will give a reading of relative humidity. A psychrometric chart is a graphical display of the properties of moist air, using axes of dry bulb temperature and absolute humidity intersected by curves of constant wet bulb temperature and relative humidity. The hand-held unit which is often used to take accommodation measurements of relative humidity is called a sling psychrometer.

A hygrometer utilizes the physical changes that occur in human hair, silk, animal membrane or other materials when they absorb moisture. Any change in length of the material, which is exposed to a free flow of air, is coupled by a linkage to an indicating or recording instrument. Electrical hygrometers use transducers of hygroscopic (water absorbing) material. Any resistance change of the material is measured in a Wheatstone bridge by an instrument calibrated for relative humidity.

OIL ANALYSIS

A bunker receipt provides certain basic information regarding the fuel delivered to a ship, e.g. specific gravity and viscosity. This relates to the fuel as it left the major supplier and not necessarily that delivered. The properties of a residual fuel will alter as a result of heat, mixing, cyclic temperatures and movement. The treatment of this fuel and its subsequent combustion may be inadequate, since the equipment cannot be properly set or tuned. Some of the possible problem areas are highlighted in Figure 3.30. Apart from the technical problems there are also economies involved in ensuring that water content is low, a fuel delivered by volume gives the correct weight, the correct and not a cheaper grade of fuel has been delivered, etc. On-board test kits are available to measure many of the important properties of fuel and lubricating oils. This will then enable the correct setting of tank temperatures, purifiers, viscometers, etc. These various kits will now be described together with the viscosity measuring instrument which is fitted in the fuel supply line to an engine.

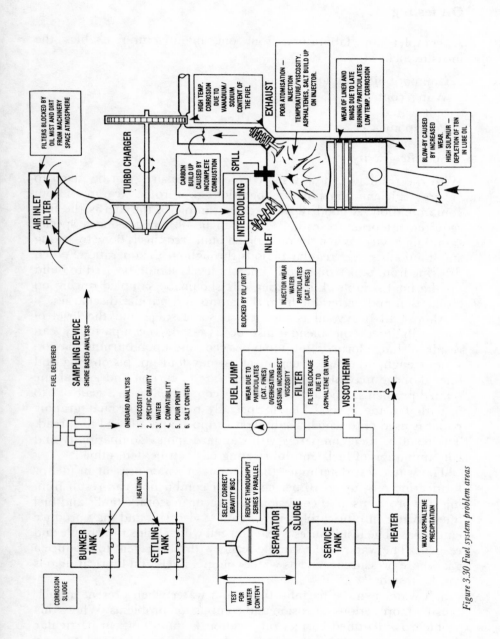

Figure 3.30 Fuel system problem areas

Oil testing

A complete oil laboratory from one manufacturer enables the measurement of

Compatibility/contamination
Water content
Salt water
Pour point
Viscosity
Specific gravity

With the results of these tests, corrective measures can be taken to ensure efficient machinery operation or protect cargoes from contamination. A good representative sample of the fuel is the first requirement prior to testing. This can be obtained using a special sampling device. When the oil is being bunkered this is done by taking small amounts over regular periods throughout the operation. When drawing from tanks, dips from different levels should be used to build up the final sample. Lubricating oils should be sampled during oil circulation and preferable from the pump and purifier discharges.

Almost all heavy oil is blended at some stage and the level of compatibility of the blend must be assessed. Incompatibility can result in sludge formation up to 6 per cent and upon burning may do serious engine damage. Fuel injectors may foul up, piston ring and liner damage may also occur, largely due to carbon and asphaltene related problems. The test kit indicates compatibility on a scale of 1 to 5, with 1 being a good blend. Specially prepared chromatographic paper is used onto which a sample is dropped and allowed to spread. The result is then compared with standard spots. Compatibility and contamination of fuels and lubricating oils can be determined.

The water test determines the amount of water present in fuel or lubricating oils, up to 10 per cent. Poor combustion can result from injector problems, and corrosion may occur in storage tanks and fuel lines. Water in lubricating oils will affect viscosity and may produce emulsions. The test kit uses a reaction cell which holds the sample and reagent. The water in the sample reacts with the reagent to produce a gas whose pressure is read as water volume. Fuels and lubricating oils can be tested.

Salt water is more harmful than fresh water when present in fuel, causing more serious corrosion and combustion problems. Where this problem is identified correct purification is important; in particular throughput, temperature and gravity disc selection. The test kit uses a tube in which the salt is extracted into water. The mixture is then separated by filtering through special paper. An indicator tube in the water changes colour in the presence of sodium chloride (salt). Fresh water, fuel oil and lubricating oil samples can be tested.

Fuel oil pour point can be determined in the range -5 to$+60°C$, by the use of a test kit. Some high pour point fuels can solidify at normal temperatures and, once solid, may be impossible to liquefy. If the pour point is near, or above, the sea water temperature then problems may well occur. Correct pour point information can ensure adequate tank heating to maintain the oil as a liquid. The test kit uses a test tube in which the sample is cooled, using a freezer aerosol, until it does not move when tilted. All fuel and lubricating oils can be tested.

Fuel oil viscosity is probably the most important measurement required. It is often the only information given on a bunker receipt. The true value is required in order to ensure correct handling, purification and precombustion temperature setting. If, for example, the fuel were overheated and gasified in the pipeline, then the fuel pumps would seize and the engine would stop. The test kit utilizes an electronically controlled heating and measuring unit, into which a sample tube is placed. The oil sample, together with a steel ball, is placed in the unit. When correctly heated, the tube is removed and inverted and the electronically controlled unit gives a digital read-out of viscosity and temperature. The test kit also enables a check to be made on viscosity index. Fuel and lubricating oil samples can be tested.

Specific gravity can be measured in the range 0.89 to 1.05. High specific gravity fuel is becoming more common and appropriate adjustments to the purification equipment, in particular, are essential. The specific gravity value also enables volume to weight conversion calculations to check delivery quantities or estimate fuel costs. The test kit comprises a thermostatically controlled heating unit into which the sample is placed. A hydrometer is then used to obtain the specific gravity reading. Fuel and lubricating oil samples can be tested.

Viscosity monitoring

Viscosity control of fuels is essential if correct atomization is to take place. Increasing the temperature of a fuel will reduce its viscosity and vice versa. As a result of the varying properties of marine fuels, often within one tank, actual viscosity must be continuously measured and then corrected by temperature adjustment.

The sensing device is shown in Figure 3.31. A small constant speed gear pump forces a fixed quantity of oil through a capillary (narrow

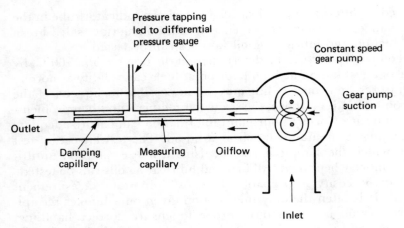

Figure 3.31 Viscosity sensor

bore) tube. The liquid flow in the capillary is such that the difference in pressure readings taken before the capillary and after it is related to the oil viscosity. A differential pressure gauge is calibrated to read viscosity and the pressure values are used to operate the heater control to maintain some set viscosity value.

ELECTRICITY

Electrical measurements of current or voltage are usually made by a moving coil meter. The meter construction is the same for each but its arrangement in the circuit is different.

A moving coil meter consists of a coil wound on a soft iron cylinder which is pivoted and free to rotate, see Figure 3.32. Two hair springs are used, one above and one below, to provide a restraining force and

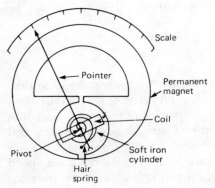

Figure 3.32 Moving coil meter

also to conduct the current to the coil. The moving coil assembly is surrounded by a permanent magnet which produces a radial magnetic field. Current passed through the coil will result in a force which moves the coil against the spring force to a position which, by a pointer on a scale, will read current or voltage.

The instrument is directional and must therefore be correctly connected in the circuit. As a result of the directional nature of alternating current, it cannot be measured directly with this instrument, but the use of a rectifying circuit will overcome this problem. This mechanism is found in galvanometers, moving coil ammeters and voltmeters and some display units in control consoles.

PHOTOELECTRIC CELLS

Photoelectric cells operate as a result of changes brought about by the incidence of light upon certain materials. They are used as sensors in equipment such as the oil-in-water monitor, crankcase oil mist detector and flame failure detector. Light is a form of radiant energy and while most of these devices use visible light some may utilize infra-red rays. This radiant energy will affect a variety of materials in different ways. Three forms of photoelectric cell are in use: photoconductive, photoemissive and photovoltaic.

Photoemissive cells utilize a film of metal such as caesium as a cathode onto which light is incident. As a result electrons flow from the cathode to an anode and a potential is created between the two. The cell is usually contained in an evacuated glass envelope. Alternatively the cell may be gas-filled, when the electron flow will ionize the gas to produce more electrons and hence an amplified signal.

Photoconductive cells use light-sensitive semiconductor materials such as cadmium sulphide, lead sulphide, selenium and germanium. The resistance between metal electrodes placed in the material will vary depending upon the amount of incident light. Considering the above materials, lead sulphide is mainly used for infra-red radiation sensing and the others for visible light radiation sensing.

Photovoltaic cells use incident light upon a junction of two different materials to produce an e.m.f. A typical cell consists of a sandwich-type construction of cadmium metal, selenium (a semiconductor material) and a thin transparent cover. Light passing through the transparent material releases electrons from the selenium which flow to the cadmium and generate an e.m.f. which can be used in a circuit which requires no other power source.

FIRE AND EXPLOSIVE GAS DETECTORS

The early detection of smoke, excessive heat, flames or an explosive atmosphere can enable rapid action to alleviate the situation. Various types of fire detector are in use which must be reliable in operation and require little maintenance. Furthermore they must not be set off by any normal occurrence in the protected space, i.e. they must be appropriately sensitive. An explosive gas detector is used to sample a suspect atmosphere for the presence of combustible gases.

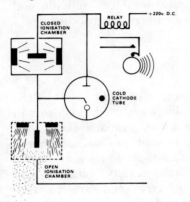 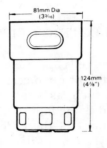

Figure 3.33 Smoke detector

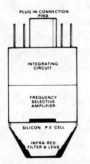 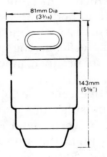

Figure 3.34 Infra-red flame detector

The smoke detector makes use of two ionization chambers, one open to the atmosphere and one closed, see Figure 3.33. The fine particles or aerosole given off by a fire alter the resistance in the open ionization chamber, resulting in the operation of a cold cathode gas-filled valve. The alarm sounds on the operation of the valve to give warning of the fire. Smoke detectors are used in machinery spaces, accommodation areas and cargo holds.

Flames, as opposed to smoke, are often the main result of gas and liquid fires and flame detectors are used to protect against such hazards. Flames give off ultraviolet and infra-red radiation and detectors are available to respond to either. An infra-red flame detector is shown in Figure 3.34. Flame detectors are used near to fuel handling equipment in the machinery spaces and also at boiler fronts.

Heat detectors can use any of a number of principles of operation, such as liquid expansion, low melting point materials or bimetallic strips. The most usual detector nowadays operates on either a set temperature rise or a rate of temperature rise being exceeded. Thus an increase in temperature occurring quickly could set off the alarm before the set temperature was reached. The relative movement of two coiled bimetallic thermostats, one exposed and one shielded, acts as the detecting element, see Figure 3.35. Heat detectors are used in places such as the galley and laundry where other types of detector would give false alarms.

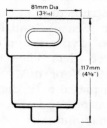

Figure 3.35 Heat detector

Associated with fire detectors is the electric circuit to ring an alarm bell. This bell will usually sound in the machinery space if the fire occurs there, and also on the bridge. Fires in other spaces will result in alarm bells sounding on the bridge.

INSTRUMENT CALIBRATION

While the carrying of spares will enable replacement of faulty instruments, the need for testing and calibration must also be met on board. Various portable test equipment is available to ensure the correct operation of electronic, pneumatic, mechanical and hydraulic instrumentation and control equipment.

A pneumatic instrument calibration and test set enables pressure gauges, differential pressure transmitters, computing relays, process controllers and control valve actuators to be calibrated to an accuracy of plus or minus 0.25 per cent. The unit comprises two dual-scale 125 mm (6 inch) gauges, one calibrated 0 to 30 lbf/in^2 and 0 to 2 kg/cm^2 and the other 0 to 400 in. w.g. and 0 to 10 000 mm w.g. Two regulated outputs of 0 to 2 kg/cm^2 and one of 0 to 400 in. w.g. are provided. This enables the simulation of a signal to a transmitter and the monitoring of its output. The only external supply required is a 2.1 kg/cm^2 (35 lbf/in^2) air supply. Four 1820 mm (6 ft) flexible plastic hoses enable the calibrator to be used where instruments are fitted in inaccessible positions.

A temperature calibration bath can be used to test various primary temperature sensing elements. The heated liquid may be oil or water and an electric heating element is used. Accurate temperature control to within plus or minus 0.01°C is possible in the range ambient to 260°C. A three-digit LED display of temperature is provided. A cooling coil is also available to enable temperature calibration down to −10°C. The cooling medium is ethanol. A circulation pump minimizes temperature variations in the bath.

Electronic instrumentation can be checked with a calibration unit which will both measure and inject constant voltage and constant current signals. Typical applications would be for controllers, indicators and recorders. The selected output is continuously variable from 0 to 199.9 mV or mA, using coarse and fine potentiometer controls. The display is a 3½ digit, 12 mm dual polarity, liquid crystal display. The various test functions are selected by push buttons. There is a 6 V maximum drive capability on the current output range and a limit of about 200 mA in the event of a short circuit. An accuracy of plus or minus 0.1 per cent of full scale deflection with a resolution of 100 mV/mA is provided. The unit is powered by two rechargeable batteries and the charging circuit is built in.

4 Control signals

The measurement of various different parameters has been considered in the previous chapter. These measuring instruments, or transducers, produce signals in various forms which may be amplified, transmitted or used in control systems. The manipulation, or handling, of these signals will now be considered. The measurement data may be in the form of electrical or pneumatic signals whose handling will be examined in two of the sections which follow. Hydraulics, fluidics and photoelectricity, as control signal media, will also be examined. Finally, digital signals, which can occur in several media, will be discussed.

ELECTRONICS

It is assumed that the reader has some knowledge of electronics and, in particular, of semiconductor devices. The atomic theory relating to the operation of electronic devices will not be considered. A brief revision of the more important semiconductor devices will be given, explaining their functions and some typical examples.

Semiconductors

A semiconductor is a material that is neither conductor nor insulator, it is somewhere in between. Reference will be made to n-type and p-type semiconductor materials. These are materials whose crystal structure and electron bonding characteristics have been changed by 'doping', or the addition of other materials. Where the crystal structure is changed to produce a surplus of electrons, it is known as an n-type material. Where the material has a deficiency of electrons, it is known as a p-type material.

83

Diode

A diode is formed at a junction of n-type and p-type semiconductor materials. It has a high resistance to current flow in one direction and a low resistance in the other. It effectively permits current flow in only

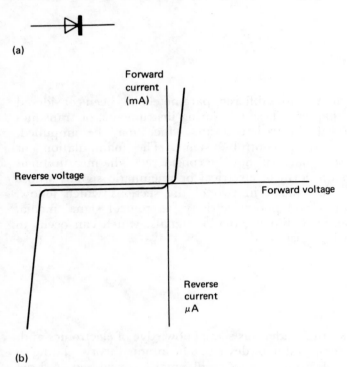

(a)

(b)

Figure 4.1 Junction diode: (a) symbol; (b) characteristic

one direction. The electrical symbol and operating characteristic are shown in Figure 4.1. The arrowhead of the electrical symbol indicates the direction of permitted current flow.

Diode applications

The most common application of diodes is in rectifiers, although the Zener diode may be used as a voltage regulator. A diode circuit may also be employed as a demodulator to recover a control signal. A rectifier converts an alternating current into a unidirectional or direct current. This can be done by suppressing alternate half-waves, i.e. half-wave rectification, or by inverting alternate half-waves, i.e. full-wave rectification.

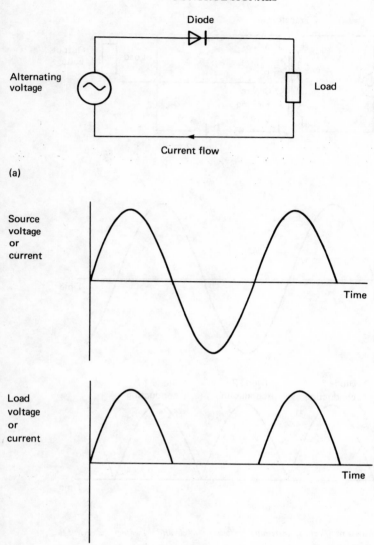

Figure 4.2 Half-wave rectification: (a) circuit; (b) voltage and current flow

A half-wave rectifier circuit is shown in Figure 4.2(a). When the source polarity is such that the diode is forward biased then current will flow. On the half-cycle when the source polarity provides a reverse bias no current will flow. The alternating source voltage and the rectified current flow are shown in Figure 4.2(b). There will be a

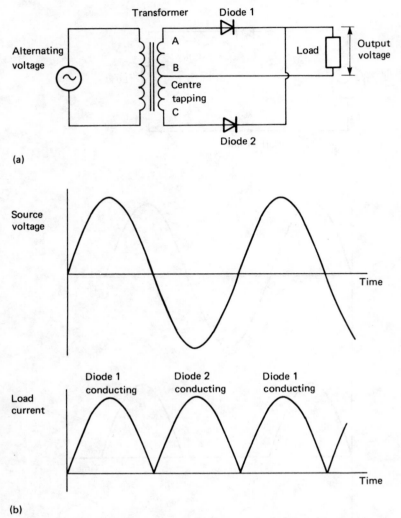

Figure 4.3 Full-wave rectification, centre-tap transformer: (a) circuit; (b) voltage and current flow

slight voltage drop across the diode and some small reverse current flow but these are usually insignificant.

Full-wave rectification is obviously more efficient and can be achieved by using two diodes in conjunction with a centre-tapped transformer, see Figure 4.3(a). When A is positive with respect to C, current will flow through diode 1 to the load and back to the centre tapping at B. When C is positive with respect to A, current will flow through diode 2 to the load and back to B. The alternating source voltage and the rectified current flow are shown in Figure 4.3(b). It should be noted that the output voltage across the load is only half the transformer secondary voltage.

A bridge rectifier enables full-wave rectification without a centre-tapped transformer but uses four diodes, see Figure 4.4. When

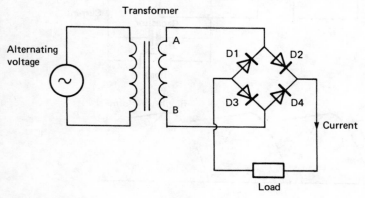

Figure 4.4 Bridge rectifier

A is positive with respect to B diode D2 will conduct current to the load and diode D3 will return the current to B. On the alternate half-cycle diodes D1 and D4 will conduct and complete the circuit, providing current in the same direction. Full-wave rectification is thus achieved and in this case the output voltage across the load is equal to transformer secondary voltage.

Full-wave rectification produces a d.c. voltage with an alternating component. It is desirable to reduce this component in order to provide a primarily d.c. voltage. This is achieved by means of filters. The simplest filter uses a capacitor in parallel with the load as shown in Figure 4.5(a). As the rectified voltage rises the capacitor is charged. As it falls the capacitor discharges and filters out, or smooths, the alternating waveform reducing it to a small ripple, see Figure 4.5(b). Capacitor input filters are made up of a capacitor connected across the output of the rectifier and a low-pass filter. The low-pass filter may be a series connected inductance or a resistance followed by a parallel connected capacitor. Appropriate values are chosen for each to provide the required ripple suppression. Choke input filters have the rectified output fed into a series inductance and a parallel connected capacitance. This device can only be used with full-wave rectification since a current must flow at all times.

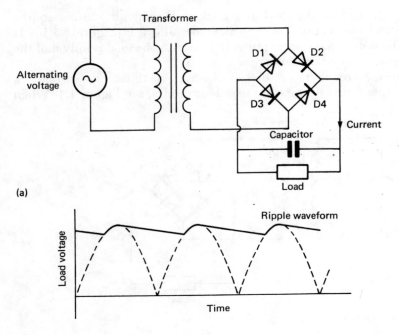

(b)

Figure 4.5 Filter circuit: (a) capacitor filter; (b) voltage waveform

Another means of providing a stabilized voltage is by the use of a Zener diode. A typical circuit arrangement is shown in Figure 4.6. When the Zener diode is operated in the breakdown region the current flowing through the diode can vary considerably, but the voltage across the diode will be virtually constant. The current supplied to the circuit will be the sum of the load and diode currents. If the load current increases, the diode current will fall and, providing it does not fall below that required for breakdown, the potential difference across the diode will be constant.

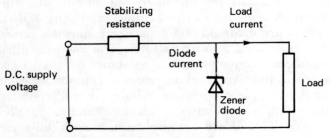

Figure 4.6 Zener diode voltage stabilizer

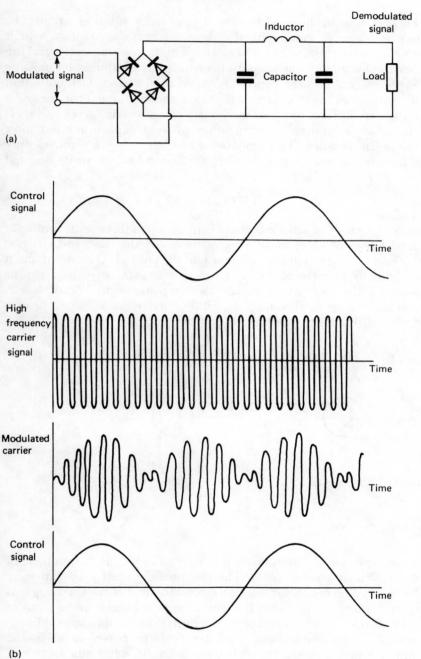

Figure 4.7 Modulation and demodulation: (a) demodulation circuit; (b) signal waveform

Diodes can also be used in detecting or demodulating circuits. In order to transmit some control signals use may be made of a high frequency carrier signal or waveform. This can be done by varying either the frequency, the amplitude or the phase with respect to some reference signal and the process is called modulation. Demodulation is the extraction of the control signal from the modulated carrier and a suitable circuit for amplitude modulation is shown in Figure 4.7(a). It is, in effect, a rectifying circuit followed by a capacitor input filter using an inductance. This smoothing or filter network removes only the high frequency carrier, leaving the control signal in its original form, see Figure 4.7(b).

Transistor

The transistor or bipolar transistor is made up of three semiconductor material regions. The middle region is called the base and the two outer regions are called the collector and the emitter. Depending upon the choice of semiconductor materials a transistor may be p-n-p or n-p-n and the electrical symbols used are shown in Figure 4.8. A transistor can be used to amplify, either currents or voltages, or as a switch, to turn large currents on and off.

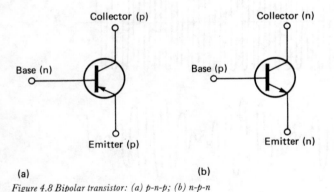

Figure 4.8 Bipolar transistor: (a) p-n-p; (b) n-p-n

Transistor static characteristics are available as a number of current against voltage plots. The measuring circuit used can have different arrangements for the transistor. Any one of the three regions may be connected such that it is common to the input and output of the measuring circuit. The common emitter connection is usual as it provides a high voltage gain and a very large power gain. In the common emitter mode the emitter current is determined, almost completely, by the base-emitter voltage.

The input characteristic shows the change in base current as the base-emitter voltage is varied. The output characteristic shows the change in collector current as the collector-emitter voltage is varied, for a constant value of base current. A family of curves is obtained when different fixed base currents are used. The output characteristic is shown in Figure 4.9, for an n-p-n transistor.

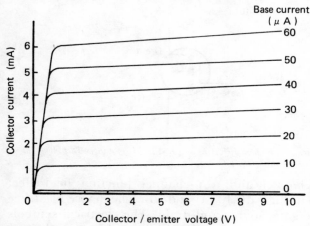

Figure 4.9 Transistor characteristics

The output characteristic shows a small leakage current for a zero base current. In a silicon transistor this will only be a few nano amperes (10^{-9}A) but will increase with temperature.

For a p-n-p transistor all the voltage polarities are reversed. The transistor can be used to amplify electrical signals when it is operated in the linear range of its characteristics. It can be operated between the cut-off points of the characteristic and thus act as a switch. These two particular applications will be discussed in later sections dealing with amplifiers and logic gates. There are also many other applications of this versatile device.

Field-effect transistor (FET)

The field-effect transistor, while performing the functions of a bipolar transistor, operates in a completely different manner. Two types exist, the junction field-effect transistor (JFET) and the metal-oxide-semiconductor field-effect transistor (MOSFET). The MOSFET type may be further classified as enhancement-type or depletion-type. All field-effect transistors may be n-channel or p-channel, depending upon the type of semiconductor material employed. The electrical

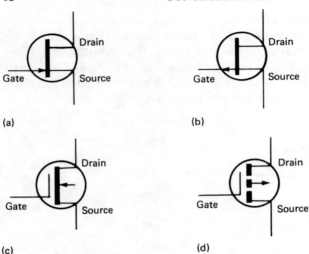

Figure 4.10 Field-effect transistors: (a) n-channel JFET (b) p-channel JFET (c) n-channel depletion-type MOSFET (d) n-channel enhancement-type MOSFET

symbols for an n-channel and a p-channel junction field-effect transistor are shown in Figure 4.10 (a) and (b). The device has three electrodes, called the gate, source and drain. The electrical symbols for an n-channel depletion-type MOSFET and an n-channel enhancement-type MOSFET are shown in Figure 4.10 (c) and (d). MOSFETs can be damaged by static or other electronic charges and should have their gate and source leads shorted together during handling or soldering.

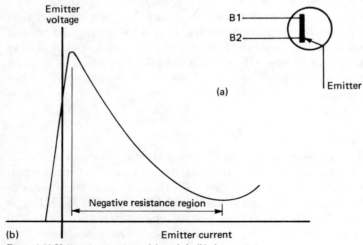

Figure 4.11 Unijunction transistor: (a) symbol; (b) characteristic

Unijunction transistor (UJT)

This device consists of a channel of n-type semiconductor material with a single junction of p-type material at about the centre. The p-type material junction acts as an emitter. The electrical symbol and operating characteristic are shown in Figure 4.11. As the emitter voltage rises it will eventually enable an emitter current to flow. The flow of the emitter current will reduce the emitter-to-B1 resistance, causing more current to flow, i.e. a negative resistance condition. This pulse of current can be used to 'fire' a thyristor. One particular use of a unijunction transistor is in an oscillator circuit which is described in a later section.

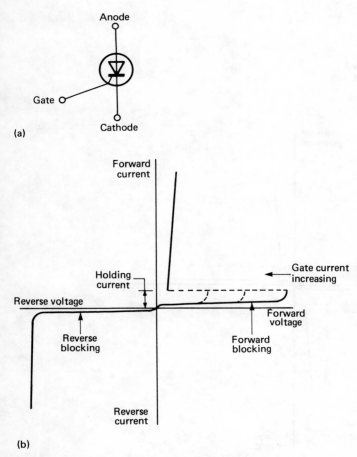

(a)

(b)

Figure 4.12 Silicon controlled rectifier: (a) symbol; (b) characteristic

Silicon controlled rectifier (SCR)

This device is also known as a thyristor and is a 'sandwich' of p-n-p-n semiconductor materials. The electrical symbol is shown in Figure 4.12(a). The gate terminal is used to 'switch on' the thyristor or make it pass a forward current. The operating characteristic is shown in Figure 4.12(b). A small gate current can be used to switch on a large load current. The load current can be switched off by interrupting the load current or reducing it below the holding current.

Where an alternating voltage is applied between the anode and cathode the SCR will act as a non-conducting diode for reverse current flow and a low voltage drop conductor for normal current flow, when the gate current is turned on. This is therefore a

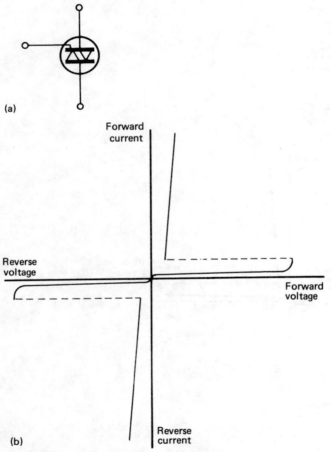

(a)

Figure 4.13 Triac: (a) symbol; (b) characteristic

controllable half-wave rectifier. If full-wave rectification is required then two SCRs are used, connected back-to-back. A single piece of silicon providing such an arrangement is called a triac. Only one gate is required, which can control the conduction of current in either direction. The circuit symbol and characteristics of a triac are shown in Figure 4.13. The triggering circuit often contains a device known as a diac. This is somewhat similar to a triac but without the gate terminal. It is designed to conduct when a positive or negative breakover voltage is exceeded. The diac will enable a voltage build-up such that a large pulse of gate current is suddenly applied to the triac.

Silicon controlled rectifiers are used in control circuits for power equipment such as motors or heaters. A motor speed control arrangement is described in Chapter 6. They are also used as power converters where, for example, electricity at a variable frequency and voltage is converted into a stable voltage and frequency. This static frequency converter is described in Chapter 6.

Amplifiers

An amplifier is used to amplify or increase a low power signal to a higher value that can be used to control or drive some load. Transistor amplifiers can be produced by the use of various circuit configurations. So far the input circuit has been considered as connected between base and emitter, i.e. the emitter is the common electrode, and this is the most common arrangement in use. The bipolar transistor can however operate with either the base, the collector or the emitter used as the common electrode. Each arrangement will enable amplification, the common base giving voltage gain and some power gain, the common collector giving current gain and power gain while the common emitter can be used for current, voltage or power amplification.

Amplifiers can be classified in a number of ways, either by function, by duty or by bias position. Function usually relates to frequency, where the amplifier may be zero, audio, radio, very high or ultra-high frequency. Zero-frequency types are used to amplify steady currents or voltages and are often referred to as d.c. amplifiers. The term d.c. is sometimes used to mean direct coupled as well as direct current (zero frequency a.c. is d.c.). All zero and low frequency amplifiers are direct coupled and used to amplify steady currents and voltages. Where duty is the classifier the apparatus or equipment will determine the type required. A voltage amplifier is designed to provide an undistorted voltage output. A power amplifier is used where considerable power is required. The bias position classification produces Class A, Class B and Class C types of amplifier. The requirement regarding distortion and efficiency of an amplifier cannot both be achieved and thus result in the class type. A voltage amplifer requires minimum distortion, regardless of efficiency. The transistor is thus biased such that the changes in collector current have the same waveform as the changes in input signal current. This is Class A mode whose efficiency is low, typically less than 20 per cent, and with a maximum of 50 per cent in terms of output to power from the supply.

Efficiency is an important consideration in a power amplifier. The bias point is therefore positioned such that the transistor is operated almost at the cut-off point. There would, therefore, be no forward biasing of the base-emitter junction. This would be Class B mode operation with collector current only present for half the input signal cycle. An efficiency range of 50 to 78 per cent is then possible. Class C mode operates the transistor beyond the cut-off point to achieve about 90 per cent efficiency, with considerable distortion. The load would normally be a tuned circuit.

A transistor voltage amplifier is shown in Figure 4.14(a). The emitter connection is common to the signal circuit and the load circuit. This configuration is known as common emitter mode or grounded emitter mode, since the emitter is connected to earth. This arrangement is usually used for voltage amplification since a small change in input voltage causes a change in input current, i.e. base current. The collector current will in turn vary, resulting in a change of potential difference across the load resstance, R_L. Since the supply voltage is fixed then the collector voltage or output signal must vary. When, for example, the input signal or base voltage increased then the base current will increase. The collector current will also increase, resulting in an increased voltage drop across the load resistance. The output or collector voltage must therefore fall. Thus as the input voltage rises the output voltage falls, i.e. they are 180° out of phase.

Auto or self-biasing is essential to ensure that temperature or component material variations do not affect the amplifier operation. The base is held at a constant negative voltage by the potential divider $(R_1 + R_2)$ which is connected across the supply. The current through the resistors is considerably larger than the base bias current in order that the voltage at the junction is almost unaffected by changes in base bias current. Any increase in collector current and thus emitter current will increase the voltage drop across the emitter resistance, R_E. With the base voltage constant, the voltage between base and emitter junction will reduce and also the bias current. The current flow through the unit will thus be stabilized. The capacitor, C_E, will effectively bypass any a.c. components of the collector

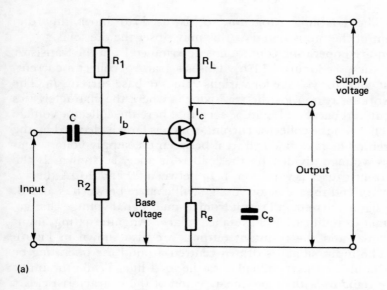

(a)

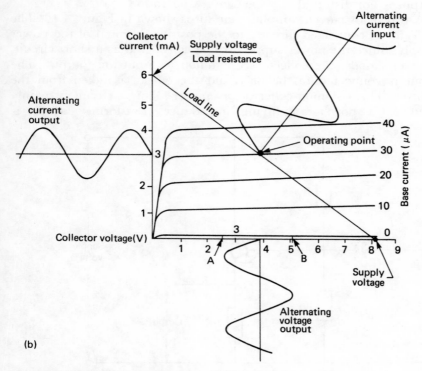

(b)

Figure 4.14 Transistor voltage amplifier: (a) circuit; (b) characteristic

current. The coupling capacitor, C, is used to block any d.c. component of the input signal as this may upset the d.c. bias.

The required operating condition is determined from the transistor characteristics, see Figure 4.14(b). This is a graph of collector current, I_c, against collector voltage for various values of base current, I_B. The normal working region for the transistor is where the characteristics are straight and parallel. It can be seen that here the collector voltage has little effect on the collector current, which is largely decided by the base current. The load line is drawn between the supply voltage and the supply voltage divided by the load resistance, as shown. If the signal current causes a variation in I_B between 20 and 40 µA then I_c will also vary and the collector voltage will change between A and B. Since the signal current will result from a small signal voltage change, then voltage amplification has taken place. An alternating input current signal and the resultant outputs are also shown in Figure 4.14(b). The input signal is drawn centred around the operating or quiescent point and perpendicular to the load line. While the input amplitude remains within the linear region of the characteristic, the output is not distorted. This is Class A operation.

A transistor current amplifier circuit is shown in Figure 4.15. The collector is connected directly to the positive terminal of the power supply. Since the power supply can be considered as a short circuit, for a.c. signals, the collector is common to input and output. The input is connected to the base and the output is taken from the emitter. This common-collector or emitter-follower circuit is mainly used as a power amplifying impedance transformer which is

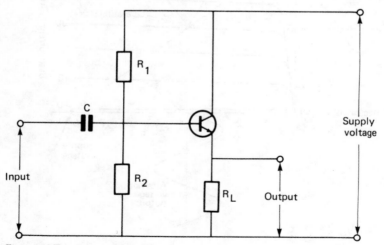

Figure 4.15 Transistor current amplifier

connected between a high impedance source and a low impedance load. A high impedance source will suffer a drop in output if current is taken from it. The current amplifier enables the supply of a high current without affecting the source. The term buffer impedance converter is sometimes used for this current amplifier.

A power amplifier will now be considered which is operated in Class B mode. Class A operation has a maximum possible efficiency of 50 per cent whereas Class B operation can be up to about 78 per cent efficient. The operating or quiescent point is brought down to the cut-off point on the load line, by suitable biasing, see Figure 4.16. A sinusoidal input then produces output current or voltage pulses which are half-sine waves. A Class B amplifier will therefore require two transistors operating in tandem in order to restore the complete waveform. They are arranged in what is called push-pull, see Figure 4.17. The arrangement is referred to as a transformer-coupled push-pull amplifier. The input signal is amplified in a driver stage and

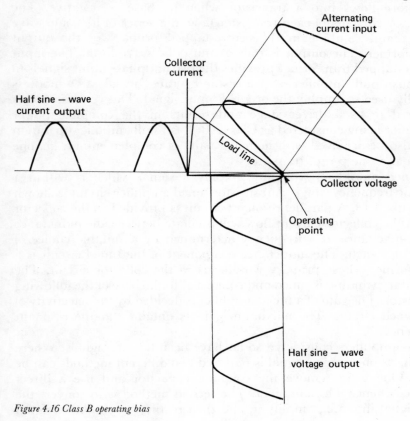

Figure 4.16 Class B operating bias

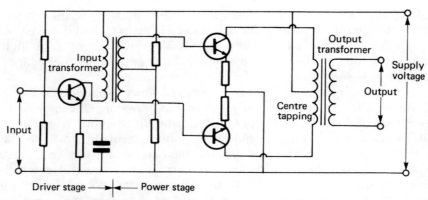

Driver stage ——→|←—— Power stage

Figure 4.17 Transistor-coupled push-pull amplifier

is applied to the primary of the input transformer. The centre-tapped secondary then produces two opposing base voltages. A base current therefore flows into a transistor when its base is negative. The collector currents of each transistor flow in a series of half-sine wave pulses and combine in the centre-tapped primary of the output transformer. The output is thus a sinusoidal wave form. The input centre-tapped transformer provides the two antiphase input signals to the push-pull amplifier. A transistor operated in Class A mode is usually used to amplify the original input signal. This combination is referred to as a driver stage and results in the complete power amplifier being considered as Class AB. Push-pull amplifier operation can also be achieved with matched pairs of complementary, i.e. one n-p-n and one p-n-p, transistors.

Tuned amplifiers will only amplify a signal which is within a specific frequency range. A transistor tuned amplifier circuit is shown in Figure 4.18. A parallel resonant circuit is provided as the collector load. The collector current flow will oscillate between the inductance and capacitance at a frequency determined by a suitable choice of values for each. The inductance component of the tuned circuit is a transformer whose primary winding is in the collector circuit. The secondary winding is tuned and connected to the base of the following transistor. The gain of a tuned amplifier is decided by the selectivity of the tuned circuit. The maximum gain is obtained at the resonant frequency.

The amplifiers considered so far have been for a.c. signals. Where amplification of a d.c. signal is required two different methods can be used. One is to remove the coupling capacitor and use a direct coupled (hence d.c.) amplifier. The second method is to convert the d.c. signal into a.c., amplify it, and then rectify the amplified signal

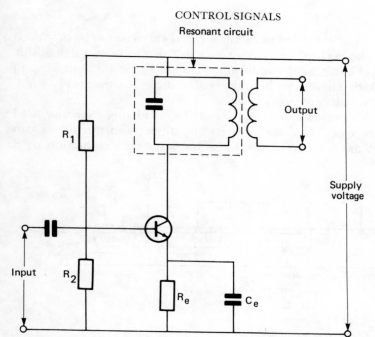

Figure 4.18 Transistor tuned amplifier

back to d.c. The direct coupled amplifier is not readily usable because of the temperature sensitivity of transistors and the small current flow that is always needed to maintain the operating point. These problems can be overcome by a difference (differential) amplifier circuit, which is often part of an operational amplifier input circuit. Operational amplifiers (op-amps), and in particular instrumentation amplifiers, are described in a later section.

When the d.c. signal is converted into a.c., this is known as 'chopping'. The three methods available are electrical, mechanical and optical. In electrical chopping the d.c. signal is shorted out periodically by using a device such as a field-effect transistor. A square wave of amplitude equal to the d.c. signal is thus produced with a frequency related to the operation of the transistor. The a.c. signal is then amplified and chopped, at the same frequency, to produce an output signal. A filtering stage smooths the output into a d.c. signal. Some operational amplifiers utilize chopping in their operation.

Integrated circuits (ICs)

A single semiconductor component can be manufactured from a small piece of silicon which has been suitably treated or doped. This

technique can be extended to enable a complete circuit to be produced
in a single silicon chip. The circuit may be referred to as a monolithic
(single-piece) integrated circuit since only a single piece or chip of
silicon is used. Modern techniques enable these ICs to be very small
in size and weight and usually low in cost.

Circuit components are produced by oxidizing, etching and
diffusing processes. Resistors, capacitors, diodes and transistors can
be produced as shown in Figure 4.19. One of the most commonly used

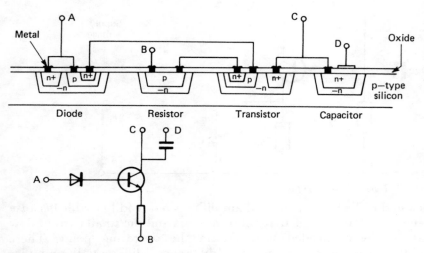

Figure 4.19 IC components

active components in early ICs was the n-p-n transistor but now the
MOSFET is used since it has the advantage of being smaller. One
particular form of MOSFET uses complementary symmetry metal-
oxide semiconductor devices in its circuitry and is referred to as
CMOS (pronounced 'seemoss'). These devices utilize mostly active
components and can thus reduce or eliminate resistors and capacitors,
which utilize considerable chip area. Integrated resistors utilize the
resistivity of a silicon layer which is usually provided as a square. A
particular resistance value is obtained by the series connection of
several individual resistor squares. Integrated capacitors may utilize
the capacitance of a reverse-biased p-n junction, as shown, or that of a
layer of silicon dioxide between two conducting areas. A fabricated
complete integrated circuit will contain the various individual
components suitably connected by a pattern of aluminium contacts
which is deposited onto the chip. A suitable package then
encapsulates the IC. Epoxy flat packs with leads from the two longest

sides are most common. The connections are usually bent at 90° to the pack for insertion into printed circuit boards (PCBs) and are referred to as dual-in-line packages (DIPs)

While ICs were originally developed to provide non-linear or digital (i.e. logic) circuits they are now used for many linear devices such as audio-frequency amplifiers, radio-frequency amplifiers and operational amplifiers. Where ICs are used, various circuit components are required, such as resistors for operational amplifiers to decide the voltage gain. Inductors cannot be provided in ICs and must therefore be external components. Where very large circuits are incorporated in a single chip the unit may be termed large scale integration (LSI) or very large scale integration (VLSI). A microprocessor is an example of VLSI.

Operational amplifiers

Amplifiers have been discussed previously and are used to process various signals by increasing, converting or altering them in some predetermined manner. Ideally the input signal should not be affected or changed and should only be amplified. Noise and distortion are inevitably added by an amplifier to the input signal. The amplifier components may have manufacturing tolerances, their values may change in time or with temperature, all of which will vary the signal gain. However, the use of negative feedback and integrated circuits can resolve most of these difficulties. A reduction in gain does unfortunately result from the application of negative feedback. An operational amplifier (op-amp) is a very high gain directly coupled amplifier device. It is able to generate a variety of different functions some of which include mathematical operations, hence the name. The gain of a typical op-amp is in the region of 200 000, ideally it would be infinite. The input impedance is around 2 000 000 ohms and again ideally would be infinite. The output impedance is low with typical values around 150 ohms or less. The operating or supply voltage is usually ±15 V. The output voltage range is around ±12 V which, considering the high gain, indicates an input voltage of ±6 µV. This is so small as to be considered as a 'virtual earth'. The input current is also so small that it is ignored. An operational amplifier is made up of three stages, which are a difference (differential) amplifier, a voltage amplifier and an output amplifier. The difference amplifier will amplify the difference between the two inputs and thus will reject interference or noise signals which occur at both terminals simultaneously.

Operational amplifier circuits for an inverting and a non-inverting amplifier are shown in Figure 4.20. The operational amplifier symbol

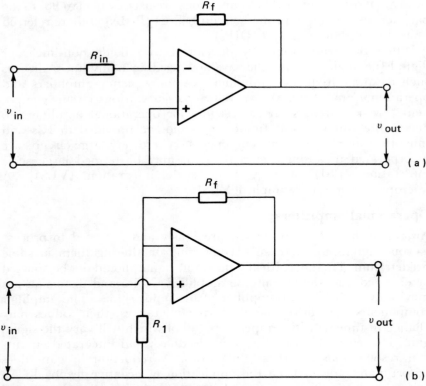

Figure 4.20 Operational amplifiers: (a) inverting; (b) non-inverting

can also be seen. In each case a large amount of negative feedback is used in order to specify accurately the voltage gain. The inverting input terminal is normally marked with a minus sign and any applied input will be inverted at the output. The non-inverting input is usually marked with the plus sign. In the inverting amplifier the input is determined by the input voltage and the resistance, R_f. The current through the op-amp is very small and therefore the output voltage will be the product of the input current and resistance, R_f. Thus

$$\text{Voltage gain} = \frac{\text{Output voltage}}{\text{Input voltage}}$$

$$= -\frac{\text{Input current} \times R_f}{\text{Input current} \times R_{IN}}$$

$$= \frac{-R_f}{R_{IN}}$$

The negative sign indicates that the output is inverted. In the non-inverting amplifier the voltage gain can be determined, after a slight approximation, in terms of R_1 and R_2.

$$\text{Voltage gain} = \frac{\text{Output voltage}}{\text{Input voltage}}$$

$$= \frac{R_1 + R_f}{R_1}$$

In the non-inverting op-amp circuit the input resistance will be a high value while the output resistance will be a low value.

A summing amplifier circuit is shown in Figure 4.21(a). An extension of the approach used for the inverting amplifier will shown that:

$$\text{Output voltage} = \text{Input current} \times R_f$$

$$= -\left(\frac{V_1}{R_1} + \frac{V_2}{R_2}\right) R_f$$

If all the resistances were equal then the output voltage would be the negative sum of the input voltages. This circuit may be arranged for unity or a particular gain and can have two or more inputs.

An integrating amplifier circuit is shown in Figure 4.21(b). The capacitor in the feedback circuit will charge and discharge at a rate related to the change of the input signal. The change in output voltage will therefore be related to the integral of the feedback current with respect to time.

$$\text{Output voltage} = \frac{1}{CR} \int v_{in} \, dt$$

A differentiating amplifier circuit is shown in Figure 4.21(c). The input voltage will be a function of time such that

$$\text{Output voltage} = R_f C \frac{dv_{in}}{dt}$$

Instrumentation amplifiers

An instrumentation amplifier is in many respects similar to an operational amplifier except that it has internal feedback. This

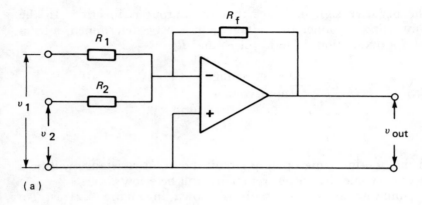

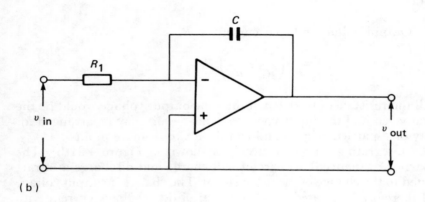

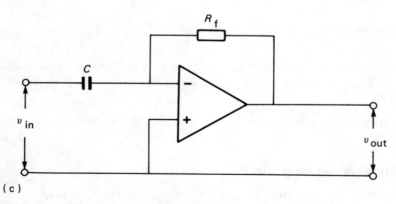

Figure 4.21 Operational amplifier circuits: (a) summer; (b) integrator; (c) differentiator

therefore eliminates the need for external feedback components with precise values. The amplifier gain can be varied between 1 and 1000 by changing the value of a single external resistor. This type of unit is used to amplify a differential input signal. It is also designed to reject noise and interference which may be present in the signal lines. The input signal is usually provided as a value which fluctuates above and below zero or ground. Any interference signals will then appear simultaneously, i.e. common-mode, and be rejected. A high common-mode rejection ratio is therefore a particular feature of instrumentation amplifiers. This is defined as the ratio of the common-mode voltage range to the peak-to-peak change in input offset voltage over the range. A high input impedance (2×10^{12} ohms) is also provided, much more than an operational amplifier connected as a difference amplifier. Typical examples of input signals would be from a thermocouple or a low impedance strain gauge. The amplifier may be an IC which is built into the transducer in order to minimize interference and provide a signal value suitable for transmission.

Voltage comparator

A voltage comparator is used to indicate when a signal exceeds a predetermined voltage level. It is available as a special purpose IC. The reference or set voltage level is fed into one terminal and a varying signal into the other. When the set value is exceeded by the varying or analogue signal, the output is a maximum or high fixed value. When the set value is not exceeded the output is a negligible value. The output is therefore a two-state signal, high or low. This device can be used with oscillators, as a logic interface or as part of an analogue-to-digital converter.

Signal generators

The conditioning of control signals occasionally requires the generation of a suitable signal. An oscillator is used for this purpose and is an electronic circuit which is designed to produce an output e.m.f. with a particular frequency and waveform. The three basic waveforms generally used are sinusoidal, repetitive pulse and sawtooth. Positive feedback is a feature of all oscillator circuits and they are available in IC form. The term *multivibrator* is used to describe an oscillator which produces a repetitive pulse or rectangular waveform. The generated signal may be used to trigger or 'fire' silicon controlled rectifiers, to 'clock' or time logical operations, etc. Three different circuit arrangements are possible to provide astable, monostable or bistable operation. The bistable multivibrator is also known as a *flip-flop* and is used in logic devices which will be discussed in a later section.

In the sine wave oscillator the feedback circuit returns a part of the output to the input and again through the amplifier with an overall zero phase shift. The oscillator thus provides its own input signal. A frequency determining network provides the initial current surge when the unit is switched on and tunes the oscillator to its particular frequency. This circuit may be an inductance-capacitance (L-C) combination, a resistance-capacitance (R-C) network or a quartz crystal. A tuned collector oscillator circuit is shown in Figure 4.22.

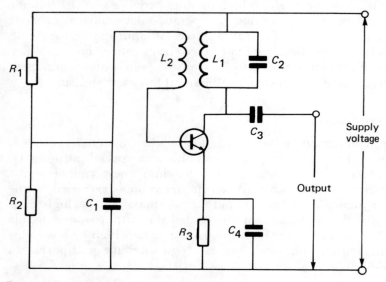

Figure 4.22 Sinusoidal oscillator

The L-C resonant circuit tunes the oscillator with the remaining elements maintaining the oscillation. An almost negligible supply current is drawn in order to maintain the oscillations. Where an IC oscillator is used, only a few discrete components are required to make up the circuit.

The non-sinusoidal oscillator can produce a sawtooth or a variety of repetitive pulse waveforms. They are sometimes referred to as *relaxation oscillators*. The circuit used is designed so that the active devices operate into saturation and then into cut-off. They act therefore as switches rather than amplifiers. The switching action between these two unstable states is determined by the charging and discharging of a capacitor. The pulse shape can be determined by varying the capacitance, the charging current or the voltage applied to the capacitor. Where a sawtooth pulse is produced it should be noted that it is not linear in shape but slightly curved, due to the exponential charging and discharging of the capacitor. A sawtooth pulse generator circuit, using a unijunction transistor, is shown in Figure 4.23 together with the waveform produced. The sawtooth can be made linear by using a constant current supply to feed the capacitor.

The term *mark/space ratio* is used in connection with regular pulse waveforms. It refers to the pulse width to distance between pulses ratio and would be unity for a square wave. The *duty cycle* is the pulse

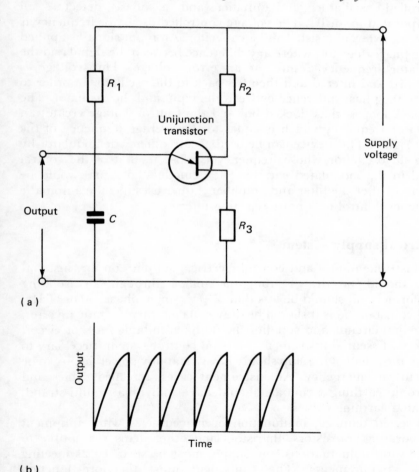

(a)

(b)

Figure 4.23 Sawtooth pulse oscillator: (a) circuit; (b) waveform

width divided by the sum of the pulse width and the distance between pulses.

A variety of ICs exist which can, by suitable external circuit connections, become oscillators. Voltage controlled oscillators, for example, may be used to generate regular pulses and triangular waves. The frequency of these waves is a linear function of the control voltage. It is also a function of an external resistor and capacitor. Applications of this device include signal generation, function generation and frequency modulation. A varying voltage signal can be readily converted into a varying frequency for transmission, i.e. FM modulation. A phase-locked loop is a combination of a voltage controlled oscillator, an amplifier and a phase detector, all incorporated in an IC. The voltage controlled oscillator frequency is set by an external resistor and a capacitor. An input signal is applied to the phase detector, where any difference between the signal and the oscillator frequency results in an error voltage. This voltage is amplified and filtered and then fed back to the oscillator in order to reduce the phase difference between the input and the oscillator. The feedback loop is thus 'locked on' and the control voltage creates an oscillator frequency which is equal to the average frequency of the input signal. This device can be used as a frequency demodulator by using an oscillator whose frequency is close to that of the control signal in the modulated carrier. The demodulated signal would be drawn off after the filter and amplifier. Other uses include automatic frequency control or a noise rejecting filter.

Electrical supply system

The instrumentation and control electrical supplies on a.c. installations should be drawn from the mains through an isolating transformer and should be less than 240 V, single phase, 50 or 60 Hz. On d.c. installations it should be drawn via a rotary or static inverter. Individual circuits and supplies should have suitable fuses or circuit breakers. Essential instrumentation and control systems necessary to ensure the safety of the ship should have a standby power facility to be used in an emergency. All instrument cases, screened cables and electronic earthing terminals should have individual, multi-strand, insulated earthing cables.

To avoid damage, malfunction or inaccuracies with equipment incorporating transistors, thyristors and other items susceptible to power supply fluctuations, the supply must be specified as meeting specific requirements. The equipment must therefore function satisfactorily within these variations. The supply frequency is permitted a continuous plus or minus 5 per cent variation or a plus or minus 10 per cent variation for up to 3 seconds. An a.c. supply voltage may vary continuously within plus 6 per cent and minus 10 per cent or a plus 20 per cent variation for one second. A d.c. supply may vary continuously by plus or minus 20 per cent. Randomly phased over or under voltage transients must also be accepted, whose amplitudes would not exceed percentages of r.m.s. values as follows: 100 per cent for 2000 microseconds, 200 per cent for 200 microseconds, 300 per cent for 20 microseconds and 400 per cent for 2 microseconds. It should be noted that modern electronic equipment would not be adversely affected by such small variations.

The performance of electronic equipment can be seriously affected by interference. It is necessary therefore to suppress this interference, which may be generated in machines or coupled inductively or capacitively into mains or signal leads from various sources. Protection can be obtained by the use of low impedance signal input circuits and d.c. current transmission of signals. Other methods include twisted, screened signal pairs, filtering and transient protection circuits on mains inputs and power supply units or high noise immunity logic circuits.

Electronic control systems are usually built up from modules and a stabilized power supply module is always part of the system. This unit provides the necessary supply stabilization protected against voltage spikes, short-circuited outputs and other hazards. Some power units have diodes built into the output circuit to enable no-break changeover to a standby supply. The output capacitors in such a unit provides sufficient energy to prevent the output voltage falling perceptibly during interruptions of up to 20 milliseconds.

PNEUMATICS

Where a control signal is transmitted by the use of a gas this is generally known as pneumatics. Air is the usual medium and the control signal may be carried by a varying pressure or flow. The variable pressure signal is most common and will be considered in relation to the devices used. These are principally position-balance or force-balance devices. Position balance relates to the balancing of linkages and lever movements and the nozzle-flapper device is an example. Force balance relates to a balancing of forces and the only true example of this is the stacked controller. Pivoted beams which are moved by bellows and nozzle-flappers are sometimes considered as force-balance devices. Fluidics is the general term for devices where the interaction of flows of a medium result in a control signal.

Air as a control medium is usually safe to use in hazardous areas, unless oxygen increases the hazard. No return path is required as the air simply leaks away after use. It is freely and readily available although a certain amount of cleaning as well as compressing is required. The signal transmission is slow by comparison with electronics, and the need for compressors and storage vessels is something of a disadvantage. Pneumatic equipment has been extensively applied in marine control systems and is still very popular.

Nozzle-flapper

The nozzle-flapper arrangement is used in many pneumatic devices and can be considered as a transducer, a valve or an amplifier. It transduces a displacement into a pneumatic signal. The flapper movement acts to close or open a restriction and thus vary air flow through the nozzle. The very small linear movement of the flapper is then converted into a considerable control pressure output from the nozzle. The arrangment is shown in Figure 4.24(a). A compressed air supply is provided at a pressure of about 1 bar. The air must pass through an orifice about 0.25 mm diameter and can then build up a back pressure behind the nozzle. Air will leak out from the nozzle through an opening which is larger than the orifice, e.g. about 0.40 mm. The position of the flapper in relation to the nozzle will determine the amount of air that escapes. If the flapper is close to the nozzle a high controlled pressure will exist; if some distance away, then a low pressure. The characteristic curve relating controlled pressure and nozzle-flapper distance is shown in Figure 4.24(b), The steep, almost linear section of this characteristic is used in the actual operation of the device. The maximum flapper movement is about 20 microns or micrometres in order to provide a fairly linear characteristic. The nozzle-flapper arrangement is therefore a proportional transducer, valve or amplifier. Since the flapper movement is very small it is not directly connected to a measuring unit unless a feedback device is used.

Bellows

The bellows is used in some pneumatic devices to provide feedback and also as a transducer to convert an input pressure signal into a displacement. A simple bellows arrangement is shown in Figure 4.25. The bellows will elongate when the supply pressure increases and

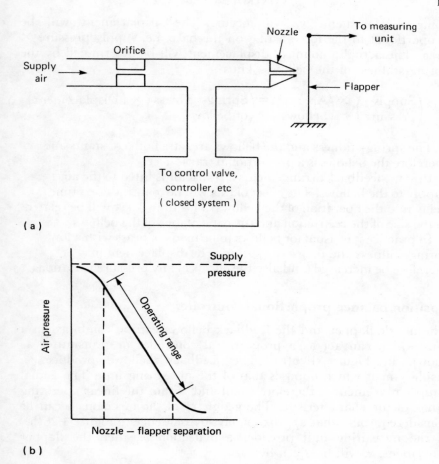

Figure 4.24 Nozzle-flapper mechanism: (a) arrangement; (b) characteristic

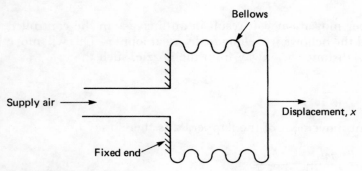

Figure 4.25 Bellows mechanism

some displacement, x, will occur. The displacement will be proportional to the force acting on the base, i.e. supply pressure × area. The actual amount of displacement will be determined by the spring-stiffness of the bellows. Thus

$$\begin{pmatrix}\text{Supply} \\ \text{pressure}\end{pmatrix} \times \begin{pmatrix}\text{Area of} \\ \text{bellows}\end{pmatrix} = \begin{pmatrix}\text{Spring-stiffness} \\ \text{of bellows}\end{pmatrix} \times \begin{pmatrix}\text{Displacement}\end{pmatrix}$$

The spring-stiffness and the bellows area are both constants and therefore the bellows is a proportional transducer.

In some feedback arrangements a restrictor is fitted to the air supply to the bellows. The effect of this will be to introduce a time delay into the operation of the bellows. This time delay will be related to the size of the restriction and the capacitance of the bellows.

In practice it is usual for bellows to be made of brass with a low spring-stiffness and to insert a spring. The displacement may therefore be increased, and also the effects of any pressure variations.

Position balance proportional controller

The nozzle-flapper and the feedback bellows can be combined in a unit which can act as a proportional controller or transmitter as shown in Figure 4.26(a). The feedback bellows produces a displacement which opposes that of the measuring unit. The actual flapper movement is therefore small and within the linear operating range of the characteristic. The geometry of the mechanism can be considered, somewhat approximately, by reference to Figure 4.26(b). If the measuring unit provides a deflection m, then the flapper movement, x, will be given by:

$$\frac{m}{l_1 + l_2} = \frac{x_1}{l_1}$$

The flapper movement will result in an increase in the controlled pressure and the bellows will elongate by an amount b. This will move the flapper a distance, x_2, away from the nozzle, such that

$$\frac{-b}{l_1 + l_2} = \frac{-x_2}{l_2}$$

The resultant movement of the flapper, x, is therefore

$$x_1 - x_2 = \frac{ml_1}{l_1 + l_2} - \frac{bl_2}{l_1 + l_2}$$

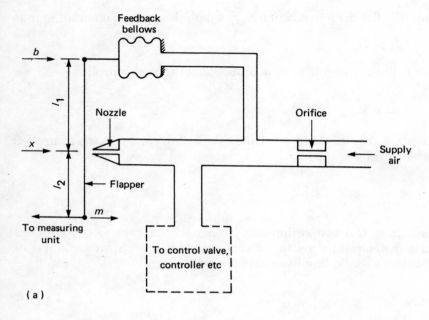

(a)

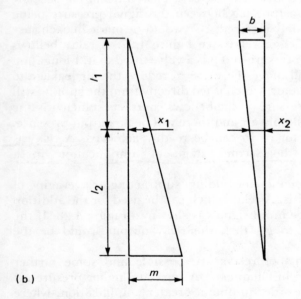

(b)

Figure 4.26 Proportional controller: (a) arrangement; (b) geometry

Since the flapper movement is very small, this may be ignored, so that

$$ml_1 = bl_2$$

The bellows movement, b, is proportional to the controlled pressure, i.e.

$$b = k \times p_c$$

where k is the stiffness coefficient of the bellows and p_c is the controlled pressure. Thus

$$p_c = \frac{l_1}{l_2} \times \frac{m}{k}$$

This, then, is a proportional controller with a gain or proportional increase determined by the linkage ratio $l_1:l_2$. The spring stiffness of the bellows would be a fixed value.

Relay

The unit described above provides a controlled pressure output. This pressure may be inadequate, in the case of a controller, to operate a correcting unit, e.g. a valve. In the case of a transmitter the low pressure will result in a time lag between the signal pressure being transmitted and ultimately received. Use would be made in each case of a pneumatic amplifier or relay, see Figure 4.27. A relay bellows receives the controlled pressure and has a valve fitted to it. Elongation of the relay bellows will move the valve to reduce the air leakage to atmosphere. The output air, which is fed directly from the supply, will therefore increase in pressure. If the bellows contracts sufficiently the valve will close off the supply air and there will be no output pressure. Amplification by a factor of 15 can be readily achieved. A relay is often considered as the second stage of amplification in a nozzle-flapper system.

Relays can also be used for the adding, subtracting or averaging of a number of input signals. A relay which can be used for the addition and subtraction of three input signals is shown in Figure 4.28. If the output were fed back to P_1, then the relay output would be the average of P_2 and P_3.

Various arrangements of relays are possible and some further examples are described in Chapter 7. A separate higher presure air supply may be used in order to obtain greater amplification, where this is required.

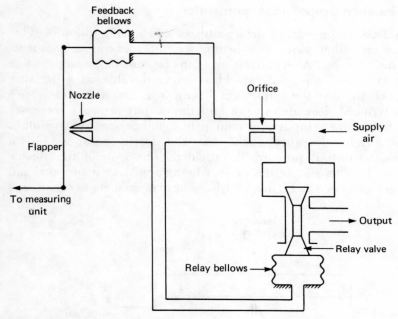

Figure 4.27 Proportional controller and relay

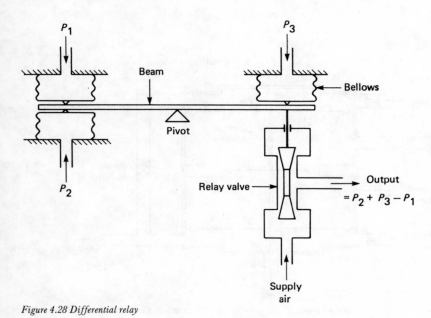

Figure 4.28 Differential relay

Force balance proportional controller

A force balance pneumatic device utilizes a balancing of forces. This may be on either side of a beam, strictly speaking a moment-balancing device. Alternatively it can be on either side of a diaphragm, see Figure 4.29(a). The measured value, as a pressure signal, acts to move the diaphragm downwards. The nozzle clearance is thus reduced, less air escapes and the output pressure increases until it balances the input. Any change in signal pressure will result in a new nozzle clearance such that the forces balance and a proportional output pressure is provided. The gain of this device would be 1. This simple device can be arranged as a proportional controller as shown in Figure 4.29(b). The arrangement is sometimes

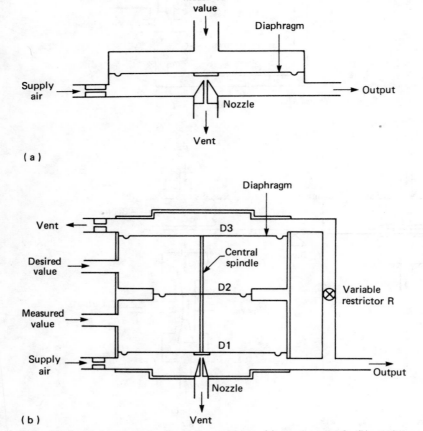

Figure 4.29 Force balance proportional controller—stack type: (a) operating principle; (b) actual arrangement

called a stack controller, since several diaphragm chambers are mounted on top of one another.

Three diaphragms, D1, D2 and D3, are joined by a central spindle and have areas in the ratio 2:1:2 respectively. Supply air acts beneath D1 and the measured value acts above. The measured value also acts beneath D2 and the desired or set value acts above. The desired or set value acts beneath D3 and the output acts above by an amount determined by the position of the variable restrictor R.

Consider R to be closed initially. When the desired and measured values are equal, the diaphragm stack is in the 'null' position and balanced. If the measured value increases by 1 unit of pressure then the output will increase by half a unit due to the relative areas of D1 and D2. This results in a controller gain of 0.5. If R is now wide open then any change in output will immediately act above D3 to further increase the output pressure. The output pressure will reach a maximum value and thus the controller gain will be high, e.g. about 40. Varying the amount of opening of restrictor R will thus determine the gain of the controller. The unit is a proportional controller, a fact that can be proved by equating the forces up and the forces down.

The diaphragms are usually made of neoprene and the absence of mechanical linkages and pivots is considered to minimize the maintenance needs of this device.

Force balance devices may also utilize the nozzle-flapper, as shown in Figure 4.30. The measured value acts within a bellows on one side of a beam and its action is opposed by a spring which positions the beam. The nozzle-flapper or nozzle-beam and a feedback bellows are located on the opposite side of the beam. In operation a change in the measured variable may cause the beam to move towards the nozzle

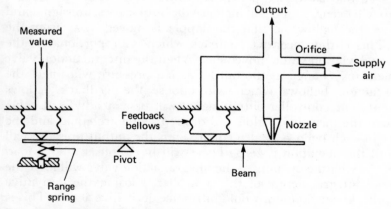

Figure 4.30 Force balance proportional controller—beam type

and thus increase the output pressure. The pressure in the feedback
bellows also increases, tending to push the beam away from the
nozzle, i.e. negative feedback. An equilibrium position will be set up
giving an output which is proportional to the measured variable. The
gain can be adjusted by moving the pivot point of the beam. The
operating range of the measured value can be varied by adjustment of
the range spring.

Three-term controller

Proportional-only control action is limited in its applications due to
offset. Offset is a sustained deviation between the actual and desired
parameter as a result of a load change. The output signal from the
controller must therefore be further conditioned to include integral or
derivative control actions, or both. Integral action occurs when the
output varies at a rate proportional to the deviation between the
desired and the actual controlled parameter. The term reset control is
also used. Derivative action occurs when the output change is
proportional to the rate of change of deviation. The term rate control
is also used. These actions, proportional (P), integral (I) and
derivative (D) are called the terms of a controller. The possible
arrangements are P, P+I, P+D, P+I+D, i.e. single-, two- and
three-term controllers.

A nozzle-flapper three-term controller will now be considered by
reference to Figure 4.31. Any difference between desired and
measured values will result in a movement of the flapper and a change
in the output pressure. If the derivative action valve is open and the
integral action valve closed, then only proportional control occurs. It
can be seen that as the flapper moves towards the nozzle a pressure
build-up will occur, which will increase the output pressure signal and
also move the bellows so that the flapper is moved away from the
nozzle. This is then negative feedback which is proportional to the
flapper or deviation value movement. When the integral action valve
is opened, any change in the output signal pressure will affect the
integral action bellows which will oppose the feedback bellows
movement. The controller output signal will be a steady fixed value
only when the measured value and desired value are equal and the
pressure in each bellows is also equal. Thus the output pressure will
vary until the deviation is zero. There will be no offset after a load
change. Varying the opening of the integral action valve will alter the
amount of integral action of the controller. Closing the derivative
action valve by any amount would introduce derivative action. This is
because of the delay that would be introduced in the provision of

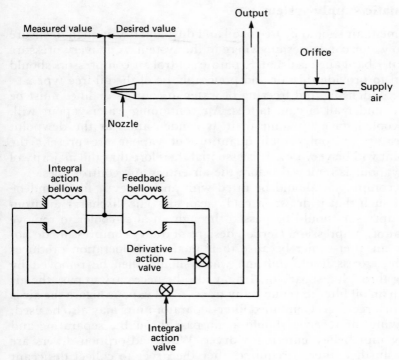

Figure 4.31 Nozzle-flapper three-term controller

negative feedback for a sudden variable change which would enable the output signal pressure to build up. If the measured variable were to change slowly then the proportional action would have time to build up and thus exert its effect. A stack controller arranged for P+I action is described in Chapter 7. Other examples of pneumatic transmitters and controllers are also described.

Pneumatic logic devices

On-off or two-position control can be utilized in logic circuits. The logic circuit is arranged to control some process or device where certain conditions must be met in a defined or logical sequence. Various pneumatic logic devices which provide gate functions, time delays, etc. are available from manufacturers. They can then be assembled into any suitable control circuit arrangement as required.

Pneumatic supply system

Instrument air should be free of oil and dust and dry enough to ensure that no water condenses anywhere in the system. A delivery pressure of about 7 bar gauge is usual. Separate control air compressors should be used to provide this air and preferably be of the oil-free type.

The condensing and freezing of water in control air lines must be avoided under all circumstances. Air containing water vapour will, when cooled, give up some of it as condensation at the dewpoint temperature. If only small quantities of vapour are present the dewpoint will be very low. It is essential therefore that the majority of water vapour is removed before the air enters any control lines.

The compressor should be fitted with an intake air filter, and be located such that it draws in cool, clean air. The discharge air from the compressor should be passed through an after-cooler to remove the heat of compression. Certain designs of rotary compressors do not require an after-cooler because their method of operation produces cool air. Excess liquid, oil and water should then be removed by passing through a separator. It may also be necessary to pass the air through an oil filter to remove any traces of oil vapour before the air is stored in a receiver. Combined filter-separator units may also be used. Air leaving the receiver should again pass through a separating and filtering unit before entering a dryer. Where adsorption dryers are used, a further filter is required after the dryer to collect desiccant

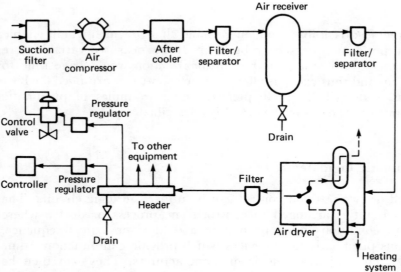

Figure 4.32 Pneumatic supply system

material. The clean, dry, oil-free air now passes to an instrument header. At entry to each instrument the air will be pressure regulated and again filtered. The complete system is shown in Figure 4.32.

A combined filter-separator or general duty air filter is shown in Figure 4.33. This unit is used to remove the majority of water and any solid particles from the air and may be fitted upstream of a dryer. Air flows through directional louvres which cause it to swirl. Any water present is thrown against the bowl wall by centrifugal force. The water drains down and collects in the bottom of the bowl beneath a baffle. The baffle isolates the water from the air stream so that it

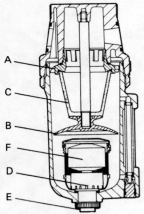

A   Louvres
B   Baffle
C   Filter element
D   Automatic drain assembly
E   Waste pipe connector
F   Float

Figure 4.33 Filter-separator unit

cannot be collected up again. The dry air then pases through a filter element to remove any solid particles. The filter element may be ceramic, wire mesh, or sintered bronze. Sintered bronze is most popular since it can provide varying grades of filtering, it does not break up and pass small particles with the air, and does not deteriorate with use. An automatic drain, in the base of the filter bowl, dumps the water as it collects. At a preset water level the float opens a pilot valve. This admits air above a piston and the drain valve is opened. The water is forced out by air pressure, the float then closes the pilot valve and thus the drain valve.

An oil removing filter is shown in Figure 4.34. The incoming air first passes through a pre-filter element to remove solid particles. The main filtration/separation element acts as a coalescer to convert the oil and water vapour into droplets. These drops are collected in a plastic sock and then drain down to the bottom of the bowl beneath a baffle. The activated carbon element in the upper chamber acts as an

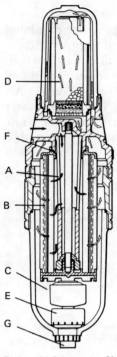

A   Pre-filter element
B   Main filtration/
    separation element
C   Liquid collecting zone
D   Activated carbon element
E   Drain mechanism
F   'O' ring
G   Waste pipe connector

Figure 4.34 Oil removing filter

adsorbent for any remaining traces of oil and hydrocarbon gases. It
also provides a back-up in the event that the lower filter unit fails or
the 'O' ring seal is damaged. The automatic liquid drain mechanism
operates as for the filter-separator.

Air can be dried by adsorption or refrigeration. Adsorption dryers
use a desiccant which collects condensed water on its surface. Two
parallel units are usually provided; one is in use while the other is
being reactivated. The quantity of water adsorbed by a desiccant is
low but the rate of adsorption is high. Typical desiccant materials
include silica gel, synthetic zealite and activated alumina. Reactivat-
ing of these units must be automatically programmed by a timer and
is accomplished by the use of heat or a flow of pre-dried air at a
reduced pressure.

Refrigerant dryers operate on an extension of the after-cooler
principle. The air is chilled to a selected temperature, the condensed
water is separated off and discharged, and then the air is reheated
prior to discharge. The resulting air will be about 96 per cent dry and
also be much reduced in oil content. A refrigerant dryer will not dry to

the same degree as an adsorption dryer but is much more economical in operation. A combination of initial refrigeration dryer and final adsorption drying is most economical for large air volumes and low temperature dewpoints.

Control air should be fed to distribution headers through lines which slope towards the header. Automatic water drain units should be fitted at the lowest points. Individual branches leading to instruments should be led from the top of the header and fitted with an isolating valve. Piping above 25 mm nominal bore should be steel tube to BS 3601 or BS 3602, seamless. Up to 25 mm nominal bore, seamless copper and copper alloy tubing to BS 2871 Part 2 should be used.

HYDRAULICS

Where a flowing liquid is used as the operating medium, this can be generally considered as hydraulic control. Hydraulics is, however, usually concerned with the transmission of power, rather than the transmission of signals.

Hydraulic systems enable the transfer of power over large distances with infinitely variable speed control of linear and rotary motions. High static forces or torques can be applied and maintained for long periods by compact equipment. The equipment itself is safe and reliable, and overload or supply failure situations can be safeguarded against. Hydraulic operation of a ship's steering gear is usual and use is often made of hydraulic equipment for both mooring and cargo handling deck machinery.

Hydraulic systems utilize pumps, valves, motors or actuators and various ancillary fittings. The system components can be interconnected in a variety of different circuits, using either low or medium pressure oil.

Circuits

The open-loop circuit takes oil from the tank and pumps it into the hydraulic motor. A control valve is positioned in parallel with the motor. When it is open the motor is stationary, when throttled or closed, the motor will operate. The exhaust oil returns to the tank. This method can provide stepless control.

The live-line circuit, on the contrary, maintains a high pressure from which the control valve draws pressurized oil to the hydraulic motor (in series with it), as and when required.

In the closed-loop circuit the exhaust oil is returned direct to the pump suction. Since the oil does not enter an open tank, the system is considered closed.

Low pressure systems use the open-loop circuit and are simple in design as well as reliable. The equipment is, however, large, inefficient in operation and overheats after prolonged use.

Medium pressure systems are favoured for marine applications, using either the open or closed circuit. Smaller installations are of the open-loop type. Where considerable amounts of hydraulic machinery are fitted the live-line circuit, supplied by a centralized hydraulic power system, would be most economical.

One type of open-loop circuit has a fixed displacement pump and a throttle or control valve connected in parallel with the hydraulic motor, see Figure 4.35. A separate valve can be used to change the

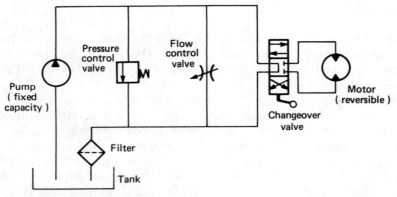

Figure 4.35 Open-loop hydraulic circuit

direction of oil flow to allow the motor to drive in either direction. This will prevent the motor being driven by the load during switching or when in neutral. A multiposition valve is usual which, for example in the case of a winch, provides hoist, lower and stop positions. Other items in the system will include a tank, a pressure control valve and a filter.

One arrangement of a closed-loop system uses a variable-delivery hydraulic pump, see Figure 4.36. Infinitely variable speed control of the motor is therefore achieved by varying the pump output volume. The pumping unit operates continuously at constant speed, even in a zero-delivery situation. A small booster pump is used to keep the system charged with oil at a fixed pressure. Reversal of the motor is achieved by a continuous movement of the pump control from forward through neutral, to reverse. Again, this arrangement prevents the load driving the motor. An expansion tank, pressure control valves and a filter are again included.

Hydraulic symbols have been used in the above two figures. Many pneumatic symbols are similar except that the arrowheads are not shaded in. The arrowhead direction distinguishes a pump from a motor. The changeover valve can have three positions with different liquid flows resulting. The broken line associated with a pressure control valve indicates the hydraulic oil which will operate the valve in the event of overpressure. There are many more symbols in use; only a few have been shown.

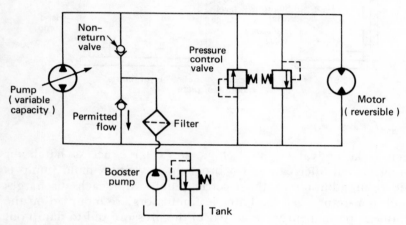

Figure 4.36 Closed-loop hydraulic circuit

In shipboard applications where many different items of equipment may have to operate simultaneously, individual units tend to be uneconomical and a ring main or central supply system can be used. Where the open-loop system is employed, several fixed displacement pumps are used, together with automatic flow control which combines the deliveries of a number of pumps to meet the maximum flow requirements, or selects only one pump for high pressure duty, as required.

If a closed-loop system with variable capacity pumps is used, it feeds a high pressure manifold. The number of pumps in use is determined by the load and each will be automatically switched on or off. The manifold acts as a ring main to supply all hydraulic services on the ship. The operation of either system can be centrally controlled from a suitable location.

Hydraulic supply systems

Depending upon the amount of hydraulic equipment in use on a ship, individual power packs or a large power plant may be fitted. The difference is largely one of size.

A fairly typical unit is shown in Figure 4.37. It is made up of a base frame upon which two electric motor driven pumps are flexibly mounted. A reservoir oil tank of appropriate capacity provides the oil supply for the pumps. This tank is fitted with suction strainers,

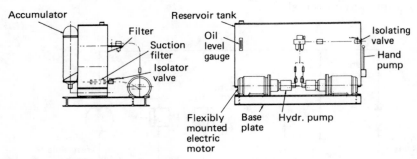

Figure 4.37 Hydraulic power pack

suction isolating valves, a level gauge, a large access hatch for cleaning, an oil filler cap and a breather or vent. A hand pump is provided in addition to the electric pumps and each discharges through non-return valves. Three accumulators are mounted on the tank; one is permanently connected to the pressure rail to damp out pressure fluctuations. The other two are fed from the pressure rail via non-return valves and can be connected to the system through an emergency valve. Double return line filters rated at 10 microns with condition indicators and alarms are also provided. A relief valve able to relieve the complete unit's capacity is also fitted.

Pressure switches may be used to provide automatic stop and start of the pumps but result in numerous stops and starts. A pressure unloading valve would enable the pump to run continuously but aeration of the recirculated oil can be a problem. Both these methods require a change in pressure to occur in order that they operate. This pressure change will adversely affect the operation of certain types of valves, in particular flow control valves. A solution to this problem is to use variable volume pumps which are pressure compensated. Any departure from system pressure would result in a pump output which is adjusted to make up the lost volume and hence the system pressure. The pump would run with zero output volume when the pressure was steady and no recirculation would take place.

The system pressure is decided according to the power and size requirements of the equipment. Three general ranges are normally considered: high (200 to 420 bar), medium (14 to 200 bar) and low (less than 14 bar). The medium pressure range is often used for marine systems but a range of values may be determined in various sub-systems. A typical mains pressure might be 200 bar, with secondary power lines at 140 bar and control lines at 70 bar.

The type of pump used in the system may be fixed or variable volume. Gear pumps are fixed volume and provide a pressure range up to 80 bar. Vane pumps are also fixed volume and provide a pressure range up to 210 bar. Piston pumps are variable volume and provide a pressure range up to 700 bar.

During operation of the hydraulic power system, oil temperature control is important. A small heater and thermostat are provided to ensure correct temperature and hence viscosity when starting. Once operating it is necessary to cool the oil, and on larger systems a cooler will be fitted. Small units may cool sufficiently by heat loss from the tank and pipework.

Correct system operation relies largely on the cleanliness of the oil in the system. Up to three different kinds of filter may be fitted in the system. Suction filters at the tank are usually coarse mesh strainers. Pressure filters are positioned in the pump discharge lines just upstream of control assemblies. Return oil filters clean the oil before it returns to the tank. Condition indicators and choking alarms are usually fitted on these filters and they will be duplex units.

Pipe and fitting materials in the machinery space are usually carbon steel. Materials for use in other areas include cupro nickel alloys, tungum (aluminium-nickel-silicon brass) and stainless steel. These materials must be used with compatible jointing methods and couplings. Cupro nickel alloys can be brazed and stainless steel welded. Tungum usually requires compression-type fittings. The question of whether or not to reuse fittings that have been disturbed is debatable. The more expensive O-ring type can readily be reused.

Equipment

The pumps used in hydraulic systems may be fixed or variable volume and, in many cases, the motor is similar in construction to the pump. A number of different pump and motor designs are described in Chapter 8. Valve-controlled hydraulic systems often make use of spool valves. These are described in Chapter 7. Satisfactory and safe operation of hydraulic systems is ensured by the use of a number of other items. Non-return valves will prevent reverse flow of oil. Pressure control valves in various parts of the system provide relief,

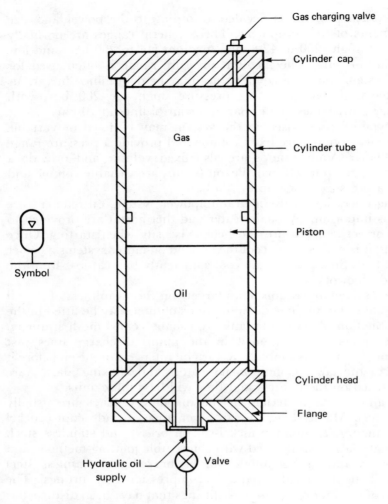

Figure 4.38 Hydraulic accumulator

unloading and pressure reduction. Accumulators are used, either to store energy, or to minimize pressure fluctuations.

One type of accumulator is shown in Figure 4.38, together with the symbol used in circuit diagrams. If the hydraulic fluid is under pressure then the gas above the piston (usually nitrogen) will be compressed. If the valve between the accumulator and the hydraulic system is now closed, then energy is stored in the accumulator. If a system power failure occurs the valve can be opened and the accumulator will provide a pressurized oil supply for emergency duties. If the valve is left open then as the system pressure falls the gas in the accumulator will expand to re-pressurize the oil and thus minimize any pressure fluctuations.

FLUIDICS

This is the technique of using the interaction of flows of a medium to bring about control actions. The media used may be gases or liquids although air is probably the most common. Use may be made of the fluid pressure or flow and it is generally accepted that fluidic devices have no moving parts other than the medium. Fluidic devices are usually made up of basic logic elements which can be suitably interconnected to provide a control circuit. The characteristics of air as the flow medium will now be considered.

Bistable

The 'Coanda effect', or wall attachment effect, relates to a high velocity jet of fluid and its tendency to attach to a nearby wall. This effect is utilized in the device shown in Figure 4.39. The device shown

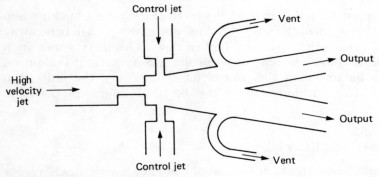

Figure 4.39 Coanda effect fluidic device

is symmetrical and the high velocity jet upon entry will bend by the Coanda effect to one side. The jet will then leave by the output on that side. If a control jet is applied to the input on the same wall side, the supply jet will be moved or switched to the opposite output. It will remain in this position until switched again. The device is therefore bistable, or a flip-flop, since it has two stable states. If the unit were unsymmetrical the supply flow would attach to the nearest wall. The application of a control jet to the input would move the supply flow to the opposite wall. However, on removal of the control jet the supply flow would revert to the original wall. This then would be a monostable device.

Proportional amplifier

Interaction between jets of air can be utilized in momentum exchange devices or in turbulence amplifiers. The momentum exchange device is shown in Figure 4.40. When no control jets are applied, the supply will divide equally on either side of the splitter. When a differential

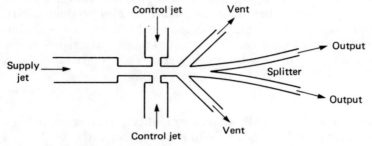

Figure 4.40 Momentum exchange fluidic device

flow is applied to the control ducts there will be a momentum exchange between all the jets. The supply or power jet will bend away from the control jet with the higher flow. This may result in a considerable change in flow between the two outputs. If the output change is greater than the control jet change then the unit is an amplifier. This arrangement is the basis of fluidic proportional devices.

Turbulence amplifier

In the turbulence amplifier the supply pipe or nozzle discharges a laminar air jet. Most of this laminar jet is collected by the output pipe, see Figure 4.41. If a small control jet discharges perpendicular to the laminar flow, then turbulence occurs and only a small part of the input jet will reach the output pipe. When the control jet is removed the laminar flow will be re-established. Several control jets can be used and this device would then become a NOR-gate logic element. A selection of symbols for fluidic elements is given in Figure 4.42.

   Air operated fluidic devices are very small and faster than pneumatic devices. Low pressure air, e.g. about 0.5–1.0 bar, is used and only in very small amounts. They can be safely used in hazardous

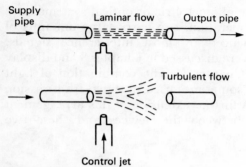

Figure 4.41 Turbulence amplifier fluidic device

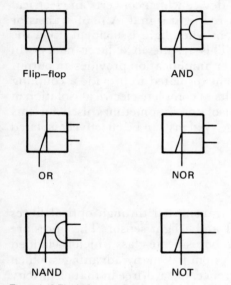

Figure 4.42 Fluidic logic symbols

environments except where air may present a hazard. Other gases could, of course, be used which are safe or inert in the particular environment. Appropriate interfacing is available to enable actuation or operation of devices or equipment.

PHOTOELECTRICITY

A large number of devices exist which convert electronic signals into light or vice versa. They are used in sensing devices, transmission and communication systems. These photoelectric or optical systems have the advantage of low power operation, can carry large amounts of information and are uninfluenced by most interference signals. Photoelectric sensing devices were discussed in Chapter 3 and display devices will be described in Chapter 7. The combination of light display and sensing devices is sometimes used in signal transmission and is called photocoupling. A further extension of this arrangement is the use of optical fibres between the devices and these two arrangements will now be considered.

Photocouplers

A light-emitting diode is a display device which converts an electrical input signal into a visible or infra-red light signal. A phototransistor will produce additional base current when light is incident upon the exposed base-collector junction. This results in a large change in collector current which upon further amplification provides an output signal. These two devices can be encapsulated to provide a coupling which transfers the signal but results in complete electrical isolation of the two systems. The term opto-isolator is sometimes used for this arrangement. High and low voltage systems can be effectively isolated by this method.

Fibre optics

Suitably modulated light can be transmitted through optical fibres positioned between a light emitter and a light sensor. The fibres are made of highly transparent sodium borosilicate glass which is cladded to reduce surface light loss. The system has many advantages which include no electromagnetic interference, hazard-free in that electricity is not carried, and it has a high bandwidth which enables several channels of high frequency data to be transmitted.

The light-emitting source may be a light-emitting diode or a laser diode. The optical fibre system can be accessed at any point for the insertion or removal of signals. Optical fibres can also be used for multiplexing, i.e. the simultaneous transmission of several signals. The signals can be time or frequency division modulated.

A fibre-optic telephone type communication system would be much safer and totally screened from interference. Fibre-optic bundles have been used to transmit light signals for oil-in-water sensing devices. This avoids the need for the electrically operated light source to be present in the hazardous space.

CODED OR DIGITAL SIGNAL TRANSMISSION

Signal transmission has so far been considered for analogue information. This means that the parameters of the signal, e.g. voltage, frequency, current, or air pressure, have been continuously varying with respect to time. Another form of signal is digital. This means that the signal is some form of pulse train with varying characteristics. In binary digital signal transmission the pulse will have two distinct values, usually a high and low value. A code must then be employed for this two-state pulse to be able to carry information. A typical example of such a code is the morse code used for telegraphy where the length of pulse duration, i.e. dash or dot, provides a code which can be interpreted as letters or numbers. A binary number code is used in electronic signal transmission. Two stable states exist, either ON or OFF. Where a low signal level condition represents OFF or 0 and a high signal level represents ON or 1, this is known as positive logic. The binary code will be discussed in a later chapter on computing. Two-state electronic devices are available which will respond to binary signals, e.g. diodes and transistors. Two-state fluidic devices are also available which will respond to binary signals. Under these operating conditions they are considered to be digital or non-linear devices. These devices are also known as logic gates or logic elements. The most common types of logic gate are the AND gate, the OR gate, the NOT gate, the NOR gate and the NAND gate.

Logic gates

All gates consist of one, two or more input terminals and one output terminal. The output for an AND gate will be 1 if A AND B are 1. For all other input combinations the output is 0. The inputs and outputs are usually displayed as a truth table which is shown, together with the AND gate symbol in Figure 4.43(a). The OR gate output will be 1 if A OR B is 1. For all other input conditions the output is zero. The truth table and OR gate symbol are shown in Figure 4.43(b). The NOT gate output will be 1 where the input is 0 or 'NOT 1' and vice versa. The truth table and NOT gate symbol are shown in Figure 4.43(c). The NOR gate output will be the opposite of the OR gate, i.e. NOT OR, and is equivalent to an OR gate followed by a NOT gate. The truth table and NOR gate symbol are shown in Figure 4.43(d). The NAND gate output will be the opposite of the AND gate i.e. NOT AND, and equivalent to an AND gate followed by a NOT gate. The truth table and NAND gate symbol are shown in Figure 4.43(e).

136

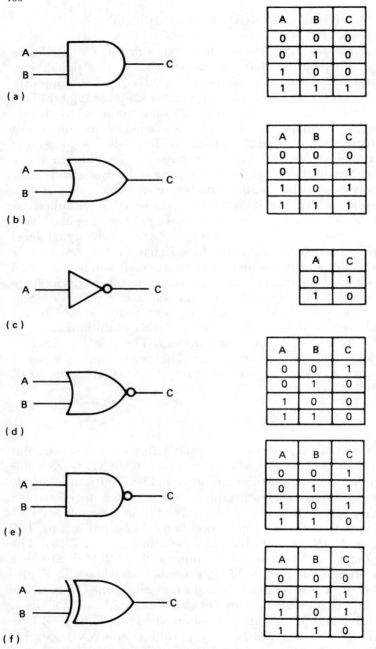

Figure 4.43 Logic gates: (a) AND gate; (b) OR gate; (c) NOT gate; (d) NOR gate; (e) NAND gate; (f) Exclusive-OR gate

Exclusive operation of a gate may be arranged, such as an Exclusive-OR gate. With exclusive operation the output will be 1 if any one input is 1 but not if more than one input is 1. The truth table and Exclusive-OR gate symbol are given in Figure 4.43(f).

The electronic circuitry necessary to achieve these various gates is usually in the form of ICs based upon NOR or NAND gates.

The practical application of logic circuits will be demonstrated by a simple example shown in Figure 4.44. Two-way switching of an electric lamp is an Exclusive-NOR gate logic situation. The switch

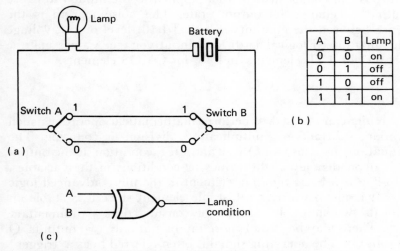

Figure 4.44 Logic example: (a) circuit; (b) truth table; (c) symbol

may be up (1) or down (0) and the lamp may be on or off. The circuit and the truth table can be examined in turn to verify this. More complex situations such as the starting of a slow speed diesel engine are also logic situations. The starting air may not be admitted to the cylinders until various conditions are satisfied. These include turning gear out, lubricating oil pressure adequate, direction of rotation correct, etc.

The different gate functions can be obtained by a variety of different electronic non-linear devices and circuits. These include diode logic (DL), resistor-transistor logic (RTL), transistor-transistor logic (TTL), direct coupled transistor logic (DCTL), emitter coupled logic (ECL) and complementary MOSFET logic (CMOS). The use of ICs has resulted in TTL, ECL and CMOS being the major systems currently in use. The term 'fan-in' of a gate refers to the number of logic inputs that can be accepted. An 'expander' device can be used to increase fan-in. 'Fan-out' is the number of similar logic loads that can be driven by a gate. This can be increased by the use of a 'buffer'. The values of fan-in and fan-out are part of the gate specification. The device speed refers to the delay in signal propagation through a logic stage and would be typically a few nanoseconds. In complex logic systems the delay can become noticeable, although increasing the power consumption will reduce it. Usually, however, it is noise rather than speed that causes problems. Increased noise immunity can be obtained by slowing the gate switching speed. A measure of the noise immunity is the voltage which when applied to the input will cause the output to change its output state. The noise margin is the difference between the guaranteed logical 1 (0) level output voltage and the guaranteed logical 1 (0) level input voltage. Values may be about 1.0 V for TTL elements and 4 V for CMOS elements.

Flip-flops

Logic circuits can be used to perform mathematical operations such as addition, subtraction, multiplication, division or counting. The logic equations used use an ON or and OFF condition at the output which is dependent upon the values or conditions of the variables. The flip-flop is a basic building element in the more advanced logic circuits. It is also known as a bistable element since it is stable on either of its two states. It can also be considered as a rudimentary memory. There may be two or more inputs but only two outputs, Q and Q̄ (not Q). The operating signal is often referred to as a 'trigger'. The trigger may result from the operation of a push-button or a number of flip-flops may be clock operated in synchronism. These clock pulses may come from an oscillator acting as a master clock.

Consider now the two NOR gates partially connected as shown in Figure 4.45(a). If the 1 input were removed the output would not change since it is held at 0 by the output from the lower gate acting as the other input. Since the lower gate input is 0 then the hanging or uncommitted input can be connected to the upper gate output, see Figure 4.45(b). This will result in no change in the output. If the 1 and 0 inputs are now removed there will be no change in the output. If either input is replaced at the same value there will be no change in output. If either input assumes a new value, i.e. the upper 1 becomes a 0, then the output will flip to a new state and hold that value. The input values are usually referred to as set (S) and Reset (R) and the outputs are Q and Q̄ (not Q). The output Q_{n+1} becomes 1 following a set input of 1 and becomes 0 following a reset input of 1. The truth table and symbol for an R-S flip-flop are given in Figure 4.46(a). The

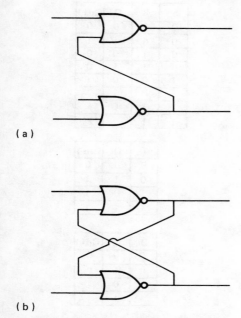

(a)

(b)

Figure 4.45 Flip-flop comprised of two NOR gates

term Q_{n+1} indicates the state of Q after an S or R input has been applied. With R and S at 1 the output state is indeterminate; furthermore it is not permissible for R and S to be 1 since this would break the logic convention.

A clocked R-S flip-flop will only change during a specified clocking or triggering transition. Edge triggering is one form where clocking takes place during the positive-going or rising edge of a pulse or the negative-going or trailing edge. Only the inputs which are present at the triggering edge of the clock will have any effect on the output. Where all the flip-flops in a chain are clocked together this is a synchronous transition. An asynchronous transition is when one device is clocked and then the next and so on. The truth table is the same as for an R-S flip-flop and the circuit symbol has an extra input labelled C.

A T or toggle flip-flop has only one input terminal and changes state each time it is clocked. It is usual for toggle flip-flops to respond only to the negative-going edge of the clock pulses. The truth table and circuit symbol are shown in Figure 4.46(b).

The D or delay flip-flop has one signal input and a clock input. A signal which occurs at the input will only appear at the output when the clock pulse occurs. The signal is therefore delayed until the clock

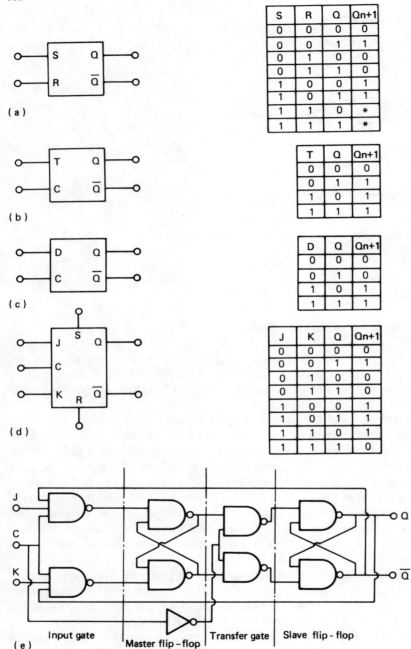

S	R	Q	Qn+1
0	0	0	0
0	0	1	1
0	1	0	0
0	1	1	0
1	0	0	1
1	0	1	1
1	1	0	*
1	1	1	*

T	Q	Qn+1
0	0	0
0	1	1
1	0	1
1	1	1

D	Q	Qn+1
0	0	0
0	1	0
1	0	1
1	1	1

J	K	Q	Qn+1
0	0	0	0
0	0	1	1
0	1	0	0
0	1	1	0
1	0	0	1
1	0	1	1
1	1	0	1
1	1	1	0

Figure 4.46 Various flip-flops: (a) R-S flip-flop; (b) T flip-flop; (c) D flip-flop; (d) J-K flip-flop; (e) master-slave J-K flip-flop

pulse occurs. The truth table and circuit symbol are given in Figure 4.46(c).

The J-K flip-flop has J and K input conditions, a clock pulse, and S and R forcing inputs. The operation and truth table indicate a similarity to the R-S flip-flop but without the indeterminate states, see Figure 4.46(d). The S and R forcing inputs will override the J-K inputs. The J-K flip-flop is versatile in that it can be connected up as any other type of flip-flop. With J and K at 0 the output is held or stored. When J and K are both 1 the output changes state with each clock pulse, i.e. a toggle. When K is made to be NOTJ by connecting an inverter between them, then the output follows J, i.e. a D flip-flop. When a flip-flop is operating at high speed, the time taken by the signal to change the output conditions can cause spurious signals. In effect this is the arrival of a second input signal before the first input has completed its action and provided an output. This is overcome by the use of a master-slave configuration, see Figure 4.46(e). The complete pulse is utilized with the rising edge operating the master flip-flop and inhibiting the slave flip-flop and the falling edge doing the opposite. The inputs to the master flip-flop can never go from 0–0 to 1–1.

Flip-flops or bistables are available as ICs, with J-K and D types being typical. They are normally provided with set (preset) and reset (clear) inputs. A latch is a logic element that stores a logic level until the next clock pulse is received. It is often used as a buffer to store data or signal levels while other parts of a system are completing their operations. Several latches are usually incorporated on a single IC. In this way amounts of digital data can be transmitted as 'words' rather than individual 'bits'. A shift register may be constructed of flip-flops. Usually D-type, operated on two-state or binary data. A shift register is a temporary storage for data which is moved between stages of the register. The data can be transferred in either direction, one bit at a time, i.e. serial-in, serial-out. It is also possible to use the preset inputs or individual flip-flops for parallel input of data to the register. ICs are available which provide shift registers able to handle a certain number of bits of input data in either serial, parallel or a combination of inputs and outputs. A group of flip-flops can also be connected to act as a counter, see Figure 4.47(a). The input is a series of pulses which represent events to be counted. This counter uses four T flip-flops and can count from 0 to 15 in binary, i.e. 0000 to 1111, after which it resets to 0. The binary coded decimal (BCD) system is described in Chapter 10. The first input pulse will set F1 to the 1 state and output A is 1. The next pulse will set F1 to 0 and F2 to 1. The output at A will now be 0 and at B will be 1. Further pulses will result

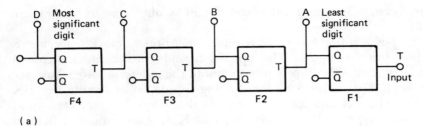

(a)

No. of high pulses	D	C	B	A
0	0	0	0	0
1	0	0	0	1
2	0	0	1	0
3	0	0	1	1
4	0	1	0	0
5	0	1	0	1
6	0	1	1	0
7	0	1	1	1
8	1	0	0	0
9	1	0	0	1
10	1	0	1	0
11	1	0	1	1
12	1	1	0	0
13	1	1	0	1
14	1	1	1	0
15	1	1	1	1
16	0	0	0	0

(b)

Figure 4.47 Counter: (a) flip-flop arrangement; (b) output table

in outputs A,B,C, and D registering as shown in the table in Figure 4.47(b). In addition to counting, the output binary code may provide data used for the control of devices such as stepping motor controllers.

5 System analysis

The examination or analysis of a control system must be undertaken in order to determine its performance. Various analysis techniques have been developed to enable the performance of a system to be evaluated with respect to a particular specification. The system must first be modelled, or represented mathematically in some way, before analysis can be attempted. The system behaviour, as a result of different inputs, is then examined, usually with respect to time. For complex systems, and where time domain analysis is difficult, use can be made of frequency response analysis. This involves determining the system response to sinusoidal inputs and avoids tedious mathematics. The frequency response results can be readily checked by experimental techniques and also graphical analysis can indicate the manner by which a system needs to be modified to meet the specification.

MATHEMATICAL MODELS

In order to analyse and design a control system a knowledge of its behaviour is required. This behaviour will be considered in a mathematical sense and a system description using mathematical terms is therefore required. The relationships between the variable quantities in a system can be expressed as mathematical equations. These equations will then form what is called a mathematical model of the system. These mathematical models are usually derived from applications of the laws of physics, e.g. Newton's law.

When a control system is analysed, two particular operating conditions may be considered, steady state and dynamic. Where the parameters of a system remain constant it is in a steady-state condition and will remain so until a change takes place. At a reasonable period after a change a stable control system will return to its steady-state condition. From the moment when a change is made until the system resumes its steady state, it is said to be undergoing dynamic or transient operation. The change may take place at the input, or it may be a disturbance within the system. The effect on the output will depend upon the system variables and possibly how they interact.

The description of a dynamic system is obtained from differential equations. These equations will contain the variables and the rates of change or derivatives of the variables in the control system. Differential equations enable the dynamic representation of a control system as a mathematical model. Ordinary differential equations are the main concern in control systems and contain a single dependent variable and an independent variable, which is usually time. The order of a differential equation relates to the index of the highest derivative. The degree is the exponent of the highest order derivative.

For example,

$$\left(\frac{d^3y}{dx^3}\right)^2 - \left(\frac{dy}{dx}\right)^3 + 2y = 0$$

is a third-order, second-degree, differential equation in which y is the dependent variable. The terms of this equation are all constant coefficients. A variable coefficient would be a function of the independent variable, e.g. $\sin t$. Where a differential equation is a summation of the dependent variable and its derivatives and equates to zero, it is considered homogenous. When equated to a constant or a function of the independent variable, it is non-homogenous. This constant or driving function is an input to the system, and examples of test inputs used are the step, ramp and sinusoidal signals.

Linearity is an important consideration in physical systems. It relates to behaviour between variables where proportionality exists over some range. A linear system may be described by algebraic equations of dependent variables no higher than first degree, or differential equations where the terms are all first degree.

For example,

$$a = 4b + 2c - 3, \text{ and}$$

$$\frac{d^2y}{dt^2} + 4\frac{dy}{dt} + 3y = 0$$

are both linear equations, whereas,

$$a = 4b^2 + 2bc - 3, \text{ and}$$

$$\frac{d^2y}{dt^2} + 4\left(\frac{dy}{dt}\right)^2 + 3y = 0$$

are non-linear.

An important property of linear systems is that the principle of superposition applies. The principle of superposition states that the response produced by simultaneously applying two different inputs or forcing functions is the sum of the two individual responses. That is, if input x_1 gives output y_1, and input x_2 gives output y_2 then input $(x_1 + x_2)$ will give an output $(y_1 + y_2)$. This enables a total control system to be considered component by component, or a complex input to be divided into several simpler inputs. Physical systems are often only linear within a certain range of operation, e.g. a transistor. While techniques are available for dealing with non-linearity, they will not be considered here. All systems will be considered to operate within their range of linearity or be 'linearized' by suitable approximations or assumptions.

Mechanical systems

Various physical systems use mechanical components to produce either translational, i.e. straight line, or rotational motion.

Translational motion will be considered first with reference to the mass-spring-dashpot system, shown in Figure 5.1. The dashpot is a

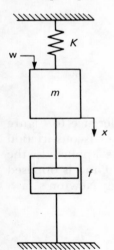

Figure 5.1 Mass-spring-dashpot system

piston in an oil-filled cylinder which provides viscous friction or damping. It effectively absorbs energy which is dissipated and lost. An external force w is applied to the mass m, causing a displacement x. Both w and x are functions of time. Applying Newton's law of motion, i.e. force = mass × acceleration, then

$$m \frac{d^2x}{dt^2} = -f\frac{dx}{dt} - Kx + w$$

or

$$m \frac{d^2x}{dt^2} + f\frac{dx}{dt} + Kx = w$$

The term, $f dx/dt$ relates to the viscous friction force, where f is the damping coefficient and dx/dt is the velocity of the piston. This force acts against the applied force w. The term Kx relates to the spring force, where K is the stiffness and x is the displacement. This force also opposes the applied force w. It should be noted that gravitational effects are not considered since the spring will be initially stretched by the action of gravity. The final equation is therefore a mathematical model of the mass-spring-dashpot system.

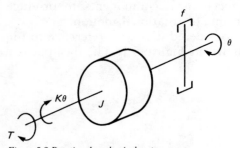

Figure 5.2 Rotational mechanical system

Rotational motion will now be considered by reference to Figure 5.2. The system consists of a load inertia J and a viscous-friction damper with damping coefficient f. A torque T is applied to the system which rotates through an angular distance, θ and is opposed by a torsional spring torque of $K\theta$. Again applying Newton's law, $J\alpha = \Sigma T$, where α is the angular acceleration, then

$$J \frac{d^2\theta}{dt^2} = T - f\frac{d\theta}{dt} - K\theta$$

or

$$J \frac{d^2\theta}{dt^2} + f\frac{d\theta}{dt} + K\theta = T$$

Electrical systems

An electric circuit or network is another type of physical system. It is comprised of resistors, capacitors and inductors, and usually one or more energy sources such as a battery or generator.

The resistors, inductors and capacitors in a circuit are considered as passive elements and their current-to-voltage relationships are shown in Figure 5.3. The active electrical elements can be considered

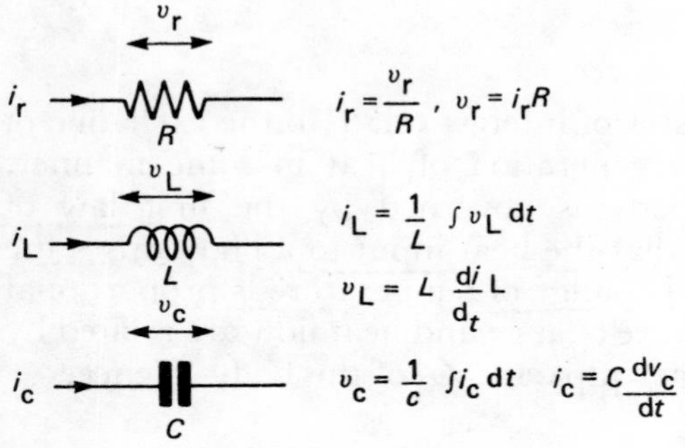

$i_r \longrightarrow \overset{v_r}{\text{WWW}}$ $\quad i_r = \dfrac{v_r}{R}$, $v_r = i_r R$
$\quad\quad\quad R$

$i_L \longrightarrow \overset{v_L}{\text{000}}$ $\quad i_L = \dfrac{1}{L}\int v_L\, dt$
$\quad\quad\quad L$

$\quad\quad\quad\overset{v_c}{} \quad\quad v_L = L\, \dfrac{di_L}{d_t}$

$i_c \longrightarrow \overset{}{\mid\mid} \quad\quad v_c = \dfrac{1}{c}\int i_c\, dt \quad i_c = C\dfrac{dv_c}{dt}$
$\quad\quad\quad C$

Figure 5.3 Passive circuit element relationships

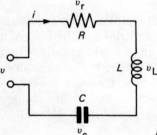

Figure 5.4 Closed-loop electrical circuit

to exist as voltage sources or current sources, where the voltage or current is considered to be constant throughout load changes. In analysing or determining the mathematical model of an electric circuit, use is made of Kirchhoff's first law which states that the algebraic sum of the voltages around a closed loop is zero. Consider the circuit shown in Figure 5.4.

$$v_r + v_L + v_c - v = 0$$

or

$$iR + L\frac{di}{dt} + \frac{1}{c}\int i\, dt = v$$

Depending upon the variable of interest, the above expression may be rearranged in a variety of forms. Use can be made of the relationship, current $i = dq/dt$, where q is the electrical charge accumulating on a capacitor, if it were required to remove the integral from the expression. The use of Laplace transforms, which will be described later, is another means of solving an expression containing differential and integral terms.

Thermal systems

The two basic thermal processes of interest relate to the exchange of heat between bodies and the generation of heat in some manner. Temperature change in a body is governed by the first law of thermodynamics. This states that the heat input to a body raises the internal energy and the rate of change of temperature is proportional to the heat flow. The temperature change and heat flow are related by a constant which is the thermal capacity, C, of the body. Hence,

$$Q = C \frac{dT}{dt}$$

where Q is heat flow, and dT/dt is the rate of change of temperature. Thermal capacity is the product of the mass and the specific heat of a body and is analogous to capacitance in an electric circuit. Heat transmission between two bodies takes place by conduction, convection and radiation. The rate of heat flow through a body is governed by its thermal resistance R. This is the temperature change which results from a unit change in the flow rate of heat. Hence,

$$R = \frac{T_1 - T_2}{Q}$$

Where $T_1 - T_2$ is the temperature change and Q is the heat flow rate. Thermal resistance is considered to be linear and is analogous to resistance in an electric circuit.

The final consideration relates to the thermal equilibrium of a system, which requires that:

Heat added = Heat stored + Heat removed or lost

If the body is small, or perfectly mixed gases or liquids are considered, then the temperature can be considered uniform throughout. A linear

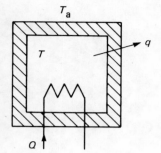

Figure 5.5 Thermal system

differential equation can then be used to describe the system. Consider the system shown in Figure 5.5. Heat is supplied to the tank of water at some rate Q. The water temperature is T and the ambient temperature outside the container is T_a. Heat is lost to the atmosphere at some rate q. Using the thermal equilibrium equation,

Heat added = Heat stored + Heat lost

then

$$Q = C\,\frac{\mathrm{d}T}{\mathrm{d}t} + \frac{T - T_a}{R}$$

where C and R and the thermal capacitance and resistance respectively. The equation may be rewritten as:

$$\frac{\mathrm{d}T}{\mathrm{d}t} + \frac{T}{RC} = \frac{Q}{C} + \frac{T_a}{RC}$$

This is a first-order differential equation with the water temperature T as the variable of interest.

Liquid level systems

The laws of fluid mechanics must now be utilized in determining suitable system equations. Certain assumptions are necessary in order to minimize the mathematics and simplify relationships. Liquid-filled tanks or other vessels are considered together with pipes and valves through which water enters or leaves. The tank is considered to have a free surface of liquid and a constant cross-section, and the connecting pipes are full of liquid.

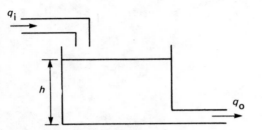

Figure 5.6 Liquid level system

Consider the tank shown in Figure 5.6. Liquid enters with a volumetric flow rate q_i and leaves at a rate q_o. The liquid level or head, h, produces the outflow which is opposed by the hydraulic resistance of the pipe and any fittings. This resistance is defined as the change in head required to produce a unit change in flow, i.e. $R = \mathrm{d}h/\mathrm{d}q$. Laminar flow occurs with low liquid velocities and flow is directly proportional to the head, thus $R = h/q$. Turbulent flow results in a more complicated relationship, developed from Bernoulli's equation. This can be linearized over a small flow range to give a relationship for resistance where $R = 2h/q$. The conservation of mass law provides the following relationship for the system:

Liquid supplied $=$ Liquid gained $+$ Liquid lost

$$q_i = A\,\frac{\mathrm{d}h}{\mathrm{d}t} + q_o$$

$$= A\frac{\mathrm{d}h}{\mathrm{d}t} + \frac{h}{R}$$

where A is the cross-sectional area of the tank. This expression is a first-order differential equation with the liquid level h as the variable of interest.

Mention has been made of analogies between capacitance and resistance in the various systems described. Similar analogies can also be made between potential and flow in each of the systems. The general form of the differential equations can be first-order for most of the systems described. In the mechanical systems if velocity rather than displacement, linear or angular, were considered, then the equations would be first-order. The standard form of a first-order differential equation is:

$$\tau\,\frac{\mathrm{d}\theta_o}{\mathrm{d}t} + \theta_o = K\theta_i$$

Table 5.1 Some system mathematical models

Mathematical model	System
$\dfrac{m}{f}\dfrac{\mathrm{d}v}{\mathrm{d}t} + v = w$	Mechanical translational; v = velocity
$\dfrac{J}{f}\dfrac{\mathrm{d}\omega}{\mathrm{d}t} + \omega = T$	Mechanical rotational; ω = angular velocity
$\dfrac{L}{R}\dfrac{\mathrm{d}i}{\mathrm{d}t} + i = \dfrac{V}{R}$	Electrical circuit with resistance and inductance
$RC\dfrac{\mathrm{d}T}{\mathrm{d}t} + T = RQ + T_a$	Thermal system
$AR\dfrac{\mathrm{d}h}{\mathrm{d}t} + h = Rq_i$	Fluid level system

where θ_i and θ_o are the input and output, K is a constant known as the gain and τ is the time constant of the system. A number of system mathematical models are shown in Table 5.1, rearranged in standard form. The significance of K and τ will be explained in a later section.

LAPLACE TRANSFORMS

Differential equations or mathematical models can be produced to represent all or part of a control system. The system response will vary according to the input received and, in order to determine this response, the differential equations must be solved. The form of the solution, since time is often the independent variable, will usually include two terms. These are the steady-state and transient solutions. The steady-state solution is obtained when all the initial conditions are zero. The transient solution represents the effects of the initial conditions. Both of these parts of the solution must be examined with respect to control systems. Classical mathematical techniques create complex solutions for linear differential equations beyond first-order. Use can be made of the Laplace transform technique to simplify the mathematics and also provide a solution in the two-term form that is required. Transforming, in this situation, involves changing differential equations into an algebraic equation in some new quantity. A useful analogy can be made to the use of logarithms where numbers are converted to a different form so that multiplication, division, raising to a power, etc., become addition, subtraction or simple multiplication. At the end of these computations the number obtained is inverse transformed or antilogged to return to the original system of numbers. It should be noted that the Laplace transform can only be used with constant coefficient linear differential equations. However, only this type of equation will be considered.

As a result of Laplace transformation, a function of time, $f(t)$, becomes a function of a new s-domain, $F(s)$. Upper case letters are always used for the transformed function. The quantity s is complex and takes the form, $s = \sigma + j\omega$, where σ (sigma) and ω (omega) are real numbers and $j = \sqrt{-1}$. The operational symbol indicating a transform is L. The actual transformation involves multiplying the function, $f(t)$, by e^{-st} and then integrating the product with respect to time in the interval $t = 0$ to $t = \infty$, i.e.

$$L\{f(t)\} = \int_0^\infty f(t)e^{-st}\mathrm{d}t = F(s)$$

The function $f(t)$ must be real and continuous over the time interval considered, otherwise the Laplace transform cannot be used.

The inverse transform is indicated by the operator L^{-1} such that

$$f(t) = L^{-1}\{F(s)\}$$

It is usual to employ tables of transform pairs for $f(t)$ and the corresponding $F(s)$. A number of examples will, however, be provided to indicate the Laplace transform technique. A short list of Laplace transform pairs in given in Table 5.2.

Table 5.2 Some Laplace transform pairs

Time function, $f(t)$	Laplace transform, $F(s)$
Unit impulse, δt	1
Unit step, 1	$\dfrac{1}{s}$
Unit ramp, t	$\dfrac{1}{s^2}$
n^{th} order ramp, t^n	$\dfrac{n!}{s^{n+1}}$
Exponential decay, $e^{-\alpha t}$	$\dfrac{1}{s + \alpha}$
Exponential rise, $1 - e^{-\alpha t}$	$\dfrac{\alpha}{s(s + \alpha)}$
Exponential $\times t$, $te^{-\alpha t}$	$\dfrac{1}{(s + \alpha)^2}$
Sin ωt	$\dfrac{\omega}{s^2 + \omega^2}$
Cos ωt	$\dfrac{s}{s^2 + \omega^2}$

Obtain the Laplace transforms of the functions

(i) $f(t) = A$, (ii) $f(t) = 1$, (iii) $f(t) = At$, (iv) $f(t) = Ae^{-\alpha t}$

assume $f(t) = 0$ for t<0 in all cases.

(i) $f(t) = A$, i.e. a step function of magnitude A.

$$L\{f(t)\} = \int_0^\infty Ae^{-st}dt = -\frac{A}{s}\cdot\frac{1}{e^{st}}\Big|_0^\infty$$

This step function is undefined at $t = 0$, but

$$\int_{0-}^{0+} Ae^{-st}dt = 0$$

Thus,

$$L\{f(t)\} = \frac{A}{s} = F(s)$$

(ii) $f(t) = 1$, i.e. a unit step function.

$$L\{f(t)\} = \int_0^\infty e^{-st}dt = \frac{1}{s}\cdot\frac{1}{e^{st}}\Big|_0^\infty = \frac{1}{s} = F(s)$$

(iii) $f(t) = At$, i.e. a ramp function.

$$L\{f(t)\} = \int_0^\infty Ate^{-st}dt = At\frac{e^{-st}}{-s}\Big|_0^\infty = \int_0^\infty \frac{Ae^{-st}}{-s}\,dt$$

$$= \frac{A}{s}\int_0^\infty e^{-st}dt = \frac{A}{s^2} = F(s)$$

(iv) $f(t) = Ae^{-\alpha t}$, i.e. an exponential decay.

$$L\{f(t)\} = \int_0^\infty A\,e^{-\alpha t}e^{-st}dt = A\int_0^\infty e^{-(\alpha+s)t}dt = \frac{A}{s+\alpha} = F(s)$$

Transform theorems

A number of theorems relating to Laplace transforms are used when solving differential equations.

Linearity theorem. Where a function is multiplied by a constant, the Laplace transform of the product is the constant multiplied by the function transform. Hence

$$L\{Af(t)\} = AF(s)$$

when the sum of two functions is transformed it becomes the sum of the Laplace transforms of the individual functions. Hence

$$L\{f_1(t) + f_2(t)\} = F_1(s) + F_2(s)$$

This is sometimes referred to as the principle of superposition.

Differential theorem. The Laplace transform of the first derivative of a function $f(t)$ is

$$L\left\{\frac{df(t)}{dt}\right\} = sF(s) - f(0)$$

Where $f(0)$ is the value of the function $f(t)$ evaluated at time $t=0$. The Laplace transform of the second derivative of $f(t)$ is

$$L\left\{\frac{d^2f(t)}{dt^2}\right\} = s^2F(s) - sf(0) - \frac{df(0)}{dt}$$

where $df(0)/dt$ is the value of the first derivative of the function at time $t=0$.

Integration theorem. The Laplace transform of the integral of a function $f(t)$ is

$$L\{\textstyle\int f(t)dt\} = \frac{F(s)}{s} + \frac{\int f(0)}{s} \, dt$$

where $\int f(0)dt$ is the value of the integral of the function evaluated at time, $t = 0$.

Initial value theorem. The value of the function $f(t)$, as time t approaches zero, is given by

$$\lim_{t \to 0} f(t) = \lim_{s \to \infty} sF(s)$$

Final value theorem. The value of the function $f(t)$, as time t approaches infinity, is given by

$$\lim_{t \to \infty} f(t) = \lim_{s \to 0} sF(s)$$

Time shift theorem. The Laplace transform of a time delayed function $f(t\text{-}\tau)$ with respect to the function $f(t)$ is,

$$L\{f(t - \tau)\} = e^{-s\tau} F(s)$$

where τ is the value of the time delay in seconds.

Solving differential equations

Where a control system is represented by a differential equation and time is the independent variable it can be solved using Laplace transforms. The first step is to transform the equation term by term, taking due account of any initial conditions. The transformed equation in s can then be solved for the variable of interest. The equation in s must then be inverse transformed to obtain the variable as a function of time. Simultaneous equations can be handled in a similar way where the solving for variable takes place in terms of s and the values obtained are inverse transformed.

The inverse transform L^{-1} is usually obtained by reference to a set of transform tables. Where this is not immediately possible the function in s must be rearranged into a suitable form. Control system response functions often appear as a ratio of polynomials, e.g.

$$F(s) = \frac{N(s)}{D(s)} = \frac{a_m s^m + a_{m-1} s^{m-1} + \dots + a_1 s + a_0}{s^n b_n + b_{n-1} s^{n-1} + \dots + b_1 s + b_0}$$

where m and n are real positive integers and all a's and b's are real constants. The highest power of s in the denominator must be greater than that in the numerator, which is usually the case with practical control systems. The partial fraction technique is the most commonly used approach when solving these functions. The denominator polynominal must first be factorized, i.e. the roots must be known. Hence

$$F(s) = \frac{N(s)}{D(s)} = \frac{N(s)}{(s + r_1)(s + r_2) \dots (s + r_n)}$$

where $-r_1, -r_2, \ldots -r_n$ are the roots of $D(s)$ which may exist as real or complex numbers. The factors of the denominator, e.g. $(s + r_1)$, should be recognizable as denominators in the table of transforms, see Table 5.2.

The partial fraction expansion will now be explained for a denominator $D(s)$ which has a mixture of roots, i.e. simple and repeated, but not complex. An illustrative example will be used.

Determine the inverse Laplace transform of the function $F(s)$, where

$$F(s) = \frac{s + 2}{s(s + 1)^2(s + 3)}$$

Expanding $F(s)$ into partial fractions:

$$F(s) = \frac{A}{s} + \frac{B}{s + 1} + \frac{C}{(s + 1)^2} + \frac{D}{s + 3} = \frac{s + 2}{s(s + 1)^2(s + 3)}$$

where A, B, C, and D are constants. The value of these constants must now be found by algebraic methods. The evaluation of residues or the 'cover-up rule' will be used.

If s is made equal to the value of any of the roots, i.e. 0, -1 or -3, then $F(s)$ becomes infinite. However, if both sides of the equation are multiplied by a factor $(s + r)$ where r is the root, then a function of s will be left which has a value at $s = -r$, or the value of $F(s)$ if the factor $(s + r)$ were covered up. Hence

$$\frac{s + 2}{s(s + 1)^2(s + 3)}(s + 3) = \left(\frac{A}{s} + \frac{B}{s + 1} + \frac{C}{(s + 1)^2} + \frac{D}{s + 3} \right) s + 3$$

Let $s = -3$, then

$$\frac{-3 + 2}{-3(-3 + 1)^2} = D = \frac{-1}{-12} = \frac{1}{12} \therefore D = \frac{1}{12}$$

Now

$$\frac{s + 2}{s(s + 1)^2(s + 3)}(s) = \left(\frac{A}{s} + \frac{B}{s + 1} + \frac{C}{(s + 1)^2} + \frac{D}{s + 3} \right) s$$

Let $s = 0$, then

$$A = \frac{2}{3}$$

Also,

$$\frac{s + 2}{s(s + 1)^2(s + 3)}(s + 1)^2 = \left(\frac{A}{s} + \frac{B}{s + 1} + \frac{C}{(s + 1)^2} + \frac{D}{s + 3}\right)(s + 1)^2$$

Let $s = -1$, then

$$\frac{-1 + 2}{-1(-1 + 3)} = \frac{-1}{2} = C \therefore C = \frac{-1}{2}$$

It is now necessary to substitute the values of A, C, and D and evaluate the equation at some convenient value, e.g. $s = 1$, in order to obtain B. Thus

$$F(s) = \frac{s + 2}{s(s + 1)^2(s + 3)} = \frac{A}{s} + \frac{B}{s + 1} + \frac{C}{(s + 1)^2} + \frac{D}{s + 3}$$

Substituting for A, C and D,

$$\frac{s + 2}{s(s + 1)^2(s + 3)} = \frac{2}{3s} + \frac{B}{s + 1} - \frac{1}{2(s + 1)^2} + \frac{1}{12(s + 3)}$$

Let $s = 1$,

$$\therefore \frac{3}{16} = \frac{2}{3} + \frac{B}{2} - \frac{1}{8} + \frac{1}{48} \therefore B = \frac{-3}{4}$$

All the constants can now be substituted into the original partial fraction expression such that

$$F(s) = \frac{s + 2}{s(s + 1)^2(s + 3)} = \frac{2}{3s} - \frac{3}{4(s + 1)} - \frac{1}{2(s + 1)^2} + \frac{1}{12(s + 3)}$$

Each of the denominators can be readily inverse transformed by reference to a table of transforms, see Table 5.2.

$$L^{-1}\{F(s)\} = f(t) = \frac{2}{3} - \frac{3}{4}e^{-t} - \frac{1}{2}te^{-t} + \frac{1}{12}e^{-3t}$$

The form of the solution can be seen to be made up of a steady-state term, i.e. $2/3$, and transient terms, i.e. the exponentials, which will all die away as the time increases towards infinity.

TRANSFER FUNCTIONS AND BLOCK DIAGRAMS

A complete control system , or any one of its constituent components, can be represented by a transfer function. This is the ratio of the output signal to the corresponding input signal for the system or component considered. It describes the way in which the signal has been transferred. Since most system components introduce a time delay into the transfer process, this dynamic aspect must be indicated or characterized in the transfer function. A differential equation will describe this dynamic characteristic, but it is not readily usable as a transfer function. A Laplace transform in the s-domain does, however, provide a transfer function which enables simple time-domain analysis of system response to a particular input signal. The transfer function of an element can be obtained by first determining the differential equation which describes its behaviour. This equation is then transformed into the s-domain assuming all initial conditions are zero. A ratio is then produced to relate the output to the input, i.e.

$$G(s) = \frac{C(s)}{R(s)}$$

where $G(s)$ is the transfer function, and $C(s)$ and $R(s)$ are the Laplace transforms of the output and input respectively. A particular element in a system can be represented as a block or rectangle which contains the transfer function.

Block diagrams

An individual block is a rectangle containing the transfer function. Lines are used to represent inputs to and outputs from the block and arrows indicate the direction of flow. A number of blocks interconnected by lines thus becomes a block diagram. This is effectively a shorthand representation of a control system or part of the system. The lines actually represent some quantity or variable in the system and the arrow indicates the direction of movement. A block diagram of a closed-loop control system is shown in Figure 5.7. A reference signal $R(s)$ is input to an error detector or summing point, which is shown by a circle containing a cross. The segments of the circle are marked with a plus or minus sign to indicate whether the input is added or subtracted. In this closed-loop system the output is fed back with a negative value as $B(s)$. The error signal $E(s)$ leaves the error detector and is input to the block with transfer function $G(s)$. The output $C(s)$ is the product of $E(s)$ and $G(s)$. The output signal, in

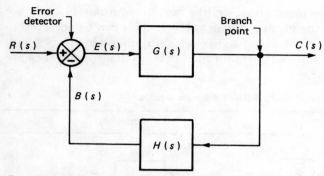

Figure 5.7 Block diagram of a closed-loop control system

addition to leaving the system, is branched off and input to the feedback transfer function $H(s)$. The feedback signal $B(s)$ which leaves is input to the error detector where it assumes a negative value. The block $G(s)$ is considered to be in the forward path and represents the feedforward transfer function, i.e.

$$\text{Feedforward transfer function, } G(s) = \frac{C(s)}{E(s)}$$

The block $H(s)$ is in the feedback path. The ratio of the feedback signal $B(s)$ to the actuating error signal $E(s)$ is called the open-loop transfer function, i.e.

$$\text{Open-loop transfer function, } = \frac{B(s)}{E(s)} = G(s)\ H(s)$$

The closed-loop transfer function is the ratio of the output, $C(s)$ to the input $R(s)$, *i.e.*

$$\text{Closed-loop transfer function } = \frac{C(s)}{R(s)} = \frac{G(s)}{1 + G(s)H(s)}$$

Reference has already been made to a number of mathematical operations. It should be realised that the block diagram is a mathematical representation with its own system of algebra. If, for example, a number of blocks are connected in cascade, i.e. the output of one becomes the input to another, their transfer functions can be combined into a single term by multiplication. From a practical point of view this is only possible where the individual blocks are non-loading or non-interacting, i.e. the output from one block is not changed by being the input to the next block. This can be achieved in electronic circuits by the use of an isolating amplifier which has a high input impedance. Some of the main rules of block diagram algebra are shown in Table 5.3.

Table 5.3 Block diagram algebra

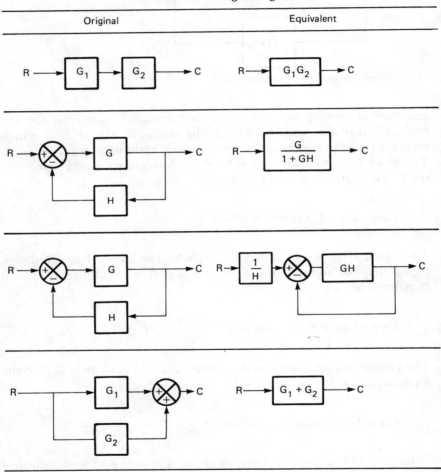

Where the block diagram representation of a control system has been drawn, it may contain various individual transfer functions, sub-loops, etc. The diagram can be reduced to a basic feedback control loop by the use of block diagram algebra. Consider the system shown in Figure 5.8(a). The cascaded blocks G_4 and G_5 are combined first and then the parallel blocks G_1 and G_2 to produce the diagram shown in Figure 5.8(b). The cascaded blocks $(G_1 + G_2)$ and G_3 are then combined and then the minor feedback loop around G_4G_5 is reduced to produce the diagram shown in Figure 5.8(c). The cascaded elements in the feedforward path are now combined to produce a basic feedback loop as shown in Figure 5.8(d). Some methods of analysis require a direct or a unity feedback loop, i.e. $H = 1$. The rearranged block diagram for unity feedback is shown in Figure 5.8(e). Alternatively, a single transfer function can be obtained for the complete system as shown in Figure 5.8(f).

SYSTEM PERFORMANCE

The output from a control system must frequently respond to changes in input. The nature of this response is important. In addition, any disturbances which may occur in a system will influence the output. A control system must therefore be analysed under dynamic or transient operating conditions. This is usually achieved by the application of certain test inputs to the differential equation which characterizes the system. Use can also be made of Laplace transforms in this analysis in order to obtain solutions to the differential equations and hence a knowledge of the system's dynamic behaviour. An initial examination of the dynamic characteristics of a system was undertaken in Chapter 2. Some of that material will be repeated here and then examined in greater detail. Absolute stability is perhaps the most important aspect of a control system's dynamic behaviour. In other words, is the system stable or unstable? The topic of stability will be dealt with separately in a later section.

Test inputs

The mathematical model of a system is subjected to certain test inputs in order to determine its transient and steady-state responses. Typical test inputs are the step, ramp and sine wave. The step input is, in effect, a sudden or abrupt change of the input signal from one steady value to another. It is used to test the response of a system to sudden change. The result is a transient and then the steady-state response of the system. The ramp input varies linearly with time and results in a response which shows the steady-state error in following the input. The sine wave input shows how the system will respond to inputs of a cyclical nature as the frequency is varied. The frequency response of the system is the result. Frequency responses have considerable practical applications in the analysis and design of control systems.

162

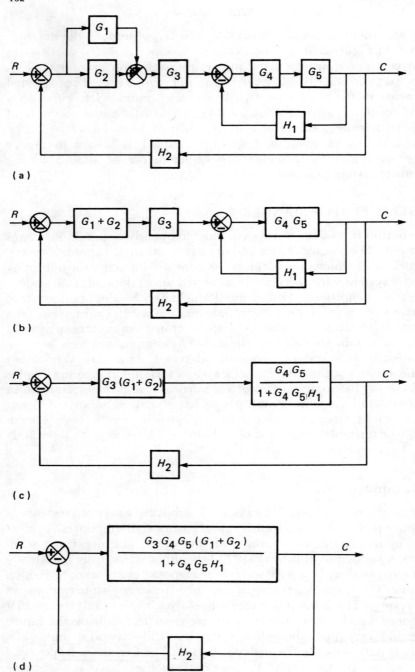

Figure 5.8 Block diagram reduction

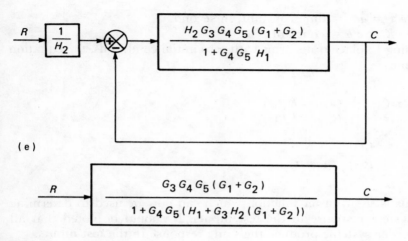

(e)

(f)

Figure 5.8 Block diagram reduction (contd.)

No system will exactly follow a changing input and dynamic specifications are usually given as parameters related to the input applied. It should be noted that many systems, although different in their physical nature, will have identical forms of response since the system dynamics are similar. It is usual, therefore, to make reference to the order of a system, using numbers from zero upwards. Systems of the same order will exhibit the same response to test inputs. Another system classification is the use of a type number, which refers to the steady-state error after certain test inputs.

System order

A zero-order system has the output directly proportional to the input under all conditions, i.e. $\theta_o = K\theta_i$, where K is a constant, θ_o is the output and θ_i is the input. The output, therefore, exactly follows the input without distortion or delay. The zero-order system therefore gives ideal dynamic performance.

A first-order system has its input and output related as follows:

$$a\frac{d\theta_0}{dt} + b\theta_0 = c\theta_i$$

where a, b, and c are constants. Expressed in a more usual or standard form, this becomes:

$$\tau\frac{d\theta_0}{dt} + \theta_0 = K\theta_i$$

where $\tau = a/b$ = time constant, in seconds
  $K = c/b$ = constant.
  Using Laplace transforms with zero initial conditions, the equation becomes

$$\tau s C(s) + C(s) = KR(s)$$
$$\therefore (\tau s + 1) C(s) = KR(s)$$

$$\therefore \frac{C(s)}{R(s)} = \frac{K}{1 + \tau s}$$

This is the transfer function which can now be used to determine the system response to the test inputs. It should be noted that all first-order systems produce the same response to the test inputs.
  Let $R(s)$ be a unit step input, i.e. $1/s$ and the gain $K = 1$. Thus,

$$C(s) = \frac{1}{s} \frac{1}{1 + \tau s}$$

$$= \frac{1}{s} - \frac{\tau}{\tau s + 1} \quad \textit{(using partial fractions)}$$

$$\therefore c(t) = L^{-1}\{C(s)\} = 1 - e^{-t/\tau}$$

The first-order system response to a step input is exponential and is shown in Figure 5.9(a). The dynamic error is the difference between the ideal and actual responses and this can be seen to decrease with time. One specification parameter used with the step input is the time constant, τ. This is the time taken to reach 63.2 per cent of the final value. This is a time, in seconds, which is independent of the size of the step change. It can be seen from the nature of the response that the step input is used to determine the transient response of the system since the steady-state response will eventually equal the input.
  Let $R(s)$ now be a unit ramp input, i.e. $1/s^2$, and the gain $K=1$. Thus,

$$C(s) = \frac{1}{s^2} \left(\frac{1}{1 + \tau s} \right)$$

$$= \frac{1}{s^2} - \frac{\tau}{s} + \frac{\tau^2}{\tau s + 1} \quad \textit{(using partial fractions)}$$

$$\therefore c(t) = L^{-1}\{C(s)\} = t - \tau + \tau e^{-t/\tau}$$

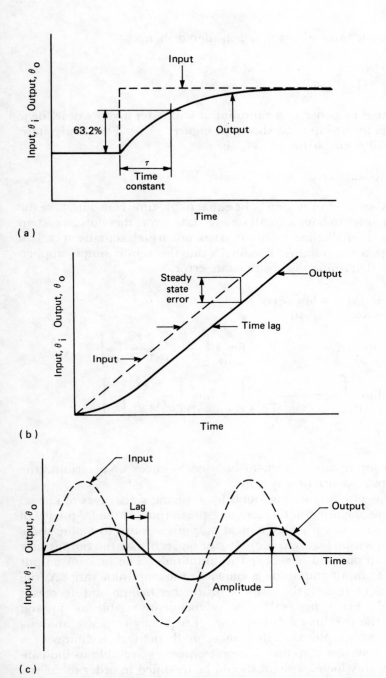

Figure 5.9 First-order system responses: (a) step response; (b) ramp response; (c) frequency response

If the dynamic error $e(t)$ is now considered then,

$$e(t) = r(t) - c(t) = t - t + \tau + \tau e^{-t/\tau}$$
$$= \tau(1 - e^{-t/\tau})$$

The system response to a ramp input will, after a short time, be a line parallel to the input, as shown in Figure 5.9(b). The steady-state error e_{ss}, will occur at time $t=\infty$, i.e.

$$\text{Steady-state error, } e_{ss} = \tau(1 - e^{-\infty/\tau}) = \tau$$

The steady-state error is seen to be equal to the time constant, τ, of the system. In order to have a small steady-state error, therefore, a system must have a small time constant. It is not usual actually to test a system with a ramp input. The final value theorem is simply applied in order to determine the steady-state error, i.e.

$$e_{ss} = \lim_{t \to \infty} e(t) = \lim_{s \to 0} sE(s)$$

$$= \lim_{s \to 0} s(R(s) - C(s)) = \lim_{s \to 0} s \left[\frac{1}{s^2} - \frac{1}{s^2(\tau s + 1)} \right]$$

$$= \lim_{s \to 0} \left[\frac{1}{s} - \frac{1}{s(\tau s + 1)} \right] = \lim_{s \to 0} \left[\frac{\tau s}{s(\tau s + 1)} \right]$$

$$= \tau$$

The ramp input can be seen to be used to check or determine the steady-state response of a system.

The frequency response is found by applying sine waves of known amplitude as the input and examining the output, as the frequency of the input wave is varied. A typical output response to a sine wave input is shown in Figure 5.9(c). It can be seen that the output lags behind the input and is reduced in amplitude. The ratio of output amplitude to input amplitude is known as the amplitude ratio. As the frequency is increased, the output falls further behind and decreases in amplitude. Frequency is thus the independent variable, as opposed to time in the previous two responses. Frequency response analysis makes use of graphical rather than mathematical techniques to determine a system response. These techniques are able to indicate the manner in which a system should be modified in order to meet a particular specification. This is not as readily possible with mathematical methods. Further consideration will be given to frequency response methods in a later section.

A second-order system has its input and output related as follows:

$$a \frac{d^2\theta_0}{dt^2} + b \frac{d\theta_0}{dt} + c\theta_0 = e\theta_i$$

where a, b, c, and e are constants. Expressed in a more usual or standard form this becomes:

$$\frac{d^2\theta_0}{dt^2} + 2\zeta\omega_n \frac{d\theta_0}{dt} + \omega_n^2 \theta_0 = K\theta_i$$

where ζ (zeta) is the damping ratio, ω_n is the undamped natural frequency in rad/second, and K is a constant which is equal to ω_n^2 if θ_o and θ_i are equal under static conditions.

Using Laplace transforms with zero initial conditions and K equal to ω_n^2 the equation becomes:

$$(s^2 + 2\zeta\omega_n s + \omega_n^2)C(s) = \omega_n^2 R(s)$$

$$\therefore \frac{C(s)}{R(s)} = \frac{\omega_n^2}{s^2 + 2\zeta\omega_n s + \omega_n^2}$$

The undamped natural frequency ω_n is a measure of the speed of response of the system. The higher the value the more rapidly the system would respond to sudden or step input changes. The damping ratio, ζ, is a measure of the damping present in the system; it is the ratio of actual damping to critical damping. The value of ζ will determine the nature of the system response to a step input. If ζ is less than 1 the system is underdamped and the response will be oscillatory. When ζ is equal to 1 the system is critically damped. No oscillations occur and there is no overshooting in the response. When ζ is greater than 1 the system is overdamped and responds slowly with no overshooting. The response of a particular second-order system is usually determined by reference to a family of curves as shown in Figure 5.10. The vertical axis is the output, usually expressed as a ratio of the steady-state value. The horizontal axis is a dimensionless variable, $\omega_n t$, which can be converted into time if the undamped natural frequency, ω_n, is known. The family of curves are drawn for different values of the damping ratio ζ. It can be seen that as the damping ratio increases the response becomes less oscillatory. At

SYSTEM ANALYSIS

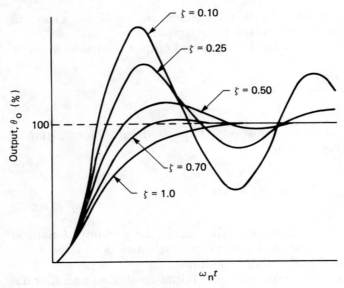

Figure 5.10 Second-order system step response

$\zeta = 1$ there is no overshoot. For ζ values greater than 1 the response is much slower.

Where a ramp input is used, the steady-state error e_{ss}, is of interest. Now

$$E(s) = R(s) - C(s) = R(s) - \frac{C(s)}{R(s)} \cdot R(s)$$

$$= R(s)\left(1 - \frac{\omega_n^2}{s^2 + 2\zeta\omega_n s + \omega_n^2}\right) = R(s)\left(\frac{s^2 + 2\zeta\omega_n s}{s^2 + 2\zeta\omega_n s + \omega_n^2}\right)$$

For a ramp input

$$R(s) = \frac{1}{s^2}$$

$$\therefore E(s) = \frac{1}{s^2}\left(\frac{s^2 + 2\zeta\omega_n s}{s^2 + 2\zeta\omega_n s + \omega_n^2}\right)$$

and,

$$e_{ss} = \lim_{s \to 0} sE(s) = \lim_{s \to 0} \frac{1}{s}\left(\frac{s^2 + 2\zeta\omega_n s}{s^2 + 2\zeta\omega_n s + \omega_n^2}\right)$$

$$= \frac{2\zeta}{\omega_n}$$

A small value of ζ and a large value of ω_n would produce a small steady-state error. A small value of ζ would however produce a large overshoot in the transient response, which may not be acceptable. Obtaining a small steady-state error and an acceptable transient response is therefore a matter of compromise.

Third and higher order equations will not be considered since most systems can be reasonably well defined using first and second-order equations.

System type

The steady-state accuracy of a control system is important and relates to the value of the steady-state error. Systems classified by type have a particular steady-state error following a test input. In a closed-loop control system the error $E(s)$ is

$$E(s) = \frac{R(s)}{1 + G(s)H(s)}$$

The steady-state error following an input $R(s)$ can be found using the final value theorem. Hence,

$$e_{ss} = \lim_{t \to \infty} e(t) = \lim_{s \to 0} sE(s)$$

$$= \lim_{s \to 0} \frac{s\,R(s)}{1 + G(s)H(s)}$$

The steady-state error therefore depends upon the Laplace transform of the input and the open-loop transfer function $G(s)H(s)$. The properties of $G(s)H(s)$ will be examined by considering it as the ratio of two factored polynomials, i.e.

$$G(s)H(s) = \frac{K(1 + T_1s)(1 + T_2s) \ldots (1 + T_ms)}{s^N(1 + T_as)(1 + T_bs) \ldots (1 + T_ps)}$$

where K and all T values are constants. The value of the index N is the type number of the system. The accuracy of a system improves as the type number increases, stability however can be a problem. Type 3 or higher is not usual because of the stability problems.

If a step input is considered then $R(s) = A/s$, and

$$e_{ss} = \lim_{s \to 0} \frac{s}{1 + G(s)H(s)} \cdot \frac{A}{s} = \frac{A}{1 + G(0)H(0)}$$

For a type 0 system, $G(0)H(0)$ will be equal to K. Thus

$$e_{ss} = \frac{A}{1 + K_p}$$

where K_p is the position error constant.

For a type 1 system, $G(0)H(0)$ will result in an infinite value. Thus

$$e_{ss} = \frac{A}{1 + \infty} = 0$$

For type 1 and higher systems, the steady-state error is zero.

If a ramp input is considered, then $R(s) = A/s^2$, and

$$e_{ss} = \lim_{s \to 0} \frac{s}{1 + G(s)H(s)} \cdot \frac{A}{s^2} = \lim_{s \to 0} \frac{A}{sG(s)H(s)} = \frac{1}{K_v}$$

where K_v is the velocity error constant.

For a type 0 system, $G(s)H(s)$ will be zero and the steady-state error will be infinite. For a type 1 system, $G(s)H(s)$ will be equal to K_v/s and the steady-state error will be A/K_v. For a type 2 or higher system the steady-state error will be 0 for a ramp input.

Performance characteristics

The performance characteristics of a control system are often specified in relation to a unit step input. For a second-order system the damping ratio and the undamped natural frequency have so far been used to describe system response. A number of other terms will now be described and are illustrated in Figure 5.11.

The rise time t_r is the time taken for the output to rise, usually from 10 to 90 per cent of the final steady-state value. The overshoot M_p is the peak value of the response curve measured from the steady-state value. The peak time t_p is the time taken by the response to reach the peak overshoot. The settling time t_s is the time taken by the response to reach and remain within a percentage tolerance band of the final steady-state value. When using these specifications it is normal practice to consider the system initially at rest with the output and all its derivatives at zero. Neither an overdamped second-order system nor a first-order system would exhibit oscillations and therefore a number of the above specifications would not be required.

There are some control systems where overshoot and oscillations

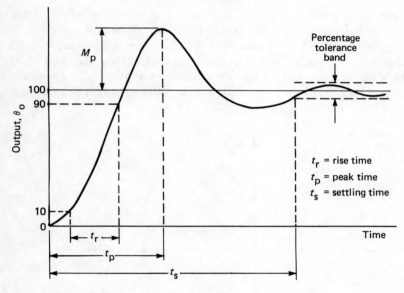

Figure 5.11 Step response specifications

cannot be tolerated, e.g. a steering gear. Otherwise the transient response must be sufficiently fast and reasonably damped, in which case a damping ratio in the range of 0.4 to 0.8 is usually desirable.

POLES AND ZEROS

Mention has already been made that the closed loop system response often appears as a ratio of polynominals, e.g.

$$F(s) = \frac{N(s)}{D(s)}$$

where $N(s)$ and $D(s)$ are the numerator and denominator polynominals, respectively. The solutions of $N(s) = 0$ are called zeros since they will result in the function $F(s)$ having a zero value. The solutions of $D(s) = 0$ are known as poles since they result in infinite values of the function $F(s)$.

Consider the function

$$F(s) = \frac{(s + 1)(s - 3)}{(s + 3)(s + 1 + j)(s + 1 - j)}$$

There are finite zeros at $s = -1$ and $s = 3$ and a zero at infinity (this will be explained in the next section). There are finite poles at $s = -3$, $s = -1-j$ and $s = -1+j$. These can be plotted in the s-plane, which has a horizontal axis, σ, which represents real values and a vertical axis, $j\omega$, which represents imaginary values; see Figure 5.12. Zeros are plotted using a circle and poles with a cross. A system can be analysed

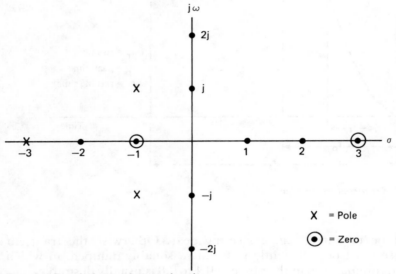

Figure 5.12 Transfer function plotting in the s-plane

to determine stability by plotting a pole-zero map and observing the location of the poles. If any pole lies in the right-hand half of the s-plane, the system is unstable. All roots with complex parts can be seen to occur in complex conjugate pairs.

It should be noted that a pole of the closed-loop transfer function is also a root of the characteristic equation. The characteristic equation is formed by equating the denominator of the closed-loop transfer function to zero. The characteristic equation can, however, be described in terms of open-loop values of poles and zeros. The closed-loop transfer function of a system can be expressed

$$\frac{C(s)}{R(s)} = \frac{G(s)}{1 + G(s)H(s)}$$

where $G(s)$ is the feedforward transfer function and $G(s)H(s)$ is the open-loop transfer function. The open-loop transfer function can be represented by a ratio of polynominals such that

$$G(s)H(s) = \frac{KN(s)}{D(s)} = \frac{K(s^m a_m + s^{m-1}a_{m-1} + \ldots + sa + a_0)}{s^n b_n + s^{n-1}a_{n-1} + \ldots + sb + b_0}$$

where K is the open-loop gain. The characteristic equation can therefore be expressed as

$$1 + \frac{KN(s)}{D(s)} = 0$$

$$\therefore D(s) + KN(s) = 0$$

The solutions to this equation are therefore dependent upon the open-loop zeros, i.e. the roots of $N(s)$, and the open-loop poles, i.e. the roots of $D(s)$. A variation of K will result in solutions ranging from the open-loop poles to the open-loop zeros or infinity. The varying of K from zero to infinity will produce a locus of the closed-loop poles in the s-plane, i.e. a root locus.

ROOT-LOCI

Root-loci are defined as plots, in the s-plane, of the poles of the closed-loop transfer function as the open loop gain is varied from zero to infinity. The system characteristic equation was shown above to be

$$1 + \frac{KN(s)}{D(s)} = 0$$

$$G(s)H(s) = \frac{KN(s)}{D(s)} = -1$$

For any point in the s-plane to be on the root-locus it must satisfy this condition. There are two conditions inherent in this equation since complex numbers are involved; these are the angle and the magnitude criteria.

The value -1 lies on the real axis and this has a phase angle of $\pm$ 180 $(2K+1)$ where $K = 0, 1, 2$, etc. Hence,

$$\angle G(s)H(s) = \pm 180(2K + 1)$$

This is the angle criterion.

The magnitude criterion requires that the magnitude or absolute value is 1, i.e.

$$|G(s)H(s)| = 1$$

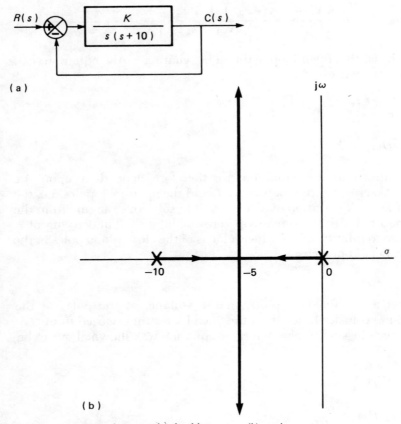

(a)

(b)

Figure 5.13 Root-locus of a system: (a) closed-loop system; (b) root-locus

A root-locus will now be plotted for the closed-loop system shown in Figure 5.13(a). The open-loop transfer function is:

$$G(s)H(s) = \frac{K}{s(s+10)} = \frac{KN(s)}{D(s)}$$

The characteristic equation is

$$D(s) + KN(s) = 0$$

i.e.

$$s(s+10) + K = 0 \quad \therefore \ s^2 + 10s + K = 0$$

The roots of this equation must now be found and plotted as K varies from zero to infinity. For $K = 0$, the roots are $s_1 = 0$ and $s_2 = -10$. These values are now plotted on the complex plane, see Figure 5.13(b). For all other values of K the quadratic equation must be solved; a selection of values are given in Table 5.4. It is not normally necessary to calculate values of the roots in order to plot the locus. A set of rules are used to determine the general shape of the locus and these will be given later in this section.

Upon inspection, the locus can be seen to move along two branches, which are marked with arrows in the direction of increasing K. Each branch begins at $K = 0$ which can be considered as the open-loop poles, i.e. poles of $G(s)H(s)$, or the closed-loop poles, i.e. $1/[1 + G(s)H(s)]$. As K increases to 25, the closed-loop poles of each branch move towards -5. The transient response for values of K up to 25 will be that of an overdamped system. For values of K greater than 25 the locus has two branches with the roots being complex conjugates. The system is therefore underdamped. At K equal to 25 critical damping occurs.

The location of the roots of the characteristic equation determines the transient behaviour of the system.

Table 5.4 Characteristic equation roots for some values of K

Gain	Characteristic equation roots	
K	s_1	s_2
0	0	−10
5	−0.53	−9.47
20	−2.76	−7.23
25	−5	−5
50	−5 + j10	−5 − j10

If all the roots are in the left-hand half of the s-plane, then all transient terms will decay and the system is stable. If any roots are present in the right-hand half of the plane, the system is unstable. The gain value for which a root existed on the imaginery axis would be a marginal stability condition.

The values of the damping ratio and the damped frequency of oscillation of an underdamped second-order system can be found from the root-locus. The characteristic equation of a second-order system is:

$$s^2 + 2\zeta\omega_n s + \omega_n^2 = 0$$

If the system is underdamped the roots will be complex conjugates, where

$$s_1, s_2 = -\zeta\omega_n \pm j\omega_n \sqrt{(1 - \zeta^2)}$$

For a given root, at a particular gain value, the distance along the horizontal axis is the real part, i.e. $\zeta\omega_n$. The vertical distance is the imaginary part, i.e. $\omega_n \sqrt{(1-\zeta^2)}$. This is shown in Figure 5.14. The location of root s_1 is defined by the angle θ, where

$$\cos\theta = \frac{\zeta\omega_n}{\omega_n} = \zeta$$

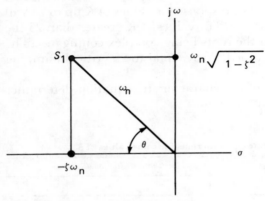

Figure 5.14 Complex root location in the s-plane

Rules for constructing root-loci

1. Obtain the characteristic equation in a form where $D(s)$; and $N(s)$ are the denominator and numerator of the open-loop transfer function.

2. Locate the open loop poles and zeros and plot in the s-plane.

3. Each locus branch will start at an open loop pole, $K = 0$, and finish at an open loop zero or infinity. The number of branches going to infinity is the number of poles p minus zeros z.

4. The loci are symmetrical about the real axis. This is because complex roots always occur in conjugate pairs. The asymptotes to those segments which tend to infinity are equally spaced by an angle $360°/(p-z)$. The negative real axis is one asymptote where the number is odd.

5. The asymptotes will meet on the negative real axis at a point, σ_m, where

$$\sigma_m = \frac{\Sigma \text{ real parts of poles} - \Sigma \text{ real parts of zeros}}{p - z}$$

6. Those parts of the negative real axis which lie on the locus can be found by moving from the origin to $-\infty$ and applying a test. Any point where an odd number of roots of poles and zeros exists to the right is on the locus. Allowance must be made for multiple roots, but complex roots have no effect since they occur in pairs.

7. Where a section of locus joins two poles there must be branches starting at each pole which meet at a common point and then follow an imaginary conjugate path.

8. A pair of conjugate branches may leave or enter the negative real axis at a point, σ_e, where

$$\sigma_e = \frac{1}{p_1 - \sigma_e} + \frac{1}{p_2 - \sigma_e} + \dots + \frac{2(a_1 - \sigma_e)}{(a_1 - \sigma_e)^2 + b_1^2} + \dots$$

$$- \frac{1}{z_1 - \sigma_e} - \frac{1}{z_2 - \sigma_e} - \dots - \frac{2(c_1 - \sigma_e)}{(c_1 - \sigma_e)^2 + d_1^2} = 0$$

where $p_1, p_2, \dots, z_1, z_2$ are the real roots of the poles and zeros and $a_1 + jb_1, \dots$ and $c_1 + jd_1$ are the complex poles and zeros. When a pole lies at the origin, then $p = 0$. This equation is usually solved by trial and error and any poles or zeros distant from σ_e can be ignored.

9(a) A locus leaves a complex pole at an angle θ, where

$$\theta = 180 - \Sigma \angle p + \Sigma \angle z$$

where $\Sigma \angle p$ is the sum of the angles of vectors from all other poles to the complex pole considered (including the conjugate), and $\Sigma \angle z$ is sum of the angles of vectors from all zeros to the complex pole.

(b) A locus approaches a complex pole at an angle θ, where

$$\theta = 180 + \Sigma \angle p - \Sigma \angle z$$

where $\Sigma \angle p$ is the sum of all the angles of vectors from all poles to the complex zero, and $\Sigma \angle z$ is the sum of the angles of all other zeros to the complex zero considered (including the conjugate).

Finally, a selection of root-loci for a number of common transfer functions are shown in Figure 5.15. Arrows are always drawn on root-loci to indicate the direction of increasing gain.

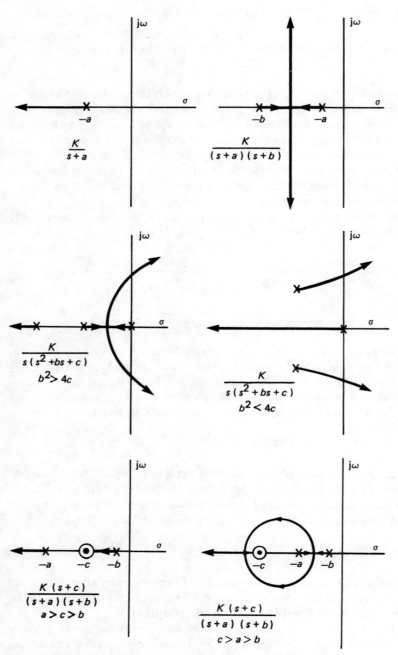

Figure 5.15 Examples of root-loci

STABILITY

The stability of a system is determined by the form of the response to any input or disturbance. Absolute stability refers to whether a system is stable or unstable. In a stable system the response to an input will arrive at and maintain some useful value. In an unstable system the output will not settle at the desired value and may oscillate or increase towards some high value or a physical limitation. More precise definitions for a stable system refer to limited or bounded inputs which produce bounded outputs or the response to a unit impulse input must decay to zero as time becomes infinite.

The input to a system will not affect or determine stability. The components of the system provide its characteristics, and hence determine stability. The solution to the differential equation describing a system is made up of two terms, a steady-state and a transient response. For stability the transient response terms must all die away as time progresses. The coefficients of the exponential terms must therefore be negative real numbers or complex numbers with negative real parts.

Characteristic equation

A general closed-loop transfer function has a transfer function as follows:

$$\frac{C(s)}{R(s)} = \frac{N(s)}{D(s)} = \frac{a_m s^m + a_{m-1} s^{m-1} + \ldots + a_1 s + a_0}{b_n s^n + b_{n-1} s^{n-1} + \ldots + b_1 s + b_0}$$

The transient response of the system can be found by equating $R(s)$ to zero, i.e.

$$(b_n s^n + b_{n-1} s^{n-1} + \ldots + b_1 s + b_0) C(s) = 0$$

Where the denominator of the closed-loop transfer function is equated to zero this is known as the characteristic equation. This expression is said to characterize the system behaviour and will enable the determination of stability. The numerator therefore has no effect on stability but will influence the total system response. The characteristic equation can now be factorized as follows:

$$(s + r_1)(s + r_2) \ldots (s + r_n) = 0$$

where $-r_1$, $-r_2$, etc. are the roots of the characteristic equation. For the system to be stable none of these roots must have positive real parts. It should be noted that the characteristic equation is formed by equating the denominator of the *closed-loop transfer function* to zero.

The roots of the characteristic equation are not always readily determined. It is however possible to determine absolute stability without actually knowing the value of the roots, by using the Routh–Hurwitz stability criterion.

Routh–Hurwitz stability criterion

This is an algebraic method of determining absolute stability in the s-domain. The presence and number of unstable roots is indicated but not their value.

The characteristic equation is first examined, i.e.

$$b_n s^n + b_{n-1} s^{n-1} + \ldots + b_1 s + b_0 = 0$$

If any term b_j is negative, the system is unstable and no further investigation is required. This is because a root with a positive real part would exist and therefore the response would not die away.

If any coefficient b_j, other than b_o, is zero, i.e. s^j does not exist, the system is unstable. A zero coefficient indicates complex roots with no real parts and hence an unstable system. The system is actually marginally stable since some responses will be bounded; however, some responses are unbounded and therefore the system is unstable.

An array is now formed as shown:

s^n	a_0	a_2	a_4 …
s^{n-1}	a_1	a_3	a_5 …
s^{n-2}	b_1	b_2	b_3 …
s^{n-3}	c_1	c_2	c_3 …

where a_n, a_{n-1}, etc. are the coefficients of the characteristic equation. The terms b_1, b_2, etc. and c_1, c_2, etc. are formed from the following expressions:

$$b_1 = \frac{a_1 a_2 - a_0 a_3}{a_1}$$

$$b_2 = \frac{a_1 a_4 - a_0 a_5}{a_1}$$

$$c_1 = \frac{b_1 a_3 - a_1 b_2}{b_1}$$

$$c_2 = \frac{b_1 a_5 - a_1 b_3}{b_1}$$

The terms in b, i.e. b_1, b_2, etc. will be continued until succeeding values are zero. The next row of coefficients in c, and any subsequent rows in d, e, etc. will be determined in a similar manner. A triangular form of array will result with one more row than the order number of the characteristic equation.

The Routh–Hurwitz criterion states that the system is stable if there are no sign changes in the first column of the array. Where one or more changes of sign occur in the first column their number equals the number of roots with positive real parts. Note that 1, −6, 4 in the first column indicates two changes of sign, whereas 3, 6, −9 is only one change of sign.

As an example, determine the stability of the system whose closed-loop transfer function is given by

$$\frac{C(s)}{R(s)} = \frac{5}{s^3 + 9s^2 + 10s + 100}$$

The characteristic equation is formed first:

$$s^3 + 9s^2 + 10s + 100 = 0$$

Upon examination it can be seen that all the coefficients are positive and there are no zero coefficients. The array is now formed:

$$
\begin{array}{c|cc}
s^3 & 1 & 10 \\
s^2 & 9 & 100 \\
s^1 & -10/9 & \\
s^0 & 100 & \\
\end{array}
$$

Two changes of sign are evident in the first column, i.e. 9 to $-10/9$ and $-10/9$ to 100. The system is therefore unstable and there are two roots with positive real parts.

Two special cases can occur in this method of analysis; a zero may occur in the first column, or a row of zeros may appear. Where a single zero occurs it is replaced by a very small positive quantity, ε, and the calculation is continued. If there is no change of sign above and below ε then a pair of imaginary roots exists. If a sign change occurs then this is a single sign change.

Where a row of zeros occurs, use must be made of the coefficients in the preceding row to form an auxiliary equation. The auxiliary equation is then differentiated and the coefficients formed are used instead of the zeros. The row of zeros indicates roots of equal magnitude but radially opposite in the s-plane. Real values would be opposite in sign and complex values would be in conjugate pairs.

In addition to the determination of absolute stability the Routh–Hurwitz criterion can also be used to find the loop gain, K, which will just produce instability. This will be illustrated by an example.

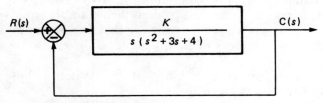

Figure 5.16 Closed-loop control system

A closed-loop system is shown in block diagram form in Figure 5.16. Find the value of K to just produce instability.

The closed-loop transfer function is given by:

$$\frac{C(s)}{R(s)} = \frac{K}{s(s^2 + 3s + 4) + K}$$

The characteristic equation is therefore

$$s^3 + 3s^2 + 4s + K = 0$$

The array is now formed:

$$
\begin{array}{c|cc}
s^3 & 1 & 4 \\
s^2 & 3 & K \\
s^1 & \dfrac{12 - K}{3} & \\
s^0 & K &
\end{array}
$$

For the system to be stable K and $(12 - K)/3$ must both be positive values. The system will just become unstable when $(12 - K)/3$ is zero. Thus

$$\frac{12 - K}{3} = 0 \quad \therefore K = 12$$

The system is therefore stable for values of K between zero and 12, i.e. $0 < K < 12$.

FREQUENCY RESPONSE ANALYSIS

The analysis methods considered so far have required the solution of differential equations. This can become a difficult or lengthy process for complex systems. Frequency response analysis does not involve the solution of differential equations. The steady-state response of a control system is measured with respect to amplitude and phase following the application of a sinusoidal input. This form of analysis therefore examines performance as a function of the frequency of the input signal, rather than as a time response. The independent variable is therefore frequency. The range of frequencies that affect a system's performance will ultimately be found.

This is the accepted practical method of determining the dynamic response of a system. The analysis also provides an indication of how the system should be changed in order to meet the performance specifications. Also, the open-loop frequency response can be used to determine absolute and relative stability of the closed-loop system. In this stability analysis there is no need to find the roots of the characteristic equation.

Use can be made of the Laplace transform of a system in order to obtain a transform in the frequency domain, e.g.

$$\frac{C(s)}{R(s)} = \frac{G(s)}{1 + G(s)H(s)}, G(s) = \frac{K}{\tau s + 1}$$

With a sinusoidal input providing a steady-state output, the s term is simply replaced by the complex operator $j\omega$:

$$\frac{C(j\omega)}{R(j\omega)} = \frac{G(j\omega)}{1 + G(j\omega)H(j\omega)}, G j\omega) = \frac{K}{\tau j\omega + 1}$$

This function may be written in polar coordinates, i.e.

$$G(j\omega) = |G(j\omega)| \angle \phi(\omega)$$

where $|G|$ is the amplitude ratio or magnitude and ϕ is the phase angle of the function $G(j\omega)$. Thus

$$|G(j\omega)| = \frac{K}{\sqrt{(1 + \omega^2\tau^2)}}$$

and

$$\phi = \angle G (j\omega) = -\tan^{-1}\omega\tau$$

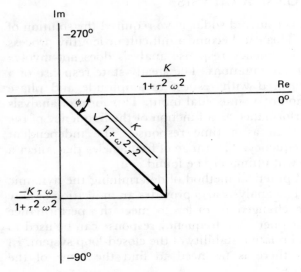

Figure 5.17 Complex plane plot of the vector $G(j\omega)$

This is plotted out on a complex or polar plane in Figure 5.17. If an input $r(t) = X \sin \omega t$ were applied, the steady-state output $c(t)$ would therefore be

$$c(t) = \frac{XK}{\sqrt{(1 + \omega^2 \tau^2)}} \sin (\omega t - \tan^{-1} \omega \tau)$$

The transfer function in the frequency domain, $G(j\omega)$, can be represented graphically in a number of ways. It has already been written in polar coordinates, i.e.

$$G(j\omega) = |G(j\omega)| \angle \phi(\omega)$$

When expressed in rectangular coordinates,

$$G(j\omega) = X(\omega) + jY(\omega)$$

where $X(\omega)$ and $Y(\omega)$ are real functions of ω.
Therefore,

$$|G(j\omega)| = \sqrt{(X(\omega)^2 + Y(\omega)^2)}$$

$$\phi = \tan^{-1} \frac{Y(\omega)}{X(\omega)}$$

For any given frequency ω_1 the function $G(j\omega_1)$ can be expressed as a vector quantity of magnitude or length $|G(j\omega_1)|$ and angle with respect to the positive real axis of $\angle\phi(\omega_1)$. A number of different frequencies, i.e. ω_1, ω_2 and ω_3, would result in separate vectors for $G(j\omega_2)$, $G(j\omega_2)$ and $G(j\omega_3)$. A locus of the end points of these vectors could be drawn for frequencies between zero and infinity. This would then be a polar plot of the transfer function, see Figure 5.18.

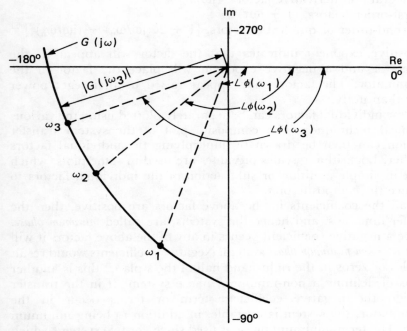

Figure 5.18 Polar plot of $G(j\omega)$

A number of different graphical methods are used to represent $G(j\omega)$ by plotting $|G(j\omega)|$ and $\angle\phi$ (ω) as ω varies. Open or closed-loop transfer functions can be plotted, although open-loop is more usual. The various plots using open-loop transfer functions are:

1. A polar diagram where $Y(\omega)$ is plotted against $X(\omega)$ as ω varies. This is also known as a Nyquist diagram.
2. Graphs of $|G(j\omega)|$ to a base of ω and $\angle\phi$ (ω) to a base of ω. The $|G(j\omega)|$ values are plotted in decibels (dB) and the ω values are on a logarithmic scale. This is also known as a Bode diagram.
3. Values of $|G(j\omega)|$ are plotted against $\angle\phi$ (ω) with ω as a parameter. The $|G(j\omega)|$ values are plotted in decibels and this plot is known as a Nichols diagram.

Basic factors of frequency response curves

The transfer function of a component or system has been shown as a factored ratio of polynomials. Four basic factors occur frequently in transfer functions in the frequency domain. These are:

1. Constant or gain, K.
2. Integral and derivative factors, $(j\omega)^{\pm 1}$
3. First-order factors, $(1 + j\omega\tau)^{\pm 1}$
4. Second-order or quadratic factors, $[1 + 2\zeta(j\omega/\omega_n) + (j\omega/\omega_n)^2]^{\pm 1}$

A positive exponent indicates that the factor will appear in the numerator and a negative exponent will place the factor in the denominator. The factors may appear raised to an integer power other than unity.

These individual factors can be separately plotted using the various graphical techniques. The composite plot of the system transfer function can then be drawn by multiplying the individual factors together. Logarithmic scales or values are used in some plots, which result in simple addition or subtraction of the individual factors to produce the composite plot.

If all the coefficients in the above factors are positive, then the transfer functions, and hence the systems, are called *minimum phase*. Where a negative coefficient occurs in any of the above factors it will result in a *non-minimum phase* system. Negative coefficients would result in poles or zeros in the right-hand half of the s-plane; this is another means of defining a non-minimum phase system. If in the transfer function the negative coefficient term or terms occur in the denominator, the system is unstable, in addition to being minimum phase. The term minimum phase is used since, for two systems which have the same magnitude characteristic, the range of phase angle for the minimum phase system is a minimum. The non-minimum system, for the same magnitude characteristic, would have a range of phase angle greater than the minimum of the other system.

Non-minimum phase systems are slow in response and therefore undesirable. An example would be a transportation lag in a control system.

Polar plots

A polar plot of a function $G(j\omega)$ is a plot of the magnitude of $G(j\omega)$ against the phase angle on polar coordinates as the frequency ω is varied from zero to infinity. The vectors $|G(j\omega)| \angle \phi (\omega)$ are therefore plotted for varying values of ω. A positive phase angle is measured anticlockwise from the positive real axis. This polar, or Nyquist, plot of the open-loop transfer function will show the frequency response over the complete frequency range. It does not, however, clearly indicate the contributions made by the individual factors. The plotting of the individual factors and the composite plot will now be described.

The gain factor K will not affect the shape of the plot but it will determine the scale of the real axis. This factor can have a considerable influence on stability. The magnitude will be constant and the phase angle is zero.

Integral and derivative factors have polar plots which are on the imaginary axis. This can be seen from

$$G(j\omega) = \frac{1}{j\omega} = \frac{1}{\omega} \angle -90°$$

and

$$G(j\omega) = (j\omega) = \omega \angle 90°$$

First-order factors produce two completely different plots depending upon whether they form part of the numerator or the denominator of the transfer function. Consider the factor $(1 + j\omega\tau)^{-1}$, i.e.

$$G(j\omega) = \frac{1}{1 + j\omega\tau} = \frac{1}{\sqrt{(1 + \omega^2\tau^2)}} \angle -\tan^{-1}\omega\tau$$

Evaluated at $\omega = 0$ and $\omega = 1/\tau$ this provides the points

$$G(j0) = 1 \angle 0°$$

$$G(j\frac{1}{\tau}) = \frac{1}{\sqrt{2}} \angle -45°$$

As $\omega \to \infty$ then $G(j\omega)$ approaches zero and the phase angle becomes $-90°$. The polar plot is a semicircle, see Figure 5.19(a). The centre is at 0.5 on the real axis and the radius is 0.5. The polar plot of $1 + j\omega\tau$ is the upper part of the line leaving 1,0 which is parallel to the imaginary axis, see Figure 5.19(b).

Second-order factors have a polar plot whose shape is somewhat

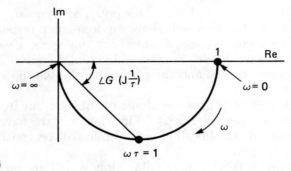

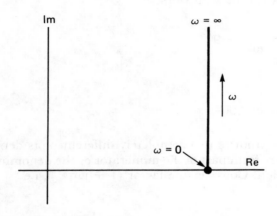

(b)

Figure 5.19 Polar plot of a first-order factor

dependent upon the damping ratio, ζ. Consider the second-order factor:

$$G(j\omega) = \cfrac{1}{1 + 2\zeta\left(\cfrac{j\omega}{\omega_n}\right) + \left(\cfrac{j\omega}{\omega_n}\right)^2} \qquad (\zeta > 0)$$

The low and high frequency points can be found as follows:

$$\lim_{\omega \to 0} G(j\omega) = 1\angle 0° \quad \text{and} \quad \lim_{\omega \to \infty} G(j\omega) = 0\angle -180°$$

The exact shape of the plot will vary according to the damping ratio but the general form can be seen in Figure 5.20(a). Where the locus

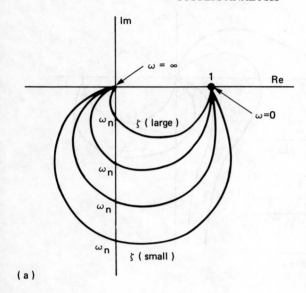

(a)

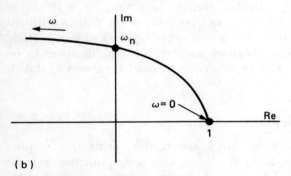

(b)

Figure 5.20 Polar plot of a second-order factor:

(a) $\dfrac{1}{1 + 2\zeta(j\omega/\omega_n) + (j\omega/\omega_n)^2}$ ($\zeta > 0$)

(b) $1 + 2\zeta(j\omega/\omega_n) + (j\omega/\omega_n)^2$ ($\zeta > 0$)

cuts the negative imaginary axis is the undamped natural frequency, ω_n. If the other form of this second-order factor is now considered:

$$G(j\omega) = 1 + 2\zeta\left(\frac{j\omega}{\omega_n}\right) + \left(\frac{j\omega}{\omega_n}\right)^2 \quad (\zeta > 0)$$

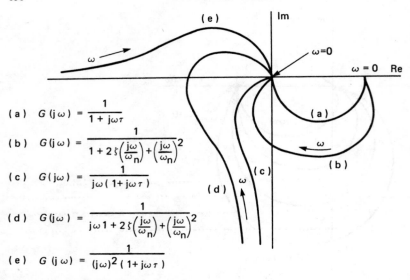

(a) $G(j\omega) = \dfrac{1}{1 + j\omega\tau}$

(b) $G(j\omega) = \dfrac{1}{1 + 2\zeta\left(\dfrac{j\omega}{\omega_n}\right) + \left(\dfrac{j\omega}{\omega_n}\right)^2}$

(c) $G(j\omega) = \dfrac{1}{j\omega(1 + j\omega\tau)}$

(d) $G(j\omega) = \dfrac{1}{j\omega 1 + 2\zeta\left(\dfrac{j\omega}{\omega_n}\right) + \left(\dfrac{j\omega}{\omega_n}\right)^2}$

(e) $G(j\omega) = \dfrac{1}{(j\omega)^2(1 + j\omega\tau)}$

Figure 5.21 Examples of polar plots

The low and high frequency points can be found as before, and the general form of the plot is shown in Figure 5.20(b).

When plotting any particular transfer function it is usual to determine the high and low frequency portions of the plot as outlined above. Direct calculation, or the use of other types of plot, e.g. Bode diagram, in the frequency range of interest, also enable them to be found. A number of polar plots of various transfer functions as shown in Figure 5.21.

Nyquist stability criterion

Stability in the frequency domain is determined using the Nyquist stability criterion. A simplified approach, which is applicable to most practical systems, will be used. A more rigorous mathematical development can be found in more specialized control texts.

A closed-loop control system is shown in Figure 5.22 and can be represented in the following general form:

$$\frac{C(j\omega)}{R(j\omega)} = \frac{G(j\omega)}{1 + G(j\omega)H(j\omega)}$$

The feedback signal $B(j\omega)$ is subtracted from the sinusoidal input $R(j\omega)$ to produce the error signal $E(j\omega)$. The error signal is modified in amplitude and phase angle by the loop gain $G(j\omega)H(j\omega)$ to become

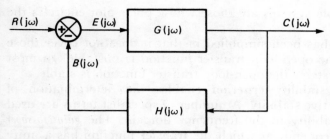

Figure 5.22 Closed-loop control system

the feedback signal. If the feedback signal achieves a phase angle which lags by 180°, it is, in effect, added to $R(j\omega)$ to produce positive feedback. If this feedback signal has an amplitude less than the error signal then the system will not be self-maintaining and is therefore stable. If the feedback signal is greater than the error signal then the input is not required, the system will maintain itself and therefore is unstable. Most practical systems will create lagging phase shifts which at some frequencies may exceed 180°. The system must therefore be designed so that at these frequencies the amplitude ratio is less than unity.

This criterion can be represented in a polar plot as shown in Figure 5.23. The $(-1 + j0)$ point indicates a unity gain at a lagging or negative phase angle of 180°. Where the plot crosses the negative real axis at a value greater than unity, i.e. the broken line, the system is

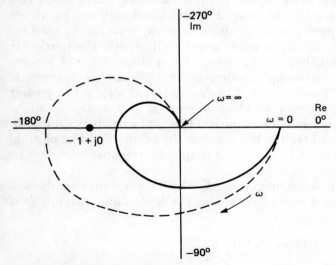

Figure 5.23 Nyquist stability criterion

unstable. Unstable systems are those whose polar plot encircles the $(-1 + j0)$ point.

This criterion has been simplified in that it does not cover those systems where the open-loop transfer function is unstable. In most simple control systems the open-loop transfer function is stable.

The Nyquist stability criterion enables the determination of absolute and relative stability. A number of specialist terms are used in relation to stability in the frequency domain. The *gain-crossover frequency* is the frequency at which the transfer function has a unity magnitude or gain. The *phase-crossover frequency* is the frequency at which the transfer function has a phase angle of $-180°$. *Gain margin* is the reciprocal of the magnitude of $G(j\omega)$ at the phase crossover frequency. *Phase margin* is the additional phase lag required at the gain crossover frequency to bring the system to instability.

Logarithmic plots or Bode diagrams

An alternative to the polar plot is the use of logarithms for the amplitude and phase angle of the transfer function, $G(j\omega)$. Two separate diagrams are drawn, each to a base of frequency ω, in a logarithmic scale. The amplitude is expressed in logarithmic terms using a unit of magnitude called the decibel (dB), where

$$\text{Logarithmic magnitude, } G(j\omega) = 20 \log_{10} |G(j\omega)| \text{ dB}$$

Since a logarithmic value is plotted, the actual scale can be linear and semilog paper is used for plotting. The horizontal scale is logarithmic and used for frequency while the linear vertical scale can be used for either magnitude (in dB) or phase angle (in degrees). The particular advantage of logarithmic plots is that the multiplication of various magnitudes becomes simple addition. Approximate or asymptotic plotting is also possible and can be corrected easily for greater accuracy. The frequency range of interest in any analysis can be plotted and even expanded if required. This is of particular value with practical systems where the lower values are of interest. The plotting of the four individual factors for a frequency response will now be considered.

A constant term has a magnitude K, which is constant regardless of frequency and has a zero phase angle. The logarithmic magnitude is given by

$$\log \text{mag } K = 20 \log_{10} K \text{ dB}$$

This is shown as a logarithmic plot in Figure 5.24(a).

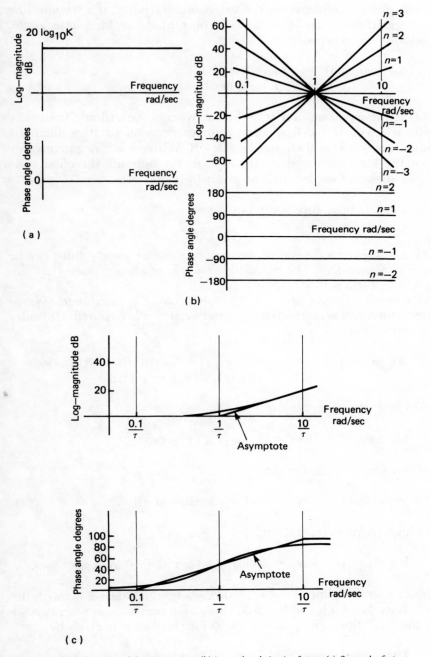

Figure 5.24 Bode diagrams: (a) constant term; (b) integral or derivative factor; (c) first-order factor

The plot of an integral or derivative factor, $(j\omega)^{\pm 1}$, is a straight line for logarithmic magnitude and a constant value for phase angle. Consider the expression

$$\log \text{mag} \ (j\omega)^n = 20 \ \log_{10}|(j\omega)^n| \ \text{dB}$$
$$= 20 \ n \ \log_{10} \ \omega \ \text{dB}$$

This is the equation of a straight line when a logarithmic frequency scale is used. If the frequency changes from ω_1 to $10\omega_1$ then the magnitude value will change by $20n$ dB. Where n is a negative value then the logarithmic plot will slope in the opposite direction. The phase angle ϕ for $(j\omega)^n$ will be given by

$$\text{Phase angle,} \ \phi \ (\omega) = n \ \tan^{-1} j\omega$$
$$= n90°$$

This is therefore a constant value regardless of frequency and n can be positive or negative. The magnitude and phase angle plots of $(j\omega)^n$ are shown in Figure 5.24(b).

First-order factors are usually plotted using approximate asymptotes which can be corrected if greater accuracy is required. Consider the expression

$$\log \text{mag} \ (1 + j\omega\tau)^n = 20 \ \log_{10}|(1 + j\omega\tau)^n| \ \text{dB}$$
$$= 20n\log_{10}\sqrt{(1 + \omega^2\tau^2)} \ \text{dB}$$

For $n = 1$, then

$$\log \text{mag} \ (1 + j\omega\tau) = 20 \ \log_{10} \ \sqrt{(1 + \omega^2\tau^2)}$$

For low frequencies, i.e. $\omega\tau<<1$

$$\log \text{mag} \ (1 + j\omega\tau) = 20 \ \log_{10} \ 1 \ \text{dB} = 0 \ \text{dB}$$

For high frequencies, i.e. $\omega\tau>>1$

$$\log \text{mag} \ (1 + j\omega\tau) = 20 \ \log_{10} \ \sqrt{(\omega^2\tau^2)} = 20 \ \log_{10} \ \omega\tau$$

This is a straight line of slope 20 dB/decade which passes through the 0 dB line. The high and low frequency asymptotes cross where $\omega\tau=1$ on the 0 dB line. The phase angle ϕ for this factor is given by

$$\text{Phase angle,} \ \phi = \tan^{-1} \ \omega\tau$$

The three points considered for the magnitude plot will have phase angles as follows:

$$\omega = 0, \phi = 0°$$

$$\omega = \frac{1}{\tau} = \omega_n, \phi = 45°$$

$$\omega = \infty, \phi = 90°$$

The magnitude and phase angle plots are shown in Figure 5.24(c), with both accurate and straight line approximations for magnitude.

Second-order factors will produce plots which vary according to the value of the damping ratio ζ. The second-order factor in control systems is usually of the form:

$$\frac{1}{1 + 2\zeta\left(\dfrac{j\omega}{\omega_n}\right) + \left(\dfrac{j\omega}{\omega_n}\right)^2}$$

If the damping ratio ζ is greater than 1, this second-order factor can be expressed as two first-order factors and plotted as outlined above. For $0<\zeta<1$ this second-order factor becomes the product of two complex conjugate factors. Thus,

$$\log \text{mag}\left(\frac{1}{1 + 2\zeta\left(\dfrac{j\omega}{\omega_n}\right)+\left(\dfrac{j\omega}{\omega_n}\right)^2}\right) = -20 \log_{10} \sqrt{\left\{\left[1 - \left(\dfrac{\omega}{\omega_n}\right)^2\right]^2 + \left(\dfrac{2\zeta\omega}{\omega_n}\right)^2\right\}} \text{ dB}$$

The asymptotic approximations are not very accurate, since they will vary with ζ. However, for low frequencies, i.e. $\omega/\omega_n \ll 1$,

$$\log \text{mag}\left(\frac{1}{1 + 2\zeta\left(\dfrac{j\omega}{\omega_n}\right) + \left(\dfrac{j\omega}{\omega_n}\right)^2}\right) \simeq -20 \log_{10} 1 \text{ dB} = 0 \text{ dB}$$

For high frequencies, i.e. $\omega/\omega_n \gg 1$,

$$\log \text{mag}\left(\frac{1}{1 + 2\zeta\left(\dfrac{j\omega}{\omega_n}\right) + \left(\dfrac{j\omega}{\omega_n}\right)^2}\right) \simeq -20 \log_{10} (\omega/\omega_n)^2 \text{ dB}$$

$$= -40 \log_{10} (\omega/\omega_n) \text{ dB}$$

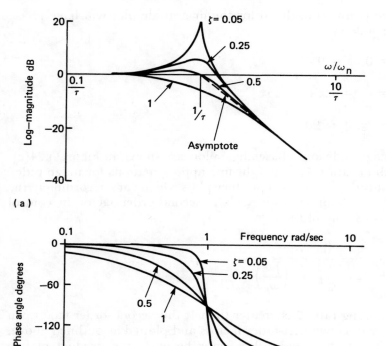

(a)

(b)

Figure 5.25 Bode diagram of second-order factor: (a) log-magnitude plot; (b) phase angle plot

The asymptotes will meet at $\omega\tau = 1$, i.e. $\omega = \omega_n$, as before, but the high frequency asymptote will slope 40 dB/decade downwards. The actual plot between the high and low frequencies will be influenced by the damping ratio ζ. A magnitude plot for various values of ζ is shown in Figure 5.25(a), together with the asymptotic approximations. The frequency ratio, ω/ω_n, is used for the horizontal scale and provides a general plot for any value of natural frequency ω_n. The phase angle ϕ for this factor is given by

$$\text{Phase angle, } \phi(\omega) = -\tan^{-1}\frac{2\zeta(\omega/\omega_n)}{1 - (\omega/\omega_n)^2}$$

The three points considered for the magnitude plot will have phase angles as follows:

$$\omega = 0, \phi = 0°$$

$$\omega = \frac{1}{\tau} = \omega_n, \phi = -90°$$

$$\omega = \infty, \phi = -180°$$

These three values are independent of ζ. A phase angle plot for various values of ζ is given in Figure 5.25(b). The magnitude and phase plots of second-order factors are usually drawn first using asymptotes and then corrected by reference to actual plots such as given above.

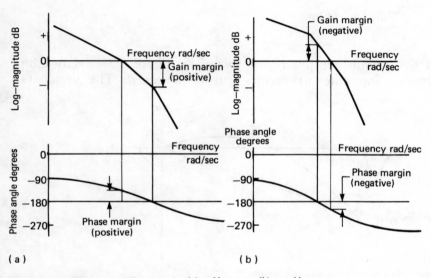

(a)   (b)

Figure 5.26 Gain margin and phase margin: (a) stable system; (b) unstable system

The determination of phase and gain margins from a Bode diagram is shown in Figure 5.26. The phase and gain crossover frequencies can be readily identified and determined. It should be noted that a positive gain margin is actually measured in negative decibels. A positive gain margin, measured in decibels, means that the system is stable. A negative value means the system is unstable. Where the phase angle of the open-loop transfer function at the gain crossover frequency is less than 180°, the phase margin is considered positive and the system is stable. A phase angle greater than 180° results in a negative phase margin and thus an unstable system.

Closed-loop frequency response

The frequency response plots considered so far have been used to determine the stability of the open-loop. These plots can also be used to determine the stability of the closed-loop by use of the Nichols chart or, somewhat approximately, from the Bode diagram.

Nichols chart
A closed-loop unity feedback system is required when using the Nichols chart. If a non-unity feedback system is being considered, it can be rearranged using block diagram algebra to obtain a unity feedback form. The closed-loop transfer function will be:

$$\frac{C(j\omega)}{R(j\omega)} = \frac{G(j\omega)}{1 + G(j\omega)}$$

In the Nyquist or polar plot shown in Figure 5.27, relationships between the different vectors can be obtained. The vector $\overrightarrow{OB}$

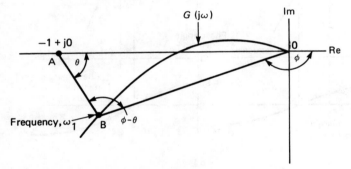

Figure 5.27 Open-loop and closed-loop relationships

represents $G(j\omega_1)$, its length is $|G(j\omega_1)|$ and the angle is $\angle G(j\omega_1)$. The vector $\overrightarrow{AB}$ represents $1 + G(j\omega_1)$, thus

$$\frac{\overrightarrow{OB}}{\overrightarrow{AB}} = \frac{G(j\omega_1)}{1 + G(j\omega_1)} = \frac{C(j\omega_1)}{R(j\omega_1)}$$

The values of magnitude and phase angle $(\phi - \theta)$ at $\omega = \omega_1$ are therefore for the closed loop. Where various frequency values are used and magnitude and phase angle are plotted, this represents the closed-loop frequency response. The magnitude of the closed-loop is defined as M and the term N is used where $N = \tan(\phi - \theta)$.

A particular transfer function, $G(j\omega)$, will have specific values of M and N. The specific value of either M or N, but not both, could however be obtained from a variety of transfer functions. It is therefore possible to plot curves of constant values of M and N as functions of $G(j\omega)$. These points when plotted in the complex or polar plane produce circles.

Logarithmic plotting is easier than polar plotting and therefore these circles of constant magnitude and phase have been translated to a logarithmic gain-phase diagram known as a Nichols chart, see Figure 5.28. Two sets of coordinates are used, one for open and one for closed-loop responses. The horizontal and vertical coordinate axes provide open-loop values. The curved lines are the M and N loci and provide the closed-loop values. When using the chart, the magnitude and phase angle values of the open-loop transfer function are plotted

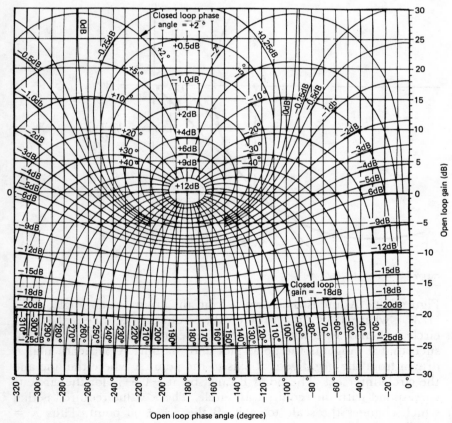

Figure 5.28 Nichols chart

for different frequencies using the coordinate axes. The locus is then drawn connecting these points. Where this locus cuts the curved lines of the M and N loci, the closed-loop frequency and phase values can be read off and then plotted in a Bode diagram form.

The M locus which tangents the open-loop plot is the maximum value of the closed-loop response response M_r, in dB. The N locus through this point gives the phase angle, and the frequency value is the resonant frequency, ω_r.

In control system design, a particular maximum response value, M_r, is usually required. This can be obtained by moving the open-loop locus up or down the Nichols chart. The necessary value of gain required by the system can then be found. Another method of doing this is by using Brown's construction. A polar plot of the normalized open-loop transfer function $G(j\omega)/K$ is first drawn, see

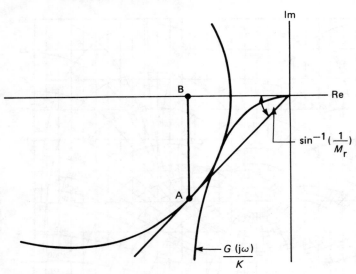

Figure 5.29 Brown's construction

Figure 5.29. A line is then drawn from the origin, at an angle, $\sin^{-1}(1/M_r)$, where M_r is a magnitude value, from the negative real axis. A circle is then drawn, with centre on the negative real axis, at a radius such that it tangents the polar plot and the line. A perpendicular is drawn from the negative real axis to the point A where the line and the circle intersect. The point B must be at $-1 + j0$ for the circle to correspond with the required M_r circle. The K value required is that which changes the scale to make B the $-1 + j0$ point. Thus $K = 1/OB$.

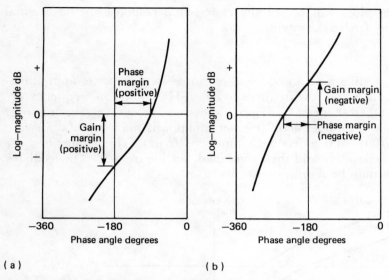

Figure 5.30 Gain margin and phase margin: (a) stable system; (b) unstable system

The determination of gain and phase margins from the Nichols chart is shown in Figure 5.30. The values of the phase and gain crossover frequencies are not readily obtainable. It should be noted that a positive gain margin is actually measured in negative decibels.

The Nichols chart is used for closed-loop systems with unity feedback. Where a non-unity feedback system is to be analysed it must be rearranged, using block diagram algebra, see Figure 5.31. The open-loop transfer function, $G(j\omega)H(j\omega)$, can then be plotted on the Nichols chart. The closed-loop response function,

$$\frac{G(j\omega)H(j\omega)}{1 + G(j\omega)H(j\omega)}$$

can then be found and plotted on a Bode diagram. The function $1/H(j\omega)$ can then be plotted on the same Bode diagram and the two plots can be added in terms of magnitude and phase angle. The

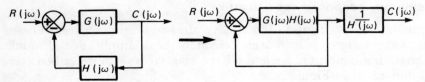

Figure 5.31 Non-unity feedback system

resulting plots will be for the closed-loop response of the original non-unity feedback system.

Bode diagram

The Bode diagram can be used for closed-loop response approximations at high and low frequency values. High and low frequency are usually taken to mean the regions above and below the gain-crossover frequency. The open-loop transfer function is made up of a forward gain, $G(j\omega)$, and a feedback function, $H(j\omega)$. These functions are plotted separately and then combined, see Figure 5.32. The feedback function may be non-unity in this case.

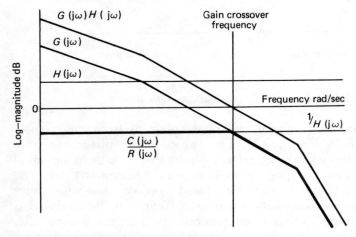

Figure 5.32 Bode diagram of a closed-loop response

At low frequencies, where $G(j\omega)H(j\omega) \gg 1$, the closed-loop transfer function becomes $1/H(j\omega)$. At high frequencies, where $G(j\omega)H(j\omega) \ll 1$, the closed-loop transfer function becomes $G(j\omega)$. These two approximations can therefore be drawn on the Bode diagram to represent the closed-loop transfer function, see Figure 5.32.

Frequency response specifications

A number of specification terms have already been described. These are phase margin, gain margin, resonant peak amplitude, M_r, and resonant frequency, ω_r. Several other terms will now be described and are illustrated in Figure 5.33.

The frequency value at whch the magnitude of the closed-loop

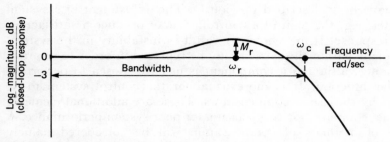

Figure 5.33 Frequency-response specifications

response is 3 dB below the zero-frequency value is called the *cut-off frequency*, ω_c. The *bandwidth* is the frequency range within which the magnitude of the closed-loop response does not drop -3 dB. The bandwidth provides an indication of the speed of response of the system. The *cut-off rate* is the slope of the logarithmic magnitude plot near the cut-off frequency.

The frequency response of a control system is related to the transient response, and for second-order systems an exact relationship exists. Where a control system can be reasonably approximated to second-order, the following correlations exist.

1. The phase margin and the damping ratio ζ are directly related.
2. For small values of ζ the value of the resonant frequency, ω_r, will describe the speed of the transient response of the system.
3. The smaller the value of ζ, the smaller is the resonant peak amplitude M_r, and the transient response maximum overshoot M_p. For very small values of ζ, M_r becomes large, whereas M_p is unity or less. It should be noted that M_r is unity for all values of ζ greater than 0.707.

Typical frequency response specifications are $0 < M_r < 1.4$ (0 dB < $M_r < 3$ dB) which corresponds to a damping ratio of $0.4 < \zeta < 0.7$. Where M_r is greater than 1.5, the transient response may produce several overshoots. The phase margin should be between 30 and 60° and the gain margin should be greater than 6 dB. The bandwidth must be wide enough to cover the frequency range of the inputs, but not higher since noise will then be a problem.

SYSTEM DESIGN AND COMPENSATION

An automatic control system must operate in a manner which meets the design specifications. These specifications can be given with respect to transient response or frequency response, using terms which have been described previously. The adjustment of a system parameter, e.g. the gain of a controller, may produce a satisfactory system response. It may however result in instability in the system. Components within the system may be replaced in order to improve performance, although a component is usually chosen to perform a particular function. It is more usual for the control system to be modified by the use of compensators. These are additional elements which make amends, or compensate, for poor system performance. A number of methods of compensation will be considered namely cascade (or series) and feedback (or parallel). The choice of method is made depending upon the changes required and the particular system. A suitably compensated system will be stable, have an acceptable transient response and a sufficient gain to reduce the steady-state error to a desirable level. All of these requirements can rarely be met simultaneously and compromises must be made.

Compensation will be considered as a means of reshaping the frequency response curves on the Bode diagram. For a small steady-state error in the lower frequency ranges, a high forward gain is required. Around the gain-crossover frequency the log magnitude plot should have a slope of about -30 dB/decade for stability. It

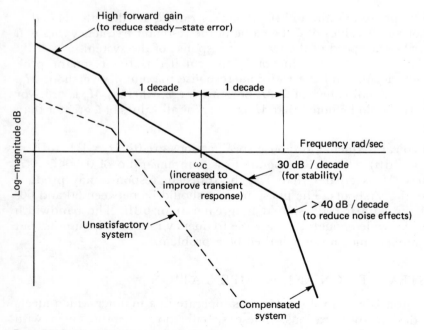

Figure 5.34 System compensation

should maintain this slope for a decade either side of the gain-crossover frequency. At high frequencies the log-magnitude plot should have a rapidly decreasing slope in order to reduce noise effects. Where the transient response of a system is unsatisfactory it may be necessary to increase the gain-crossover frequency. These various compensations to a system are summarized in Figure 5.34. In a practical sense the compensator in a system is usually a controller. The output from the controller can be adjusted to provide a suitable performance in terms of the system specification or operation. Use can also be made of lag and lead networks to provide suitable system compensation.

Series compensation

The most common form of series compensator in marine systems is a controller. Consider the compensated closed-loop control system shown in Figure 5.35. The transfer function of the controller, G_c, is

$$G_c = \frac{M(s)}{E(s)} = \frac{M(s)}{R(s) - B(s)}$$

This is also known as the controller action and can take one of several forms. The basic actions are proportional (P), integral (I) and derivative (D). A controller can be single-term, i.e. P; or two-term, i.e. P+I or P+D; or three-term, i.e. P+I+D.

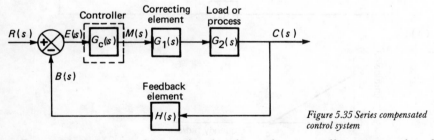

Figure 5.35 Series compensated control system

Proportional control or action is where the controller output signal is proportional to the error. The response is considered to be immediate and there is no delay between changes in input and output. The transfer function of a proportional controller is

$$G_c(s) = \frac{M(s)}{E(s)} = K_p \text{ or } G_c(j\omega) = \frac{M(j\omega)}{E(j\omega)} = K_p$$

where K_p is the proportional gain.

The frequency response characteristics of proportional control are a constant magnitude ratio and a constant zero phase angle. Proportional control cannot completely eliminate error and an offset or steady-state error occurs with a proportional-only controller.

The use of proportional plus integral (P+I) controller action will remove offset and hence improve the steady-state response of the system. Integral action is where the output changes at a rate proportional to the error, i.e.

$$\frac{\mathrm{d}m(t)}{\mathrm{d}t} = K_i e(t) \text{ or } m(t) = K_i \int e(t)\mathrm{d}t$$

$$\therefore \ M(s) = K_i \frac{E(s)}{s} \text{or } M(j\omega) = K_i \frac{E(j\omega)}{j\omega}$$

where K_2 is the integral action factor.

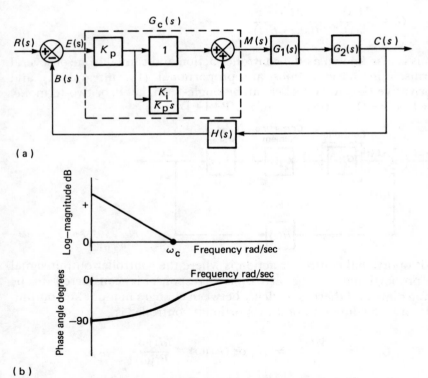

(a)

(b)

Figure 5.36 Proportional plus integral controller compensation: (a) block diagram; (b) Bode diagram

The controller action will therefore continue as long as an error exists. When combined with proportional control action the system block diagram will appear as shown in Figure 5.36(a). The transfer function of the P+I controller is

$$G_c(s) = \frac{M(s)}{E(s)} = K_p(1 + \frac{K_i}{K_p s}) = K_p\left(1 + \frac{1}{T_i s}\right)$$

or $\quad G_c(j\omega) = \frac{M(j\omega)}{E(j\omega)} = K_p\left(1 + \frac{1}{T_i j\omega}\right) = K_p\left(1 + \frac{1}{j\omega/\omega_c}\right)$

where ω_c is the frequency for the value $1/T_i$, i.e. a corner frequency and T_i is the integral action time. The Bode plot for this controller is shown in Figure 5.36(b). The constant, T_i, or frequency, ω_c, must be chosen to produce a satisfactory transient response and avoid possible instability.

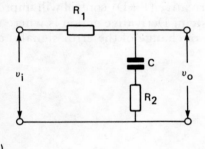

(a)

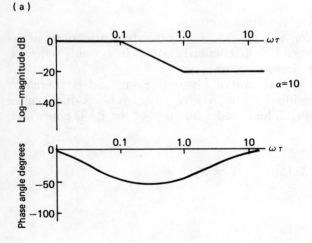

(b)

Figure 5.37 Lag compensation network: (a) circuit; (b) Bode diagram

An electrical network can be used to approximate P+I controller action and would act as a lag compensator. The circuit of a lag compensation network is shown in Figure 5.37(a). The transfer function is

$$G_c(j\omega) = \frac{1 + j\omega\tau}{1 + j\omega\alpha\tau}$$

where $\tau = CR_2$ and $\alpha = (R_1 + R_2)/R_2$.

The Bode diagram for this unit is shown in Figure 5.37(b), where a normalized frequency scale of $\omega\tau$ is used. The variation in lagging phase angle can be seen with a maximum value occurring between the corner frequencies. The lower corner frequency on the log-magnitude plot occurs at $\omega\tau = 1/\alpha$ and the higher corner frequency at $\omega\tau = 1$. The log-magnitude plot has a $-20\,\mathrm{dB/decade}$ slope between the corner frequencies.

The use of proportional plus derivative (P+D) control will improve the transient performance of a system. Derivative action is where the output is proportional to the rate of change of the error signal, i.e.

$$m(t) = K_d \frac{de(t)}{dt}$$

$$\therefore M(s) = K_d \, s \, E(s)$$

$$\text{or } M(j\omega) = K_d \, j\omega \, E(j\omega)$$

where K_d is the derivative action factor.

This controller action will provide a considerable correction before the error becomes large. It is particularly useful in systems where a sudden load or input change occurs.

Derivative control action cannot be used alone and is therefore combined with proportional action, to give a system block diagram as shown in Figure 5.38(a). The transfer function of the P+D controller is

$$G_c(s) = \frac{M(s)}{E(s)} = K_p\left(1 + \frac{K_d}{K_p} s\right) = K_p(1 + T_d s)$$

or

$$G_c(j\omega) = \frac{M(j\omega)}{E(j\omega)} = K_p(1 + T_d j\omega) = K_p\left(1 + \frac{j\omega}{\omega_c}\right)$$

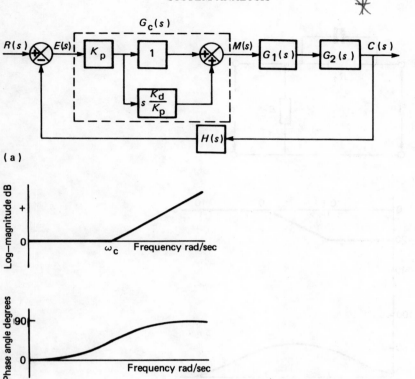

(a)

Figure 5.38 Proportional plus derivative controller compensation: (a) block diagram; (b) Bode diagram

where ω_c is a corner frequency for the value $1/T_d$ and T_d is the derivative action time. The Bode plot for this controller is shown in Figure 5.38(b). Since derivative action will amplify unwanted noise signals, it is usual to limit the gain at higher frequencies.

An electrical network can be used to approximate P+D controller action and would act as a lead compensator. The circuit of a lead compensator is shown in Figure 5.39(a). The transfer function is

$$G_c(j\omega) = \frac{1}{\alpha}\left(\frac{1 + j\omega\tau}{1 + \dfrac{j\omega\tau}{\alpha}}\right)$$

where $\tau = CR_1$ and $\alpha = (R_1 + R_2)/R_2$.

The Bode diagram for this unit is shown in Figure 5.39(b) where a normalized frequency scale of $\omega\tau$ is used. The variation in leading phase angle can be seen, with a maximum value occurring between

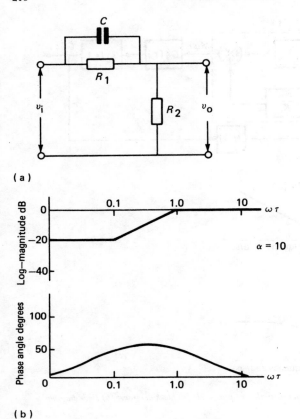

(a)

(b)

Figure 5.39 Lead compensation network: (a) circuit; (b) Bode diagram

the corner frequencies. The lower corner frequency on the log-magnitude plot occurs at $\omega\tau = 1/\alpha$ and the higher corner frequency at $\omega\tau = 1$. The log-magnitude plot has a 20 dB/decade slope between the corner frequencies.

A three-term or P+I+D controller combines the above-mentioned actions. This type of controller will be used in process control where large transfer lags exist. The transfer function of a three-term controller is

$$G_c(s) = \frac{M(s)}{E(s)} = K_p \left(1 + \frac{K_i}{s} + K_d s\right)$$

or

$$G(j\omega) = \frac{M(j\omega)}{E(j\omega)} = K_p \left(1 + \frac{1}{j\omega/\omega_{CI}} + \frac{1}{j\omega/\omega_{CD}}\right)$$

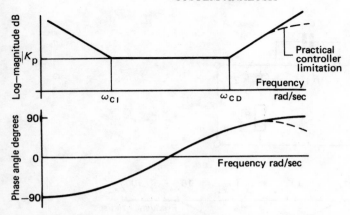

Figure 5.40 Bode diagram for a proportional plus integral plus derivative controller

where ω_{cI} and ω_{cD} are the corner frequencies for integral and derivative action respectively. The Bode diagram for this unit is shown in Figure 5.40. It is usual in a practical controller to limit the derivative action as shown, to minimize noise effects. Integral action is also known as reset action. Derivative action is also known as rate action.

An electrical network can also be used to approximate P+I+D controller action and would act as a lag-lead compensator. The circuit of a lag-lead compensator is shown in Figure 5.41(a). The transfer function is

$$G_c(j\omega) = \left(\frac{1 + j\omega\tau_2}{1 + j\omega\alpha\tau_2}\right)\left(\frac{1 + j\omega\tau_1}{1 + \dfrac{j\omega\tau_1}{\alpha}}\right)$$

where $\tau_1 = R_1 C_1$, $\tau_2 = R_2 C_2$ and $\alpha = \dfrac{R_1 + R_2}{R_2}$.

The Bode diagram for this unit is shown in Figure 5.41(b). The log-magnitude plot is seen to have a zero value at high and low frequencies. The phase angle is also zero at high and low frequencies.

When using lag, lead or lag-lead compensators the uncompensated system response must first be plotted on a Bode diagram. If a particular compensator is chosen then its response can be plotted on a Bode diagram. The combined plot is found from the sum of the two individual plots, both in terms of log magnitude and phase angle. The combined plot will then be examined to determine if it meets the system specifications. Alternatively, the uncompensated system plot is

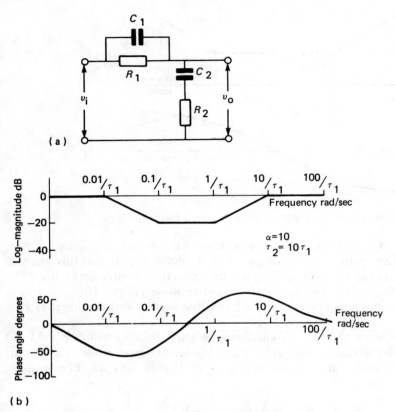

Figure 5.41 Lag-lead compensation network: (a) circuit; (b) Bode diagram

drawn and then a plot which will meet the system specifications. The difference between the two plots will be the plot of the compensator. The nature of the compensator plot will possibly determine its type and then the values of log-magnitude and phase angle will result in particular values of, for example, α and τ for a lead compensator.

Feedback compensation

Derivative or velocity feedback is a common feature of many speed and position control systems. The principle and use of feedback in a control system have been previously described. Feedback applied around a particular element or group of elements will improve system performance. The feedback path may incorporate proportional action or lag, lead or lag-lead actions as described earlier for series compensation. A block diagram of feedback compensation is shown in

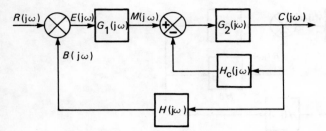

Figure 5.42 Feedback compensated control system

Figure 5.42. The open-loop transfer function of this system can be simplified to

$$\frac{B(j\omega)}{E(j\omega)} = \frac{G_1(j\omega)\,G_2(j\omega)\,H(j\omega)}{1 + G_2(j\omega)H_c(j\omega)}$$

It is not possible simply to sum the log magnitude and phase angle of the system and the compensator with feedback compensation. Use can, however, be made of the low and high frequency approximations in relation to the inner loop transfer function. Thus, if $G_2(j\omega)\,H_c(j\omega) \ll 1$, i.e. high frequency, then

$$\frac{C(j\omega)}{M(j\omega)} \simeq G_2(j\omega)$$

and if $G_2(j\omega)H_c(j\omega) \gg 1$, i.e. low frequency, then,

$$\frac{C(j\omega)}{M(j\omega)} \simeq \frac{1}{H_c(j\omega)}$$

This leaves undetermined the condition $G_2(j\omega)H_c(j\omega)=1$, but enables some useful information to be found.

Derivative or velocity feedback is the use of a derivative compensating signal in a feedback path. A block diagram of such a system is given in Figure 5.43(a). The compensating signal is proportional to the derivative of the output, and the transfer function of the compensator, $H_c(j\omega)$, is,

$$\frac{B(j\omega)}{C(j\omega)} = H_c(j\omega) = j\omega K_d$$

where K_d is the derivative gain constant.

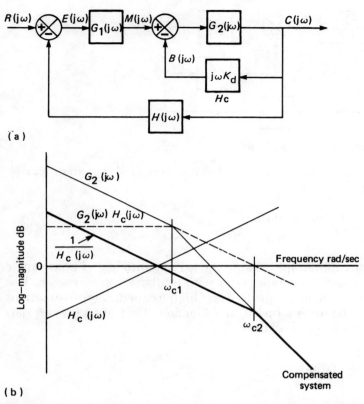

(a)

(b)

Figure 5.43 Derivative feedback compensated control system: (a) block diagram; (b) Bode diagram

The effect of derivative feedback on the frequency response of the system can be seen in the Bode diagram in Figure 5.43(b). The feedback response $H_c(j\omega)$ is added to the forward gain $G_2(j\omega)$ to give a combined gain $G_2(j\omega)H_c(j\omega)$ for the inner loop. The high and low frequency approximations enable plotting of the compensated response $C(j\omega)/M(j\omega)$. When the compensated and uncompensated system responses are compared it can be seen that the cut-off frequency has been extended from ω_{c1} to ω_{c2} and the low frequency gain has been reduced.

When considering position or velocity servomechanism control systems the velocity feedback is usually provided by a tachogenerator (see Chapter 6). The velocity feedback acts as a practical form of damping in that the damping ratio can be increased by increasing the derivative gain constant. The maximum overshoot and the steady-state error of the system can therefore be reduced and the undamped natural frequency ω_n is unaffected.

6 Process and kinetic control

Closed-loop control systems may be divided into kinetic and process control. A third category of electrical control, consisting of voltage and current regulators and feedback amplifiers, will not be considered separately as these units normally form part of kinetic and process control systems. A kinetic control system is used to control displacement, velocity or acceleration of a mechanical component. Kinetic control systems are often referred to as servomechanisms or simply servos. Process control is used to maintain at some desired value a variable such as temperature, pressure, flow or liquid level. Either control system may be continuous or discontinuous in its action.

PROCESS CONTROL

All control systems share certain features. They all function by moving information around the system. The information is used to produce a control action in which energy is transferred to or from the controlled object. Process control systems have the extra feature in that the controlled object is moved from one place to another. Usually the controlled object is a material undergoing a process of physical or chemical change. There are often a number of important variables in the process with feedback loops used to control them. In many cases it may not be possible to obtain a direct or immediate feedback of the controlled variable. The control system must then be modified accordingly. In every system the effect of the time taken for the material to move from one place to another must be taken into account.

As an example, consider a boiler. Water is converted into steam which leaves the boiler and passes to a turbine. After leaving the turbine the exhaust steam is condensed back into water and returned to the boiler to continue the cycle. The temperature of the steam cannot be measured at the place where the water receives the energy (the boiler tubes), but instead must be measured at the drum outlet or perhaps even at the turbine. The energy received by the water is determined by the flow of fuel into the burners. It is transferred by the hot gases from the point of entry of fuel to the point of transfer of energy into the water. The time taken for the gases to move from the burners to the tubes and the time taken for the steam to travel from the tubes to where the temperature is measured are both important characteristics of the system.

The function of process control is to maintain, at some desired value, variables such as temperature, pressure, flow and liquid level. This can be achieved either manually or automatically depending upon the arrangements made in the control system. It is usual to consider that all forms of control act in a loop. This loop is made up of several basic elements, a detector, a transmitter, a comparator, a controller and a correcting unit, all of which surround the process and provide a controlled condition. This arrangement results in an automatic closed loop if the elements are all connected together and the controlling action takes place without human involvement. A manual closed loop would exist if one element, e.g. the controller, was replaced by a human operator.

In a closed-loop control system it can be seen that the control action is dependent on the output. In achieving control of the system the actual items of equipment which make up the basic elements include a detecting or sensing element from which a signal is fed to a transmitter, see Figure 6.1. From the transmitter the signal is passed to the comparator. In the comparator, a desired or set value of the controlled condition is compared with the measured value signal. Any deviation or difference between the two values will result in an output

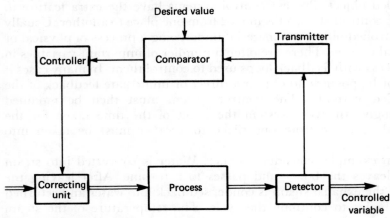

Figure 6.1 Elements in a control loop

signal to the controller. The controller will then act depending upon the output signal and send a signal to the correcting unit, which is often a valve. The correcting unit will then increase or decrease its effect on the process to achieve the desired value of the system variable. The term 'plant' is also used with reference to process control. This is the installation in which the process is carried out. It does not include the sensing and measuring devices, the controller or the actuator, but it does include the actual correcting element.

Control loop characteristics

Within a process control loop there are inevitably time lags or delays occuring during measurement and transmission of signals. There are two types of delay or lag which occur in a process: those associated with a transfer of energy, and those associated with a transfer of material. The physical size of the plant is often such that it takes a relatively long time for energy to be transferred or for materials to move from one point to another. Time delays may be expressed in minutes rather than seconds and also angular frequency may be expressed in radians per minute. These delays produce what is known as the transfer function of the unit or item, i.e. the relationship between the output and input signals. A knowledge of these various process and control system relationships is therefore necessary in order to achieve the desired degree of control.

Inherent regulation

The process itself will possess some inherent regulation. This is its ability to reach an equilibrium state after a disturbance, in the absence of any controlling signal. The more inherent regulation there is in the process the easier it is to control. In order to understand the process property of inherent regulation, consider an open tank of water fed by a constant supply Q_s. Water leaves the tank through a valve at a rate Q_0. The level or head of liquid will settle at some value h such that $Q_o = Q_s$. If the supply were increased to some new value Q_s' the level of water would rise. The amount of water leaving the tank would then increase, since outflow is proportional to the square root of the head of liquid until $Q_o' = Q_s'$. This system would possess inherent regulation since an equilibrium condition has been reached in the absence of any external control action.

Process reaction rate

This is the greatest possible rate of change of the controlled condition as a result of a particular step change at the correcting unit. The degree of control that is possible for a process can often be determined from the process reaction rate. This reaction rate is largely governed by the capacity and the resistance of the process.

Capacity is the ratio of quantity to potential of a process or system. When considered in electrical terms this would be capacitance in farads, where quantity is measured in coulombs and potential in volts. Thermal capacity in joules/°C would arise from heat quantity in joules and potential in degrees Centigrade. Capacity has the effect of delaying the reaching of the value of potential. For a single-capacity process the reciprocal of the process reaction rate is the capacity lag.

In the sense of process control, *resistance* is an opposition to flow, and is measured as the potential change necessary to produce a unit change in flow. In electrical terms this is voltage (volts) divided by current (amps), i.e. ohms. In heat terms this would be degrees Centigrade per watt.

Distance velocity lag

This is the pure time delay resulting from the elapsed time between a process disturbance and its detection, as a result of the finite distance the disturbance must travel. There is theoretically no alteration in the magnitude of the disturbance as it travels to the detecting unit. One way to arrive at the mathematical representation of a pure time delay is to consider its effect on a sinusoidal signal. It is the same as a pure phase lag whose value is proportional to frequency. When the sinusoidal signal is represented on a complex plane, the extra phase shift may be seen to be achieved by multiplying the signal vector by the vector $e^{-j\omega T}$. This confirms the Laplace transform result, e^{-sT}, which can be obtained from the definition of the transform, see Chapter 5.

Transfer lag

A transfer or exponential lag occurs when energy is transferred through a resistance to or from a process with capacity. For a temperature controlling system, the heat transfer resistance from the heater to the liquid and its thermal capacity would result in a transfer lag. A time constant is associated with a transfer lag and its determination can be seen by reference to Figure 6.2(a) and (b), for step and ramp inputs. If a sinusoidal input were used, the transfer lag would cause a phase shift and a reduction in amplitude (attenuation), see Figure 6.2(c). A quadratic lag is a more complex delay with a second-order, underdamped type of response. It is due to elements possessing more than one type of energy storage, e.g. mass and elasticity.

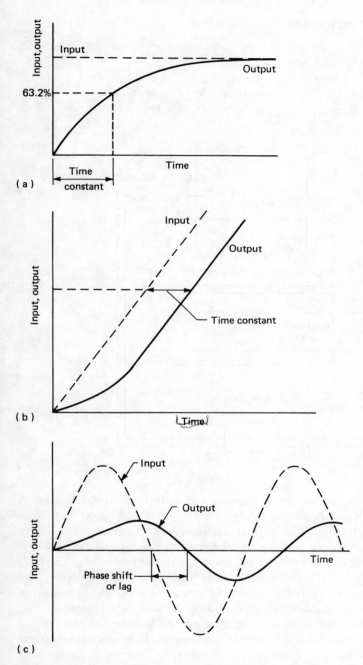

Figure 6.2 Transfer lag: (a) step input; (b) ramp input; (c) sinusoidal input

Control loop response

The response of a process or a particular element in a control system will depend upon the various lags that occur.

If a complete process, e.g. oil cooling, is considered, see Figure 6.3, a number of lags will be seen to affect the system response. A distance velocity lag will occur on the supply side as a result of the time taken

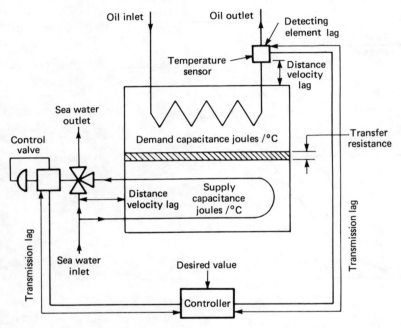

Figure 6.3 Control system lags

by the sea water in travelling from the valve to the heat exchanger. A similar lag will occur on the demand side as the cooled oil travels to the detecting element. The supply capacity will cause a time delay as the heat exchanger cools down or conversely heats up. There will also be a transfer lag as heat energy passes through the material of the heat exchanger tubes. A transmission time lag will occur between the detecting element and the controller unit. There will also be a detecting element lag for the temperature measuring element.

Good control system design requires a prior knowledge of as many of these lags as possible. Where they cannot be determined they must be minimized by reducing piping distances, process capacity and resistance values, etc.

Stability of process control systems

The pure time delay has a very significant effect on the stability of a system. Stability in this sense is considered as the ability of a system to settle down after a disturbance or change to a value at or near the desired value.

The use of a controller providing one or more continuous control actions is usual to bring about a suitable system response. This is discussed in detail in Chapter 5.

Types of control action

Control action results from a difference between any momentary value of the controlled condition and its desired value, i.e. a deviation. The correcting action is brought about by the controller and can occur in various forms. The manner of the controller action will determine how well the process is controlled, i.e. the output maintained as close to the desired value as possible. The controller input is the output from the measuring unit and there will be a range of measured values that the controller is designed to handle. The controller output is a function of plant deviation and it also has a design range. These various types of controller action will now be examined.

Two-step or on-off controller action

In this the simplest of control actions two extreme positions of the correcting element are possible, either on or off. Where the correcting element is, for example, a valve it could be open or closed. It is also possible for any two other predetermined valve positions to be used, e.g. 1/3 open and 2/3 open.

Consider, for example, the oil cooler shown in Figure 6.3. The correcting element action and the measured value response is shown in Figure 6.4(a). As the measured value (oil temperature) rises above its set point (desired oil temperature) the correcting element operates (the valve closes the bypass, forcing the sea water to flow through the cooler). The various lags in the process will result in a continuing temperature rise which will gradually be arrested by the controlling action. As the cooling takes effect, the temperature peaks and then falls until it passes below the desired value. At this point, the valve opens the bypass but, as before, there is a noticeable delay before the measured value is affected. The continual oscillation about the desired value that occurs in on-off control may be acceptable, particularly if the size of peak deviation can be kept reasonably small.

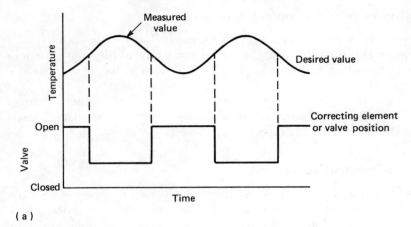

(a)

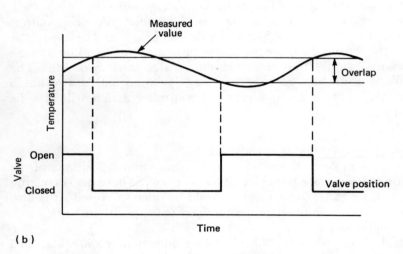

(b)

Figure 6.4 Two-step or on-off controller action: (a) without overlap; (b) with overlap

The correcting element will not often close at exactly the same deviation as it opens. The difference between the deviation required to open a valve and that to close it is called the differential gap or overlap, see Figure 6.4(b). The effect of overlap is to increase the amplitude of the variable variation but reduce the amount of operation of the regulating element.

Two-step action is mainly used for processes with a high demand-side capacity and a low supply-side capacity, i.e. a large hot water tank with a small heater.

Proportional controller action

This is a form of continuous control in which any change in controller output is proportional to the deviation between the controlled condition and the desired value, see Figure 6.5. The mathematical equation for proportional action (P) is

$$m = -K_1 e$$

where m is the change in the controller output signal, e is the deviation and K_1 is a constant known as the proportional action factor. The minus sign indicates that the control action is opposite in direction to the deviation.

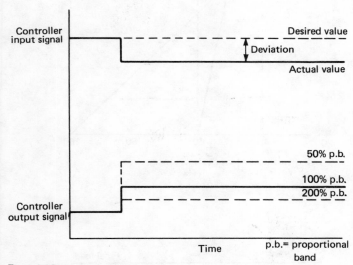

Figure 6.5 Proportional controller action

The *proportional band* is the amount by which the input signal value must change to move the control element between its extreme positions, e.g. fully closed to fully open for a valve, see Figure 6.6. The desired value is usually located at the centre of the proportional band. Where the proportional bandwidth is narrow, a large controlling movement is obtained for a small deviation. This results in very sensitive control, with possible instability and hunting.

Offset is a sustained deviation as a result of a load change in the process. It is an inherent characteristic of proportional control action. Consider, for example, a proportional controller acting on a feed water valve supplying a boiler drum. If the steam demand (i.e. load)

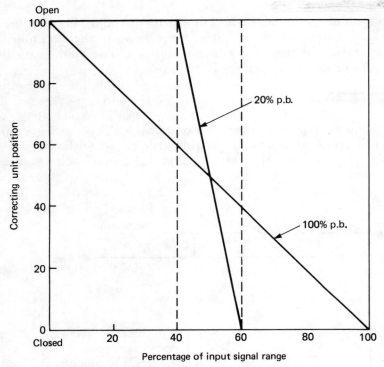

Figure 6.6 Proportional band

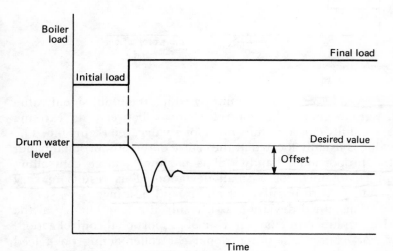

Figure 6.7 System response to proportional controller action

increased, then more feed water would be required to stop the drum emptying. Only when the level has dropped, i.e. a deviation has occurred, can the feed water valve open further. An equilibrium position will occur when the feedwater valve opens an amount to match the new steam demand. The drum water level will, however, have fallen to some value below the desired value. The difference between the two levels, desired and actual, is the offset, see Figure 6.7. The next load change will bring about a new offset and so on. The set value with a proportional controller needs to be different from the desired value because of offset. *Set value* is the value of the controlled condition to which the comparing element of a controller is adjusted after each load change in order to achieve the desired value. Except when referring to proportional controllers, set value and desired value are usually considered as the same. A narrow proportional band will result in a small value of offset.

The proportional band is defined in terms of the normal ranges of controller input and output. When a deviation equal to the full range of input produces a full range of output, the proportional band is 100 per cent. When the full range of output is produced by a deviation equal to only half the full range of input, the proportional band is 50 per cent.

Most controllers can be considered as amplifiers in that the ratio of change in output to corresponding change in input, i.e. the gain, is greater than 1. In process control, where the units of input and output are often different, it is useful to express both changes as percentages. If, for example, a level controller with a scale range of 0–5 m has a full output range, i.e. 100 per cent, for a level deviation of plus or minus 0.2 m about a desired value of 1.5 m, then

$$\text{Change of output} = 100\%$$
$$\text{Change of input} = \frac{2 \times 0.2 \times 100}{5} = 12.5\%$$
$$= \text{Proportional band}$$

Therefore,

$$\text{Gain} = \frac{100}{12.5} = 8$$

or

$$\text{Gain} = \frac{100}{\text{Proportional band (\%)}}$$

The term proportional control factor is sometimes used instead of gain.

Integral controller action

Integral or reset action occurs when the controller output varies at a rate proportional to the deviation between the desired value and the measured value. This type of controller action is used in conjunction with proportional control in order to remove offset. The mathematical equation for integral action is

$$\mathrm{d}m/\mathrm{d}t = -K_2 e$$

thus

$$m = -K_2 \int e \,\mathrm{d}t$$

where m is the change in controller output signal, e is the deviation and K_2 is a constant known as the integral action factor.

Integral action time relates to a controller having proportional and integral action (P+I) and is the time interval during which the integral action signal increases by an amount equal to the proportional action signal for a constant deviation. This is illustrated in Figure 6.8. When a sudden deviation occurs at time T_1, the

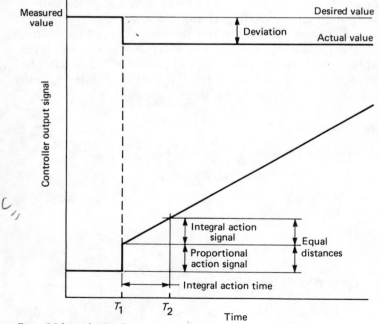

Figure 6.8 Integral action time

controller will produce a step output as a result of proportional action. If deviation is assumed constant, then integral action will produce an output signal which increases at a constant rate. At some time T_2, the output signal will have doubled in value.

The interval $T_2 - T_1$ is known as the integral action time and has the value K_1/K_2, since

Proportional output signal, $m_p = -K_1e$

Rate of change of integral output signal, $\dfrac{dm_1}{dt} = -K_2e$

Now $dm_1 = m_p$ in period $dt = T_2 - T_1$; i.e.

$$\frac{m_p}{T_2 - T_1} = -K_2e \quad \therefore \frac{m_p}{m_p/T_2 - T_1} = \frac{K_1e}{K_2e} = \frac{K_1}{K_2}$$

$$\therefore \frac{K_1}{K_2} = T_2 - T_1 = \text{Integral action time, } T_I$$

Integral action in a controller reduces the gain and introduces an extra time lag. Integral action time must be set correctly for the particular process; too long and the system will take a long time to stabilize; too short and overshoot and hunting will occur.

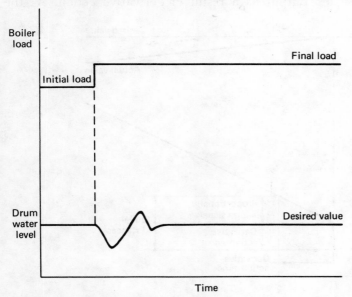

Figure 6.9 System response to proportional plus integral controller action

Consider now a proportional plus integral action controller acting on a feed water valve supplying a boiler drum. The controller action will now bring the water level back to its original desired value with no offset, see Figure 6.9.

Derivative controller action

Derivative or rate action is where the output signal change is proportional to the rate of change of deviation. This action is particularly useful where a process has long time delays between changes in the measured value and their correction.

The mathematical equation for derivative action is

$$m = -K_3 \, \mathrm{d}e/\mathrm{d}t$$

where m is the change in controller output signal, e is the deviation and K_3 is a constant known as the derivative action factor.

Derivative action time relates to a controller having proportional and derivative action and is the time interval during which the derivative action signal increases by an amount equal to the proportional action signal for a constantly changing deviation, i.e. a ramp input. This is illustrated in Figure 6.10. When a constant rate deviation occurs at time T_1, the controller is considered to produce an instantaneous step output as a result of derivative action. As the

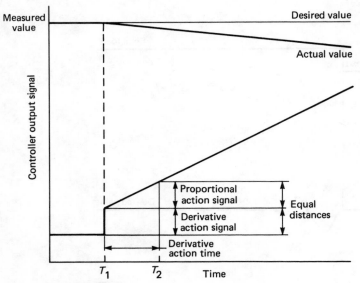

Figure 6.10 Derivative action time

deviation continues proportional action will produce an output signal which increases at a constant rate. At some time T_2 the output signal will have doubled in value. The interval $T_2 - T_1$ is known as the derivative action time and has the value K_3/K_1, since

Derivative output signal, $m_0 = -K_3 \, de/dt$
Proportional output signal, $m_p = -K_1 e$

Now $m_D = m_p$ and deviation $= e$ in period $dt = T_2 - T_1$

$$\therefore \frac{m_0}{m_p} = \frac{K_3}{K_1 e} \frac{e}{T_2 - T_1} \quad \therefore T_2 - T_1 = \frac{K_3}{K_1} = \text{Derivative action time, } T_d$$

Derivative action in a controller increases the gain in relation to how fast the deviation increases. Correct setting is again important for the particular process; the greater the derivative action time the greater the effect. Derivative action is usually combined with proportional (P+D) or proportional plus integral (P+I+D) in order to obtain a relatively fast response and zero steady-state deviation.

Multiple term controllers

Reference is often made to the number of terms of a controller. This means the various actions—proportional (P), integral (I) and derivative (D). A two-term controller can be P+I or P+D and a three-term controller P+I+D.

The output $c(t)$ from a P+I controller may be written in terms of the deviation $e(t)$ as

$$c(t) = -K_1(e + \frac{1}{T_I} \int e \, dt)$$

and the controller transfer function is

$$G_{P+I}(s) = -K_1 \left(1 + \frac{1}{T_I s}\right)$$

where T_I is the integral action time.

The output $c(t)$ from a P+D controller may be written in terms of the deviation $x(t)$ as

$$c(t) = -K_1 \left(e + T_d \frac{de}{dt}\right)$$

and the controller transfer function is

$$G_{P+D}(s) = -K_1(1 + sT_d)$$

where T_d is the derivative action time.

The output $c(t)$ from a P+I+D controller may be written in terms of the deviation $e(t)$ as

$$c(t) = -K_1(e + T_d\frac{de}{dt} + \frac{1}{T_I} \int edt)$$

and the controller transfer function is

$$G_{P+I+D}(s) = -K_1(1 + sT_d + \frac{1}{sT_I})$$

The various controller actions in response to a process change are shown in Figure 6.11. The improvement in response associated with the addition of integral and derivative action can clearly be seen.

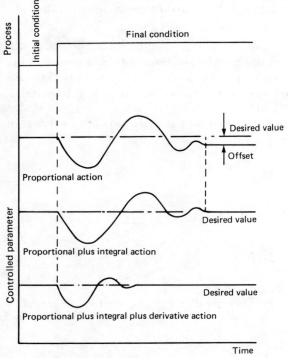

Figure 6.11 Controller action response

Multi-loop control systems

So far, process control has been considered using a single control loop. It is sometimes necessary to employ multi-loop control systems in order to achieve satisfactory control.

The two-tank system shown in Figure 6.12(a) may be considered, in the first place, as a process with level of tank 2 being the variable controlled by a single loop. Each tank will represent a capacity and

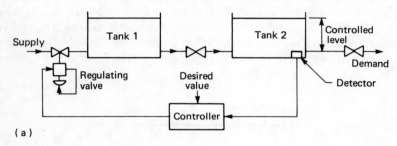

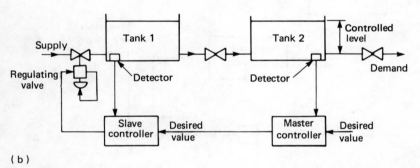

Figure 6.12 Single and multi-loop control: (a) single loop; (b) cascade control

the valve between is a resistance. The regulating valve will have difficulty in maintaining the level in tank 2 because there are two capacities and a resistance in the system which will introduce considerable time lags. A cascade control system for the same process is shown in Figure 6.12(b). There are two controllers in the system: a master and a slave. The slave controller measures and controls the level in tank 1. The desired value for this loop is provided by the master controller which is sensing the level in tank 2. The complete slave controller loop may be considered as the correcting unit for the master controller. With the cascade control arrangement a single capacity control loop around tank 1 can quickly detect and react to supply variations. This will minimize any effect on tank 2 and also reduce any time lags. The actions required by master controllers will usually be P+I and D if time lags are still present outside the slave controller loop. The slave controller will usually have only P or possibly P+I actions.

Ratio control is another form of cascade control where the relationship between a controlled variable and an uncontrolled variable is maintained at some desired ratio, see Figure 6.13. The master controller provides a desired value signal to the slave controller which is related to the measurement of flow A. The slave controller will control flow B in such a manner that it retains a desired ratio between flow A and flow B.

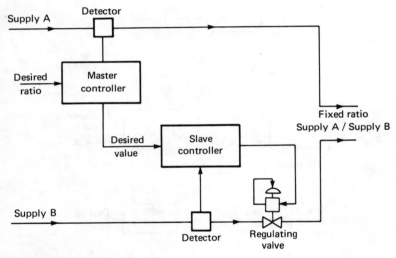

Figure 6.13 Ratio control

Split range control is another form of multi-loop control. With this arrangement the output signal from a single controller is split into two or more ranges to operate correspondingly more correcting units. The range of the output signal will determine which of the correcting units will be operated to bring about the desired action.

Feedforward control is used to anticipate and correct for large disturbances in a process. The disturbance input is measured as it enters the system and is used to supplement the output from a feedback controller, see Figure 6.14. Ideally the signal from the feedforward controller should cancel the effect of the disturbance. In

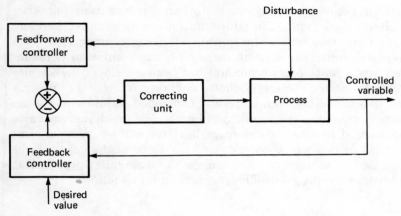

Figure 6.14 Feedforward control

practice, reasonable compensation is achieved and the feedback loop will remove any remaining effects.

Actual examples of each of these multi-loop systems are given in Chapter 9.

Controller adjustment

A controller must be correctly set in order to achieve a suitable system response. This response usually requires accuracy, stability and a suitable speed. These requirements are often in conflict with one another. Where the proportional band is too narrow or the integral action is excessive, the controlled variable will oscillate about the desired value. If the proportional band is too wide, stability is

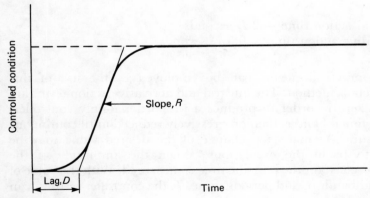

Figure 6.15 Process response

achieved but recovery time after a disturbance is increased and offset occurs after a load change. Suitable controller settings must therefore be made in order to achieve optimum system performance.

While trial and error may ultimately produce optimum perform-ance settings a more precise method has been developed by Ziegler and Nichols. The Ziegler–Nichols method utilizes the process response to a step change and a typical controlled condition variation with time is shown in Figure 6.15. The percentage change in valve position needed to produce the reaction curve will be considered as ΔV. The lag or delay is D seconds and the slope of the curve or the reaction rate is R in units of percentage of the scale range per second.

The settings for the controller are then found as follows:

For proportional-only action:

$$\text{proportional band} = \frac{R \times D}{\Delta V} \times 100\%$$

For proportional plus integral action:

$$\text{proportional band} = \frac{R \times D}{\Delta V} \times 110\%$$

$$\text{integral action time} = 3.33\ D \text{ seconds}$$

For proportional plus integral plus derivative action:

$$\text{proportional band} = \frac{R \times D}{\Delta V} \times 83\%$$

$$\text{integral action time} = 2\ D \text{ seconds}$$
$$\text{derivative action time} = 0.5\ D \text{ seconds.}$$

A more practical means can be employed in the use of this Ziegler–Nichols method. The integral and derivative action terms are reduced to zero in order to produce a proportional-only controller. The proportional band is then progressively reduced until continuous cycling occurs. A small step change of the desired value may be necessary to begin the oscillations. When the amplitude of the oscillation is constant the periodic time is measured. With the value of proportional band, B, and periodic time, T, the controller settings can be determined.

For proportional-only action
   proportional band = 2 $B\%$
For proportional plus integral action
   proportional band = 2.2 $B\%$

$$\text{integral action time} = \frac{T}{1.2} \text{ seconds}$$

For proportional plus integral plus derivative action
   proportional band = 1.67 $B\%$

$$\text{integral action time} = \frac{T}{2} \text{ seconds}$$

$$\text{derivative action time} = \frac{T}{8} \text{ seconds}$$

A small amount of trimming around these settings will result in optimum performance. It should be noted that this method is suitable only for a continuous process. It would not be acceptable, for example, where any auto-start with zero overshoot was required.

The setting and adjustment of a controller is a skilled operation requiring considerable time and a knowledge of the plant and its characteristics. It may be useful to consider, in a practical sense, the actions and interactions that result from the individual controller terms. Consider therefore a three-term proportional plus integral plus derivative controller. The integral action is first reduced to a minimum (in older controllers a resistance is set at maximum). Derivative action is then reduced to a minimum (in older controllers a resistance is set to minimum). Now, with proportional action only, a value of about 200 per cent proportional band would initially be chosen. A step input would then be introduced by momentarily altering the desired value setting. The settling time would then be measured. The proportional band value would then be reduced in steps until the system did not settle. A slight increase in the proportional band would then provide the correct setting for minimum offset and minimum stabilization time. If a proportional plus integral controller is now considered, the proportional band would be set at the value determined above and the integral action time would be set at maximum. The integral action time is then progressively reduced until oscillations begin. A slight increase in the integral action time will provide the correct setting for zero offset and stability. For proportional plus derivative control action the proportional band setting that produced oscillations is used. With this value fixed the derivative action time is increased from the minimum value up to a value which will remove the oscillations. The proportional band is now reduced slightly and the oscillations produced are again removed by adding derivative action. The proportional band value is slightly increased to provide the correct setting for minimum overshoot and the minimum stabilization time. A proportional plus integral plus derivative controller is set initially as for a proportional plus derivative controller. The value of derivative action time is also used as an initial setting for the integral action time. The integral action time is then varied until a minimum overshoot and minimum stabilization time is obtained.

KINETIC CONTROL

Where a system is used to control displacement, velocity or acceleration of a unit or load then this is kinetic control. A servomechanism is an automatic kinetic control system which usually includes an amplifier in the forward path such that a small input will control a large output. The basic elements in the system are an actuator, a transducer or monitor, and a controller. There may be a requirement for data processing of the input depending upon the nature of the system. A servomechanism is usually classified according to the operating medium of the servomotor, e.g. hydraulic or electric. A servomotor is a device providing translation or rotational motion and is simply a motor which is suitable for use in a servomechanism. While a number of different linear actuators exist, e.g. hydraulic rams, most servomotors are rotary devices.

Servomechanism analysis

The various mechanical, electrical or hydraulic components of servomechanisms can be described by mathematical models as

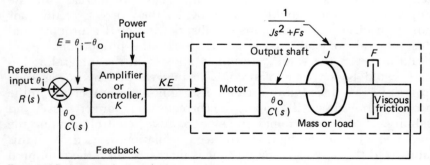

Figure 6.16 Position control servomechanism

outlined in Chapter 5. The servomechanism can then be considered as a control loop and analysed in terms of performance and stability.

A position control servomechanism will be considered and is shown in Figure 6.16. The reference input or desired position is θ_i, the output shaft position is θ_o and any difference between the two, θ_i-θ_o, will act as an error signal. The error signal is fed into an amplifier, which may also have an input of a power source. The motor develops a torque which is considered proportional to the input signal. The motor torque will position the mass or load at some angle θ_o and the viscous friction will oppose the movement. The system is considered ideal in that transfer delays and non-linearities are not considered. The motor torque, T_m, is considered proportional to the error signal, hence

$$T_m = K(\theta_i\text{-}\theta_o)$$

where K is the gain of the amplifier and motor. This is therefore a proportional control system.

The viscous friction of the load F is considered to act as a retarding torque T_f where

$$T_f = F\frac{\mathrm{d}\theta_0}{\mathrm{d}t}$$

The net or resultant torque T_r, acting on the load, is therefore

$$T_r = T_m - T_f$$
$$= K(\theta_i - \theta_0) - F\frac{\mathrm{d}\theta_0}{\mathrm{d}t}$$

The load J will be accelerated such that

$$T_r = J\frac{\mathrm{d}^2\theta_0}{\mathrm{d}t^2}$$

since Newton's Second law states that $T = J\alpha$ where α is acceleration

$$\therefore J\frac{\mathrm{d}^2\theta_0}{\mathrm{d}t^2} = K(\theta_i - \theta_0) - F\frac{\mathrm{d}\theta_0}{\mathrm{d}t}$$

$$\text{or } J\frac{\mathrm{d}^2\theta_0}{\mathrm{d}t^2} + F\frac{\mathrm{d}\theta_0}{\mathrm{d}t} + K\theta_0 = K\theta_i$$

Using Laplace transforms this would be

$$(Js^2 + Fs + K)C(s) = KR(s) \tag{1}$$

This is a second-order control system which has been analysed earlier in its standard form, i.e.

$$(s^2 + 2\zeta\omega_n s + \omega_n^2)C(s) = \omega_n^2 R(s)$$

By rearranging Equation (1) into the same form and comparing coefficients, it can be seen that

$$\omega_n = \surd(K/J); \; \zeta = F/2\surd(JK)$$

The significance of the various terms F, K and J on the values of natural frequency ω_n and damping ratio ζ can readily be seen. The second-order system response to step and ramp inputs has been described earlier.

The step input will result in an underdamped, critically damped or overdamped system response depending upon the value of the damping ratio ζ. The undamped natural frequency ω_n is the frequency of oscillation of the system response if there were no damping. The higher the value of ω_n the faster the system response. Since damping is always present in practical systems the damped natural frequency ω_d is of interest, where $\omega_d = \omega_n\surd(1 - \zeta^2)$. When ζ is equal to or greater than 1 the system is critically damped or overdamped and will not oscillate.

A ramp input is used to test the steady-state error of the response. The ramp input can be considered as $r(t) = \omega t$, where the gradient of the ramp or the velocity of the input is ω. The steady-state error e_{ss} is therefore

$$e_{ss} = F\omega/k \quad \text{or} \quad e_{ss} = 2\zeta\omega/\omega_n$$

and is sometimes called the velocity lag of the system.

In order to obtain a suitable system response with either form of input some compromise is necessary. For a reasonable transient response following a step input, ζ must not be too small and ω_n must be reasonably large. The steady-state error can be made small by using a large gain value K. This would, however, make ζ small and increase the maximum overshoot. The system response can be further improved by the use of other types of control action.

The use of proportional plus derivative control action can be

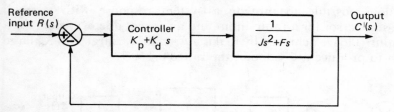

Figure 6.17 Error-rate damping

considered as a means of improving system response. The derivative term can also be said to provide 'rate of error' and this type of control action is often called error-rate damping. Consider the system shown in Figure 6.17. The transfer function of the controller is given in a slightly different form from that used in earlier work, but can be related as follows:

$$K_p + K_d s = K_p(1 + T_d s) = K_p(1 + \frac{K_d}{K_p} s)$$

where K_p and K_d are the proportional gain and derivative action factors respectively and T_d is the derivative action time.

The closed-loop transfer function of the system is therefore

$$\frac{C(s)}{R(s)} = \frac{K_p + K_d s}{J s^2 + (F + K_d)s + K_p}$$

or

$$\left[s^2 + \left(\frac{F + K_d}{J} \right) s + \frac{K_p}{J} \right] C(s) = (K_p + K_d s)R(s)$$

By comparing coefficients with the standard form equation it can be shown that

$$\zeta = \frac{F + K_d}{2\sqrt{(K_p J)}}$$

and the steady-state error for a ramp input, $r(t) = \omega t$, is

$$e_{ss} = \left(\frac{F + K_d}{K_p} \right) \omega$$

It is now possible to provide a system response with a small steady-state error for a ramp input and an acceptable overshoot for a step input. This is achieved by making F small, K_p large and K_d large enough to produce a ζ value in the range 0.4–0.7.

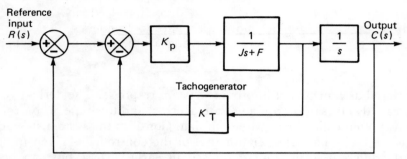

Figure 6.18 Velocity feedback

A tachogenerator may be used to provide velocity feedback in order to improve the system response. The arrangement is shown in Figure 6.18. The tachogenerator provides a feedback signal related to speed and has a gain, K_T. The closed-loop transfer function of the system is

$$\frac{C(s)}{R(s)} = \frac{K_p}{Js^2 + (F + K_pK_T)s + K_p}$$

or

$$\left[s^2 + \left(\frac{F + K_pK_T}{J} \right) s + \frac{K_p}{J} \right] C(s) = K_p R(s)$$

By comparing coefficients with the standard form equation it can be seen that

$$\zeta = \frac{F + K_pK_T}{2\sqrt{(K_pJ)}}$$

and the steady-state error for a ramp input, $r(t) = \omega t$, is

$$e_{ss} = \left(\frac{F + K_pK_T}{K_p} \right) \omega$$

A comparison between the expressions obtained for these terms and those using proportional plus derivative control will show that they are identical if $K_p K_T$ is made equal to K_d. The improvement in system response would therefore be obtained in a similar manner, i.e. choosing F small, K_p large and K_T large enough to produce a ζ value in the range 0.4–0.7.

For example, the block diagram of a position control system is shown in Figure 6.19. If there is no derivative feedback, find the damping ratio, ζ, and the undamped natural frequency, ω_n. What would be the steady-state error following a unit ramp input? What

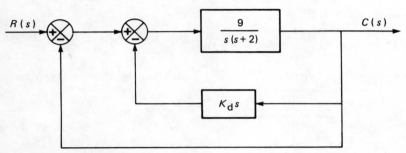

Figure 6.19 Position control system

will be the damping ratio of the system when the derivative feedback constant K_d is set at 0.25? What will the steady-state error now be following a unit ramp input? How can the steady-state error with derivative feedback be made the same as that without derivative feedback?

With no derivative feedback

$$\frac{C(s)}{R(s)} = \frac{9/s(s+2)}{1 + 9/s(s+2)} = \frac{9}{s^2 + 2s + 9}$$

Comparing coefficients with the standard form $s^2 + 2\zeta\omega_n s + \omega_n^2$,

$$\omega_n^2 = 9$$

∴ undamped natural frequency, $\omega_n = 3$ rad/s and $2\zeta\omega_n = 2$.

∴ damping coefficient, $\zeta = 1/3 = 0.33$.

The steady-state error e_{ss}, following a unit ramp input, is given by

$$e_{ss} = \frac{2\zeta\omega_n}{\omega_n^2} \times 1 = \frac{2}{9} = 0.22$$

Now, with derivative feedback

$$\frac{C(s)}{R(s)} = \frac{9}{s^2 + (9K_d + 2)s + 9}$$

Comparing coefficients with the standard form $s^2 + 2\zeta\omega_n s + \omega_n^2$

$$2\zeta\omega_n = 9K_d + 2$$

and since $K_d = 0.25$

Damping ratio, $\zeta = 4.25/6 = 0.71$

The steady-state error e_{ss}, following a unit ramp input is given by

$$e_{ss} = \frac{2\zeta\omega_n}{\omega_n^2} = \frac{4.25}{9} = 0.47$$

In order to reduce this steady-state error to 0.22, and retain the damping coefficient ζ at 0.71, the proportional gain of 9 must be increased to a higher value, K_p, and the derivative feedback K_d will be different. Thus

$$\frac{C(s)}{R(s)} = \frac{K_p}{s^2 + (K_p K_d + 2)s + K_p}$$

Comparing coefficients with the standard form $s^2 + 2\zeta\omega_n s + \omega_n^2$

$$2\zeta\sqrt{K_p} = 2 + K_p K_d$$
$$\therefore 2 \times 0.71 \times \sqrt{K_p} = 2 + K_p K_d$$

The steady-state error e_{ss}, following a unit ramp input, is given by

$$e_{ss} = \frac{2 + K_p K_d}{K_p}$$

and this is to be 0.22.

Solving the above two equations gives

Proportional gain constant, $K_p = 41.66$, and
Derivative gain constant, $K_d = 0.17$

Multiple inputs

A servomechanism may have more than one input since an applied load torque may also exist in addition to the reference input. In a position control system such as a steering gear this may be a heavy sea acting on the rudder. In a speed control system this would be a change in load on the engine.

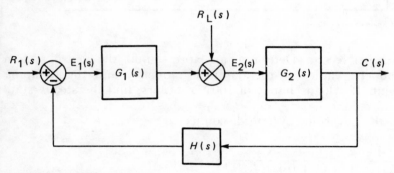

Figure 6.20 Multiple inputs

Consider the system shown in Figure 6.20. The load torque R_L may be a positive or negative value. Considering the complete system, then

$$C(s) = G_2(s)E_2(s) = G_2(s)[G_1(s)E_1(s) + R_L(s)]$$

and $E_1(s) = R_1(s) - H(s)C(s)$

$$\therefore C(s) = G_2(s)[G_1(s)(R_1(s) - H(s)C(s)) + R_L(s)]$$

$$\therefore C(s)(1 + G_1(s)G_2(s)H(s)) = G_1(s)G_2(s)R_1(s) + G_2(s)R_L(s)$$

$$\therefore C(s) = \frac{G_1(s)G_2(s)}{1 + G_1(s)G_2(s)H(s)} \cdot R_1(s) + \frac{G_2(s)}{1 + G_1(s)G_2(s)H(s)} \cdot R_L(s)$$

A similar result could have been obtained by considering $R_1=0$ and then $R_L=0$, in each case obtaining the transfer function. The principle of superposition enables the addition of the two to give an overall system transfer function.

For example, the block diagram, Figure 6.21, shows a speed control system for an engine with an inertia of $5\,kg\,m^2$ and viscous damping of $25\,Nm$ per radian per second. The engine response is described by the transfer function G_1 and the governor is adjusted so that every radian per second change in speed results in a regulating lever movement of $2°$. A trial run of the engine with the governor system disconnected showed that $1°$ of rotation of the regulating lever changed the speed by

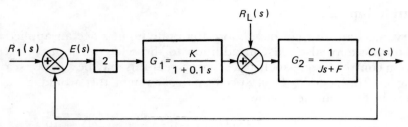

Figure 6.21 Speed control system

2 radians per second. Determine an expression for the control system and find the values of the damped frequency and the damping coefficient. If a load change of 100 Nm occurs, find the steady-state error.

With the governing system disconnected

$$\frac{C(s)}{R(s)} = \frac{2}{1} = \frac{K}{(1 + 0.1s)(Js + F)}$$

and in the steady-state condition $s \to 0$ as $t \to \infty$

$$\therefore \quad \frac{2}{1} = \frac{K}{F}$$

Considering the speed control system:

$$\frac{C(s)}{R(s)} = \frac{\dfrac{2K}{(1 + 0.1s)} \cdot \dfrac{1}{(Js + F)}}{1 + \dfrac{2K}{(1 + 0.1s)} \cdot \dfrac{1}{(Js + F)}} = \frac{2K}{0.1Js^2 + (J + 0.1F)s + (F + 2K)}$$

Substituting $J = 5$ kg m^2, $F = 25$ Nm per rad/s and $K/F = 2$

$$\frac{C(s)}{R(s)} = \frac{100}{0.5s^2 + 7.5s + 125} = \frac{200}{s^2 + 15s + 250}$$

Comparing coefficients with the standard form $s^2 + 2\zeta\omega_n s + \omega_n^2$ gives

$$\omega_n^2 = 250$$
$$\therefore \quad \omega_n = 15.8 \text{ rad/s}$$

and

$$2\zeta\omega_n = 15$$
$$\therefore \text{ Damping coefficient, } \zeta = 0.47$$

Now

$$\text{Damped frequency, } \omega_d = \omega_n\sqrt{(1 - \zeta^2)} = 15.8\sqrt{[1 - (0.47)^2]}$$
$$= 13.95 \text{ rad/s}$$

Considering the (step) change in load:

$$\frac{C(s)}{R_L(s)} = \frac{\dfrac{1}{Js + F}}{1 + \dfrac{1}{Js + F} \cdot \dfrac{2K}{1 + 0.1s}} = \frac{1 + 0.1s}{0.1Js^2 + (J + 0.1F)s + F + 2K}$$

Since $R_1(s) = 0$, $E(s) = -C(s)$ and $R_L(s) = \dfrac{100}{s}$

$$\therefore E(s) = \frac{-100}{s} \frac{1 + 0.1s}{0.1Js^2 + (J + 0.1F)s + F + 2K}$$

Steady-state error, $e_{ss} = sE(s)$ (as $s \to 0$)

$$= \frac{-100}{F + 2K} = \frac{-100}{125}$$
$$= -0.8 \text{ rad/s (a reduction)}$$

Position control

Where a system brings about control of position or displacement, in a linear or angular sense, this is position control.

An example of a somewhat old-fashioned d.c. position control servomechanism is provided by the Ward-Leonard electric steering gear system, see Figure 6.22(a). A continuously running motor generator set has a directly coupled exciter to provide the field current of the generator. The exciter field is part of a control circuit, although in some circuits control is directly to the field current of the generator with the exciter omitted. When the control system is balanced there is no exciter field, no exciter output and no generator output, although it is continuously running. The main motor which drives the rudder has no input and thus is stationary. When the wheel on the bridge is

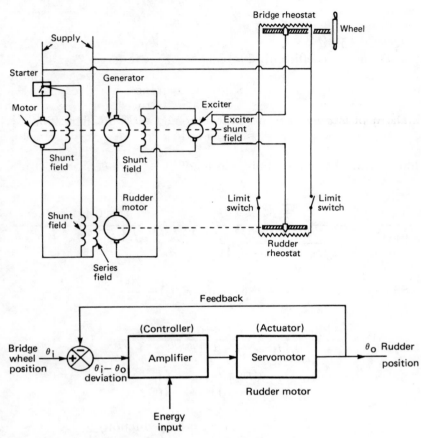

Figure 6.22 Ward Leonard electrical steering gear: (a) circuit diagram; (b) block diagram

turned, and the rheostat contact moved, the control system is unbalanced and a voltage occurs in the exciter field, the exciter, and the generator field. The generator then produces power which turns the rudder motor and hence the rudder. As the rudder moves it returns the rudder rheostat contact to the same position as the bridge rheostat, bring the system into balance and stopping all current flow. A block diagram representation of this system is given in Figure 6.22(b). The output torque of the servomotor is proportional to the deviation and this is therefore proportional control.

The d.c. stepper motor is being increasingly used with computer controlled servomechanisms. The computer provides digital signals, i.e. pulses, which the stepper motor converts into rotation of its shaft. For each pulse received by the motor its output shaft will rotate through a fixed angle. The pattern of pulses received can be used to control both the position and velocity of the output shaft and hence the load. With this type of motor there is no requirement for feedback and any error is related only to a single step and is not cumulative. The motor stator has a number of poles (often eight are used) and their polarity is changed by electronic switches. This results in a rotation of the average north-south polarity of the stator. The rotor is normally a permanent magnet whose north pole will align with the stator's south pole. Therefore, as the stator field moves through small steps, the rotor will also rotate in a stepwise manner. The motor is controlled by the drive circuitry, which creates a current flow in the stator windings. The motor torque, and to some extent acceleration, is proportional to the current flow. When a pulse is fed into the circuit a series of gates and flip-flops activate transistor switches in a sequence to cause appropriate movement of the motor.

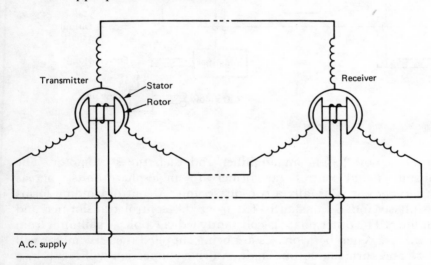

Figure 6.23 Synchros

Synchros, which are alternating current devices, can be used in position control systems. A typical arrangement is shown in Figure 6.23. This unit combines the working principles of the motor and the transformer. Stator windings and rotor windings are used as in a motor while these windings also act as a primary and secondary as in a transformer. In the transmitter a secondary voltage is induced in the stator which is dependent upon the rotor position. This voltage when applied to the receiver stator causes it to align with the transmitter. When both rotors are aligned the voltage induced in the receiver cancels out that of the transmitter. The synchro unit can, however, only provide a small torque at the receiver and is limited in its useful applications.

A synchro control transformer is often used instead of the receiver in servomechanisms. The arrangement is shown in Figure 6.24. The transmitter-control transformer operates in much the same way as the synchro described earlier except that the control transformer rotor

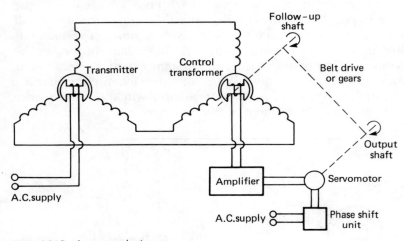

Figure 6.24 Synchro servomechanism

output is now fed to an amplifier and then the servomotor. The transmitter and control transformer are single-phase units whereas the servomotor is usually a two-phase unit. A control winding forms one phase and is constantly fed from the control transformer and amplifier. The other phase is constantly fed via a phase shift unit from the mains. When both phases are being supplied the servomotor will rotate and turn the output shaft. A drive connection will result in a similar rotation of the follow-up shaft. When the transmitter and control transformer rotors are aligned no output voltage will be supplied to the control winding of the servomotor and it will stop. The constantly fed motor winding creates heat which effectively limits the a.c. servomotor to 200 W (¼ hp) maximum size.

Alternating current signals are used for actuation and monitoring of a.c. servomechanisms. The basic signal is usually modified or modulated with respect to a function such as position, speed, etc. The original unmodified signal is called the carrier and has a constant frequency. The servo is required to respond to the modified signal but not the carrier itself. The modulated carrier is therefore the carrier

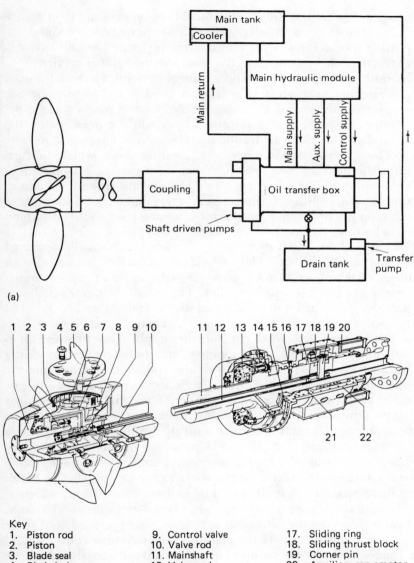

(a)

Key
1. Piston rod
2. Piston
3. Blade seal
4. Blade bolt
5. Blade
6. Crank pin
7. Servomotor cylinder
8. Crank ring

9. Control valve
10. Valve rod
11. Mainshaft
12. Valve rod
13. Main pump
14. Pinion
15. Internally toothed gear ring
16. Non-return valve

17. Sliding ring
18. Sliding thrust block
19. Corner pin
20. Auxiliary servomotor
21. Pressure seal
22. Casing

(b)

Figure 6.25 Controllable pitch propeller: (a) hydraulic circuit; (b) general arrangement

with the control information added on. Three types of modulation are possible, namely amplitude, phase and frequency modulation. Amplitude modulation is used in control systems. Demodulation is the extraction of the control signal from the modulated carrier.

Hydraulically operated position control systems are usually used for the steering gear on a ship. Linear motion is provided by the ram-type steering gear and rotary motion by the rotary vane type. The desired movement is determined by a wheel movement on the bridge and an electric or hydraulic signal transmission system may be used. The control signal moves the floating lever which in turn operates the floating ring or slipper pad of a variable displacement hydraulic pump. The pumping action then results in a movement of the rams or vane of the steering gear. A return linkage or hunting gear mounted on the tiller will reposition the floating lever so that pumping ceases when the required rudder angle is reached.

The controllable pitch propeller is another hydraulically operated position control system. The individual propeller blades are all simultaneously moved through an arc in order to vary the pitch angle, and hence the pitch, of the propeller. The hydraulic circuit is shown diagrammatically in Figure 6.25, and also a general arrangement of the propeller and shafting. When a pitch demand signal is received a spool valve is operated which controls the supply of low pressure oil to the auxiliary servomotor. The auxiliary servomotor moves the sliding thrust block assembly to position the valve rod which extends into the propeller hub. The valve rod admits high pressure oil into one side or the other of the main servomotor cylinder. The cylinder movement is transferred by a crank pin and ring to the propeller blades. The propeller blades all rotate together until the feedback signal balances the demand signal and the low pressure oil to the auxiliary servomotor is cut off. To enable emergency control of propeller pitch in the event of loss of power, the spool valves can be operated by hand. The oil pumps are shaft driven. The control mechanism, which is usually hydraulic, passes through the tailshaft and operation is from the bridge. Varying the pitch will vary the thrust provided, and since a zero pitch position exists the engine shaft may turn continuously. The blades may rotate to provide astern thrust and therefore the engine does not require to be reversed.

Speed control

The control of linear or angular speed (velocity) in a system is known as speed control. Diesel engines and steam turbines utilize governors for speed control, and a number of other functions. Governors will

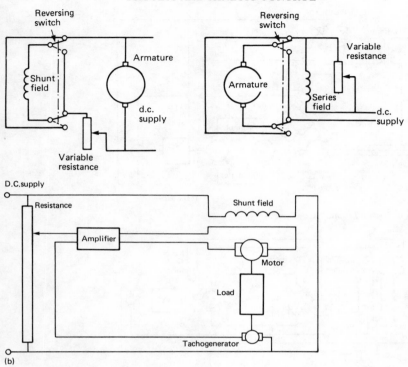

Figure 6.26 Speed control of d.c. motors: (a) manual; (b) automatic

therefore be dealt with in a separate section. The speed control of
electric motors will be considered in this section.

Speed control of d.c. motors can be obtained by varying the
armature or field current. An arrangement for speed control of shunt
and series motors using varying field current is shown in Figure
6.26(a). The speed of a motor may be affected by a variation in the
load. This can be corrected automatically by the use of feedback, see
Figure 6.26(b). The desired speed is represented by an input voltage.
A tachogenerator is driven by the motor output and produces a
voltage proportional to speed. The difference between the desired
speed voltage and the actual speed voltage is amplified to provide the
voltage supplied to the motor. Armature voltage control will give a
much wider range of speed control but on larger motors a
considerable power loss may occur in the armature resistance. The
Ward-Leonard system of speed control was developed to overcome
this problem, see Figure 6.27. The system is made up of a driving
motor which runs at almost constant speed and powers a d.c. motor
whose speed is to be controlled. When the generator field current is

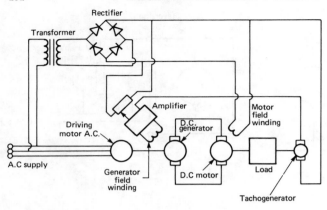

Figure 6.27 Ward Leonard speed control

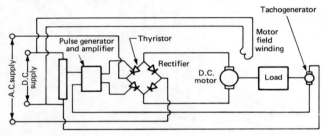

Figure 6.28 Thyristor speed control

varied the output will change. The controlled motor can thus have its speed smoothly varied from zero to full speed. A tachogenerator produces a voltage related to motor speed and acts as a feedback control in the event of load changes. Since control is achieved through the generator field current then the control equipment required is only for small current values. The motor has a constant excitation; its speed and direction are thus determined by the generator output. The driving motor for this system can be a d.c. motor or an a.c. motor since its function is only to drive the generator.

Thyristors (silicon controlled rectifiers) offer a speed control system for use with various sizes of motors, see Figure 6.28. Armature current control is provided by two thyristors. An a.c. supply is rectified by a bridge which uses two half-wave rectifiers and two thyristors. A tachogenerator provides an output voltage proportional to speed and this, together with a desired speed d.c. voltage, is fed into a pulse generator. This unit amplifies the error signal and produces pulses to trigger the thyristors. The armature voltage is thus adjusted to maintain the motor speed. Thyristors can be similarly employed to regulate the current flowing in the motor field and hence control speed. Thyristors, as with all semiconductor devices, must be protected from current and voltage surges (see Chapter 4).

Modern electronic techniques enable a.c. induction motors to be used in speed control systems. The ship's supply, which may not be as stable in voltage or frequency as that ashore, is first rectified to provide a d.c. supply. This is then used as the power supply of an oscillator using high power electronic devices. These may be thyristors (for powers up to 1.5 MW or more) or transistors (for powers up to a few tens of kW). The high power oscillator output is controlled in frequency and voltage by a feedback system. The motor speed is varied by changing the oscillator output frequency. The motor current necessary to obtain the desired torque (at small values of slip) is normally obtained by maintaining the voltage almost proportional to frequency.

Use is made of this static frequency converter in some shaft generator systems. Here a drive is taken from the main engine and used to power a generator. The various operating conditions of the ship will inevitably result in variations of the shaft speed. A generator whose output was provided directly would have unacceptable fluctuations in voltage and frequency. The generator output is therefore fed into the static frequency converter. It is rectified into a variable d.c. voltage and then inverted back into a three-phase a.c. voltage. A feedback system within the oscillator inverter results in a constant output voltage and frequency. Some shaft generators can be arranged to run as motors in order to provide an emergency drive. The auxiliary diesel generators are used to provide the electrical power. The static frequency converter is now operated in a reverse sense in that the auxiliary generator output is rectified and then fed to the power oscillator before passing to the shaft motor.

Governors

A governor is used to maintain engine speed within certain prescribed limits throughout the operating power range. In addition to speed control, modern governors also provide other control functions such as load control and fuel limitation, which will protect an engine from adverse operating conditions. Where a direct coupling exists between an engine and a propeller the unit is naturally regulated. This is because the torque law of the propeller intersects the torque curves of the engine in such a way that stability results. However, in the event that the engine becomes separated from the propeller, it is considered wise to have a separate overspeed shutdown device provided, in addition to the the governor.

An inertia governor or overspeed trip will stop an engine when its speed is about 15 per cent above the rated value. It consists of a bolt assembly located in some rotating component driven by the engine. A spring holds the bolt in place against the action of centrifugal force during the normal range of engine speed. If the engine overspeeds, the bolt head will project and trip a lever. This lever will shut off the fuel to the engine and must then be manually reset. This device will only protect against overspeed.

The desired engine speed is set by the engine control and the governor will then maintain this speed within specified limits by

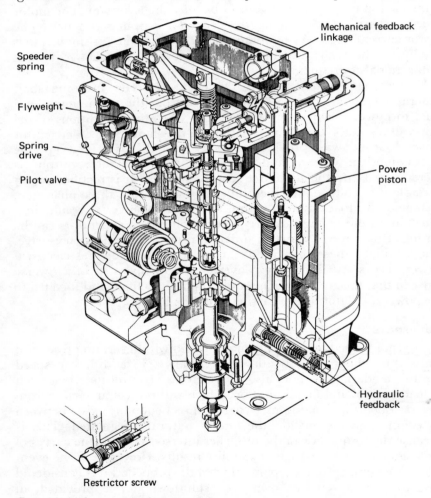

Figure 6.29 (a) Governor: general arrangement

varying the fuel supply to the engine. A governor is made up of a
speed error detector, a servomechanism and a compensation
mechanism. The speed measurement system uses rotating flyweights
which are driven by the engine and able to move outwards under the

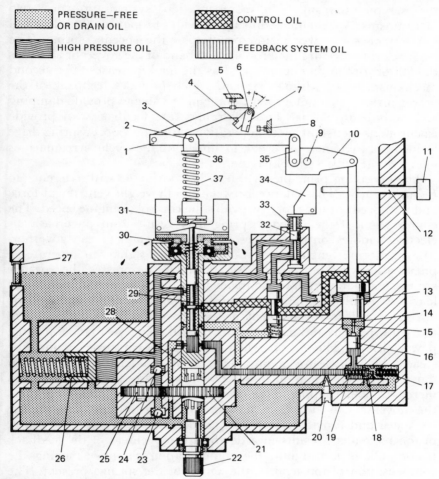

Figure 6.29 (b) Governor: operational schematic
1. Droop lever. 2. Droop lever pin. 3. Speed control lever. 4. Speed stop lever, minimum. 5. Speed stop minimum.
6. Speed control shaft. 7. Speed stop lever, maximum. 8. Speed stop, maximum. 9. Output shaft. 10. Output
lever. 11. Manual shutdown button. 12. Manual shutdown rod. 13. Power piston. 14. Wire strut. 15.
Shutdown, secondary. 16. Feedback piston. 17. Compensation spring. 18. Compensation piston. 19.
Compensation spring. 20. Restrictor screw. 21. Oil pump, driven. 22. Drive shaft. 23. Oil pump check valve,
inlet. 24. Oil pump check valve, outlet. 25. Oil pump idler. 26. Accumulator piston. 27. Oil level sight glass.
28. Rotor. 29. Pilot valve. 30. Rotor drive spring. 31. Flyweight. 32. Shutdown valve, primary. 33. Shutdown
valve, primary return spring. 34. Shutdown valve, primary, lever. 35. Droop link. 36. Speeder spring carrier,
upper. 37. Speeder spring.

action of centrifugal force; see Figure 6.29(a). A speeder spring provides an opposing force, which is related to the desired speed, to restrict the flyweight motion. Any speed error will result in flyweight movement and subsequent operation of the engine fuel controls via the servomechanism. The compensation system provides two mechanisms. A mechanical linkage provides proportional feedback of the servomotor power piston position to the speeder spring. The feedback ratio decides the proportional band of the governor and thus the fall or 'droop' in engine speed as the load increases. The second mechanism is a hydraulic system, which provides feedback of the power piston rate of movement to the pilot valve to provide damping and stabilizing effects. This hydraulic rate feedback can provide isochronous (constant speed) operation without droop. A spring drive is incorporated in a governor to filter out the cyclic irregularities which occur with a diesel engine.

The operating principles will now be considered with reference to Figure 6.29(b). The balance between the flyweight centrifugal force and the speeder spring force provides the control of engine speed. The compression of the speeder spring may result from pneumatic or electric remote control devices or manual action at the governor. Many marine engines use a pneumatic signal to operate a pneumatic/hydraulic position servo which compresses the speeder spring in a manner related to the engine control lever. An increase in load will result in a fall in engine speed and the flyweights will be forced inwards by the action of the speeder spring. The pilot valve will move downwards and high pressure oil will then flow to the top of the power piston. The piston will now move downwards against the steady high pressure maintained on its underside. The piston movement operates an output lever which rotates the output shaft to increase the fuel supply to the engine. An additional linkage transfers the movement to the top of the speeder spring to slightly reduce the set speed and provide a stabilizing droop characteristic. The power piston movement results in a downward movement of the feedback piston. Oil is forced into the compensation chamber moving the compensation piston against the action of the springs present. The pressure in the feedback system now forces the pilot valve up against the speeder spring which is currently out of balance. The pilot valve movement cuts off the oil supply to the power piston, which limits its movement. The feedback system pressure slowly leaks away through a restrictor screw, until it becomes atmospheric. The pilot valve is then in equilibrium with the engine running steadily at a new, slightly reduced speed as a result of the increased load.

Isochronous or constant speed governing is also possible, for use with electricity generating machines, to ensure constant frequency of the supply. An increase in load, for example, will cause the engine speed to fall and the flyweights will move inwards under the action of the speeder spring. The pilot valve moves downwards and high pressure oil then flows to the top of the power piston. The power piston moves down and turns the output shaft so that the fuel supply is increased. The feedback piston, which is connected to and located beneath the power piston, also moves down and displaces oil. The compensation piston is thus moved to the right and the pilot valve is forced upwards to shut off the oil supply to the power piston. The movement of the compensation piston results in oil draining past the restrictor screw until the feedback pressure falls to zero. The forces on the pilot valve will by then have reached equilibrium and the engine will be running at its set speed. A load decrease will result in a reversal of most of the above actions, again to result in the engine running at its set speed. This is, in effect, proportional plus integral (P+I) control action.

A number of auxiliary features may be provided in main propulsion engine governors to suit certain starting and operational conditions. A torque limit arrangement will limit fuel as a function of the governor speed setting. As the load increases with additional submergence of the propeller in rough weather, the governor will increase the fuel

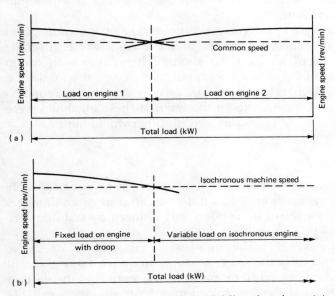

Figure 6.30 Parallel operation: (a) two engines with different droop characteristics; (b) an isochronous machine and a machine with droop

supply until the fuel limit is reached. At this limit the speed will drop until the engine and propeller torques are equal. A microswitch is usually provided which operates a contact when at the fuel limit and provides indication. The engine can then be seen to be running at the set speed or with limited fuel at a lower speed. A manifold fuel pressure limiter will limit fuel as a function of the turbocharger discharge air pressure. This will ensure that there is always sufficient air available to burn the fuel, particularly during starting and low speed operation. A solenoid shutdown may also be provided, which will shut the engine down when energized or de-energized.

The parallel operation of two or more diesel engines presents a particularly difficult speed control problem. The droop or change in engine speed as a result of a load change has already been mentioned. This droop is usually about 4 per cent for a full load change and can be varied within the governor. In order to ensure load sharing between diesel engines operated in parallel their droop characteristics must be appropriately matched. For equal load sharing their droop characteristics must be identical.

Consider two identical machines with different droop characteristics, see Figure 6.30(a). When operating in parallel, either as alternators or by feeding into a common gearbox, their common speed will result in an unequal sharing of the load. Only with identical droop characteristics can the common speed be achieved with equal loading on each machine.

If one machine were operated isochronously, i.e. at constant speed without droop, and one with droop, then the isochronous machine would have to accept all load variations. The engine with droop would have a fixed load at the isochronous speed and this could not vary, see Figure 6.30(b). If both machines were operated isochronously, then each would try to take all the load. If these machines were generators then one would generate and the other would motor.

Roll stabilization

The motions of the ship in a seaway can result in various undesirable effects, examples of which are human discomfort and cargo damage. Only the rolling of a ship can be effectively reduced by stabilization. Active or fin stabilization will now be considered.

The actions of waves on a ship in a seaway result in rolling. If the rolling couple applied by the sea can be opposed then the vessel will be stabilized. The rolling acceleration, velocity, angle and the natural list of the vessel must all be determined in order to provide a suitable control signal to activate the fins. The stabilizing power results from

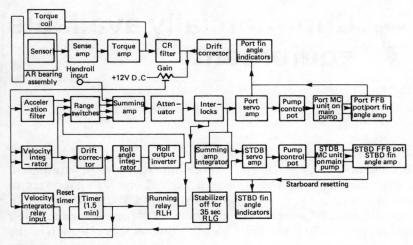

Figure 6.31 Stabilizer control system

the lift on aerofoil fins located on opposite sides of the ship. The angle of the fins is controlled in order to produce an upward force on one side of the vessel and a downward force on the other. The resulting couple will oppose the couple-inducing roll.

One type of control unit uses an angular accelerometer which continuously senses the rolling accelerations of the ship, see Figure 6.31. The sensor is supported on air bearings to eliminate friction and provide fine resolution of the signal. Air for the accelerometer is provided by a small oil-free compressor via filters and driers and the system is sealed in operation. The accelerometer output signal is proportional to the rolling acceleration of the ship. This signal is first electronically integrated to give a rolling velocity signal and then integrated again to give a roll angle signal. Each signal can be adjusted for sensitivity and then all three are summed. The summed signal is fed to a moving coil servo valve which is located in the hydraulic machinery which drives the fins. The stroke of the hydraulic pumps and the overall gain of the system can each be adjusted. A fin angle transmitter is provided for each fin to provide a feedback to the servo valve. This type of stabilization will provide roll reduction in excess of 90 per cent at resonance and where low residual roll occurs over a wide range of frequencies. However, at low speed the stabilizing power falls off and when the vessel is stopped no stabilization is possible.

7 Commercially available equipment

In this chapter it is proposed to examine examples of equipment commercially available and in actual use. Many manufacturers of control equipment exist, some specializing in a particular medium such as hydraulic oil, others offering a number of control media. Their interpretations of the basic principles are different. A selection of the variations available will therefore be considered. It is by no means comprehensive but it is hoped to be representative.

The exercise of control involves sensing, transmission, comparison, controller action and subsequent actuator and correcting element operation. Some units will undertake only one of these functions, in others several may be combined. The parameter being measured and the nature of the control required will, to a large extent, determine how this is achieved.

A number of on-off controllers are first considered. Individual items of equipment which transmit, compare and control are then described. Correcting units are considered in Chapter 8. The different control media used provide a convenient means of classification into pneumatic, electronic and hydraulic.

ON-OFF CONTROLLERS

Most on-off controllers will sense, compare and bring about a control action. The control action may be the opening or closing of a valve, the starting or stopping of an electric motor, or any two-position action which will regulate the controlled parameter. On-off control is the simplest of control actions and, where acceptable, should be used.

A pressure controlled electrical changeover switch is shown in Figure 7.1(a). The system pressure is controlled by some electrically operated device such as a motor. The system pressure acts on a bellows which is compressed externally by the main spring. The adjusting spindle enables the spring counter pressure to be set. A lever transfers the net force of the main spring and bellows to the main arm.

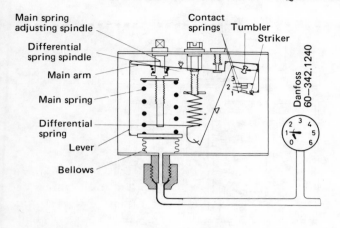

(a)

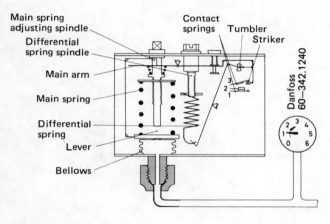

(b)

Figure 7.1 Pressure controlled on-off switch: (a) falling pressure; (b) rising pressure

The main arm is pivoted and at its opposite end acts on a tumbler and the electrical switch contacts. The tumbler is held in position by a compressive force transferred from the adjustable differential spring. The main arm can be in one of two positions. As shown, the upper two electrical contacts are closed and the main arm is in its lowest position.

As the system pressure falls, the bellows contracts and the force on the left-hand side of the main arm increases. The force applied to the tumbler moves upwards, reducing its moment arm about the tumbler pivot. The differential spring force and its moment about the tumbler pivot will become dominant. The tumbler will snap over to a new position, where the differential spring force now acts in line with the

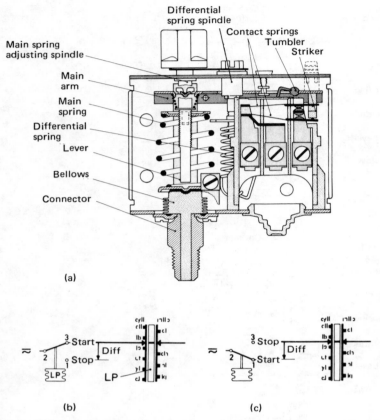

(a)

(b)   (c)

Figure 7.2 Pressure controlled on-off switch: (a) general arrangement; (b) low pressure control; (c) high pressure control

tumbler pivot and therefore exerts no moment. The component parts then adopt the positions shown in Figure 7.1(b), with the lower electrical contacts now closed. The system pressure must now rise to overcome the force of the main spring. When the pressure has risen sufficiently the tumbler will snap back to its previous position. The differential spring has no effect on this action, since its moment acts in line with the tumbler pivot point. The small striker is actuated by the tumbler to give a quick make or break of the spring-loaded electrical contacts.

The physical appearance of the above unit can be seen in Figure 7.2(a). If used for low pressure control in, for example, a refrigeration plant, the bellows would be connected to the suction side of the refrigerant compressor. The low pressure setting is determined by the adjusting spindle. When the pressure falls the circuit between contacts 2 and 3 is broken to stop the compressor, see Figure 7.2(b). The differential spindle sets the differential pressure at which the compressor will start up again (start pressure = stop pressure + differential).

A unit used for high pressure control would have a suitable bellows connected to the discharge side of the refrigerant compressor. The high pressure setting is determined by turning the adjusting spindle. When the pressure rises, the circuit between terminals 1 and 2 would be broken and the compressor would stop, see Figure 7.2(c). The differential spindle will determine the pressure at which the compressor would start up again (start pressure = stop pressure − differential).

A thermostat can use the same operating principle as the unit described above. A filled bulb and capillary tubing will supply the bellows. Any change in temperature will cause the bellows to expand or contract and the unit to operate as described earlier. The adjusting spindle will increase or decrease the cut-in and cut-out temperatures. The differential spindle will adjust the temperature difference between the cut-in and cut-out temperatures. Where, for example, the thermostat was controlling an air-conditioned cabin the cut-in temperature would result in a supply of cold air until the room cooled down to the cut-out temperature.

PNEUMATIC EQUIPMENT

Compressed air for many years provided all that the marine control situation required. It is clean, relatively safe, reliable, straightforward to understand and can be maintained by ship's personnel. It is now being superseded in many situations by solid state electronic devices in recently completed vessels. However, much of it remains 'afloat' and its understanding is a necessity for the serving marine engineer.

Transmitters

The most commonly transmitted parameters are temperature, pressure and differential pressure. Differential pressure provides a measurement which can be used as taken or for the measurement of liquid level or liquid flow.

The Babcock Controls Miniline transmitter can be used to transmit pressure or temperature measurements depending upon the sensing element employed. It will also provide a direct indication of the

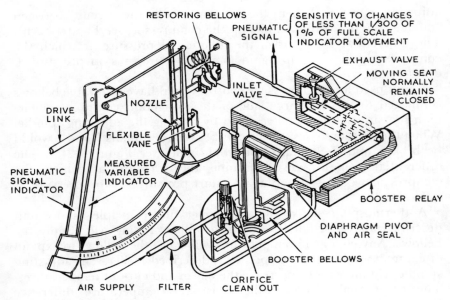

Figure 7.3 Miniline transmitter

measured parameter. The operation of the unit is described with reference to Figure 7.3. The measured variable brings about a movement of the drive link which in turn moves the vane with respect to the nozzle. An air pressure change occurs in the booster bellows. A proportional, amplified pneumatic signal is produced in the booster relay and passes to the restoring bellows and also provides the transmitted pneumatic signal. The restoring bellows moves the pneumatic signal indicator and holds the transmitter in balance when

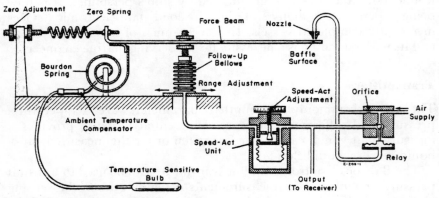

Figure 7.4 Sensaire temperature transmitter

the output signal is proportional to the measured variable. The measured variable signal is provided by a Bourdon tube, the free end of which moves the drive link. For pressure transmission, the Bourdon tube is operated directly by the medium. For temperature transmission, a closed, non-diffusing helium gas-filled system comprised of a temperature sensing bulb and capillary tubing is used.

The Taylor Sensaire temperature transmitter is shown in Figure 7.4. A mercury-filled bulb and capillary tubing forms the sensing element and operates a Bourdon spring. A change in temperature will move the force beam to change the nozzle-baffle gap. This will change the nozzle back pressure and also change the relay output pressure signal i.e. the transmitted signal. This pressure signal is also passed through a Speed-Act unit to a follow-up bellows. The follow-up bellows will reposition the force beam and equilibrium will be reached when the measured signal and bellows signal are proportional. The Speed-Act unit reduces the delay in system response to changes by introducing a delay in action of the follow-up bellows (derivative action).

A Taylor pressure transmitter is shown in Figure 7.5. An increase in the measured pressure, acting on the measuring element bellows, develops force against the base of the force beam. Since the flexure pivot is offset, an anticlockwise torque is produced which moves the force beam to the left. As the nozzle-baffle gap reduces the nozzle back

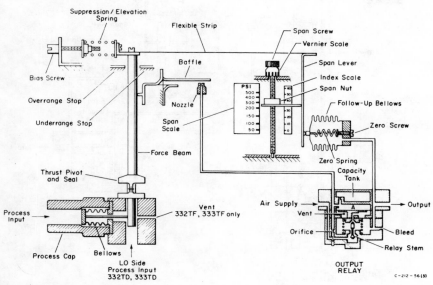

Figure 7.5 Pressure transmitter

pressure increases and is fed to relay chamber A. As the pressure in chamber A increases, the diaphragm assembly moves the relay stem downwards, closing the vent port and opening the air supply port to increase the output. The output increases until it balances the downward force in the diaphragm assembly. This output pressure is fed to the follow-up bellows which moves the span lever and, via a flexible strip, the force beam. The nozzle-baffle gap is restored and equilibrium is established between the measuring element and follow-up bellows forces. The suppression-elevation spring is used to bias the output to compensate for any initial pressure present.

The use of a differential pressure measuring element enables the above instrument to be used for just such measurements, see Figure 7.6. An increase in differential pressure will cause movement of the lower end of the force beam to the right and the region above the pivot

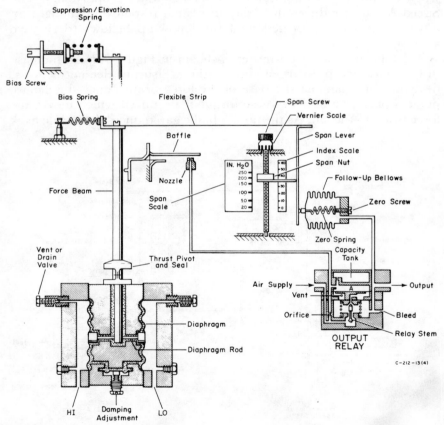

Figure 7.6 Differential pressure transmitter

will move to the left. Further operations will take place in a similar manner to those described above for the pressure transmitter.

A differential pressure measurement can be used directly to give a pressure difference or a measurement of liquid level. It can also be used to give a measurement of flow rate but here the relationship is non-linear and in fact involves a square root term. Some differential pressure measuring devices therefore extract a square root reading of the measured value in order to provide a linear signal related to fluid flow. In the Babcock Controls Miniline square root converter a horizontal beam receives the measured signal from a drive link, see Figure 7.7. The beam movement results in a change in the nozzle vane

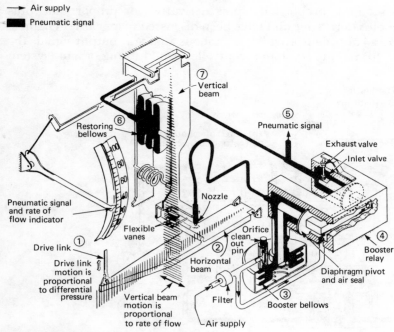

Figure 7.7 Miniline square root converter

relationship and a pressure change in the booster bellows. A proportional, amplified signal is produced in the booster relay and passes to the restoring bellows, and it also provides the transmitted pneumatic signal. The restoring bellows moves a vertical beam which restores the nozzle-vane relationship and equilibrium returns. Movement of the vertical beam also provides an indication of the transmitted signal. The converter is designed such that the vertical beam must move a distance proportional to the square root of the distance moved by the horizontal beam. Thus a pneumatic signal corresponding to rate of flow (the square root of differential pressure) is transmitted.

Controllers

The controller will receive either a transmitted or a direct signal related to the measured parameter. This signal must then be compared with the set or desired value and, if required, some controller output signal provided. The nature of the controller output signal can vary in its response to the input depending upon the various actions provided. These can be proportional only, proportional plus integral, proportional plus derivative, or proportional plus integral plus derivative and have been discussed in an earlier chapter.

Where a controller provides continuous analogue output signals the transfer from auto to hand controller could bring about system

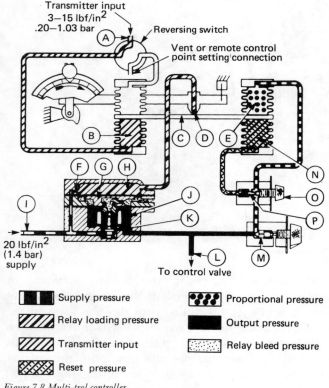

Figure 7.8 Multi-trol controller

disturbances. Some means of balancing prior to transfer may be necessary in older equipment to enable 'bumpless' transfer. More modern equipment may be provided with a comparator unit, or some means whereby the manual and automatic signals follow one another. If a change to manual is made, the output of the memory remains at the value of the controller output at the instant of switching. When the memory is in the 'hold' state its output may be varied by hand control signals. Switching back to auto is similarly 'bumpless'.

The Fisher Multi-trol receiver-controller is shown in Figure 7.8, and is two-term, providing proportional plus integral action. Control air is supplied at point 1 and after passing through the orifice at F will fill the chamber H and the piping to the nozzle. Depending upon the nozzle-plate relationship air will escape from the nozzle and a pressure less than the supply will be established. The transmitted pressure signal is input at A and will pass to bellows B. Output pressure from the controller is delivered to the control valve at L. If an increase in pressure signal from the transmitter occurs then bellows B will push up the plate C towards the nozzle D. This will cause a pressure build-up in chamber H and the relay diaphragm assembly G will be pushed down. The supply air will then be able to pass through the open relay supply valve at K into the chamber J. As the pressure in chamber J builds up, the diaphragm assembly will move up and close the relay supply valve. The increased pressure in chamber J will be passed to the control valve actuator. At the same time the pressure through the proportioning valve E is moved down by the increased pressure and moves the plate away from the nozzle thus stopping the pressure build-up to the control valve. The pressure in the line leading to bellows E will slowly leak through the reset valve P and will build up a pressure in bellows N. The upward movement of bellows N will change the nozzle-beam relationship to bring about another pressure build-up which will result again in an increased pressure to the control valve. This pressure build-up in the system will continue until the pressure from the transmitter is decreased and the system is brought back to its set point, i.e. equilibrium in the controller. It should be noted that all the actions previously described will act continuously and simultaneously. The set point or desired value can be adjusted at the controller unit or remotely by connections into the vent point.

Where a manual operating back-up is required the controller output pressure would be fed into a three-way valve. The output would then pass through to the regulating unit in the 'auto' mode. A separate pressure supply, which could be controlled by a hand-operated valve, would provide the other input to the three-way valve.

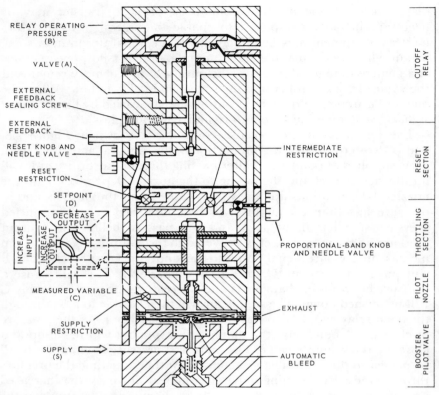

Figure 7.9 Nullmatic controller

The controller output and the manual pressure input would each have indicating pressure gauges that must be balanced prior to change-over from auto to manual or vice-versa.

The Moore Products series 502 Nullmatic controller is a two-term device with a built-in cut-off relay, see Figure 7.9. It operates on the null balance principle, in that equal and opposite forces result in a zero movement of the controller parts.

Consider first the action as a proportional-only controller, with the reset needle valve fully closed. The desired and measured values are supplied on opposite sides of the small centre diaphragm in the three-diaphragm stack. The outer two diaphragms are identical but have twice the area of the centre diaphragm. With desired and measured values equal the diaphragm stack is in the null position and balanced, since the output pressure, intermediate and integral chamber pressures are all equal. If the measured variable pressure increases by 1 unit then the output will increase by half a unit. This is because the net downward movement can only be half because of the difference in area of the centre and outer diaphragms. The widest proportional band of 200 per cent is thus established with the proportional band needle valve closed. If the proportional band needle valve had been wide open an instant output pressure increase would have occurred. This pressure increase now acting in the intermediate chamber would have moved the stack further down, creating even more output pressure. A small error signal will therefore produce a large change in output, i.e. minimum proportional band of about 2 per cent giving almost on-off action. Intermediate settings of the proportional band needle valve will provide different pressures in the intermediate chamber as a result of error signals. The intermediate restriction is fixed in size.

The rate of output pressure change is determined by the integral needle valve. Air will flow in or out of the integral reference chamber through this needle valve. An equal pressure must be present on the other side of the diaphragm in the integral chamber which receives supply air through the fixed integral and intermediate restrictions and exhausts to atmosphere. While an error signal exists the diaphragm stack will be moved away from the null position. The pressure in the intermediate, integral and integral reference chambers will be varying at a rate according to the integral needle valve setting. When the output signal acts on the regulating element and brings the measured and setpoint signals to equal values the diaphragm stack will be returned to the null balance position. There will then be no pressure differential across the integral needle valve or the restrictions.

The cut-off relay is used to shut off the controller output internally and also opens a bypass around the integral needle valve. This would be the situation when the controller was set to manual. In this way 'bumpless' transfer between automatic and manual and vice versa is possible since the blocked internal controller output signal is continuously matched to the manual loading pressure. The controller is shown set for internal feedback with the external feedback line plugged. The unit can be rearranged for external feedback where this is desired.

Indicators

The display or indication of measured and set values of the process variable will be required at some control station. The indicator may be integral with the controller and both may be present in the machinery control room. The controller may however be located near to the regulating unit and only indication or indication and remote adjustment may be present in the control room.

The Taylor 1410 Series indicating controller uses a full view scale and contains the indicating and control units in a single housing. It is intended to describe only the indicating mechanism. The measured variable indicating pointer and remote set pointer movements are provided by a servomechanism referred to as a 'vector servo' because of its principle of operation. Two forms are available, a single bellows unit for full range process or set pointer movement, and a dual bellows unit for deviation pointer movement.

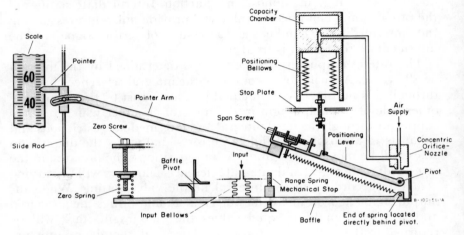

Figure 7.10 Vector servo indicator

The servo shown in Figure 7.10 operates on the force balance principle where the input signal pressure is detected by a nozzle-flapper arrangement. The flapper movement may cause pressure increase or reduction in the positioning bellows. An increasing input pressure will move the flapper away from the nozzle, reducing the pressure in the positioning bellows. The upward movement of the bellows will lift the pointer arm and produce a higher reading on the scale. The range spring will provide a feedback force to return the flapper to its original position and the unit to equilibrium. Since the range spring provides an effective feedback force which is a vector of the range spring force, the unit is known as a 'vector servo'. The deviation servo would have two bellows, one on either side of the baffle pivot, and thus the effective input force is due to the difference between the set and measured values.

The set pointer movement has a separate vector servo. The set point is adjusted by a thumb-wheel on the front of the instrument through a positive drive belt. Increasing the set point extends the range spring of this servo and decreases the nozzle-flapper gap. What was previously an input bellows is, for this unit, an output pressure signal which passes to the controller module. The increased pressure in the positioning bellows will act as a feedback to reposition the nozzle-flapper and bring about equilibrium of the unit.

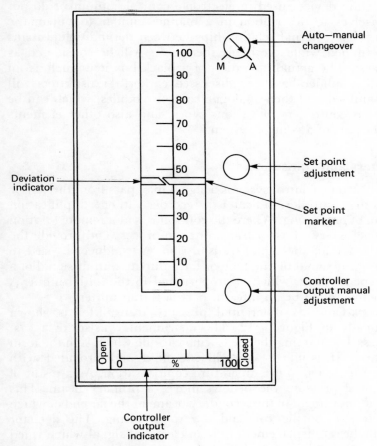

Figure 7.11 Pneumatic controller faceplate

The faceplate of a fairly typical indicating pneumatic controller is shown in Figure 7.11. A set point adjustment knob enables any particular value to be set and displayed. The deviation indicator will move according to any existing deviation and should ultimately align itself with the set value marker. In the auto mode the output indicator will show the percentage opening of the correcting unit. If the auto-manual knob is moved to manual then the controller output knob can be used to vary the position of the correcting unit.

ELECTRONIC EQUIPMENT

The solid state devices used in electronic control equipment do not lend themselves to description in a manner similar to pneumatic equipment. The external relationships between the individual items will be examined while the items themselves will be considered as 'black boxes'. The actual operation of a black box item such as an operational amplifier has been discussed earlier. Transmitters will first be examined and then analogue control modules, which can be built up into controllers of various types, and also other elements which form part of a control system.

Transmitters and transducers

In many electronic control systems a signal may pass from the sensor straight to the controller, indicator or recorder without amplification or any form of processing. Where the controller is at a remote location it may be necessary to use a transmitter to process and provide the power necessary for the signal transmission. A tranducer is used to change an input signal of one type or form into an output signal of a different type or form, which is proportional to the initial input. A transducer may often be an integral part of a transmitter.

A Babcock-Controls differential pressure transmitter is shown diagramatically in Figure 7.12. The instrument consists of a cast pressure vessel containing the measuring capsule which is in the form of a bellows. It is filled with silicone fluid and provided with over-range protection and temperature compensation. As a result of the differential pressure the bellows moves a primary beam. This brings about movement of the secondary beam, at the far end of which is a detector, a moving coil and a zeroing spring. The detector converts the beam displacement into an electrical signal which is fed to an oscillator/amplifier and then to the moving coil where it creates a feedback force. The feedback force opposes the movement of the beam so as virtually to restore the beam to its previous position. There will be a very small displacement (to provide the amplifier input required) but the overall mechanism is that the force produced by the coil balances that produced by the bellows. Hence the coil current is a measure of the bellows force. The small current from the coil is converted to a d.c. output signal of 0–10, 0–20 or 4–20 mA for

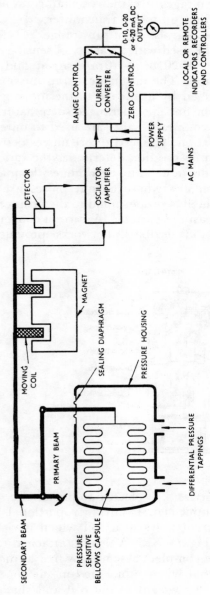

Figure 7.12 Differential pressure transmitter

transmission by the current converter. The power supply provides the necessary low voltages to the oscillator/amplifier and current converter and is built in to the transmitter.

The Babcock-Controls Minitran range of electronic inductive transmitters can be used with a variety of sensing elements. The unit provides either a 4–20 or 0–10 mA signal and uses the variable inductance principle. The mechanical transmission from the sensing element is connected by a linkage to the moving ferrite core of the electronic unit. The linkage is arranged such that friction is reduced to a minimum and counter-weights are used to minimize the effects of attitude and vibration. The ferrite core moves between two coils on a hinge system and its position determines the ratio of inductances of the coils. This inductance ratio determines the mark-space ratio of a square wave oscillator whose output pulses are integrated into a voltage output which is proportional to the position of the ferrite core and hence the measured variable. A current converter provides linear output current and feedback networks provide range and zero adjustments.

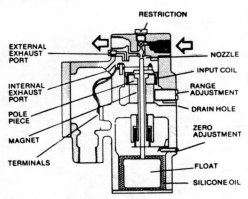

Figure 7.13 Electric-to-pneumatic transducer

The Moore Series 77 electric-to-pneumatic (E/P) transducer converts a d.c. input signal into a proportional pneumatic output signal. Input current flows to a coil which is rigidly fastened to a centre shaft, see Figure 7.13. A float is attached to the lower end of this shaft and the complete assembly is free to move vertically. The float is sized so that when submerged in silicone fluid the resultant buoyancy equals the weight of the coil and shaft. The assembly is therefore in a state of neutral buoyancy, and the silicone fluid also provides viscous damping to make it relatively insensitive to shock and vibration. A permanent magnet produces a magnetic field which surrounds the coil. The input current to the coil moves the coil assembly closer to the nozzle. The top end of the centre shaft moves to restrict the flow of air from the nozzle. Air is supplied to the nozzle via a restriction and an output pressure will build up depending upon the restrictive effect of the centre shaft. A balance will be created between centre shaft position and output pressure and then output pressure will be directly proportional to the input current. Zero adjustment is made by varying the spring force on the moving coil assembly. Range adjustment is made by changing the gap between the permanent magnet and the end of the range screw adjustment. This screw shunts off a portion of the magnetic field and hence its effect on the coil. A voltage to current converter can be used where a voltage input is to be used with this device.

The Moore Model 781 pneumatic-to-electric (P/E) transducer converts a standard range of pneumatic signals into any one of a number of standard d.c. electrical signals. The pneumatic input actuates a capsule that is connected to the lower plate of an air-spaced variable capacitor, see Figure 7.14. The gain of amplifier A_s is

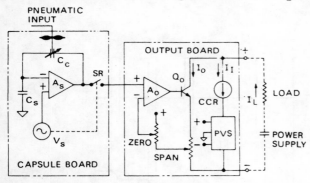

Figure 7.14 Pneumatic-to-electric transducer

controlled by C_c. The a.c. reference voltage V_s is amplified by A_s and then converted into a d.c. signal by the synchrono rectifier SR. The current output board contains a constant current regulator, CCR, that controls the idle current I_i, driving a precision voltage source, PVS. The PVS provides operating and reference voltage for the entire transducer (see Zener diode, Chapter 4). The idle current is maintained at a constant value of approximately 3.8 mA, independent of supply and load changes. The load current I_L, which is composed of I_o and I_i, is controlled by amplifier A_o and drive transistor Q_o. When calibrated, the span and zero adjustments provide a d.c. signal at the negative input of A_o which equals the d.c. signal received from the capsule assembly.

Pulse controller

Reference has already been made to 'bumpless' transfer between auto and manual modes of control. One way of achieving this with electronic equipment is by the use of a pulse controller. This unit provides an output that is not position conscious and consists only of raise, lower or zero signals.

The pulse controller only provides an output signal when a movement of the actuator is required. These signals are in the form of constant amplitude but varying duration. Consider a step change in the set value signal of a process with reference to Figure 7.15. The

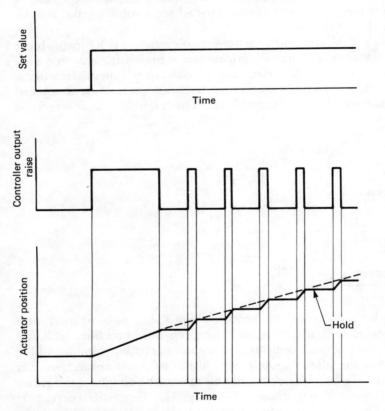

Figure 7.15 Pulse controller operation

deviation or error signal passing to the pulse controller will result in a raise or lower series of output pulses. A long duration pulse will occur first, followed by a series of small duration pulses. The actuator will move at a constant velocity while the pulse exists. The actuator therefore responds with a large movement and then a series of small steps which closely follow an ideal controller response, as shown. When a zero signal exists the actuator will hold its last position. Transfer to manual control is therefore instant and bumpless. Pulse controllers also provide a fail-safe condition of 'as-is'.

Bumpless transfer is of particular importance where sequence control or computer supervised control is operating. The constant switching off-line and on-line of various loops will require this facility.

Analogue control modules

The Babcock-Bristol Series 4 Electronic Analogue Control System provides a variety of modular elements which can be built up to meet almost any control requirement. In general each module has a single function although in some cases, such as the 'multiplier/divider/square root extractor' module, the external wiring may decide the function. All module input/output signals are based on a zero to $+5\,V$ d.c. signal range, which is measured with respect to a common connection.

A system block diagram and the actual modules employed are usually in close correspondence. The signal flow is further mirrored in the module interconnections. At the design stage this enables a straightforward hardware build-up of a proposed system.

While all internal computation uses the zero to $5\,V$ d.c. signals, the actual input and output signals can vary. Range card modules enable the system to accept input signals of 4–20, 0–20, and 0–10 mA, or a 0–5 V signal. Outputs can be 4–20 mA or 0–5 V continuous signals, in electrical pulse form or as a mechanical output, e.g. stepper motor shaft position. Some of the various modules will now be described. It is not proposed to consider these devices in other than a black box sense, in that their internal workings will not be described.

The Analogue Controller Module provides proportional plus integral $(P+I)$ control action by the use of a 0–5 V output signal and is primarily intended for use where control terms are set from external signals.

The local proportional, integral and set value controls are situated on the front plate together with test points for set value and output, see Figure 7.16(a). The use of suitable internal wiring connections enables the control terms and set value to be adjusted externally as a possible option, if required. Derivative action on the measured value signal can be obtained by using an additional module. The output voltage is limited to the range 0–5 V. The upper and lower limits may be set to any values in this range by applying voltages from an

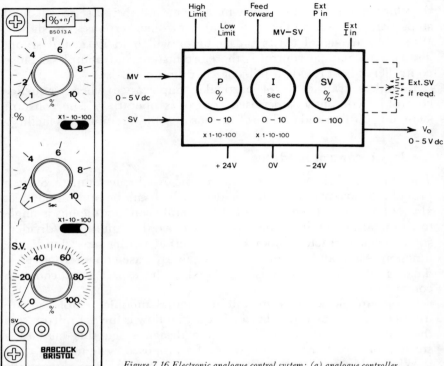

Figure 7.16 Electronic analogue control system: (a) analogue controller

external source. A feedforward terminal enables a 0–5 V feedforward signal to be added to the output of the controller. To enable auto-to-manual transfer without the need for prior balancing, a digital memory module is used. The memory output follows the controller output when on auto. When a change to manual is made, the output of the memory remains at the value of the controller output at the instant of switching.

The Pulse Controller Module, see Figure 7.16(b), is a two-term proportional plus integral controller which provides an output signal suitable for the operation of stepping motors, which are used as input transducers to pulse-pneumatic convertors and electro-hydraulic actuators. Two inputs of 0–5 V can be accepted, one for set value and one for the measured value signal. The various proportional band, integral action time and set value local controls are situated on the front plate. When used with a stepping motor, the motor acts as an integrator which eliminates integral saturation and provides drift-free manual control independent of the controller circuit. Derivative

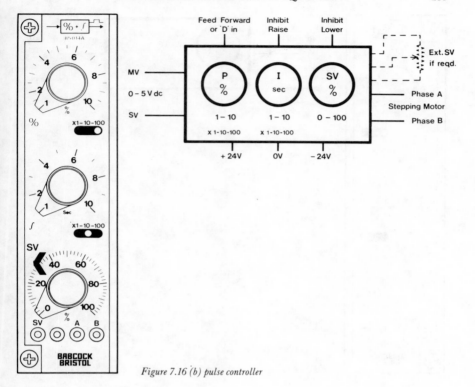

Figure 7.16 (b) pulse controller

action on either the deviation or the measured value signal can be obtained by using an additional module, see Figure 7.16(c).

Other modules provided as standard units include amplifiers, multipliers, dividers, square root extractors, limiters, high/low signal selectors, etc. A voltage source module is used to provide a 0–5 V signal which can be preset to provide a set value or biased control signal. Adjustment or setting may be locally at the module or by an external potentiometer, if required. A stabilized power supply module is also available to provide 5 A at +24 V and −24 V to meet the requirements of all the system modules. It also acts as a convenient power source for electronic transmitters. This unit is designed to protect against mains voltage spikes, short-circuited outputs, wide supply voltage variations and other hazards. 'SUPPLY ON' and 'OUTPUT AVAILABLE' indicator lamps are provided together with output voltage test points. Relay contacts provide remote alarms on mains supply failure or fuse failure, and warn when one or both outputs have fallen below their preset voltages. It is usual to provide

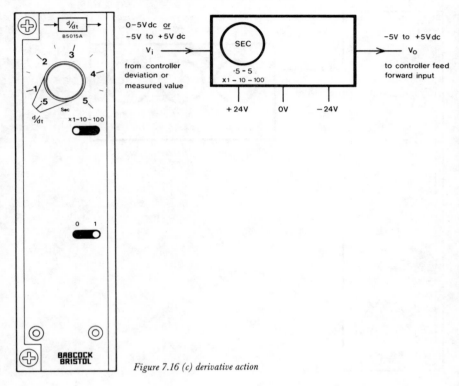

Figure 7.16 (c) derivative action

an independent standby supply for control systems, which could be an identical unit fed from a separate mains supply. If necessary, storage batteries with regulators and charger units can be used to provide standby d.c. supplies. Diodes are built into the output circuit to enable automatic no-break changeover between main and standby supplies.

An integrated monitoring and test facility is provided as part of this system to enable complete electronic checks of modules. No additional measuring instruments are necessary. Each module is fitted with colour coded test points which provide access to the 0–5 V computation signals and the pulsed stepping motor drive signals. Measurements are made using wander plugs which are on extending coiled leads. Read-out is given on a digital voltmeter or a stepping motor meter. The test panel and wandering leads are permanently installed in the upper bay of the system cubicle.

With a suitable grouping of modules it is possible to obtain a variety of control system configurations from on/off control through single modulating loops and cascade systems to complex feedforward, feedback and adaptive systems. The transmission of measurement and control signals to alarm, data-logging and computer systems is simplified and also the integration of command signals from such equipment into the modulating loops is facilitated. The range of modules will meet most practical requirements for process control. While all input signals are from the same general range, i.e. 4–20 mA usually, these are converted into a 0–5 V value by suitable range cards. All signal manipulation is therefore at the same level and interfacing is straightforward. The use of a common reference line means that a one-signal wire connection between modules is used, which enables simple interpretation of control diagrams from the flow format to actual wiring or installation diagrams. A system of graphical signals and part numbers on each module ensures easy identification for positioning of modules and ordering of spares.

The Moore Products Synchro 350 range offers a variety of different analogue controllers with various functions. The function modules Series 380 provides a complete line of standard plug-in modules to provide all the signal conditioning, computation and alarm functions that are necessary in a modern electronic control system.

The Synchro 350 controller has a modular construction using all plug-in components. Every controller uses the same chassis and base board into which standard modules can be plugged. A program board determines the function of a base board. Thus to assemble any required type of controller the correct program board must be attached and the appropriate modules plugged in. Flexibility in converting controller actions is possible and options such as feedforward compensation, alarms, input or output isolation can be added or deleted. The controller module can be removed, on line, with the controller set to 'manual' or the manual control unit can be removed with the controller set to 'automatic'.

A single-loop controller with set point tracking is shown diagramatically in Figure 7.17. Standard modules are shown shaded (1,2,7,8) while spaces are available for other optional modules (3,5,6). The power supply module will accept 120, 220 or 240 V a.c. inputs, which it converts to +26 V, +8 V and −6 V d.c. for use within the controller as well as external to it. The process variable input and the common terminals receive a supply from a process transmitter which may be a 4–20, 1–5 or 10–50 mA d.c. signal. The actual input to the controller and indicator becomes a 0–5 V d.c. signal. The process input signal and the setpoint are displayed on the duplex bar-graph indicator. The interface and tracking module generates the setpoint for the controller. When the control station is in manual it tracks the

284

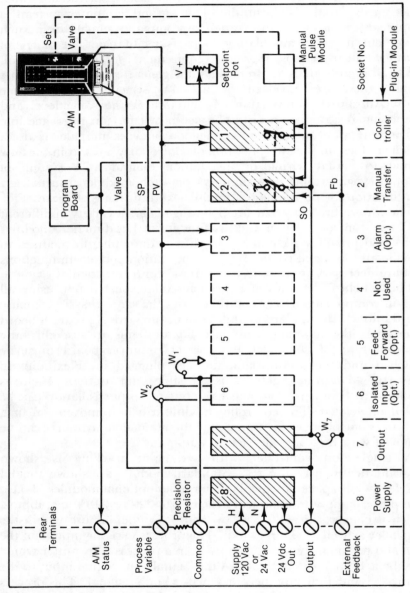

Figure 7.17 Single-loop controller

process variable signal. When switched to auto it stops tracking and holds, as a setpoint reference, a signal corresponding to the last value assumed by the process variable. Any further setpoint changes are made by turning the setpoint knob which will generate up or down pulses to change the stored count and thus the setpoint from the interface and tracking module.

The analogue controller module compares the process input to the setpoint and acts to maintain the process at setpoint. The controller module can provide proportional integral and derivative actions. The output signal is 1–5 V d.c. which is connected to the output module and the manual transfer module. The output module provides load buffering for the controller module. The manual transfer module enables bumpless switching from auto to manual by continuously tracking the controller output when on auto. When on manual the output is changed by turning the knob marked 'value' on the indicator panel. This generates up or down pulses to change the output.

The optional modules for input and output isolation may be used where earth loops are a problem. The alarm module may be used to provide an absolute value (high-low) alarm action or deviation alarm action. The feedforward modules provide feedforward compensation where this is required.

The setpoint tracking feature is required in standby synchronizing applications where a control loop can be operated from various locations by control stations connected in parallel. Any station can be made the active one, which places the other in the standby synchronizing state. In this state, although off-line, it is fully synchronized to the movements of the active controller. The two stations might be a local control position and a central control room. The inactive station controller will have the setpoint, value loading and controller reset all tracking the respective signals from the active station.

A semi-automatic diagnostic module tester is also available for trouble-shooting and maintenance. The module tester automatically guides the operator through a test point sequence, analyses the circuit and identifies faults. No knowledge of electronics or the circuitry is required to do the testing. A small calibrator module is also available which can be plugged into a controller. This enables calibration of the indicator, the controller and any alarm module fitted. The calibrator can be plugged in with the controller on-line or off-line and checks can be made without disrupting operations while on-line.

Series 380 is a range of electronic function modules, including signal converters, alarm relays and computation modules, that plug into standard enclosures. The function modules are used in electronic process control systems to provide a flexibly structured system which can meet any control requirements. Modules available include high-low limits, high-low signal selectors, adder-subtractor, multiplier/divider, square root extractor, etc.

Indicators

Electronic indicators can be incorporated in a controller module or they can be provided as a separate display unit. They have the advantage of having no moving parts which would require lubrication and maintenance.

A cathode ray tube (CRT) may be used to provide a display of a voltage waveform, as a video display unit (VDU) for a computer, or as a television monitor.

The cathode ray tube produces light on the screen by the action of a beam of high velocity electrons which strike the phosphor-coated inner surface of the screen, see Figure 7.18. The beam is moved under

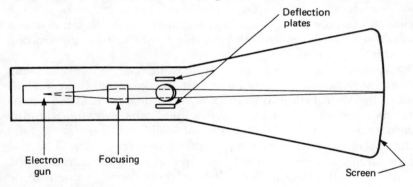

Figure 7.18 Cathode ray tube

the control of voltages applied to the horizontal and vertical (x and y) deflection system. This system may be electrostatic for narrow angle oscilloscope displays of waveforms or it can be electromagnetic for a wide-angle television-type display for a VDU or TV.

Waveform displays are produced by applying the input voltage to the vertical (Y) deflection system while the horizontal (X) deflection system moves the beam at a constant speed across the tube to provide a 'timebase'. TV type displays are produced by making the beam move back and forth across the screen in the form of a 'raster'. This is a set of lines completely covering the screen at a fixed rate. The 'raster' can be seen on any TV by increasing the brightness sufficiently, although it is normally kept at a very low brightness level.

The input voltage to the display affects the brightness of the raster. The input signal and the raster have to be synchronized so that the effect of the input voltage occurs at the correct point on the screen during each complete raster scan.

By this means an image generated by a camera, or a set of characters from a computer character generator, can be reproduced on the screen. The input signal, called a composite video signal, must contain all the necessary timing information to ensure that correct synchronization occurs.

Cathode ray tube systems are complex, but very useful when large amounts of information need to be displayed.

Where a numeral is required in a single panel, e.g. temperature display, use can be made of numerical indicators. Early devices which performed this function included neon discharge tubes and edge-lit acrylic plates. Modern systems use solid state devices such as light-emitting diodes and liquid crystal displays.

The cold cathode numerical indicator is a neon discharge tube containing ten wire electrodes shaped into the figures 0 to 9, each having its own connector pin. The displayed figure is seen as a red glowing shape when its input pin is energized. Another device uses a sandwich of ten thin acrylic plates each with a figure engraved upon it. When any particular plate is edge-lit the engraved figure is seen.

Solid state illuminators are now almost exclusively used for small panels. Light-emitting diodes (LEDs) are semiconductor diodes which radiate light in the visible region when energized. A red display is usually given. Liquid crystal displays (LCDs) are liquid crystal

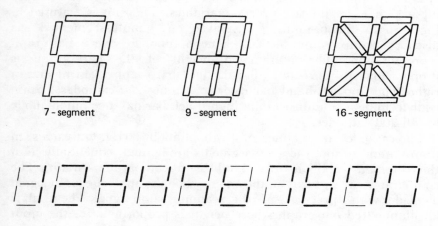

7 - segment   9 - segment   16 - segment

7 - segment numeral display

Figure 7.19 Multiple segment display

cells whose light transmitting properties vary with the applied electric field. Numbers or letters may be displayed by the use of an array of straight lines, see Figure 7.19. Depending upon the number of segments the character set will vary in appearance and available symbols. The display may be a single digit or several digits positioned together on one integrated circuit. Reference is occasionally made to 3½-digit displays. These are four-digit displays where the left-hand digit is only able to display plus, minus or one. The other three digits can display any number from 0 to 9; a decimal point is usually available on each display. These units operate on low voltages and are fully compatible with solid state integrated circuits.

Another display method is the use of a dot matrix. A dot pattern, perhaps seven dots high and five dots wide, provides a matrix where any number of the 35 light points may be illuminated. This display method is also used by printers to provide written data. Here a print head will actuate wires or needles to impact on a carbon and thus write figures or letters. Some examples of a dot matrix character set are given in Figure 7.20.

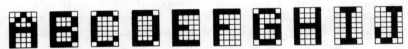

Figure 7.20 Dot matrix display

The Moore Products Co. Model 375C Electronic Vertigauge unit uses a digital principle of operation to provide an analogue indication of one or two electronic inputs. It will accept a variety of standard input signals to indicate process variables. The unit is featured in Figure 7.17. Each input is displayed on a multi-segmented gas discharge lamp, somewhat like a neon tube, to give a bar-graph representation. The illuminated height of the bar graph is proportional to the input signal. The bar-graph element has a right-hand and left-hand bar each containing 200 cathodes 2.5 mm wide forming a column 100 mm high. Each bar has a common anode for all 200 cathodes.

The cathodes are scanned at a rate of about 60 Hz. On each scan from bottom to top, the neon segments are ignited sequentially until the common anode is turned off by a comparator circuit. The comparator circuit turns off the anode when the analogue input signal coincides with a precise 1–5 V d.c. scanning ramp signal. The result is an illuminated bar-graph whose height is proportional to the input signal.

Light-emitting diode bar displays are also in use. They may be incorporated into a single integrated circuit along with the encoding/decoding circuitry so that an analogue input voltage is displayed in bar-graph form.

HYDRAULIC

The controller in some hydraulic systems is the variable stroke pump, which is described in Chapter 8. Valve controlled high pressure oil supplies often make use of spool valves which are, in effect, controllers.

Spool valve

A simplified form of spool valve is shown in Figure 7.21. The spool position may be controlled by a mechanical linkage to the error detecting unit or by some other control medium such as an electric solenoid. When the spool is in the mid-position both channels 1 and 2

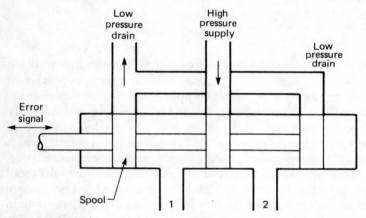

Figure 7.21 Spool valve

are closed off. When the spool is moved to the right, the high pressure supply is directed into channel 1 and exhausts from channel 2. When the spool is moved to the left, the supply is fed into channel 2 and exhausts through channel 1. Where the valve opening, i.e. the spool movement, is small, it is assumed that the rate of flow of oil is proportional to the valve opening.

A commercially produced proportional directional spool valve is shown in Figure 7.22. The unit comprises a pilot control valve, proportional solenoids and a main valve and spool. When the

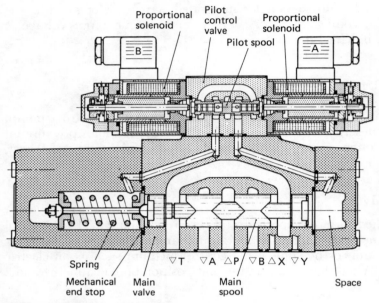

Figure 7.22 Proportional directional valve

solenoids are de-energized the main spool is held in the centre position
by the spring and the end-stop. When solenoid A is energized the pilot
spool is moved to the right. Pilot oil, supplied internally from channel
P or externally from channel X, is now fed via the pilot control valve
into the space (8) and moves the main spool to the left, a distance
proportional to the electric input signal. The main spool therefore acts
as an orifice with an opening having progressive flow characteristics.
The return of the pilot spool to its starting position and the main spool
to the centre position is independent of pilot pressure. The control
lands of the main spool, with their special control slots, remain in
engagement with the control edges in the valve housing in all possible
positions of the valve spool. The inlet and outlet are therefore
continually throttled.

8 Correcting units

The correcting unit in a control loop can take many forms. It may be a valve, a damper, a louvre or in some cases a motor. The control valve is the most common correcting unit found in marine control systems and will therefore be considered in some detail. It is usual to consider a control valve or other correcting unit to be made up of two distinct parts; the actuator or motor element, which provides the operating force; and the valve body or correcting element, through which the controlled fluid flows. Movement of the valve or other unit will require considerable force in most situations. This can be provided by compressed air, hydraulic power or in some cases electricity. Compressed air powered or pneumatic actuators are often found in marine applications.

ACTUATORS

An actuator will be selected according to the type of valve it is to operate and the motion required. It must generate a sufficient force to overcome the reaction forces created by a valve and provide an appropriate stroke. It must be compatible with the operating signal source, act with a suitable speed of response and in the event of supply failure must leave the valve in the most desirable condition. Three particular types of actuator will be considered. They are classified by the operating medium employed, namely compressed air, electricity and hydraulic oil.

Pneumatic

Pneumatic actuators usually appear as diaphragm or piston operated devices. The diaphragm actuator has a relatively short stroke and this limits its applications. It is however quite adequate for most globe-type valve operating applications. The piston actuator can have a very long stroke and provides large forces for valve operation.

Diaphragm

This consists essentially of a flexible synthetic rubber diaphragm which forms part of a pressure-tight chamber, see Figure 8.1. The diaphragm movement is opposed by a spring. In the unit shown, an air pressure signal from the controller acts on the top of the

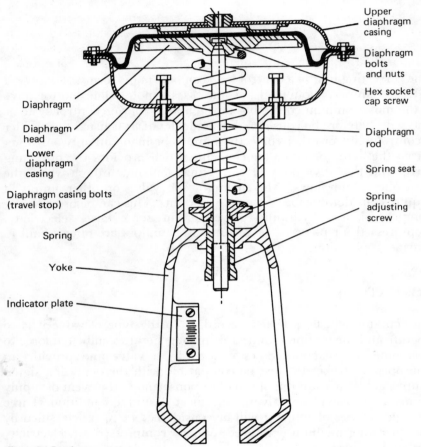

Figure 8.1 Diaphragm actuator

diaphragm. The diaphragm movement is transmitted via the diaphragm head to the diaphragm rod or stem, which moves down. The lower end of the spring, which opposes the stem movement, is fitted into a carrier or seat on the yoke of the actuator. The spring force can be adjusted by the screw below the spring carrier, although once set by the manufacturer this should not normally require alteration. The lower diaphragm casing nuts also double as stops to limit the travel of the diaphragm. Some actuator designs arrange for an air supply to the underside of the diaphragm in order that an increase in air pressure will move the stem upwards. Automatically controlled valves must also have a means of hand control or a hand-operated bypass to enable their operation in the event of a control air failure. Marine applications usually employ a hand control or 'jack' which operates directly on the diaphragm or by a side linkage onto the spindle. Full travel of the valve will be obtained with an air pressure change from 20 to 100 kPa (0.2–1.00 bar) which is the standard output range for pneumatic controllers. The actuator in operation is required to provide a pressure-stroke characteristic which is a straight line, i.e. linear. This will require a large diaphragm of constant area, a spring with a linear force-deflection characteristic and minimum friction in the assembly. All of these requirements can be met to within small tolerances, the smaller the tolerance the more expensive the unit. The stroke is usually limited to about 90 mm in order to avoid non-linearities in the diaphragm and spring behaviour.

Piston type

Pneumatically operated piston actuators are used to provide a high stem force and a long stroke. They can, like diaphragm actuators, be installed on rotary shaft control valves by the use of a suitable linkage. High pressure air, up to about 1000 kPa (10 bar), can be directly applied without the need for pressure regulators and this will give maximum thrust output with a fast response. The operating direction can be easily changed by a slight modification to the valve positioner and double-acting operation is usual. In the event of supply failure the actuator can be arranged to fail safe in either the open, closed or 'as-is' condition.

Piston actuators operate as a result of a pressure imbalance created by a supply pressure on one side of the piston and the releasing or absence of pressure on the opposite side.

A double-acting piston actuator is shown in Figure 8.2. Pressure-tight chambers are formed above and below the piston and receive their operating air supply via relays. The controller or operating instrument signal is supplied to a bellows, any movement of which will change the position of a pivoted beam. The bellows is shown positioned for a direct-acting valve movement, i.e. an increase in supply air pressure will move the actuator stem downwards. The bellows can be positioned above the beam to provide reverse-acting operation. When the bellows is receiving a constant input signal pressure the beam will be stationary. This is because the supply

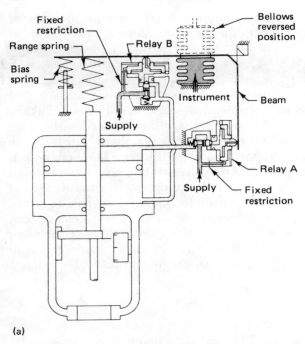

(a)

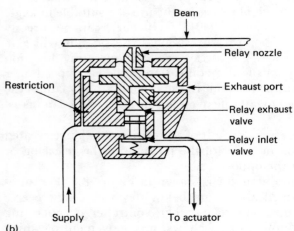

(b)

Figure 8.2 Piston actuator: (a) arrangement; (b) detail of relay

pressure will vent through the relay nozzle faster than it enters
through the restriction, and the relay inlet and exhaust valves will
both remain closed. If now an increase in controller signal pressure
occurs the beam will be moved to block the nozzle on relay A. The

pressure within relay A increases and the inlet valve opens to provide supply air to the top of the piston. At the same time the pressure within relay B will fall and the exhaust valve opens to release air from beneath the piston and enable it to move down. As the piston moves down, a range spring fastened to the extended piston rod will move the beam until both relays are again venting more air than they receive and their respective inlet and exhaust valves will, once again, be closed. This feedback arrangement ensures exact positioning without overcorrection for a particular controller signal. If a reduction in controller signal pressure occurs then the beam will move to cover the nozzle on relay B and uncover that of relay A. Relay, piston and feedback actions are now opposite to those for downward piston movement.

Single-acting actuators are sometimes used when a spring would provide the return motion. Only relay A would be fitted and the space below the piston would vent to atmosphere.

Hydraulic

Hydraulic control systems are to be found in many forms and these were discussed in Chapter 4. Various types of pump and motor are to be found in the different systems and a number of these will now be described. One major difference in operation is whether they are fixed or variable stroke.

Fixed stroke pump

A fixed stroke pump will provide a pressurized supply of hydraulic oil. Suitable circuit arrangements then have to be made to control the oil supply and thus the system. Fixed-stroke pumps may use gears, screws, vanes or fixed-stroke axial pistons to provide a high pressure oil supply.

In gear pumps, a pair of gear wheels, one driving and one driven, will mesh together in a closely fitting housing. Oil is trapped between the teeth and the casing. Two separate paths of oil then pass to the outlet and are discharged.

Internal gear pumps operate in a similar way, using a circular gear rotating within an elliptical casing. A single path of oil trapped between the gear teeth and the casing is pumped to the outlet.

Screw pumps use two, or sometimes three, helical rotors which externally mesh in a closely fitting casing.

A simple vane pump consists of a rotor which runs eccentrically within a circular casing. Several vanes are located in slots within the rotor and are free to slide radially. As the rotor turns, the vanes are

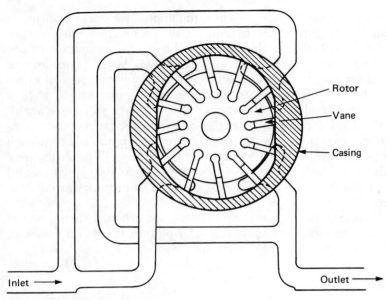

Figure 8.3 Balanced vane pump

held against the casing wall by centrifugal force and create continuously expanding and contracting volumes. Suction and discharge ports can be appropriately located to produce the pumping action. Out-of-balance forces are a problem in this arrangement and therefore an elliptical casing is used. Diametrically opposite suction and discharge ports then enable a double pumping action, with balanced forces on the rotor, see Figure 8.3.

Variable stroke pump
Various designs of variable stroke pumps exist, with the radial piston or 'Hele-Shaw' and the axial piston or swashplate being probably the most common. The hydraulic motor version would be identical in construction and simply operated as a reverse pump.

A radial piston pump is shown in Figure 8.4. Within the casing a short length of shaft drives the cylinder body which rotates around a central valve or tube arrangement and is supported at the ends by ball bearings. The cylinder body is connected to the central valve arrangement by ports which lead to connections at the outer casing for the supply and delivery of oil. A number of pistons fit in the radial cylinders and are fastened to slippers by a gudgeon pin. The slippers fit into a track in the circular floating ring. This ring may rotate, being

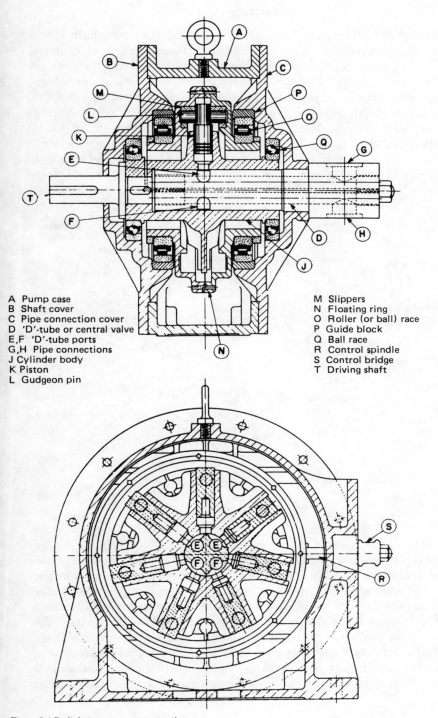

A Pump case
B Shaft cover
C Pipe connection cover
D 'D'-tube or central valve
E,F 'D'-tube ports
G,H Pipe connections
J Cylinder body
K Piston
L Gudgeon pin

M Slippers
N Floating ring
O Roller (or ball) race
P Guide block
Q Ball race
R Control spindle
S Control bridge
T Driving shaft

Figure 8.4 Radial piston pump—construction

supported by ball bearings, and can also move from side to side, since the bearings are mounted in guide blocks. Two spindles which pass out of the pump casing control the movement of the ring.

The operating principle will now be described by reference to Figure 8.5. When the circular floating ring is concentric with the central valve arrangement the pistons have no relative reciprocating motion in their cylinders, see Figure 8.5(a). As a result no oil is pumped and the pump, although rotating, is not delivering any fluid. If, however, the circular floating ring is pulled to the right then a relative reciprocating motion of the pistons in their cylinders does occur, see Figure 8.5(b). The lower piston, for instance, as it moves

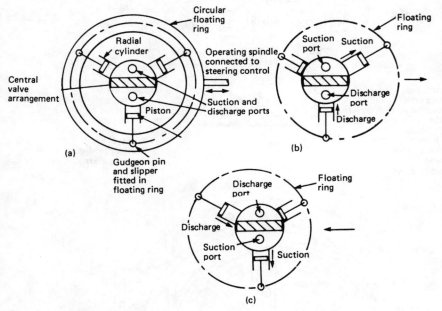

Figure 8.5 Radial piston pump—operation

inwards will discharge fluid out through the lower port in the central valve arrangement. As it continues past the horizontal position the piston moves outwards, drawing in fluid from the upper port. Once past the horizontal position on the opposite side, it begins to discharge the fluid. If the circular floating ring were pushed to the left then the suction and discharge ports would be reversed, see Figure 8.5(c).

The construction and operation of an axial piston pump can be seen by reference to Figure 8.6. Multiple pistons are positioned axially in a rotor which is connected to the prime motor by a drive shaft. Each

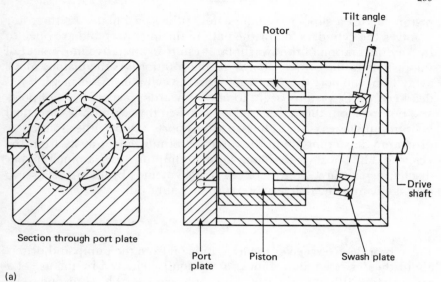

Section through port plate

(a)

Rotor

Tilt angle

Drive shaft

Port plate

Piston

Swash plate

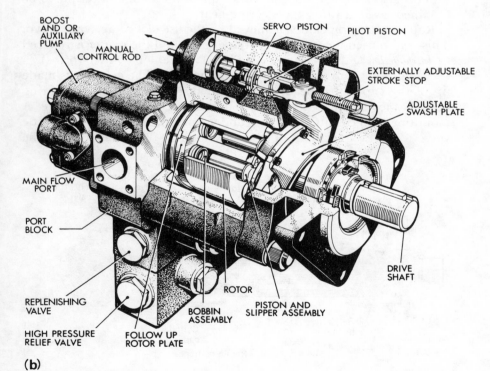

BOOST AND OR AUXILIARY PUMP

MANUAL CONTROL ROD

SERVO PISTON

PILOT PISTON

EXTERNALLY ADJUSTABLE STROKE STOP

ADJUSTABLE SWASH PLATE

MAIN FLOW PORT

PORT BLOCK

REPLENISHING VALVE

HIGH PRESSURE RELIEF VALVE

FOLLOW UP ROTOR PLATE

BOBBIN ASSEMBLY

ROTOR

PISTON AND SLIPPER ASSEMBLY

DRIVE SHAFT

(b)

Figure 8.6 Axial piston pump: (a) operation; (b) construction

piston carries a slipper running against the swashplate. As the rotor revolves the cylinders follow the path of the inlet port and are open to it. Any inclination of the swashplate results in a relative movement of the pistons in the cylinder bores during rotation. As the pistons move away from the port they draw in oil to the cylinder. After passing top dead centre the pistons begin to move towards a separate set of ports and pump oil out through these ports. When the swashplate is vertical no pumping takes place. The two sets of ports can be either suction or discharge depending upon the direction of movement away from the vertical. The boost or auxiliary supply pump provides a much higher discharge pressure. Control of the arrangement is by an integral servo arrangement using delivery pressure hydraulic oil.

Servo motors
The motor device receives the hydraulic oil from the pump and brings about the desired action. Linear actuation is achieved by the use of a ram or jack, although the use of multiple rams enables a torque to be obtained, as in a ram-type steering gear.

Rotary actuation can be achieved by the use of a rotary vane servo. This is also used for steering gear operation and the reader is referred to *Introduction to Marine Engineering* by D.A. Taylor (Butterworths).

A hydraulic ram unit is shown in Figure 8.7. The cylinder is made up of the cap, tube, head, piston and piston rod. A gland bearing permits movement of the piston rod and seals against oil leakage. A mounting flange is fitted to the cylinder cap and an adjustable throttle valve enables variation of the cushioning. Tie rods clamp the

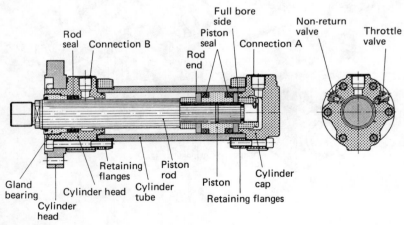

Figure 8.7 Hydraulic ram unit

assembly together and piston and rod seals prevent leakage from the pressurized spaces. Feeding oil to connection A causes the cylinder rod to extend, while oil to connection B causes it to retreat. The extending force is greater than the retracting force since the oil can act on a larger area. Extension is, however, slower for a particular rate of flow since piston speed is inversely proportional to area.

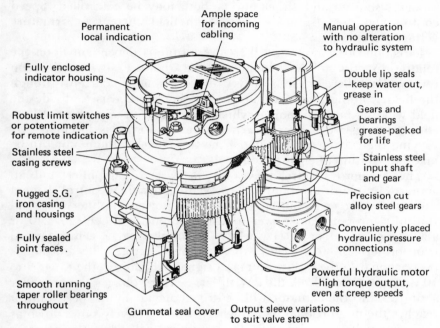

Permanent local indication

Ample space for incoming cabling

Manual operation with no alteration to hydraulic system

Fully enclosed indicator housing

Double lip seals —keep water out, grease in

Robust limit switches or potentiometer for remote indication

Gears and bearings grease-packed for life

Stainless steel casing screws

Stainless steel input shaft and gear

Rugged S.G. iron casing and housings

Precision cut alloy steel gears

Fully sealed joint faces

Conveniently placed hydraulic pressure connections

Smooth running taper roller bearings throughout

Powerful hydraulic motor —high torque output, even at creep speeds

Gunmetal seal cover

Output sleeve variations to suit valve stem

Figure 8.8 Hydraulic rotary valve actuator

A rotary valve actuating device is shown in Figure 8.8. The hydraulic motor drives the input shaft and, through a system of gears, the output sleeve. Rotation of the output sleeve will result in opening or closing of the valve. Manual operation of the actuator and valve is achieved by the square drive on the input shaft. A local valve position indication is given on the unit cover. Remote indication is provided by limit switches or a potentiometer located within the actuator casing. This actuating unit can be used on all lift-type valves, e.g. globe and gate, in all types of remote operated systems, e.g. bilge, ballast and cargo pumping.

Electric

Both d.c. and a.c. motors are commonly used in control actuating systems. Special motor designs may be used for control purposes where an a.c. supply is used. High rotor acceleration as a result of large torque and low inertia is possible with a.c. motors which are to be intermittently used. A solenoid is another form of electric actuator, providing a linear, and usually short, operating stroke.

When d.c. motors are used they may be arranged for series, shunt or compound operation. Usually the field and armature are fed from separate sources and either one or both may be controlled. Speed control can then be achieved through field current or armature voltage variation.

Direction of rotation and therefore torque is dependent upon the relative directions of the field flux and the armature current. Direction reversal can therefore be achieved by reversing the current through the field winding or the armature. Another method is to divide the field winding into two halves which are wound in opposition. When equal currents are present in each half then no torque is developed. By varying the relative magnitude of the two currents the motor can be made to run in either direction.

The Foxboro Electric drive system uses an amplifier and an actuator unit to bring about a 90° movement of a final control element such as a damper or butterfly valve. The power amplifier is a solid state d.c. proportional power unit. The input is either 120, 240 or 480 V a.c. at 50 or 60 Hz, which is supplied to a centre-tapped transformer for 0 to 90 V d.c. motor control. The output is proportional to the input command signal, which is in the range 2 to 10 V d.c. or 4 to 20 mA d.c.. With large error voltages the amplifier saturates and the actuator will be driven at maximum speed until it reaches the proportional region where it progressively slows down as the error voltage is reduced. The amplifier will drive the actuator motor in the correct direction until the actuator position feedback signal equates the command signal. The electric motor-driven rotary actuator operates over 90° with a torque output dependent upon the supply voltage. Movement of the actuator results in a feedback signal to the amplifier or actual position. A manual handwheel override is provided with a positive declutching mechanism. The amplifier can arrange for the actuator to hold in position in the event of the command or input signals being lost or falling below some fixed level. Manual control is then available either locally or remotely.

Where a constant speed a.c. drive is required the three-phase squirrel cage motor is usually used. Single-phase induction motors can be used, such as the split-phase motor or the capacitor start motor (where an auxiliary winding is supplied via a capacitor). In each case the motor starts as a crude two-phase induction motor and when up to speed it switches to become a single-phase motor running at its rated speed. The single-phase motor is particularly useful for on-off control situations.

The Rotork rotary valve actuator uses a three-phase squirrel cage motor, see Figure 8.9. The motor combines low inertia with a high torque and a special lost motion drive arrangement provides a hammer blow once the motor is running. A worm gear drive enables the valve to be opened fully or 'inched' to any position. The gearbox is oil filled and O-ring seals are used to ensure no oil leakage. Torque and limit switches are operated by the motor-driven worm shaft. The limit switches provide end-position signalling and the torque switch will switch off the motor at a set torque value. A mechanical position pointer is located at the end of the worm shaft, to show whether the

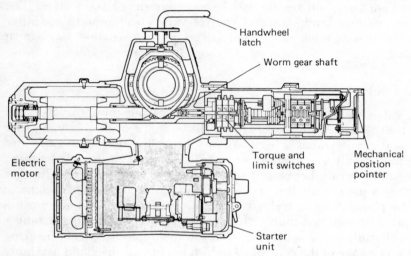

Figure 8.9 Electric rotary valve actuator

valve is open, closed or in an intermediate position. A local operation handwheel is provided which, when engaged by a latch, will declutch the motor drive. Once the motor is started it will re-engage unless the handwheel latch is padlocked into place. A starter unit is shown connected to the actuator in Figure 8.9. This provides all the necessary controls such that the unit needs only a three-phase power supply in order to operate. Any remote indication, control or interlocks can be provided by appropriate wiring into the starter unit.

Linear movement can be obtained with electric motor actuation by the use of suitable gearing arrangements. A simple device providing a linear stroke is the solenoid. This consists of a cylindrical coil in which an iron plunger or core is free to move. When a supply is provided to the coil it becomes an electromagnet which can be designed to provide a constant inward or outward motion of the plunger.

VALVE BODY

The actuator yoke is fastened onto the valve body and the valve spindle fastens onto the actuator stem. Most control valves are of the straight-through globe valve type, although three-way valve bodies have certain mixing applications. Butterfly valves are used in some systems where high flow capacities exist and a minimum valve pressure loss is required. Since their operation requires a rotary stem movement they will be discussed separately in a later section. The actual selection and sizing of control valves will be outlined after detailed descriptions of the valve and its construction have been given.

Globe valve

The valve body provides a pressure-tight casing through which the controlled fluid passes, see Figure 8.10. A single or double valve disc and seat arrangement is used to control the fluid flow. The valve and seat may result in a metal-to-metal surface contact or 'soft-seating', using a nitrile or other elastomeric material to form the seal. This disc or plug is usually shaped to provide the required flow characteristic for the plant. Alternatively, a cage with specially shaped entry ports will also provide a suitable characteristic. A gland sealing arrangement or stuffing box is fitted around the valve spindle. While ensuring that no leakage of the controlled fluid takes place, this gland assembly must not produce a heavy or varying frictional load on the actuator as both would affect the valve characteristic. The assembly is normally flanged and bolted into the pipeline, although smaller valves may have screwed ends. A number of aspects of globe valve body design will now be examined in more detail. These are bonnets, operating action, disc or plug shaping and gland sealing arrangements.

The selection of the valve body material will be based upon the pressure, temperature, corrosive and erosive properties of the flowing liquid. Some of these requirements may result in the use of special metals and alloys but usually cast iron and cast carbon steel can be used. Some of the more commonly used materials and their properties will now be described.

Cast carbon steel is the most popular steel material for services involving the control of air, saturated or superheated steam,

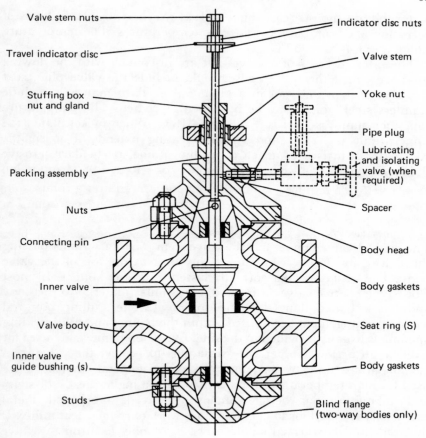

Valve stem nuts

Indicator disc nuts

Travel indicator disc

Valve stem

Stuffing box
nut and gland

Yoke nut

Pipe plug

Lubricating
and isolating
valve (when
required)

Packing assembly

Spacer

Nuts

Body head

Connecting pin

Body gaskets

Inner valve

Seat ring (S)

Valve body

Inner valve
guide bushing (s)

Body gaskets

Studs

Blind flange
(two-way bodies only)

Figure 8.10 Valve body

non-corrosive liquids and gases. It can be used in the temperature
range −29 to +540°C, although prolonged exposure above 413°C is
not advisable. Cast chrome-moly steel has improved corrosion and
creep resistance because of its additives. It is often used for high
pressure steam, oils, gases, sea water and other mildly corrosive
liquids. Its operating temperature range is from −29 to +593°C. Cast
stainless steel, which has been heat treated, is used for valves
controlling oxidizing or very corrosive fluids. Its operating range is
from −253 to +815°C. Cast iron is an expensive, ductile material
which is used for valves controlling steam, water, gas and
non-corrosive fluids. Its operating temperature range is from −101 to
+232°C. Cast bronze is sometimes used for valve bodies but more
often for valve trim parts. It is used for valves controlling steam, air,

water, oil and non-corrosive gases. It is resistant to certain types of corrosion and suitable for cryogenic temperatures. The temperature range is −198 to +232°C.

The internal parts of a valve that are in contact with the flowing fluid are called the trim. These would include the valve plug, seat ring, cage, stem and pin in a globe valve. Trim materials include stainless steel which may be hardened or coated. The temperature range for stainless steel is −268 to +316°C. When nickel plated the upper limit is 427°C and chrome plating extends it to 593°C. Elastomer trim is used when controlling some, particularly erosive fluids. Neoprene has a temperature range of −40 to +93°C and nylon is −73 to +93°C.

Valve body bonnets

The control valve bonnet has the valve stem (or rotary shaft) passing through it and forms a pressure-tight cover at the top of the valve body. The actuator yoke normally fastens onto the bonnet. In most globe-type control valves it is made of a similar material to the body and has a bolted flanged connection to it. The stuffing box and packing arrangement are housed within the bonnet and a lubricating opening is usually provided in the side. Extension bonnets are used for either high or low temperature situations to protect the valve stem packing from the extreme temperatures. Cast metal extensions are used for high temperature work as they have a higher heat emissivity and therefore cool better. Smooth surfaced, fabricated metal extensions are used for low temperature work to reduce heat influx. If the cold fluid is warmed sufficiently a frost may form on the valve stem, which will score the packing and cause leakage. In both cases the material should be thin to reduce heat transfer by conduction. Stainless steel, having a lower coefficient of thermal conductivity, is to be preferred to carbon steel. Extension bonnets in low temperature situations may have insulation fitted to further protect against heat influx. A bellows seal bonnet is used where absolutely no leakage along the valve stem can be allowed. The valve stem and bellows are surrounded by a metal cylinder which has the bellows sealing it at the upper end, see Figure 8.11. The lower end of the cylinder is securely sealed and fastened to the valve body. The other end of the bellows is sealed around the valve stem when it is in its lowest position. Any upward movement of the stem will result in a compression of the bellows but no possible leakage since the bellows moves with the stem. A standard stuffing box assembly is also fitted above the bellows to protect against a failure or rupture of the bellows. Bellows seal

1 Bonnet
2 Bushing (extension bonnets only)
3 Packing flange
4 Packing flange stud
5 Packing flange nut
6 Packing set (TFE V-ring packing only)
7 Packing ring (not req'd for TFE V-ring packing)
8 Lantern ring (not req'd for TFE V-ring packing)
9 Packing ring (not req'd for TFE V-ring or TFE-impregnated asbestos packing)
10 Special washer (TFE V-ring packing only)
11 Packing box ring
12 Upper wiper (not req'd for laminated-graphite packing)
13 Packing follower
14 Pipe plug (not req'd with lubricator or lubricator/isolating valve)
15 Yoke locknut

16 Pipe plug (tapped extension and bellows seal bonnets only)
17 Bellows seal adapter (bellows seal bonnet only)
18 Anti-rotator (bellows seal bonnet only)
19 Travel stop (bellows seal bonnet only)
20 Bellows seal assembly (bellows seal bonnet only)
21 Anti-rotator gasket (bellows seal bonnet only)
22 Bonnet gasket (bellows seal bonnet only)
23 Cap screw (bellows seal bonnet only)
24 Connection stud (bellows seal bonnet only)
25 Cap screw
26 Hex nut
27 Pipe nipple (lubricator/isolating valve only)
28 Warning plate (bellows seal bonnet only)
29 Drive screw (bellows seal bonnet only)

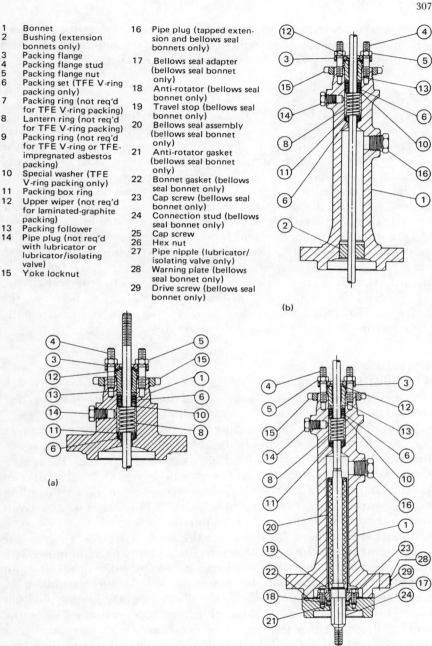

Figure 8.11 Valve bonnets: (a) plain bonnet; (b) extension bonnet; (c) bellows seal bonnet

bonnets are limited in application to 20.7 bar at 21°C and subsequent pressure reductions as the temperature rises. Considerable care and attention must be paid to this assembly once installed.

Valve operating action

The valve disc in a control valve can be made to increase or decrease flow as the controller pressure signal increases. A direct-acting valve is arranged to decrease the flow or close as the pressure on the diaphragm is increased. Another term used is air-to-close (ATC) and such an arrangement means that the valve will be open in the even of air failure, i.e. fail-safe open. A reverse-acting valve will open as the pressure on the diaphragm is increased, i.e. air-to-open or fail-safe closed. The particular application of the control valve in a system will decide the choice of action and fail-safe condition required. It is also possible with the use of locking valves on the diaphragm supply air to trap air and have the valve 'fail-safe as-is'. Some valve bodies are arranged with a removable bottom flange below the valve disc assembly. The actuator yoke assembly can be attached here and the valve, in effect, operated upside-down. Where the valve was originally direct-acting it now becomes reverse-acting.

Valve disc or plug

The valve disc of a globe-type control valve is the movable part which provides a variable restriction to fluid flow. Various plug or disc designs are available which produce different flow characteristics, enable different methods of guiding or alignment with the seat ring, or have a certain shut-off capability. The valve disc will be designed initially for either two-position or throttling control. If it is a two-position type then the actuator will locate the valve at two particular points of its travel, usually open or closed. In throttling control applications the valve plug may be positioned at any point within the travel of the valve as required.

The shape of the valve disc, and the flow past it for a particular valve lift, result in the valve characteristic. This, when combined with the characteristics for the other items in the system, will result in an overall characteristic for the plant or unit being controlled. A single-seated valve has one disc and will close tightly against the fluid flow. However, there is a considerable force applied to the disc by the flowing fluid and this force must be overcome by the actuator. In a double-seated valve the fluid flow divides to pass through the upper and lower openings. Since they are approximately equal in area, then the liquid pressures are balanced and operate in opposite directions.

The lower valve disc is slightly smaller since it must pass through the upper valve seat when installed. A smaller actuating unit can therefore be used. The double-seated valve does not shut off the fluid flow as effectively. This is a result of spindle expansion, due to temperature change, which will move one disc off its seat. This is rarely a problem since most control valves have an operating range which does not include the fully closed position.

The disc is shaped in order to provide a varying orifice area as the valve opens or closes. The relationship between valve lift and fluid flow rate is called the valve characteristic. Three common characteristics are quick-opening, linear and semi-logarithmic; they are shown in Figure 8.12. The quick-opening, bevel or mitre valve has

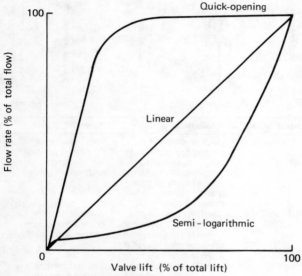

Figure 8.12 Valve operating characteristics

a small lift but the flow area increases rapidly as the valve opens. A minimum obstruction to flow is provided with this type of valve and it is usually used with on-off or two-position controllers. Over most of the range of opening, the flow-lift relationship is linear. The linear characteristic valve gives a flow against valve lift relationship which is almost a straight line throughout. At 20 per cent lift the flow rate is 20 per cent of the maximum, at 60 per cent the flow rate is 60 per cent of the maximum, and so on. This is achieved by shaping of the disc opening or a contoured disc. The actual angles of the V-port or the shaping of the disc sides will provide this or a variety of other

characteristics. The equal-percentage or semi-logarithmic characteristic valve movement results in equal percentage changes in the flow
rate. This means that for a 10 per cent change in valve travel for a
high flow rate, for example 80 per cent, the flow rate will change by 20
per cent, and for a low flow rate of 10 per cent, the flow rate will also
change by 20 per cent. Suitably shaped V-ports or contoured discs are
used for this valve also. A selection of various valve disc or plug
shapes is shown in Figure 8.13.

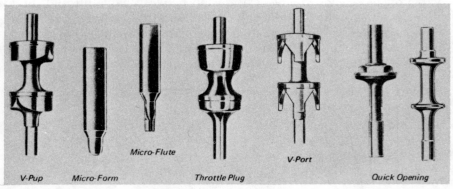

Valve plug style	Flow characteristic	Application	Remarks
V-Pup Micro-Form Micro-Flute	Equal percentage	Used where large percentage of pressure drop is absorbed by system itself. Also used where highly varying pressure drops can be expected.	Very popular for throttling applications. Generally top or top and bottom guided.
Throttle plug V-Port	Modified parabolic	Used on pressure and flow control applications where the major system pressure drop is available at the control valve.	Top and bottom guided. Metal or composition seating.
Quick opening	Quick opening	Used for two-position (on-off) service where the valve is required to be in one of two positions with no throttling of the flow.	Top and bottom guided. Metal or composition seating.

Figure 8.13 Valve plug types

Another method of characterizing control valves is to have a
cylindrical valve plug which moves within a cage. The cage has ports
or flow openings in the wall. As the valve disc moves away from the
seat the ports are opened to permit fluid flow through the valve.
Various standard designs of cage are available to produce
quick-opening, linear, or equal-percentage valve characteristics, see
Figure 8.14. This cage-guiding arrangement provides other advantages in that the maintenance and replacement of internal parts is
simplified and valve characteristics can easily be changed by

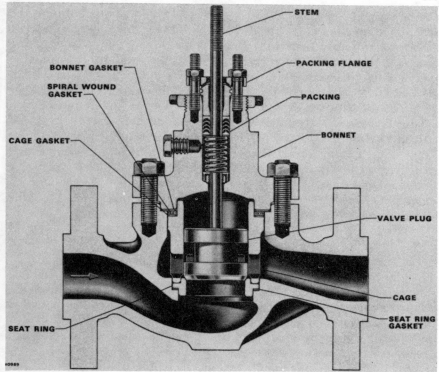

STEM

BONNET GASKET

SPIRAL WOUND
GASKET

CAGE GASKET

PACKING FLANGE

PACKING

BONNET

VALVE PLUG

CAGE

SEAT RING
GASKET

SEAT RING

Figure 8.14 Control valve with cage

installing a different cage. Special cage designs are also available to combat cavitation or reduce noise.

It should be noted that all these characteristics relate to the valve alone and are obtained when there is a constant pressure drop across the valve. When considering the control system or plant as a whole then the valve will contribute some proportion of the total pressure losses. If the loss is only 25 per cent and it has a linear characteristic then the system characteristic will be similar to that of a quick-opening valve. A valve with an equal-percentage characteristic would, in the same system, produce an overall characteristic of linear form. Where the majority of the system pressure drop occurs across the valve its characteristic would therefore provide an almost linear system characteristic.

The valve disc, when operating, must be correctly aligned with the seat and guided in its movement to ensure correct operation. This can be achieved in a number of ways one of which, cage guiding, has already been described. Top-and-bottom guiding uses bushes in the bonnet and bottom flange to locate the valve stem. Top guiding is the use of a single extended bush in the bonnet or valve body.

A top guide together with a fluted valve disc moving in the seating ring is a slight variation giving effectively top and bottom guiding.

The valve disc in certain control applications may be surrounded by a restricted-capacity trim. The reduced flow rate resulting may be required to reduce inlet and outlet fluid velocities, to enable a much stronger valve construction while still maintaining valve travel and capacity relationships, to enable system capacity to be increased at a later stage by the removal of the trim, or simply to avoid fitting expensive reducers in the pipeline. A conventional globe-type valve body can easily be fitted with a seat having a smaller port area and a valve plug to suit the smaller port. The necessary inserts are available to reduce down to about 40 per cent of the original capacity.

Gland sealing

The gland fitted around the valve spindle must effectively seal against leakage of the controlled fluid. The packing used must not, however, create too high a friction load on the spindle or a load which varies as the spindle moves. The type of packing may be dictated by upper or lower temperature limits; it may be adjustable or spring loaded when fully screwed down.

The packing arrangement within the stuffing box may permit adjustment or may be fully screwed down. In either case there may be a spring at the bottom of the stuffing box to keep the packing rings compressed against the valve spindle. A number of different packing arrangements are shown in Figure 8.15.

PTFE (polytetrafluoroethylene, trade name Teflon) is a plastic material with an inherent ability to minimize friction. It is moulded into V-shaped rings which are self-adjusting in the stuffing box. No lubrication is necessary but the valve stem must be extremely smooth to ensure a good seal. If the packing rings or the stem is scored then leakage will occur. The recommended temperature limits for this material, which is resistant to most known chemicals, are -40 to $+232°C$. Where asbestos is impregnated with PTFE a compressible packing is produced with low friction qualities. Rings of square cross-section are used and it is normal to provide lubrication. A lantern ring is fitted to enable the entry of the lubricant and care must be taken during assembly to ensure that the lubricator and lantern ring line up. The gland assembly will provide for adjustment in service to correct any minor leaks. The recommended temperature limits for the use of this material are -73 to $+232°C$. Graphited

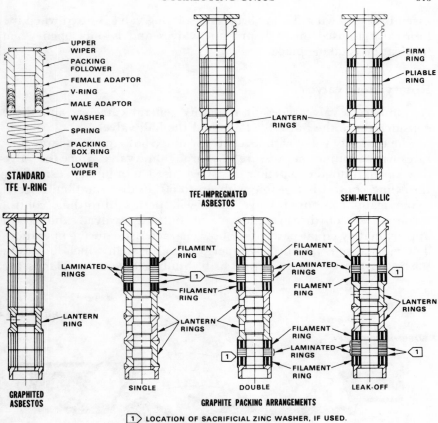

Figure 8.15 Packing material arrangements

asbestos is a formed ring packing made up of asbestos fibre, lead wool, flake graphite, some metal particles, and neoprene as a binder. It is particularly suited to systems containing steam, oil or compressed air. It can be compressed to correct small leakages but must be lubricated to reduce friction and improve sealing. The upper limit of use is again 232°C. Semi-metallic packing rings have an asbestos core which is covered with shredded or braided aluminium foil. It is used for high temperature and high pressure applications, particularly where the valve stem surface is less than perfect. The upper limit of use is 482°C and lubrication should be provided.

Where lubrication is required for a packing material it is usually silicone grease, which reduces friction and improves the valve stem action up to temperatures of 260°C. It is usually supplied through a screw-operated injector which feeds into the stuffing box; a typical assembly is shown in Figure 8.10. An isolating valve is fitted when the lubricator is used on high pressure valves and is only open when lubrication is taking place.

Rotary stem valves

A number of valve types fit into this general category and those considered are the butterfly valve and the ball valve.

The butterfly valve with its centrally hinged disc permits large flow rates with a minimum pressure loss through the valve. Since the valve disc opens into the pipeline the space used is minimal. On-off or throttling control is possible with up to 60° of disc rotation. Special dynamically contoured valve discs will permit throttling control through 90° of disc rotation. The butterfly valve exhibits an approximately equal-percentage flow characteristic during operation. The valve disc is fastened by taper pins to the shaft which locates in bushes in the body, see Figure 8.16. Stuffing boxes and glands are

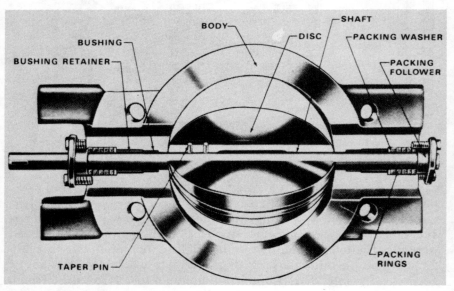

Figure 8.16 Butterfly valve

fitted where the shaft leaves the body to prevent fluid leakage. Packing materials used are similar to those described earlier for control valve bodies but no spring loading is used and all glands can be adjusted. Since only rotary motion is involved, nitrile rings are used in some stuffing box arrangements.

The conventional swing-through disc has a small clearance between the disc and valve body resulting in slight leakage when shut. For on-off service, and when throttling, the disc will only move through 60°. This limit results from the torque-position characteristic which rises with increasing angle of valve opening. The principal consideration for actuator sizing is the torque required when opening or closing the valve against the shut-off pressure drop in the pipeline. A dynamically contoured disc will enable on-off or throttling control through 90°. This type of disc must however be correctly positioned such that the wider edge opens downstream. A conventional disc can open or close upstream or downstream. Various disc-seat configurations are possible depending upon the shut-off requirements or the process fluid. The usual arrangement is a small clearance between the metal seat to enable the disc to swing through. Some leakage is inevitable with this method. A step-seat design has the seat and disc stepped such that the disc closes against the step and improved shut-off is provided. Where the process fluid is likely to deposit solids in the pipeline a tapered body bore is provided in the valve to give a small shear area and the disc has a knife-edge. Elastomer-lined body bores provide excellent shut-off capabilities at the expense of increased actuator torque. Nitrile, neoprene and viton are typical lining materials and the disc edge is chrome plated where cast iron or steel discs are used. Alternatively, the disc may be made from stainless steel.

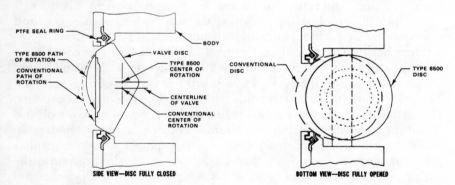

Figure 8.17 Comparison of disc actions

Eccentric-disc type butterfly valves provide excellent shut-off against high pressure drops since the disc moves away from the seal as it opens. A comparison between the conventional and eccentric disc movements is shown in Figure 8.17. The eccentric disc can have either a PTFE (elastomer) seal ring or a metal seal ring fitted, as shown.

Flow direction is with the conical disc face upstream and a linear flow characteristic is provided through 90° of rotation.

Ball control valves are another type of rotary stem valve but in this arrangement the ball remains in constant contact with the seal during rotation. This results in a good shut-off capability and the seal ring may be elastomer or metal. The ball arrangement permits an unrestricted straight-through flow and therefore a high capacity. One particular design has a patented V-notch in the ball, which produces an equal-percentage flow characteristic through the 90° of rotation.

Rotary stem valves can be used for three-way flow applications. Two valves would be used, operated in tandem by a single actuator with a suitable linkage connection. Operation of rotary stem valves is by conventional diaphragm or piston actuators which have a lever linkage mechanism to provide the rotational movement.

VALVE POSITIONERS AND BOOSTERS

Acceptable performance of a control system requires careful design, taking into account the static and dynamic characteristics of the various components and the process being controlled. It may be considered necessary to fit valve positioners to control valves to ensure accurate location of the valve disc. Problems such as valve stem friction loads due to packing, valve disc imbalance, and hysteresis in the diaphragm and return spring can also be overcome by the use of a valve positioner. Usually associated with valve positioners and occasionally fitted independently a pneumatic isolating amplifier or volume booster may be used to speed up the valve movement.

Simulation and experimental work has however revised the 'rules' with regard to the fitting of valve positioners and volume boosters. Where packing friction is considerable and the system response fast, the fitting of a positioner can result in poorer system control and instability. Simply fitting a volume booster alone provides an improved control performance since its response to the controller signal is more precise. On control systems with a slow response the fitting of a valve positioner and perhaps a volume booster is beneficial to the performance. It is also beneficial where the controller output is split into ranges for more than one valve, where an increased thrust is required which normal supply pressure cannot provide and where long controller to instrument pipelines are involved and a fast response is required.

A valve positioner suitable for a diaphragm-actuated control valve is shown in Figure 8.18. When the controller pressure signal increases,

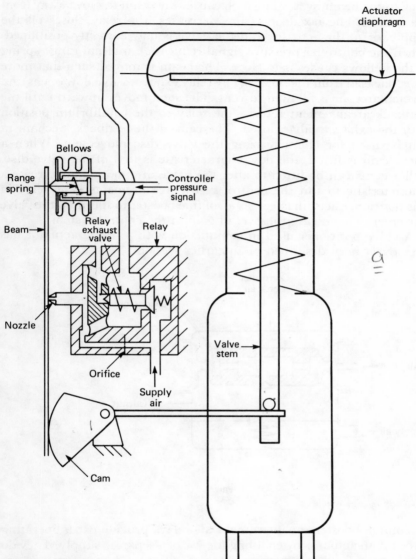

Figure 8.18 Valve positioner

the bellows expands and moves the beam which restricts the nozzle. The pivoting arrangement is not shown but it enables the movement as described. The nozzle pressure increases and the relay operates to provide supply air to the diaphragm actuator. The actuator stem moves down (assuming it is direct-acting). The stem movement is fed back to the beam by a cam which causes the beam to move away from the nozzle. The nozzle pressure decreases, the relay closes off the supply air to the actuator and the valve is now correctly positioned. When the controller pressure signal reduces an internal range spring in the bellows causes it to close. The beam is moved such that more air is released from the nozzle. The relay exhaust valve now opens and the actuator air is allowed to vent. The stem moves upward until the feedback arrangement returns the relay to the equilibrium position with the exhaust valve closed. The cam in the feedback mechanism can be used for characterizing the valve disc movement. When a linear cam is fitted, the flow characteristic is that of the valve disc. Other cams can be fitted to alter the valve disc motion and create a characteristic to suit the control system requirements. The relay in this positioner acts, in effect, as a volume booster to speed up the valve movement or increase the overall gain in the control system.

A valve positioner used in conjunction with a piston actuator has previously been described in an earlier section.

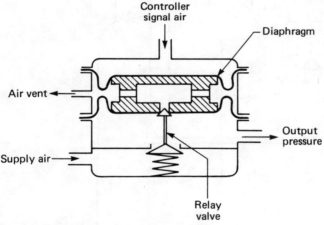

Figure 8.19 Volume booster

Volume boosters or instrument air relays provide extra operating force for an actuator by enabling the use of a separate supply. They do not have a feedback from the stem position and therefore are not positioners. One design is shown schematically in Figure 8.19. The controller signal air acts on the upper diaphragm. The supply air enters through a port but can only pass to the outlet, and thus the actuator, when the relay valve is open. The output pressure acts within the relay on a lower diaphragm. In an equilibrium situation the relay valve has the supply air inlet valve closed and also the output air vent closed. An increase in the controller pressure signal will push down the upper diaphragm and also the lower diaphragm. The exhaust valve remains closed while the supply inlet valve opens to admit air to the actuator. As the output air pressure increases, the lower diaphragm moves up and the supply inlet valve will close under the action of the spring. The relay will then be in equilibrium once more. A drop in the controller signal pressure will result in the output pressure pushing up both diaphragms and the release of air from the actuator. When the controller pressure and output pressure are in equilibrium the diaphragms will have moved down again and the vent valve will be closed.

ACCESSORIES

A number of items related to control valves come under this general heading. They are handwheels for manual operation, hydraulic snubbers to dampen valve disc movement, and lock-up and fail-safe arrangements in the event of supply failure.

A facility for the manual operation of control valves is essential. This is usually provided by a handwheel which may be top or side mounted. Space restrictions usually result in top-mounting, particularly for pneumatic diaphragm-actuated control valves. Pneumatic piston-actuated valves must have side-mounted handwheels since the

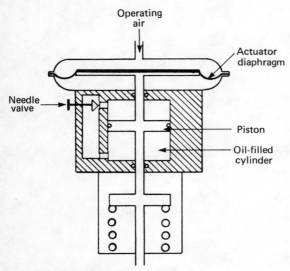

Figure 8.20 Hydraulic snubber

valve positioner is mounted on the top. Both types of handwheel can also act as travel stops, the side-mounted handwheel limiting in both directions whereas the top-mounted handwheel will only limit in one direction.

A hydraulic snubber is usually provided on control valves which operate under severe conditions. A piston attached to the valve stem moves in an oil-filled cylinder and provides a damping action on the stem movement, see Figure 8.20. A needle valve in the oil flow passage enables the amount of damping to be varied. A snubber may be fitted on a pneumatic diaphragm- or piston-actuated control valve.

Pneumatic lock-up and fail-safe systems serve to bring about a particular valve position in the event of power failure. The lock-up system is used to hold the valve in its last position in the event of supply failure. Fail-safe systems are arranged to move the valve disc to the open or closed position in the event of supply failure. If the valve fully-open position is the fail-safe condition then, in the event of supply failure, the valve will be moved to this position. An arrangement to provide a fail-safe downward movement of the

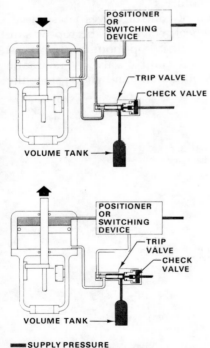

SUPPLY PRESSURE
TOP CYLINDER PRESSURE
BOTTOM CYLINDER PRESSURE
DIRECTION OF AUTOMATIC PISTON MOTION   *Figure 8.21 Fail-safe valve operation*

actuator is shown in Figure 8.21. A volume tank is charged with supply pressure and on supply failure will provide the pressurized air to move the actuator to the fail-safe position. When the supply is resumed the volume chamber is recharged and automatic actuator positioning will continue.

SELF-ACTING CONTROL VALVES

Some simple single-variable control applications make use of self-acting valves which have no separate source of power. The fluid being controlled provides the means by which a controlling action is achieved.

Pressure regulator

This unit is used to deliver a constant, reduced pressure air supply to controllers or instruments. The general arrangement is shown in Figure 8.22. High pressure air enters the valve chamber and will cause the valve to move down, away from its seat. The air then passes through to the outlet side and also to an opening into the diaphragm chamber. The outlet air now acts on the diaphragm to push it up and close the valve. The spring pressure acting down will determine the equilibrium situation and thus the output air pressure. If the reduced pressure were to rise above the set point, the diaphragm would lift off the valve stem and open an orifice. This would release the air into the spring case and then to atmosphere. The body may be die-cast aluminium or, in some cases, cast iron. The valve plug may have an elastomer insert or be made of aluminium or brass. The diaphragm is usually made of nitrile and the valve stem is stainless steel.

Temperature regulator

Automatic temperature control of fluids can be achieved by the use of three-port valves arranged either to mix or divert. Where two ports act as inlets the valve is a diverter. The appropriate mixing or diverting action is achieved by a rotor whose angular movement determines the proportion of flow between the ports. In operation the rotor will automatically position itself so that the coolant is proportioned between the cooler and the cooler bypass system. The coolant temperature may be sensed either within the valve, i.e. direct operation, or remotely, resulting in pneumatic operation.

Direct operation is brought about by a sealed capsule containing a

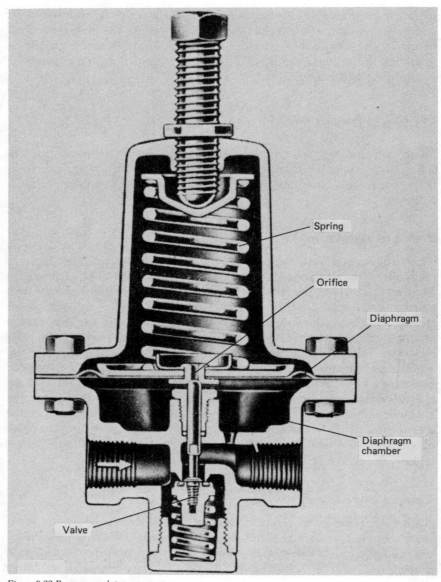

Figure 8.22 Pressure regulator

wax mixture. When heated, the mixture rapidly expands and this expansion is transmitted via a plunger and linkage to a rotor which operates in a three-port valve body, see Figure 8.23. The rotor movement determines the extent of opening of the two lower ports of

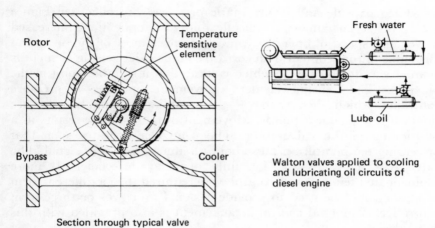

Rotor

Temperature
sensitive
element

Bypass

Cooler

Section through typical valve

Fresh water

Lube oil

Walton valves applied to cooling
and lubricating oil circuits of
diesel engine

Figure 8.23 Direct acting valve

the valve. The temperature range of a valve is determined by the wax
mixture in the capsule. An external lever enables the automatic
mechanism to be overridden and permits manual operation. No
external actuating power source is required for this type of valve and
it will operate in any position.

The basic three-port valve body can be designed for pneumatic
operation with temperature sensing by a remotely positioned

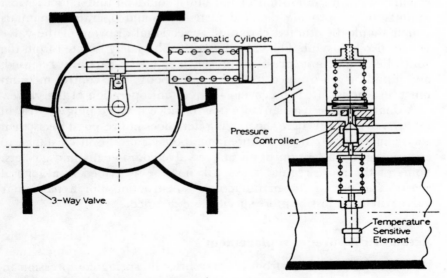

Pneumatic Cylinder.

Pressure
Controller.

3-Way Valve.

Temperature
Sensitive
Element

Figure 8.24 Pneumatically operated direct-acting valve

wax-filled capsule and a pneumatic pressure controller, see Figure 8.24. This arrangement provides flexibility in applications, increased power and speed of operation and it removes most of the operating mechanism from contact with corrosive fluids. The sensing element is again a wax-filled capsule which is located at a suitable point in the pipeline. The sensing element movement operates a pressure controller which then sends a corresponding pneumatic pressure signal to the piston actuator. Movement of the actuator results in a positioning of the valve rotor. The controller operates such that increasing temperature brings about a reducing pressure signal. The valve will then fail-safe, i.e. fully open to the cooler. If more sophisticated temperature control were required then a different form of sensor could be used to provide a signal to a two- or three-term controller. A manual control arrangement is also provided with this valve design.

Another design, similar to the pneumatically operated valve, is operated by gas pressure. A particular application of this is in refrigeration and air-conditioning systems, which will be described in Chapter 9.

CONTROL VALVE MAINTENANCE

Before any attempt at maintenance is made, the fundamental construction and operation of the unit should be understood. Most manufacturers provide detailed instruction and operation manuals which should be studied carefully. A sectional drawing of the valve would also be useful. The valve must then be safely isolated from the controlled fluid, any pressure present should be carefully released, any liquid or gas drained from the valve body. The control medium must also be isolated to prevent inadvertant operation of the valve.

A control valve uses an actuator to move a valve plug or disc in relation to a seat. Where the moving item does not respond freely then servicing is required. A maintenance policy may be in existance to ensure regular attention to all major valve components and gaskets. Some of the more regular tasks will now be described in a general sense. The use of the manufacturer's instructions for a particular valve will doubtless be more specific and detailed.

Actuator diaphragm replacement

With the valve isolated from all pressure, the spring compression in the main spring must be relieved as much as possible. The upper diaphragm case is then removed. With direct-acting actuators the diaphragm can then be removed and replaced. On reverse-acting actuators, the diaphragm assembly must first be dismantled in order to change the diaphragm. Moulded diaphragms are usually used since they provide a greater travel and ensure a more even loading during valve travel. A flat sheet diaphragm can be used as an emergency repair but this should be replaced at the earliest opportunity with the moulded type. When reassembling the diaphragm case, the cap screws should be tightened firmly and evenly around the circumference.

Stem packing replacement

When leakage occurs around the valve stem, or maintenance work has disturbed the packing, it may need to be replaced. The valve should be isolated and all the pressure released before the packing nuts are loosened.

Split-ring packing can be removed with the use of a narrow sharp tool without removing the valve stem. This must be done with care in order not to score or scratch the stem. The best method for removing packing is to separate the valve stem and actuator stem connection. The actuator is then removed from the valve body. The valve bonnet is then removed and the valve plug and stem is withdrawn. A rod, slightly larger in diameter than the stem, can now be inserted through the bottom of the packing box to push out the packing at the top. It is unwise to use the valve stem as the threads may be damaged. The packing box should then be inspected for scratches or anything that may damage new packing. The valve plug, seat ring and trim parts can also now be inspected and then the valve and bonnet reassembled. The bonnet bolts should be tightened so as to evenly load the gasket. The new packing rings should then be slid down the stem, in order and the correct way around. The packing follower, flange and packing nuts are then fitted into place. Where spring-loaded PTFE V-ring packing is used the packing nuts must be fully tightened; for other types a pressure sufficient to prevent leakage in service is sufficient. The actuator is now replaced and set for the correct valve travel.

Threaded seat ring replacement

Screwed-in seat rings are used on many sliding stem control valves. Where the seat becomes damaged and does not seal it will require removal and replacement. If the seat ring has been tack-welded in place, the welding must first be cut away. Some penetrating oil should then be applied to the threads. A seat ring puller is then used to unscrew the seat ring. Where this is not available a lathe or boring mill may be used. The seat ring is unscrewed by a bar contacting lugs on the seat, enabling it to turn. The threads in the body should be thoroughly cleaned before a new seat ring is fitted. The new seat ring should then be tack welded in place and the valve body reassembled.

Seat grinding

The valve plug and seating surfaces of metal-to-metal seating valves will require grinding-in when leakage becomes excessive. Deep marks or nicks in either surface should be machined out or the item replaced. Grinding compounds can be used for small indentations and to produce a good mating seal between the two surfaces. White lead should be applied to the seat to avoid excessive cutting during grinding. In valves with cages the whole assembly must be in place to position correctly the valve plug and seat ring. A special grinding tool will have to be made which fastens onto the valve plug stem. The top ring of a double-ported valve body will usually grind faster than the bottom ring. Grinding of the bottom ring must then be continued with a polishing compound being used on the top ring. Where only one seat is being ground the other must not be left dry. Grinding will be continued until both seating surfaces are clean and free of blemishes and the plug seals when closed.

Valve packing lubrication

Semi-metallic packing requires the use of a lubricator and it is recommended for graphited asbestos and PTFE-impregnated asbestos packing. An appropriate lubricant should be used, depending upon the service conditions. The lubricator must first be completely filled with lubricant. The isolating valve (where fitted) is opened and then the lubricator bolt is rotated one complete turn. This will force lubricant into the packing box and the isolating valve should then be closed.

Stem connection and adjustment

Certain maintenance tasks require the separation of the actuator and the valve. Reassembly must be undertaken with care, and also the valve travel may require resetting or, at least, checking. Care must be taken during these operations to ensure that the valve stem is not scratched, otherwise leakage may result. Where a bellows seal bonnet is used, the stem must not be rotated during assembly or adjustment. Other types of valve and bonnet assembly may be rotated to enable small adjustments of travel. The valve plug, however, should not be in contact with the seat when any rotation is made.

Reference should be made to Figure 8.1 and 8.7 for the various parts which will now be mentioned. The valve body and actuator should be mounted and fastened together. The actuator stem must now be moved such that the valve is in its closed position, i.e. fully down for a push-down-to-close valve. The valve plug must now be moved to the closed position to contact the seat ring. The actuator should now be moved down a further 4 mm and then the connecting nut or assembly secured. The actuator should now be operated to check the travel and also to ensure that the valve plug seals before the end of actuator travel. Slight adjustments of travel may need to be made, and the connecting device usually permits this as a result of turning the stem, except where bellows seal bonnets are used. The indicator plate on the valve stem may need repositioning by loosening the locknuts and moving the plate. The valve travel should now be checked against the signal range desired. Rotary shaft valves will have the valve disc and shaft marked to enable straightforward assembly. Lever linkages are usually provided with a turnbuckle to enable fine adjustment. This is best done with the valve out of the pipeline to enable careful measurements to be taken.

CONTROL VALVE SELECTION

The selection of a control valve should be made by providing the best available combination of valve body style, material and trim construction design for the required service. The system operating pressures and capacity requirements must also be considered in selecting a control valve. When consulting a manufacturer, the following information should be available:

1. type, temperature, viscosity and specific gravity of the fluid;
2. inlet and outlet pressures at the valve;
3. the pressure drop during normal flow and shut-off;
4. inlet and outlet pipeline size and type of connections;
5. degree of superheat or existence of flashing, if known, and any noise restrictions which may exist.

When ordering a control valve, some or all of the following information will have to be given:

1. item number, valve type number, quantity and valve size according to the manufacturer's catalogue;
2. valve body construction, e.g. angle, double-port;
3. body material and end connections;
4. valve plug or disc style, guiding, port size and trim material;
5. valve plug action, e.g. direct or reverse acting, and action required on air failure, e.g. open, close or remain 'as-is';
6. flow action, i.e. flow tends to open or flow tends to close the valve;
7. bonnet style, e.g. plain or extension, and packing material to be used;
8. actuator size and any accessories required;
9. operating signal and range.

A number of these requirements have already been discussed and consideration will now be given to valve sizing, flashing and cavitation.

Valve sizing

Using a valve which is the same size as the system piping will rarely result in satisfactory control of the system. Too small a valve will not pass the necessary amount of liquid. Too large a valve may produce system instability as it attempts to control with very small changes in lift.

Bernoulli's equation for the conservation of energy is used as the basis for valve sizing. Most manufacturers use a basic liquid sizing equation:

$$Q = C_v \sqrt{\frac{\Delta p}{G}}$$

where Q = capacity through the fully open valve, in US gallons per minute, C_v = valve sizing coefficient, determined experimentally for each style and type of valve using water as the test fluid, Δp = pressure drop across the valve in p.s.i. and G = specific gravity of the fluid.

In the SI system of units, this equation is

$$Q = A_v \sqrt{\frac{\Delta p}{\varrho}}$$

where Q = volumetric flow rate through the fully open valve, in m^3/s, A_v = valve flow coefficient, Δp = pressure drop across the valve, in Pa, and ϱ = density of the fluid, in kg/m^3.

When controlling any liquid other than water, or liquids behaving like water, a viscosity correction will have to be made. Most control valve manufacturers provide information in the form of tables or charts to make this correction.

Flashing and cavitation

These are physical phenomena which tend to limit flow through a control valve and can also cause damage to the valve and adjacent piping.

As liquid flows through a restriction, e.g. the valve port, the flow stream narrows. It has its smallest cross-sectional area at a point called the vena contracta, and a considerable increase in velocity and decrease in pressure occurs here. Further downstream from the vena contracta the velocity will reduce and the pressure will increase. If the pressure at the vena contracta falls below the vapour pressure of the liquid, bubbles will form in the flowing liquid. If the pressure at the valve outlet remains below the vapour pressure of the liquid, the process is said to have 'flashed'. If the pressure downstream rises above the vapour pressure of the liquid, the bubbles will collapse or implode, producing cavitation. Both phenomena will result in erosion of the valve disc, seat and sometimes adjacent pipework. Flashing damage leaves a smooth surface while cavitation leaves a rough surface.

A valve recovery coefficient can be used in association with the pressure drop across the valve in order to correctly size a valve and avoid flashing or cavitation problems.

9 Control systems

Various control systems as found on board ship will now be described. The systems described will be representative but not necessarily the same as those found on every ship at sea. Consideration will be given first to systems fitted in a ship related to its main propulsion machinery. Various auxiliaries and their control systems are next considered. Air conditioning and refrigeration control systems are then described. Deck machinery and their control systems are examined and then finally bridge control of main machinery and propulsion systems.

BOILER AND TURBINE CONTROL SYSTEMS

The production of steam in a boiler and its subsequent use in a steam turbine and recirculation through a closed-feed system results in a variety of different control systems which will be considered in turn.

Boiler water level

A modern high pressure, high temperature watertube boiler holds a small quantity of water and produces large quantities of steam. Very careful control of the drum water level is therefore necessary. The reactions of steam and water in the drum are complicated and require a control system based on a number of measured elements.

When a boiler is operating, the water level in the gauge glass reads higher than when the boiler is shut down. This is because of the presence of steam bubbles in the water, a situation which is accepted in normal practice. If however there occurs a sudden increase in steam demand from the boiler, the pressure in the drum will fall. Some of the water present in the drum at the higher pressure will now 'flash off' and become steam. These bubbles of steam will cause the drum level to rise. The reduced mass of water in the drum will also result in more steam being produced, which will further raise the water level. This effect is known as 'swell'. A level control system which used only level as the measured value would close the feed water control valve, when it should be opening it.

When the boiler load returns to normal the drum pressure will rise and steam bubble formation will reduce, causing a fall in water level. Incoming cold feed water will further reduce steam bubble formation and what is known as 'shrinkage' of the drum level will occur.

The problems associated with swell and shrinkage are removed by the use of a second measuring element, 'steam flow'. A third element, 'feed water flow', is added to avoid problems that would occur if the feed water pressure were to vary.

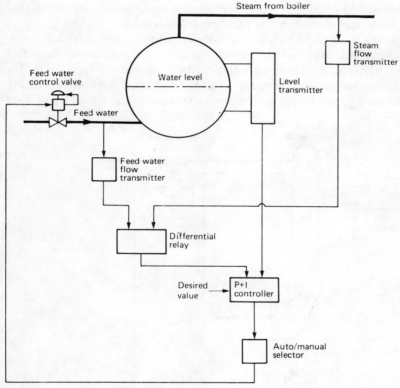

Figure 9.1 Three-element boiler water level control

A three-element control system is shown in Figure 9.1. The measuring variables or elements are 'steam flow', 'drum level' and 'feed water flow'. Since in a balanced situation steam flow must equal feed flow, these two signals are compared in a differential relay. The relay output is fed to a two-term controller and comparator into which

the measured drum level signal is also fed. Any deviation between the
desired and actual drum level and any deviation between feed and
steam flow will result in controller action to adjust the feed water
control valve. The drum level will then be returned to its correct
position.

A sudden increase in steam demand would result in a deviation
signal from the differential relay and an output signal to open the feed
water control valve. The swell effect would therefore not influence the
correct operation of the control system. For a reduction in steam
demand, an output signal to close the feed water control valve would
result, thus avoiding shrinkage effects. Any change in feed water
pressure would result in feed water control valve movement to correct
the change and maintain the correct drum level.

In the mass level feedwater control system the mass of feedwater in
the boiler is inferred from a measurement of the pressure differential
between the steam drum and the bottom of the water header. By
maintaining the mass of water present in the boiler at a constant value
then the feedwater flow is approximately equal to the steam flow. This

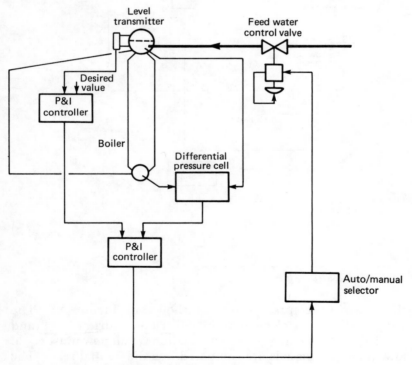

Figure 9.2 Mass/level feedwater control

will result in a good system response under transient conditions. A level control is also provided, which acts as a master signal to counteract the effect of the steeply rising steady-state characteristic of this system. In the system, shown in Figure 9.2, the measured value signal for level is compared with a desired value in the level controller. Any deviation results in an output which acts as a variable desired value for the mass controller which also receives a measured value signal of water mass, inferred from the differential pressure cell. The mass controller output signal will act upon the feedwater control valve. This control system is considered to have a performance equal to the three-element control system. It has the advantage of a simpler installation since it does not require steam flow or feed water flow measurements to be taken. It has the disadvantage of not having a steam flow signal available for other systems such as combustion control.

Steam temperature

Steam temperature control of high pressure superheated steam is necessary to avoid damage to the metals used in a steam turbine.

One method of control is shown in Figure 9.3. Steam from the primary superheater may be directed to a boiler drum attemperator

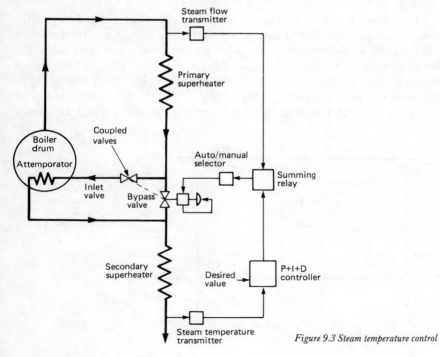

Figure 9.3 Steam temperature control

where its temperature will be reduced. This steam will then be further heated in the secondary superheater. The steam temperature leaving the secondary superheater is measured and transmitted to a three-term controller, which also acts as a comparator. Any deviation from the desired value will result in a signal to a summing relay. The other signal to the relay is from a steam flow measuring element. The relay output signal provides control of the coupled attemperator inlet and bypass valves. As a result the steam flow is proportioned between the attemperator and the straight-through line. This two-element control system can adequately deal with changing conditions. If, for example, the steam demand suddenly increased, a fall in steam temperature might occur. The steam flow element will, however, detect the load change and adjust the amount of steam attemperated to maintain the correct steam temperature.

Exhaust steam pressure

Exhaust steam for various auxiliary services may be controlled at constant pressure by appropriate operation of a surplus steam (dump) valve or a make-up steam valve. A single controller can be used to operate one valve or the other in what is known as 'split range control'.

The control arrangement is shown in Figure 9.4. The steam pressure in the auxiliary range is measured by a pressure transmitter. This signal is fed to the controller where it is compared with the desired value. The two-term controller will provide an output signal which is fed to both control valves. Each valve is operated by a different range of pressure, with a 'dead band' between the ranges so that only one valve is ever open at a time. Thus if the auxiliary range

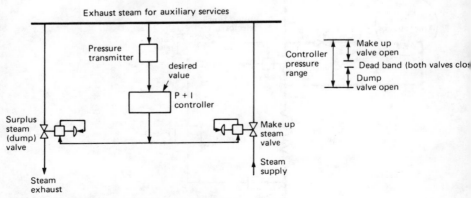

Figure 9.4 Exhaust steam pressure control

pressure is high the dump valve opens to release steam. If the pressure is low the make-up valve opens to admit steam.

This split range control principle can be applied to a number of valves if the controller output range is split appropriately.

Boiler combustion control

The essential requirement for a combustion control system is to proportion correctly the quantities of air and fuel being burnt. This will enable complete combustion, a minimum of excess air and acceptable exhaust gases. The control system must therefore measure the flow rates of fuel oil and air in order to regulate correctly their proportions.

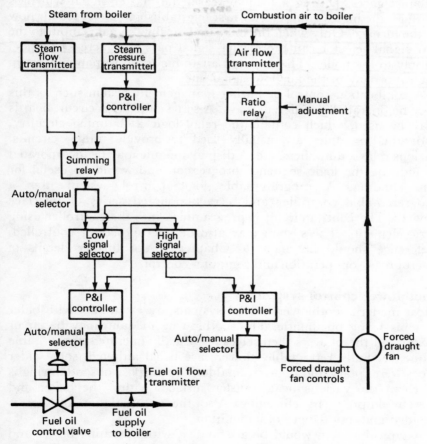

Figure 9.5 Combustion control system

A combustion control system capable of accepting rapid load changes is shown in Figure 9.5. Two control elements are used, steam flow and steam pressure. The steam pressure signal is fed to a two-term controller and is compared with the desired value. Any deviation results in a signal to the summing relay.

The steam flow signal is also fed into the summing relay. The summing relay, which may add or subtract the input signals, provides an output which represents the fuel input requirements of the boiler. This output becomes a variable desired value signal to the two-term controller in the fuel control and combustion air control loops. A high or low signal selector is present to ensure that when a load change occurs the combustion air flow is always in excess of the fuel requirements. This prevents poor combustion and black smoky exhaust gases. During a load increase, the master signal will pass through the high signal selector first to establish an increased air flow in the furnace. Only when the increased air flow signal is input to the low signal selector can the master signal pass and increase the fuel supply to the boiler. The required air-to-fuel ratio is manually set in the ratio relay in the air flow signal line.

A combustion control or burner management system such as this may be operated in different ways. A series of printed circuit boards may be used, which contain the relay logic and timing circuitry. Individual modules are usually used to provide timing circuits, various relays, amplifiers, etc. A display module may be incorporated to indicate the logic sequence progression and would be useful for fault finding. A programmable logic control system uses a programmable controller and a rack-mounted series of interface devices. The control circuit is programmed into the controller using logic elements. The system may also be microprocessor controlled. Reference should be made to Chapter 10 for further details of microprocessor operation and computer control.

Sootblower control system

Most modern sootblower control systems are electronic, with older systems being pneumatic. The sootblowing medium may be air or steam and the blowers themselves are usually operated in a suitable sequence. Fully retractable blowers are usual although some older types were rotary and non-retractable. The purpose of sootblowing is to clean the various heat transfer surfaces within the boiler and thereby improve its efficiency. Also the accumulation of soot is avoided and any danger of its ignition.

A typical system would be at standby, with operating power and control power available at the panel. All alarms would be healthy, all sootblowers would be fully retracted, the main steam valve would be shut and all drain valves would be open. With one or more of the control sequence select buttons pressed, the control sequence start button is then pressed. The 'sequence run' light is illuminated and the main steam valve opens fully. The sootblowing system pipework is now charged with steam which exits, together with any condensation, through the open drain valves. The valves remain in this position until the warming period time has elapsed and no further condensation occurs. The drain valves close as the first selected sequence is initiated. The first selected blower in this first sequence will now operate. An electric motor will move the blower forward into position, sootblowing will take place and the blower will now operate, continuing the sequence until it is finished. When the last selected blower has completed its operation the main steam valve will close and the drain valves will open. The steam is now back on standby.

This system may be controlled by a programmable logic controller or a microprocessor.

Three modes of operation are available in this system: auto, local and manual. A preference order is given to mode selection, with local control being first preference, manual control second and auto control third. This enables personnel working at, or near, the blowers to be in control of blower operation. Control sequences are usually provided to cover every required blowing pattern within the boiler. The various sequences can be selected singly or as a number of sequences in their numerical order. The sequence is generally to blow economizers or air heaters first, in order to clear a path for subsequent soot that is blown. The blowers nearest to the furnace are then blown and subsequent blowers leading to the economizers. The economizer blowers will then be operated again.

Various alarm and indication lamps and controls are provided, e.g. low steam pressure alarm, blower motor stall alarm, sequence lamps, etc. The operator is thus fully aware at all times of the system status.

Deaerator level control

This is an important level control system in a steam plant. When a vessel is steaming at full speed the boiler will contain a minimum mass of water, due to the presence of large numbers of steam bubbles. If the speed is reduced then the boiler must receive more water to maintain its correct operating level, as many of the steam bubbles will collapse. A storage tank containing hot deaerated feed water is therefore necessary to supply to or receive water from the boiler. This tank is normally integrated with the deaerator and its level is automatically controlled. There will also be feed supply variations to

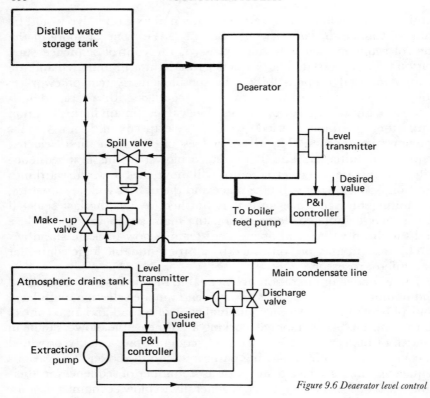

Figure 9.6 Deaerator level control

correspond with the steam supply variations due to changing turbine
loads.

One method of providing this level control is shown in Figure 9.6. A
differential pressure cell is used to measure the water level in the
deaerator and transmits a signal to a P+I controller. The controller
provides a signal to one of two valves which operate in split range
control. If the water level in the deaerator rises, due to an increase in
boiler load, the spill valve will open and water will pass to the distilled
water storage tank. If the deaerator water level falls, due to the boiler
requiring more feed water, then the make-up valve will open to pass
water from the distilled water tank to the atmospheric drain tank. A
dead band ensures that both valves will not be open at once. The
atmospheric drain tank level will thus rise and the water will be
pumped out into the main condensate line. A pressure cell and P+I
controller are used to provide level control on the atmospheric drains
tank. The discharge valve from the extraction pump will be suitably
throttled by the controller. High and low level alarms are also fitted to
this tank.

Feed recirculation control

The boiler feed water from the condenser acts as a cooling medium for the air ejectors and other units in the closed feed system. The feed water in turn is heated as it flows. During reduced power operations or manoeuvring the supply of feed water may not be sufficient to perform the cooling function adequately. Some recirculation of feed water back to the condenser is therefore required.

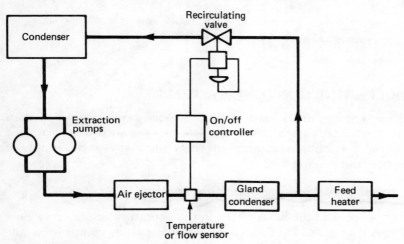

Figure 9.7 Feedwater recirculation control

One method of automatically achieving this is shown in Figure 9.7. A flow or temperature sensor is placed in the main feed water line and passes a signal to the on/off controller which, in turn, operates the recirculating valve. If the feed water flow rate is too low or the temperature is too high, the recirculating valve will open to establish a sufficient flow through the system.

Gland steam control

Steam is prevented from leaking out of the rotor high pressure end, and air is prevented from entering the low pressure end, by the use of glands. A combination of mechanical glands and a gland sealing system is usual.

The gland steam control system maintains a constant pressure in the receiver, see Figure 9.8. A three-way valve is controlled by the pressure within the receiver. The valve operates to admit low pressure steam into the receiver when the pressure falls during reduced load operation. During full load operation the valve will dump steam to the gland condenser in order to release the excess pressure.

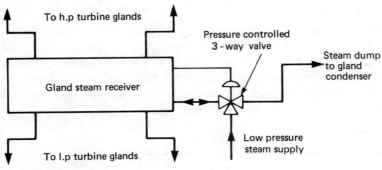

Figure 9.8 Gland steam control

DIESEL ENGINE CONTROL SYSTEMS

The diesel engine, in its many forms, is more easily controlled than turbine machinery. Various systems will be examined that deal with the control of starting, stopping and reversing and also the supply of lubrication and cooling media.

Slow speed diesel engine operating system

A variety of control media are used in the operating system for a slow speed diesel engine. These include lubricating oil, compressed air, and a variety of mechanical linkages and drives.

For starting, the direction of rotation is set by the telegraph reply lever in the system shown in Figure 9.9. This results in movement of a linkage, which positions the reversing valve appropriately. Control oil can then flow through the safety interlock and then to the starting lever blocking device. The starting lever is then free to move. The control oil will also have moved a slide valve to supply oil to the cut-out servomotor. This servomotor frees the fuel control linkages. The fuel or speed setting lever will have been set at a position between 2.5 and 3.0 on a full range of 10. The auxiliary load indicator is now free to move to the same setting and the governor will control the fuel supply to the pumps.

The starting lever is held in the OFF position by a spring. When it is moved to the START position, a pilot air valve is lifted. With the turning gear out, compressed air can pass from the receiver through the blocking valve and into the pilot valve. This pilot air can now pass to the starting air control valves and to the actuating valve of the automatic starting air shut-off valve. This shut-off valve now opens, admits starting air to the manifold, to the starting air valves and to the control valves. The control valves are forced into contact with the

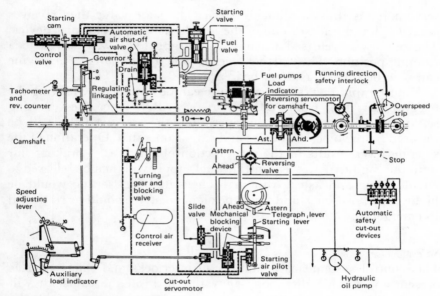

Figure 9.9 Slow-speed diesel control system

starting cam and a starting air valve will be opened and followed by others in the appropriate sequence for the engine rotation desired. The engine rotates under the action of the starting air, fires, and the starting lever is returned to the OFF position by the spring. The pilot valve closes, the line is vented, and the starting air control valve will then move away from the cam. The starting air valves will then cease to operate. The automatic shut-off valve will also close in the absence of pilot air, and the starting air manifold pressure will gradually be relieved through leakage points in the starting air valves.

With the engine running ahead it can be made to run astern by first bringing the telegraph reply lever to STOP. The fuel or speed setting lever is also brought back to about position 3.0. With the telegraph lever at STOP, the starting lever is fixed in the OFF position by the blocking device. The reversing valve is also brought into the stop position and the oil pressure to the reversing servomotor on the camshaft is relieved. The slide valve then operates under the action of its spring and the cut-out servomotor is relieved of pressure. The various mechanical linkages now move to cut off fuel injection.

The oil pressure beneath the piston of the blocking device is relieved when the slide valve moves and the starting lever is now held in position by two interlocks. Once the engine speed has dropped sufficiently, the telegraph lever is positioned ASTERN. The reversing servomotor is thus positioned astern. The slide valve then receives control oil and releases one of the interlocks on the blocking device. The other was released when the telegraph lever was moved to a running position. The starting lever is now free to move. The engine can now be started as described earlier.

A more rapid reversing manoeuvre can be obtained by moving the telegraph straight from AHEAD to ASTERN. Once the reversing servomotor has completed its operation, the starting lever will be released by the blocking device and can be operated. Operation of the starting lever results in the introduction of astern (i.e. braking) air until the engine rotates astern. The fuel supply will then be released to enable firing and astern running. The initial fuel setting would be higher, say position 5, and this type of manoeuvre should be restricted to emergencies.

Safety devices

This control system has a number of interlocks and safety devices present. A running direction safety interlock on the camshaft will ensure that the engine is rotating in the direction required by the telegraph lever, before any fuel is admitted. Safety cut-outs will operate in the event of loss of lubricating oil pressure, cooling water supplies or overheating. The engine cannot start if any of these faults exist since the blocking device will hold the starting lever. If the engine is running the slide valve will operate and the cut-out servomotor will cut off the fuel supply to the engine. These cut-outs can be overridden in an emergency so that the engine will continue to operate. An overspeed trip is located at the end of the camshaft. This mechanical device will cut off the fuel supply in the event of overspeeding. Emergency control arrangements are also provided which enable engine starting, direction selection and speed setting without any control media other than levers.

Recent developments

The control system described above is that of a Sulzer RND engine. More recent engine designs from this manufacturer, and others, have replaced many of the mechanical valves, e.g. starting lever blocking devices, with a number of circuits which use pneumatic logic elements. These logic elements were, at first, connected together by individual copper pipes. Use is now made of a pneumatic 'printed circuit'. This is a composite plastic sheet with pre-machined integral connecting passages for the pneumatic logic elements. Direction selection is, on some engines, obtained by a separate lever, rather than using the telegraph reply lever. Engine starting may be a press-button instead of a lever, but will still be suitably interlocked to avoid incorrect operation. The overspeed unit is currently a tachogenerator which, when operated, will cut off the fuel supply.

The principal mechanical items, e.g. the starting air control valves, the automatic shut-off valve, the camshaft reversing servomotor, the reversing valve and the safety running direction interlock have all been retained in the latest range of Sulzer engines. Use is still made of the same three control media, e.g. mechanical linkages, compressed air and hydraulic oil. If anything, fewer mechanical linkages now exist, although those used for emergency operation will always be retained. The pneumatic system is two separate circuits, one for starting air and one for control air. The starting air system has changed little through the various engine designs. The control air system is confined to the normal control of engine direction selection, starting and speed control and associated functions for engine room and bridge remote control. The hydraulic oil control system includes the engine direction control and safety interlocks to prevent almost every possibility of incorrect engine operation. Lubricating oil is used because of the need for engine shut-down in the event of loss of lubricating oil supply. This is also the safest medium in that air leakages into the crankcase could cause explosions under adverse conditions.

Lubricating oil temperature control

This method of temperature control uses a single measuring device located at the oil inlet to the engine, see Figure 9.10. A three-way valve is provided in the oil supply line to the cooler to enable bypassing, if required. The cooler is provided with a full flow of sea water, which is not controlled by the system. The temperature sensing element on the lubricating oil inlet to the engine provides a signal to a two-term (P+I) controller. The controller is provided with a desired value and any deviation between it and the input signal will result in an output to the three-way control valve. If the temperature is low, more oil will bypass the cooler and its temperature will therefore increase. If the temperature is high, then less oil will be bypassed, more will be cooled and the temperature will fall. A simple system such as this can only be used after careful analysis of the plant conditions and the correct sizing of equipment fitted.

The lubricating oil system will also have a low level alarm on the drain tank and a high differential pressure alarm fitted across the duplex filters. A pressure switch located after the pumps will provide

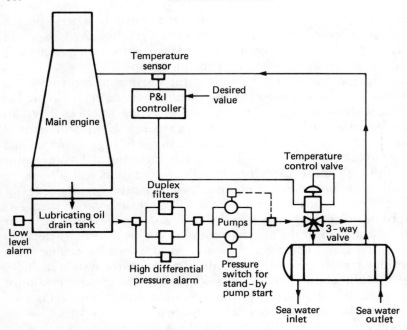

Figure 9.10 Lubricating oil temperature control

an automatic start-up of the standby pump in the event of low
pressure.

Cooling water temperature control

Accurate control of diesel engine cooling water is a requirement for
efficient operation. This can be achieved by a single controller under
steady load conditions, but because of the fluctuating situation during
manoeuvring a more complex system is required.

The control system shown in Figure 9.11 uses a combination of
cascade and split range control. Cascade control is where the output
from a master controller is used to adjust automatically the desired
value of a slave controller. It is used in order to rapidly detect load
changes in the engine and provide precise temperature control. It will
also rapidly detect and react to changes in sea water temperature.
Cascade control was discussed earlier in Chapter 6. The master
controller obtains an outlet temperature reading from the engine
which is compared with a desired value. Any deviation acts to adjust
the desired value of the slave controller. The slave controller also
receives a signal from the water inlet temperature sensor which it
compares with its latest desired value. Any deviation results in a

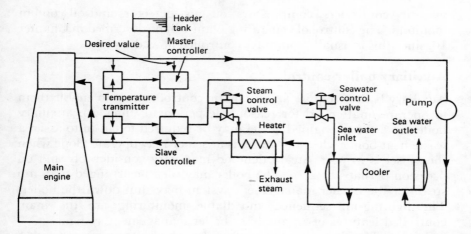

Figure 9.11 Cooling water temperature control

signal to two control valves arranged for split range control. If the cooling water temperature is high, the sea water valve is opened to admit more cooling water to the cooler. If the cooling water temperature is low, then the sea water valve will be closed in. If the sea water valve is fully closed, then the steam inlet valve will be opened to heat the water. Both master and slave controllers will be identical instruments and will be two-term (P+I) in action.

Fuel valve cooling water temperature control

This independent system is necessary in order to avoid possible contamination from leaking fuel oil. The controller obtains a temperature signal which is sensed at the water inlet to the fuel valves. It then operates two valves which are arranged for split range control. One valve admits steam to a heater and is used when warming-through the engine. The other valve is a three-way type which will vary the amount of water which enters or bypasses the cooler in a similar arrangement to that described earlier for lubricating oil cooling. A dead band ensures that the two valves cannot be open together.

AUXILIARY EQUIPMENT CONTROL SYSTEMS

A number of items of auxiliary equipment and their associated control systems will now be described. These include auxiliary boilers, viscosity controllers, compressors, oil mist detectors and oil content monitors. The control of generating plant will be described in Chapter 10, since this is usually computer controlled nowadays.

Auxiliary boiler control

Auxiliary boilers require an automatic control system to enable them to operate unattended for reasonable periods of time. An auxiliary boiler on a diesel engined vessel may be required to cut-in to assist a waste heat boiler when the vessel is at sea or may operate alone when the vessel is in port. Steam demand may vary considerably and on occasion perhaps be zero. The boiler may then be arranged to dump steam or the burner management system may shut down the boiler. The lighting-up sequence and flame monitoring are the main controlled features of an auxiliary boiler management system.

An on-off system will now be describd which uses a burner with a fixed capacity. When light-up is required the closure of the mains switch energizes the fuel oil pump and the heater, see Figure 9.12(a). The oil recirculates back to the pump suction due to the position of the solenoid operated changeover valve. The high temperature cut-out will disconnect the heater circuit should the oil become too hot. When the fuel oil reaches a suitable temperature the low

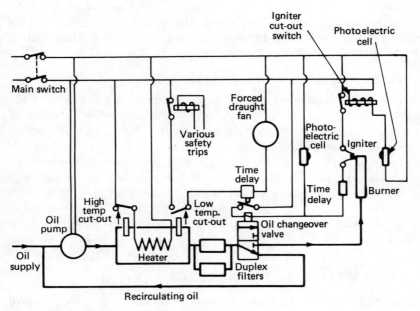

Figure 9.12 Auxiliary boiler control: (a) on-off system

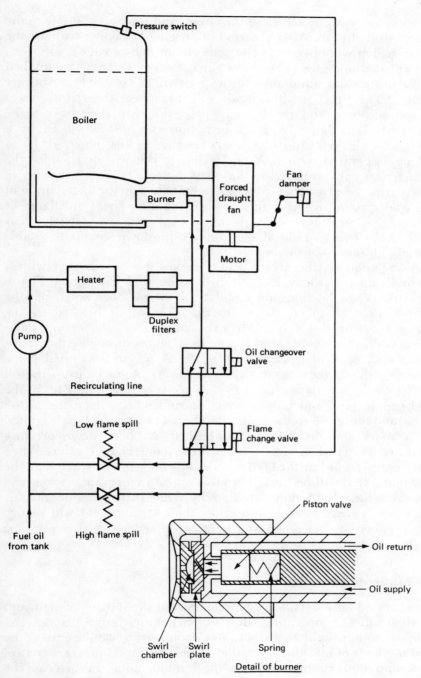

Pressure switch

Boiler

Forced draught fan

Fan damper

Burner

Motor

Heater

Duplex filters

Pump

Oil changeover valve

Recirculating line

Low flame spill

Flame change valve

High flame spill

Fuel oil from tank

Piston valve

Oil return

Oil supply

Swirl chamber

Swirl plate

Spring

Detail of burner

Figure 9.12 (b) high-low flame system

temperature cut-out will close the circuit and provide a supply to the forced draught fan. After a period of purging the boiler with air the delay switch will operate to close the circuit and provide a supply to the solenoid-operated changeover valve. Fuel oil will now be supplied to the burner and simultaneously a spark will be created at the burner igniter. The timer in this circuit will disconnect the spark after a reasonable time and the light-up procedure will then have to be repeated. If a flame is established, however, this is sensed by a photo-electric cell and the spark circuit is disconnected by a solenoid-operated switch. A photo-electric cell will de-energize the changeover valve solenoid in the event of flame failure. A number of safety trips are also provided which operate to stop the forced draught fan and change over the fuel to recirculating. These are flame or combustion air failure, high steam pressure and low water level. A time delay exists in the flame failure shut-down circuit to enable initial lighting-up of the boiler.

A variation on the above system makes use of a burner with a spring-loaded piston valve and two flame spill valves, see Figure 9.12(b). When heating and circulating, the oil does not reach the burner swirl chamber. Access to this chamber is blocked by the spring-loaded piston valve. When the changeover valve operates and directs oil to the burner the oil now recirculates through either a low flame spill or a high flame spill valve. A solenoid-operated flame change valve determines which is used. At initial light-up the oil passes to the low flame spill valve. A pressure now builds up in the fuel supply pipe and burner which is sufficient to open the piston valve and admit oil to the swirl chamber. The atomized oil is ignited by a spark and the flame is established. A boiler steam pressure operated switch then acts to control the flame change valve. When steam pressure is low the high flame spill will be in use, when high the low flame spill will be used. The steam pressure operated switch also provides forced draught fan flap movements to provide the air quantities necessary for combustion. This arrangement will reduce the number of shut-down and lighting-up sequences that must be performed by the control system.

Compressor operation

Compressed air must always be available for the starting of main and auxiliary diesels, operating whistles, pneumatic control devices, etc. Its provision, usually by two or three compressors, can be ensured by two methods of machine operation. These are on-off pressure control and continuous running with loading and unloading. In each case the

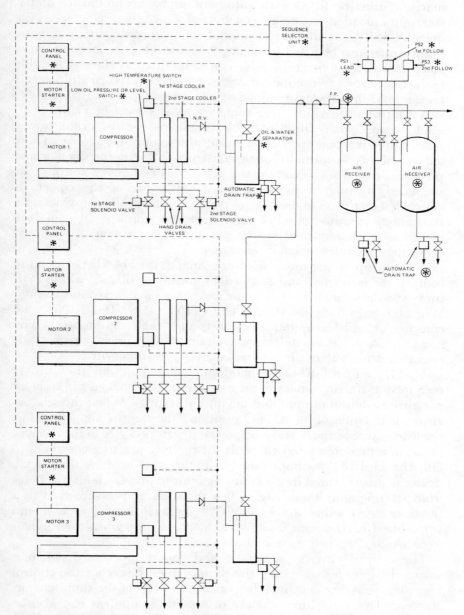

Figure 9.13 Compressor control (PS: pressure switch. NRV: non-return valve. FP: fusible plug.)

machine must be fitted with automatic unloaders to ensure that it starts up unloaded, i.e. no air is delivered. Once running at speed the machine will 'load' and begin to produce compressed air. Automatic drains must also be fitted to ensure the removal of moisture from the stage coolers. A non-return valve is usually fitted as close as possible to the discharge valve of the compressor to prevent return airflow. It is an essential fitting where unloaders are used.

A control system for three compressors is shown in Figure 9.13. Each compressor is fitted with two solenoid-operated drain valves, one for the first stage cooler and one for the second stage cooler. These valves, being of normally open construction, vent the coolers and pressure spaces of the compressor while it is stationary and provide unloaded starting. Periodic automatic draining of the coolers is controlled by timers in the control panel. The controller provides auto continuous running, hand or auto start and stop operation of each compressor. A sequence switch permits the selection of lead and following machines or hand operation.

With the operating mode selector switch in the HAND position the compressor is started and stopped by means of the START/STOP press switches located on the motor starter or at a remote station. With the selection of AUTO CONTINUOUS RUNNING, the compressor will automatically start and run continuously. The compressor will load and unload automatically since the solenoid-operated drain valves are controlled by a pressure switch.

AUTO START-STOP operation will result in the LEAD compressor starting and stopping at the predetermined air receiver pressure switch minimum and maximum settings. When the selector switch is in either of the AUTO positions, the compressor selected as the lead machine starts and loads when the air pressure in the receiver drops to a predetermined value. If the receiver pressure continues to fall, the FOLLOW compressors will start and load. A time delay device is incorporated in the control circuit to prevent both machines from starting simultaneously. When the receiver pressure rises to a predetermined value the FOLLOW compressors will unload and stop. The LEAD compressor will unload and stop when the receiver pressure has reached its maximum value.

The control unit is pneumatic and contains pressure switches, solenoid valves for operating the drain valves, relays for the control logic, transformers and time delay relays to prevent the simultaneous starting of two machines. Safety protection equipment can also be incorporated in the control unit. This provides shut-down, lock-out and an alarm lamp in the event of low lubricating oil pressure or high temperature.

Heavy fuel oil separation

Heavy fuel oil presents various problems in its handling, cleaning and ultimate combustion. Changes in refinery techniques are resulting in quality changes in the heavy fuel oil being supplied to ships. These quality changes will now be considered in so far as they affect the pretreatment and cleaning of the oil. The major change is the increase in density which has required a redesigning of the conventional centrifuge. The generally accepted maximum density limit for purifier operation is $991 \, kg/m^3$ at 15°C. Correct separation is dependent upon the interface between oil and water being correct inside the bowl. This interface position is controlled by a suitable gravity disc and it is this disc which sets the upper density limit for purification.

In the ALCAP separation system the separator has no gravity disc. The self-cleaning separator normally operates as a clarifier. Clean oil is discharged from the oil outlet and separated sludge and water collect at the periphery of the bowl. When the separated water reaches the disc stack, some water will escape with the cleaned oil. The increase in water content is immediately sensed by the water transducer which is installed in the clean oil outlet, see Figure 9.14.

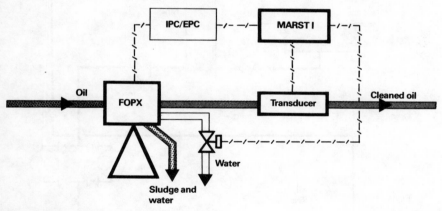

Figure 9.14 Fuel oil separation control

The signals from the water transducer are transmitted to the MARST 1 microprocessor. At a predetermined water content the microprocessor will begin the automatic discharge of water either through the sludge ports of the bowl or the water drain valve. The water and sludge will be discharged from the bowl as long as the sludge discharge is not more than once in 15 minutes. If the water reaches the disc stack in less than 15 minutes after a sludge discharge it is discharged through the water drain valve.

The separator in the system is neither a clarifier nor a purifier. It operates similarly to a clarifier but water can be discharged via a water paring disc when the water drain valve is opened. The water transducer makes a measurement based on capacitance. An inner and an outer concentric pipe are insulated from one another and form a circular capacitor through which the oil flows. The transducer registers current changes due to variations in water content. An oscillator and a test control card are housed in a box fitted to the transducer and the unit requires no calibration. The microprocessor interprets the signals from the water transducer and controls the discharge of water from the separator. Also the operation of the transducer is checked every six seconds by the microprocessor, which can be linked up with an external computer.

The presence of catalyst fines is another fuel quality problem. Catalysts are used in the refining process, from which small particles or fines break off. These fines remain in the fuel and must be removed

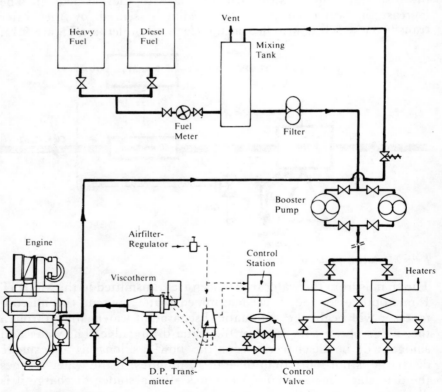

Figure 9.15 Viscosity control

by separation. The ALCAP system has shown significant improvements in separation efficiency with regard to catalyst fines.

Viscosity control

The measuring unit used in viscosity control has been described in an earlier chapter. The actual system to bring about automatic viscosity control will now be considered.

A typical system is shown in Figure 9.15. The differential pressure signal from the measuring unit is fed to a transmitter and then to a control station, i.e. P+I controller. Any deviation from the desired value within the controller will bring about a signal to the control valve. The control valve movement will result in either an increase or decrease in the steam supply to the fuel oil heaters. This will result in either an increase or decrease in the fuel viscosity. In order to obtain a stable control of viscosity the measuring unit should be located close to the heater outlet flange.

Oil mist detector

The presence of oil mist in the crankcase of an engine is the result of oil vaporization caused by a hot spot. Explosive conditions can result if a build-up of oil mist is allowed. The oil mist detector, working on the principle that oil mist density is proportional to optical obscurity, samples the oil mist in the crankcase in a regular repetitive sequence. The sample is measured by passing it through a measuring chamber that has a light source at one end and a photo-cell at the other. The output signal from the photo-cell represents oil mist and is compared with threshold levels set during commissioning. If the thresholds are exceeded an alarm indicates the need for an engine slow down and an immediate investigation of engine condition.

The flow system for this microprocessor controlled unit is shown in Figure 9.16. Microprocessors are described in Chapter 10. Initially a supply of air is passed through the measuring chamber and the signal from the photo-electric cell is stored in the data memory, as a reference. Each of the sample valves is now opened in turn and the output signal for each is stored in the memory. The average value of this set of data is then calculated. All subsequent sampling will now result in the new average value being compared with the previous average. If the value is greater this is then compared with a threshold which was set during commissioning. If the threshold is exceeded a purge cycle is undertaken to check the value and, if still excessive, an alarm is given. Where the value is not excessive it is used to update the average, which is then displayed. Where no excessive level is

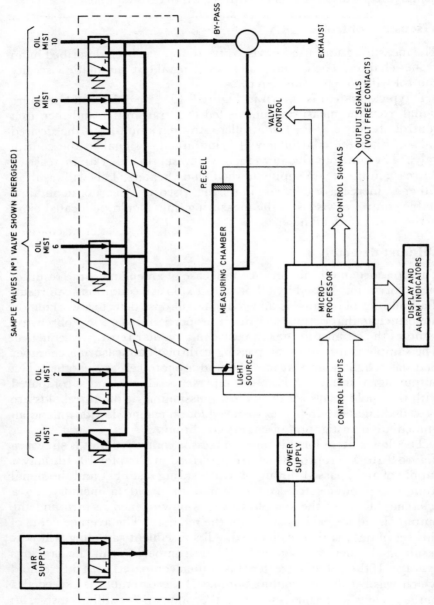

Figure 9.16 Crankcase oil mist detection

found the next sample valve opens and the procedure is repeated. At intervals of 10 minutes, the air supply valve opens and a new reference signal is generated. This will ensure compensation for the presence of oil mist on the optical surfaces, temperature variations and changes in output from the light source. Once the reference signal has been memorized the sampling cycle continues from where it was broken off.

Oil content monitoring system

International legislation relating to oil pollution is now very stringent in the limits set for oil discharge. Clean water, suitable for discharge in coastal waters, is defined as that containing less oil than 15 parts per million. Gravity type oil/water separators cannot meet these requirements unless operated in conjunction with some form of filter. The legislation further requires a continuously operating monitoring unit and an alarm system to warn of excessive oil levels.

One type of suitable monitoring system for bilge water discharge is shown in Figure 9.17. When the bilge pump is started the 'Oilcon' monitoring unit is also brought into action. This unit will function automatically once the alarm level has been set at either 15 or 100 p.p.m. This is to suit the area of coastal or ocean waters into which the bilge water will be discharged. Also the sampling point must be selected. The monitoring unit will then first flush itself with fresh water to clear all pipelines and the measuring chamber. The operation of the measuring unit has been described in an earlier chapter on instrumentation. Sampling of the bilge water then takes place from the selected sampling point. The amount of oil present is displayed on the monitor and also on the recorder. Where the level is acceptable the overboard discharge valve is now opened and the bilge water is pumped overboard. If the monitored oil level rises to an excessive level, the monitor will simultaneously initiate audible and visual alarms, divert the bilge water discharge to a settling or slop tank and continue to monitor the recirculated bilge water. The bilge pump must then be stopped manually. When the bilge pump is stopped the monitoring unit closes down after flushing itself with clean water.

The discharge/recirculating valve is pneumatically actuated as a result of action by electro-pneumatic equipment within the monitoring unit cabinet. The sampling valve and the clean water flushing valve are also pneumatically operated. The system can be further arranged with a manual override, remote discharge/recirculating valve position indication and complete system start-up as a result of a high level bilge alarm.

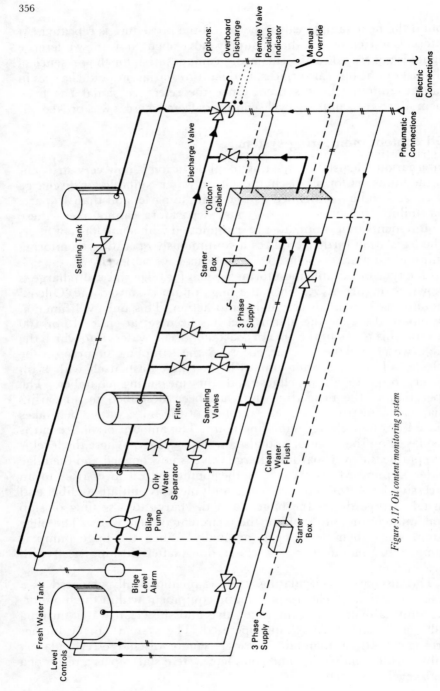

Options:
Overboard
Discharge
Remote Valve
Position Indicator

Manual
Override

Electric
Connections

Pneumatic
Connections

Discharge Valve

Settling Tank

"Oilcon"
Cabinet

Starter
Box

3 Phase
Supply

Filter

Sampling Valves

Oily Water
Separator

Clean Water
Flush

Bilge Pump

Starter
Box

Bilge Level
Alarm

3 Phase Supply

Fresh Water Tank

Level Controls

Figure 9.17 Oil content monitoring system

A similar type of unit can be used to monitor ballast water discharge from oil tankers. The use of such a device is required by international legislation, which limits oil discharge to 60 litres during one nautical mile of travel in the ocean. Coastal discharges must again be less than 15 p.p.m.

REFRIGERATION AND AIR-CONDITIONING CONTROL

Refrigeration is a process wherein the temperature of a space or its contents is reduced and maintained below that of their surroundings. Air conditioning is the control of temperature and humidity in a space together with the circulation, filtering and refreshing of the air. The control aspects of these processes will now be examined.

The basic refrigeration cycle operates by the controlled flow of high pressure liquid refrigerant into a chamber called an evaporator. The liquid refrigerant expands into a gas and the energy for this expansion comes from the gas itself. The temperature of the gas falls and, provided the temperature difference is large enough, heat will be transferred from the space which is to be cooled. The gas then returns to the compressor for recompression. Before it is released into the evaporator the compressed gas is cooled and liquefied in a condenser. The complete cycle as used for a small refrigerated cargo space or provision room is shown in Figure 9.18. The twin circuit arrangement for each evaporator provides flexibility and duplication in the event of one system failing. The back pressure valve maintains a minimum constant pressure or temperature in the evaporator when working a space in high temperature conditions, to prevent under-cooling of the

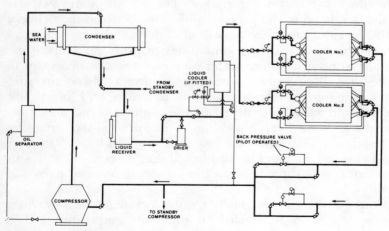

Figure 9.18 Refrigeration cycle control

cargo. The liquid cooler is necessary where an abnormal high static head has to be overcome between the machinery and the coolers. In this vessel the liquid is sub-cooled to prevent it flashing off before reaching the thermostatic expansion valve.

The expansion valve or regulator meters the flow of refrigerant from the high pressure to the low pressure side of the system. It may be of the thermostatic type as shown in Figure 9.19. The bulb senses the

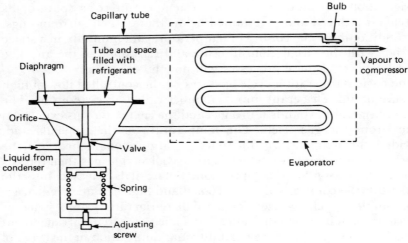

Figure 9.19 Thermostatic expansion valve

temperature of the refrigerant at the outlet from the evaporator and opens or closes the valve accordingly. The design of the valve is critical and is related to the pressure difference between the delivery and expansion side. Therefore it is essential that the delivery pressure is maintained at or near the maximum design pressure. Thus, if the vessel is operating in cold sea water temperatures it is necessary to recirculate the cooling water to maintain the correct delivery pressure from the condenser. If this is not done, the valve will 'hunt' and refrigerant liquid may be returned to the compressor suction. It is usual to have a solenoid valve in the liquid line prior to the expansion valve or regulator. This shuts or opens as determined by a thermostat in the cooled space. It may also be used to shut off certain circuits in the evaporator when the compressor is operating on part-load conditions.

Refrigerated cargo vessels usually require a system which provides for various spaces to be cooled to different temperatures. The arrangements used can be considered in three parts: the central

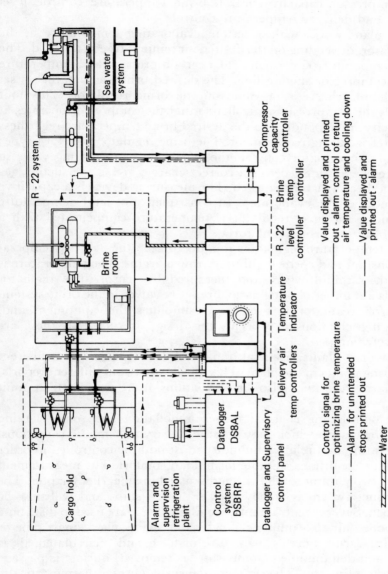

Figure 9.20 Cargo refrigeration control

primary refrigerating plant, the brine circulating system, and the air circulating system for cooling the cargo in the hold. The complete system can be seen in Figure 9.20. The control regulating functions are compressor capacity control, brine temperature control, level control and delivery temperature control.

The plant works with a certain evaporating temperature in the evaporator, depending on the desired air temperature in the hold. The brine temperature corresponds to a certain pressure and temperature in the compressor suction line. The desired brine temperature is set with thumb-wheels as a value on the brine regulator. This unit controls the compressor controller so that the compressor operates at a capacity corresponding to the desired brine temperature regardless of the refrigerating requirement. The brine regulator is of P+I type.

The level regulator controls the expansion or regulating valve so that the evaporator receives a correct charge, giving the suction gas the superheat which is required. The measuring device is a capacitive transducer in the evaporator. In consequence of large temperature differences, the level regulator is temperature compensated with a signal from the brine regulator.

The temperature regulator attempts to keep the delivery temperature constant and correct within narrow margins. The temperature is set with a thumb-wheel and measured by sensor. The regulator controls a number of pneumatic three-way valves in the brine system. An on/off regulator is used as it simplifies the equipment and, although oscillations can occur, the design is such that these are effectively damped.

In modern plants, use is also made of data-loggers to log different measuring points in the plant. This device writes out different reports, and alarm recorders also list deviations from programmed limit values.

Air conditioning is usual in accommodation and some working spaces for vessels which may operate in varying climatic conditions. Temperature and relative humidity must both be controlled in order to provide conditions suitable for human comfort. The measurement of these two parameters has been discussed in an earlier chapter. The single duct system is widely used on cargo ships and will now be described. Several central units, see Figure 9.21, are used to distribute conditioned air to a number of cabins or spaces via a single pipe or duct. In warm climates a mixture of fresh and recirculated air is cooled and dehumidified (some water is removed) during its passage over the cooling coil. The refrigeration system uses a thermostatically controlled regulating valve. The cooling effect of the unit may need to be reduced if the demand is low and the hot gas bypass provides this

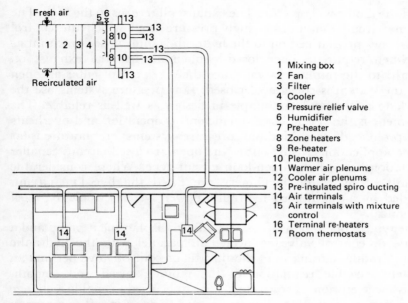

Fresh air

Recirculated air

1 Mixing box
2 Fan
3 Filter
4 Cooler
5 Pressure relief valve
6 Humidifier
7 Pre-heater
8 Zone heaters
9 Re-heater
10 Plenums
11 Warmer air plenums
12 Cooler air plenums
13 Pre-insulated spiro ducting
14 Air terminals
15 Air terminals with mixture control
16 Terminal re-heaters
17 Room thermostats

Figure 9.21 Air-conditioning control

facility. In cold climates the air is humidified by steam jets which will be controlled by a humidity sensor and controller (humidistat). Heating of the air may be by steam, hot water or electrical heaters using a temperature sensor and controller (thermostat). Within the controlled space, e.g. a cabin, control is by variation of the volume flow of air.

HYDRAULIC DECK MACHINERY CONTROL

The operations of mooring, cargo handling and anchor handling all involve controlled pulls or lifts using chain cables, wire or hemp ropes. The drive force and control arrangements adopted will influence these operations. Hydraulic equipment is being increasingly used and the systems used together with their control will now be considered.

Hydraulic systems are made up of an oil tank, pumps, control valve, hydraulic motor and pipework. The oil tank and pump are common to all equipment, acting as a central pumping unit, employing either low or medium pressure oil supplies.

The open-loop circuit takes oil from the tank and pumps it into the hydraulic motor. A control valve is positioned in parallel with the motor. When it is open the motor is stationary; when throttled or closed the motor will operate. The exhaust oil returns to the tank. The live line circuit maintains a high pressure from which the control valve draws pressurized oil to the hydraulic motor in series with it as and when required. The closed-loop circuit has the exhaust oil returned to the pump suction. Since the oil does not enter an open tank, the system is considered closed. Low pressure systems use the open-loop circuit and are simple in design as well as reliable. The equipment is, however, large, inefficient in operation and overheats after prolonged use. Medium pressure systems are favoured for marine applications, using either the open or closed circuit. Smaller installations are of the open-loop circuit type. Where considerable amounts of hydraulic machinery are fitted the live line circuit, provided by a centralized hydraulic power system, would be most economical.

One type of open-loop circuit has a fixed displacement pump and a throttle or control valve connected in parallel with the hydraulic motor. Gradual closing in of the throttle or control valve permits an infinitely variable regulation of the motor's speed and smooth, stepless acceleration. A separate valve can be used to enable a change of direction of oil flow to allow the motor to drive in either direction and will prevent the motor being driven by the load when switching or positioned in neutral. A multiposition valve is usual, which provides, for example in the case of a winch, hoist, lower and stop positions. Other items in the system will include an expansion tank, pressure control valves and a filter.

One arrangement of a closed-loop system uses variable delivery hydraulic pumps and fixed delivery motors. Infinitely variable speed control of the motor is therefore achieved by varying the pump output volume. The pumping unit operates continuously at constant speed, even in a zero-delivery situation. A small booster pump is used to keep the system charged with oil at a fixed pressure. Reversal of the motor is achieved by a continuous movement of the pump control from forward, through neutral, to reverse. It is not possible for the load to drive the motor with this arrangement. An expansion tank, pressure control valves and a filter are also included in the system.

In shipboard applications, where many different items of equipment may be operated at once, individual units would be uneconomical and a ring main or central supply system would be used. Where the open-loop system is employed, several fixed displacement pumps are used together with automatic flow control. The automatic flow control combines the deliveries of a number of pumps to meet the maximum flow requirements or selects only one pump for a high pressure duty. If a closed-loop system with variable capacity pumps is used, it feeds a high pressure manifold. The number of pumps in use is determined by the load and each would be automatically switched on or off. The high pressure manifold would act as a ring main to supply all hydraulic services on the ship. The operation of either system can be centrally controlled from a suitable location.

CARGO TANK VALVE CONTROL

Cargo pumps and piping systems are installed on tankers to discharge and load the liquid cargo. Separate ballast pumping systems are also used for ballast-only tanks which are filled during ballast voyages. Most piping systems use several ring mains along the tank length, with branches off to the individual tanks. Several cargo pumps are used and by various arrangements of the valves in the system any pump could discharge any tank. Isolating valves, usually in pairs, can also enable a particular 'parcel' of oil to be separately loaded and discharged without contamination. The control and operation of these many valves is usually hydraulic and will now be examined.

The hydraulic ring main employs a system similar to that described earlier for deck machinery. Actuators have been described in an earlier chapter. Control arrangements for the operation of the actuator can be one of two types. Manual control using hydraulic valves ensures a positive opening or closing action of the valve but results in a large control panel. Alternatively, explosion-proof solenoid valves may be mounted on the deck near to the valve and an electric push-button in the control room would be used for valve operation. Valve position indication is an essential requirement of any cargo valve control system. This can be achieved in many ways, such as using indicating cylinders whose pistons operate limit switches, pneumatic bellows which indicate according to the air pressure present due to actuator movement, or, where permitted, electrical indication from actuator-operated potentiometers.

A central cargo valve control system would be based upon the control console, see Figure 9.22. In the system shown, valve actuation control and position indication is accomplished electrically. The valve actuating medium is hydraulic but others can be used. The various types of valves have either linear or rotary actuators. A hydraulic power pack provides the necessary pressurized oil supply with associated control equipment. A pneumatic tank level indicating panel is shown, although this could be an electronic unit supplied by float gauges, which were described in an earlier chapter.

364

1 Control console, pneumatic, hydraulic, electric or various combinations.
2 Globe or angle valves, complete with hydraulic actuator, electro/hydraulic operation, electrical indication.
3 Pneumatic tank and/or draft level indication.
4 Gate valves complete with hydraulic actuator, electro/hydraulic operation. Electrical indication.
5 Valve chest complete with pneumatic actuator, pneumatic operation and indication.
6 Hydraulic power pack and control valves.
7 Butterfly valves complete with pneumatic actuator, pneumatic operation and indication.
8 Butterfly valves complete with hydraulic actuator, electro/hydraulic operation. Electrical indication.
9 Globe or angle valves complete with pneumatic actuator, pneumatic operation and indication.

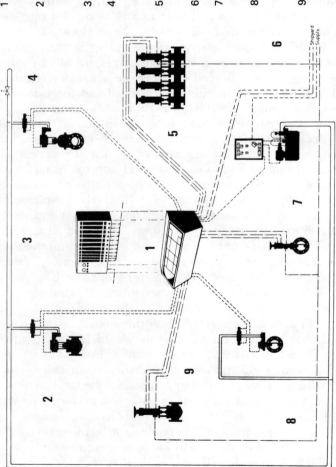

Figure 9.22 Central cargo valve control

BRIDGE CONTROL

Where machinery is operated from a machinery space this will be done by a trained engineer. The various preparatory steps and logical timed sequences of events, which an engineer will undertake, cannot be expected to occur when equipment is operated from the bridge. Bridge control must therefore have built into the system appropriate circuits to provide the correct timing, logic and sequence. There must

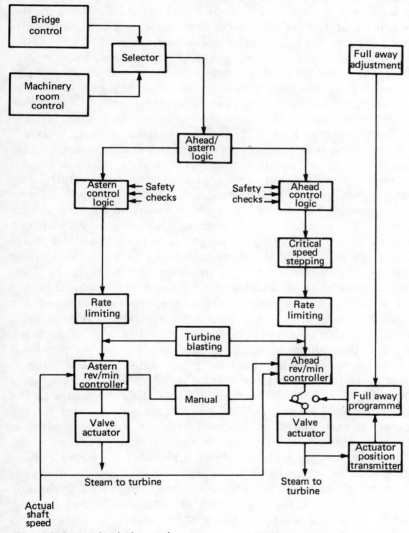

Figure 9.23 Steam turbine bridge control

also be protective devices and safety interlocks built into the system. Bridge control is, therefore, automatic remote control. The provision of bridge control is one of the essential requirements for UMS (Unattended Machinery Space) operation. Bridge control systems are available for the operation of steam turbine or diesel main machinery and also controllable pitch propellers. The steering gear has always been a bridge controlled item of machinery.

A bridge control system for a steam turbine main propulsion unit is shown in Figure 9.23. Control of the main engine may be from the bridge control unit or the machinery control room. The ahead/astern logic unit ensures that the correct logical sequence of events occurs over the appropriate period. Typical operations include the circulating of lubricating oil through the turbine and the opening of steam drains from the turbine. The timing of certain events, such as the opening and closing of steam valves, must be carefully controlled to avoid dangerous conditions occurring or to allow other system adjustments to occur. Protection and safety circuits or interlocks are input to the logic unit to stop its action if, for example, the turning gear is still engaged or the lubricating oil pressure is low. The critical speed stepping unit prevents continuous operation of the turbine in any critical speed range, where one exists. The rate limiter is used to limit the rate of change of the turbine speed within the design constraints of the boiler, turbine and gearing torque. The turbine blasting unit ensures that if the turbine is stopped it automatically receives blasts of steam at timed intervals to prevent rotor distortion. The full-away programmer unit is provided to accelerate the shaft revolutions from the full-ahead to the full-away condition. This unit will result in a control system utilizing the manoeuvring valve position as opposed to shaft speed. A control system acting in this way will ensure more stable conditions in the boiler and turbine. A feedback signal of actual shaft speed completes the control loop for all operations except when the full-away programmer is in operation.

A bridge control system for a slow speed diesel main engine is shown in Figure 9.24. Control may be from either the bridge or the machinery control room. The desired engine speed is set by the particular telegraph position. Engine revolutions can be adjusted in steps to correspond with the telegraph position or stepless control can be achieved by moving the handgrip through 90°. The desired speed is transmitted as a current signal to an electric-to-pneumatic converter. The pneumatic signal then acts on the governor via a pneumatic amplifier. The engine starting system provides a choice of either a normal or a heavy start. A heavy start would be used for an emergency start, a third attempt, or when reversing a rotating engine.

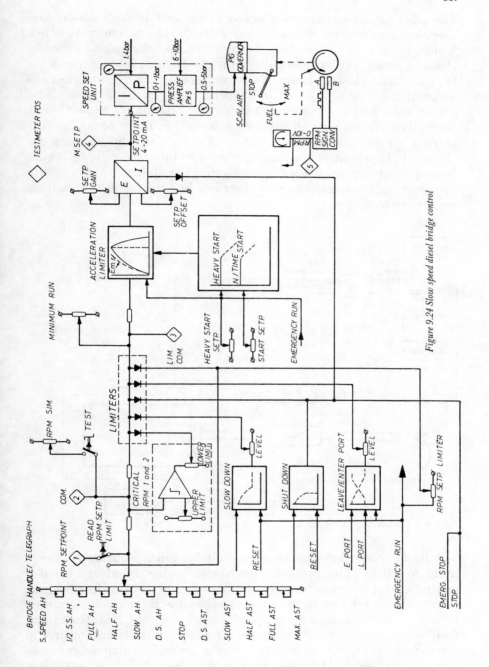

Figure 9.24 Slow speed diesel bridge control

The start sequence may be blocked under certain fault conditions. The running direction of the engine is detected by two microswitches A and B. A critical speed limiter ensures that the engine speed is always outside the critical range. Programs are provided for Slow Down, Shut Down, Enter Port and Leave Port sequences to automatically slow down or run-up the engine speed. The acceleration limiter ensures that no rapid variations of engine speed occur. It is non-linear and allows a faster run-up at lower speeds. During emergency operation an especially fast run-up may be obtained. This control system is designed to interface with an engine having extensive pneumatic manoeuvring equipment. Many of the necessary safety interlocks will therefore be built in to the existing engine controls.

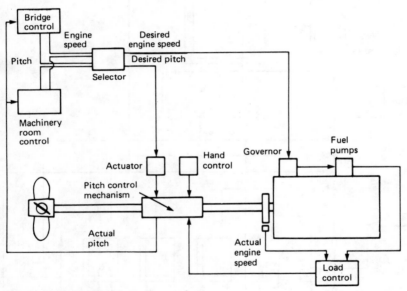

Figure 9.25 Controllable pitch propeller control

A bridge control system for a controllable pitch propeller is shown in Figure 9.25. The propeller pitch and engine speed are usually controlled by a single lever (combinator). The control lever signal passes via the selector to the engine governor and the pitch operating actuator. Pitch and engine speed signals will be fed back and displayed at both control stations. The load control unit ensures a constant load on the engine by varying propeller pitch as external conditions change. The input signals are from the fuel pump setting

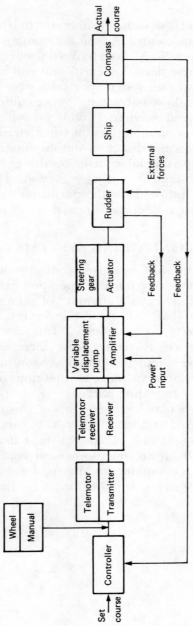

Figure 9.26 Steering gear control

and actual engine speed. The output signal is supplied as a feedback to the pitch controller.

The steering gear is of course bridge controlled and is arranged for automatic or manual control. A typical automatic or auto pilot system is shown in Figure 9.26. A three-term controller provides the output signal where a course deviation exists and will bring about a rudder movement. The various system parts are shown in terms of their system functions and the particular item or equipment involved. The feedback loop between the rudder and the amplifier (variable delivery pump) results in no pumping action when equilibrium exists in the system. External forces can act on the ship or the rudder to cause a change in the ship's actual course, resulting in a feedback to the controller and subsequent corrective action. The controller action must be correctly adjusted for the particular external conditions to ensure that excessive rudder movement does not occur.

INTEGRATED MONITORING SYSTEMS

The ultimate goal in the centralized control room concept will be to perform and monitor every possible operation from this location. This will inevitably result in vast amounts of information reaching the control room, more than the engineer supervisor might reasonably be expected to observe continuously. Integrated monitoring and recording systems are therefore being increasingly used. Various sensors monitor the complete plant either continuously or at regular intervals and give alarm warnings of conditions outside the set limits. The data-logging or recording part of the system then gives an output reading of the particular fault. Systems of this complexity are often microprocessor-based and may incorporate computer control. Some individual control systems, e.g. the oil mist detector, have already been mentioned which are microprocessor controlled. The microprocessor, its use in a computer, and its application to both simple and complex control systems will be discussed in detail in the next chapter.

10 Computer control

A computer is a device which accepts data, performs appropriate operations on this data and then provides the results. Where the input data is in the form of discrete signals which represent numerical values, it is a digital computer. If the data is in the form of continuously varying quantities such as voltage, it is an analogue computer. The digital computer has virtually replaced the analogue computer and will therefore be considered in more detail.

The use of computers for measurement, monitoring and various forms of control is then described by reference to actual systems. Finally simulation, and in particular a diesel plant simulator, is explained in some detail.

ANALOGUE AND DIGITAL SIGNALS

Control signals have so far been considered in terms of their operating media. They can also exist in analogue or digital form, depending upon how the signal is to be used, or manipulated, in the system. The difference in form between these two types of signal will now be considered together with conversion between them.

A transducer converts an input signal into an output signal of a different form. In an analogue transducer the input and output signals are continuous functions of time. The signal may have any value within the physical limitations of the system. A digital transducer has input and output signals which only occur at discrete, i.e. separate, intervals of time. Furthermore, the signal magnitude can only exist at particular discrete levels. An analogue-to-digital transducer has an input signal which is a continuous function of time and an output signal which only occurs at discrete intervals of time and levels of magnitude. A digital-to-analogue transducer has input signals which occur at discrete intervals of time and levels of magnitude and the output is a smooth continuous function of time.

The majority of transducers used in measuring systems produce analogue output signals. Where these are to be input to a digital

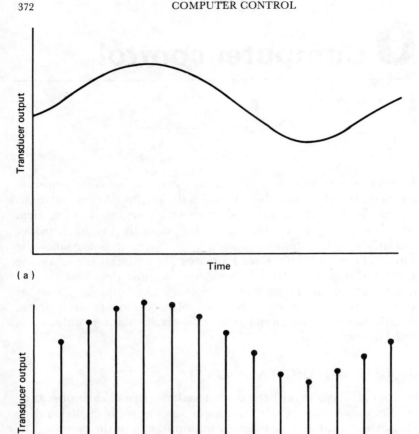

Figure 10.1 Analogue-to-digital signal conversion

controller or computer, then a conversion must be made. The conversion of an analogue signal to a digital, i.e. binary number, signal involves some approximation since the analogue signal can have an infinite range of values and the binary number formed by a finite set of digits is limited. The approximation process is known as quantization. This process will be described by reference to Figure 10.1. An analogue signal is shown in Figure 10.1(a) and can be seen to be smooth and continuous. A discrete-time signal is shown in Figure

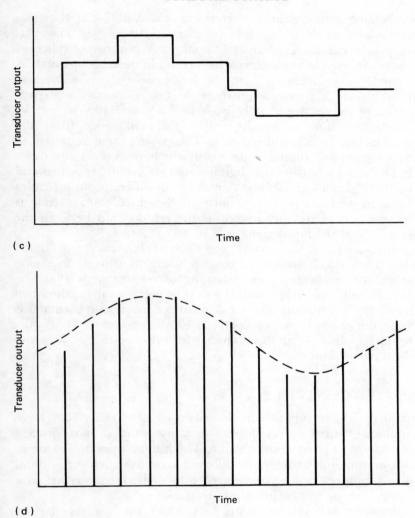

Figure 10.1 Analogue-to-digital signal conversion (contd.)

10.1(b) with values occurring only at specific intervals of time. In Figure 10.1(c) the signal has been quantized. The input magnitudes are divided into intervals of time, which are not necessarily equal. Within the interval all input magnitudes are equated to a single value. This single value is then the digital approximation of the analogue input signal. Finally, in Figure 10.1(d) the signal has been quantized in both amplitude and time. The original analogue input has been superimposed to show that an approximation does occur.

Many analogue-to-digital converters are now available as ICs or as an encapsulated module. A number of external devices are, however, necessary in order for the unit to function. A number of different techniques are used in converters which result in descriptions such as 'high speed', 'high accuracy', etc. An analogue-to-digital converter will usually have a specification incorporating a number of terms. Input voltage ranges are usually $-5\,V$ to $+5\,V$ or $-10\,V$ to $+10\,V$. The conversion time is usually stated and will range from 100 nanoseconds up to 50 milliseconds. This is the time required to generate a complete digital code word which represents the input signal. The word length of the digital output is usually specified and may be 8, 10, 12, 14 or 16 bits. A number of different output codes may be used and the particular form of 'weighted' binary code is usually specified. This output code is the relationship between the output code and the input signal.

Digital-to-analogue converters are likewise ICs or encapsulated modules. They do, however, all operate using the same conversion technique, which involves the switching of resistor networks. The specification will similarly detail the output voltage range, the word length and the input code. The term 'settling time' is also used and is usually in the range 15 nanoseconds to 40 microseconds. This is the time required following an input change for the output to change and settle by a particular amount.

COMPUTER CONTROL

The majority of control systems described earlier in this book have used analogue controllers. A closed loop is used and, in most process control systems, a fixed desired value. The human operator becomes the coordinating link between the different systems to achieve optimal control. Computers can be introduced into such systems either in a supervisory role or to provide direct control.

In computer supervisory control (C.S.C.) the various desired values are outputs from a computer to controllers, see Figure 10.2. The individual controllers then operate their control loops as independent systems. The actual measured values of the various processes are also input to the computer. A program within the computer will enable the display of information, the changing of desired values in the controllers to ensure optimum operation, and probably the logging of information or data. The controllers will usually have pulse outputs so that they can be switched on-line and off-line without the need for balancing. The human operator may be able to make minor changes to the computer program but usually the

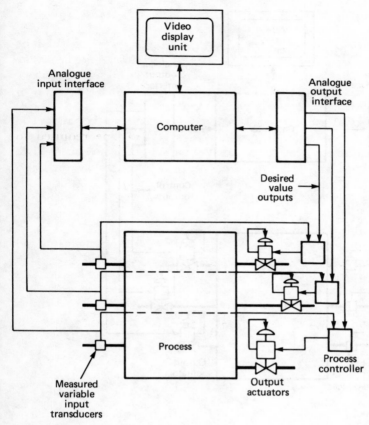

Figure 10.2 Computer supervisory control

computer is simply operating in a supervisory capacity. The individual control systems operate independently and, in the event of a computer failure, their controllers can have desired values set by hand. This system arrangement is inevitably expensive, since individual controllers are provided as well as the computer. The method of operation also results in an element of redundancy since the computer and the controllers often operate in parallel. The system reliability is high and, in the event of computer failure, the local controllers will still function. Most data-logging systems are effectively computer supervisory control. The computer will undertake certain programmed tasks but it does not make decisions or actually control. It does, however, provide the information necessary for the human operator to make decisions regarding the efficient or optimal operation of the plant.

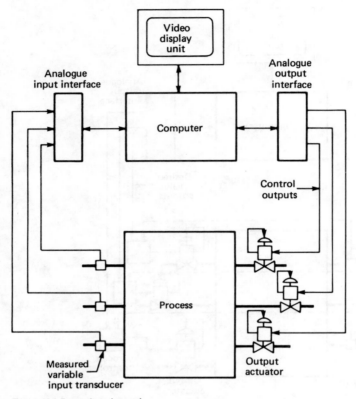

Figure 10.3 Direct digital control

Direct digital control (D.D.C.) is achieved when the computer acts as a controller for numerous systems, see Figure 10.3. It receives inputs of actual measured values and outputs controlling signals to actuators. The computer or digital controller operates using numbers in a binary code. Complex computations can be achieved with any required degree of accuracy at very high speed. The program or instructions for a digital controller can be changed easily and thus the nature of the output to an actuator. A central computer can be used to provide operating instructions or programs to enable efficient or optimal operation of the plant. Decision making is also an important feature of digital controllers. Programs can be produced to enable the complete start-up of main propulsion machinery, electrical power supply, etc. A failure in the computer would result in a loss of control and it is only as a result of the much reduced cost of microprocessors and microcomputers that this system is now feasible. Redundant microprocessors are usually fitted in these systems and each microprocessor is capable of continuously self-checking its operation and will transfer control to the redundant unit in the event of a fault. There is still a requirement for manual back-up facilities and alternative power supplies when this method of control is used.

ANALOGUE COMPUTING

An analogue computer operates with a parameter which is continuously varying in amplitude. It is usual to make use of electrical analogues which use varying voltage signals to represent the system variables. An analogue, or analogy, is a representation or similarity in a particular respect, although there may be differences in physical form. It has been shown earlier that mathematical models or analogues may be produced to represent physical systems such as the liquid flow from a storage tank. The mathematical operations are then undertaken by the analogue computer. This representation or simulation of the mathematical operations produces results without actually solving the mathematics. The basic mathematical operations which can be carried out on an analogue computer include addition, subtraction, multiplication, division and integration. It is also possible to generate the various input functions, e.g. ramp.

The principal components of an analogue computer are operational amplifiers, resistors, capacitors and diodes. Various electronic circuit arrangements of these units will provide the mathematical operations mentioned earlier. Summing and integrating amplifiers, for example, were discussed in Chapter 4. Non-linear functions are to be found in many engineering systems and these can be represented by non-linear elements such as diodes. Examples of non-linearity include backlash in a gear train and saturation in amplifiers.

The analogue computer is made up of a number of physical elements which can then be suitably connected using a patch panel. These will include a number of amplifiers, an input function generator and an output display unit. Additional elements are used to provide mathematical functions such as multiplication, squaring and square root determination. Various non-linear units, stabilized d.c. supplies and a number of potentiometers complete the system.

The analogue computer has previously served as a valuable aid for the design and analysis of control systems. It is, however, being rapidly replaced by digital computers, which are faster and cheaper. Digital computers are also more versatile in that their programs can be easily changed, for example to cater for varying control conditions. Analogue computers will not be considered further.

DIGITAL COMPUTING

A digital computer can be considered as a very fast electronic calculating machine. Information is fed into the machine, it is processed according to a set of instructions, or program, and an output or solution is provided. In addition to understanding what a computer is and how it works, there is almost a new language or jargon to be learnt.

A computer is made up of five main parts, each with an individual function. These are a control unit, an arithmetic and logic unit, a memory, input and output units. These items interrelate as shown in Figure 10.4. Any connecting link between the various parts is called a *bus*. The control unit, the memory and the arithmetic and logic unit are grouped together and known as the *central processing unit* (CPU).

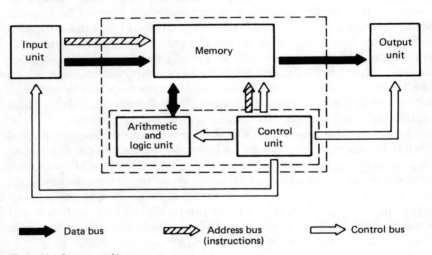

Figure 10.4 Computer architecture

Where all the items of the CPU are incorporated on a single chip or large scale integrated (LSI) circuit it is called a microprocessor. A microcomputer has a CPU which is a microprocessor.

Hardware is the general term used to describe the physical devices which surround and support a computer. The programs which instruct a computer and provide operating systems are called *software*.

The information which is fed into a computer is usually either instructions or data. Instructions are commands which require a transfer of information within the machine or the performance of arithmetic or logical operations. Data are numbers which are used as operands by the instructions. Any number, letter or symbol that a computer can store or process is called a character. All characters must first be suitably coded for use within a computer by making them into binary digits or bits. Binary coding is used since the digital circuits need have only two stable states, on or off. The translation of letters A to Z and numbers 0-9 (*alphanumeric* information) to and from binary is performed within the computer. Reference will be made later in this section to various electronic devices such as bistable elements, which were discussed in Chapter 4.

Central processing unit

The central processing unit is the brain in a computer system. However, it cannot think and operates according to a set of instructions or a program. When a program has been fed into the CPU it can operate. The program is stored in the memory and is retrieved as required by the control unit. The arithmetic and logic unit will perform operations as directed by the program.

The memory is where programs and data are stored. First the program must be placed in the memory to provide instructions on how to deal with the input. The input data must then be stored until it is to be processed. A storage area must also be provided for intermediate results of the processing. The final results or data must then be stored prior to transfer to the output unit. The main memory, or primary storage, is able to operate very fast and is where programs and data are stored during their execution. Secondary storage areas located outside the computer are sometimes used for large quantities of data that are seldom used; these may take the form of discs or magnetic tapes. The main memory is made up of large numbers of storage cells each of which can store one binary digit, or *bit*, of information. These cells are usually dealt with in multiples called a *location*, *byte* or *word*. Large computers may have 32 bits per word while microcomputers usually have 8 or 16 bits per word. In order that a word may be stored or retrieved from the memory, each location is given a distinct name known as an *address*. A particular word can be obtained from the memory by specifying the address and giving a control command to retrieve. Instructions and data can be stored in the memory, when the term 'written in' is used, or removed from the memory, when the term 'read out' is used. A memory where instructions or data can be written in or read out is called a random access memory (RAM). These memory cells are made up of bistable elements. A memory from which it is only possible to read out is called a read only memory (ROM). These are memory cells whose contents have been fixed, usually during manufacture. The time required to

access one word from the memory is called the *memory cycle time* and is
in the order of one microsecond or less. A *register* is a special memory
unit which is used for short term, high speed storage. Certain registers
are dedicated to a particular use, such as the program counter and the
instruction register. A number of general purpose registers are also
available which may be used, for example, to temporarily store a
frequently used operand. The program counter is a register which
contains the address of the next instruction. It is updated by adding
one each time the central processing unit collects an instruction. The
instruction register holds the instruction that is currently being
executed.

The control unit is required to coordinate and supervise all the
operations of the various components in the system. It also organizes
and controls the flow of data around the system. A program
instruction is selected from the memory, interpreted and then an
appropriate signal is passed to other units to carry out the instruction.
Data flow around the system is usually from input, via the control
unit, to the memory and then to and from the arithmetic and logic
unit. Finally, the data will leave the memory and pass to an output
unit. A group of wires over which electrical signals is passed is called a
bus. Three distinct types are used, namely address bus, data bus and
control bus. The address bus is unidirectional since it is only used to
select an address. The data bus and control bus are bidirectional in
their transfer of signals. A data bus will typically be 8 bits or 1 byte
wide. The address bus may be 16-bit, which will enable the accessing
of $2^{16} = 65\,536$ bytes of memory. This number is usually expressed as
64K, where $1K = 1024$. The RAM and ROM memory sizes are
usually given in terms of K, e.g. 64K RAM, 16K ROM. The various
operations carried out within the central processing unit are cyclic
and therefore need a precise form of time control. The clock pulse
generator is an oscillator that provides this time base. The control
unit will also accept 'interrupt' and 'wait' requests. An interrupt will
result in the master program being stopped in such a way that data is
preserved and when the interrupt is over the master program
operations will continue. A wait request may be made to enable a
slower unit to catch up or be ready to participate in the program.
During a wait request the central processing unit will 'tick over' until
the slower unit is ready.

The binary data from memory undergoes various manipulations in
the arithmetic and logic unit (ALU). After any particular operation
the new data is returned and stored in the memory or a register.
Binary data is used since the digital circuit need have only two stable
states, on or off.

A brief comparison between decimal numbers which use a base of 10 and binary numbers with their base of 2 will now be made. The number 2345 as a decimal number is understood with reference to the base 10 and the position of the numerals, i.e.

$$2345 = 2 \times 10^3 + 3 \times 10^2 + 4 \times 10^1 + 5 \times 10^0$$

A binary number 11010 should be understood in the same manner, with reference to the base 2 and the position of the numerals, e.g.

$$11010 = 1 \times 2^4 + 1 \times 2^3 + 0 \times 2^2 + 1 \times 2^1 + 0 \times 2^0$$
$$= 16 + 8 + 2 \text{ (as a decimal number)}$$
$$= 26 \text{ (as a decimal number)}$$

The basis of all arithmetic operations is addition. The addition of two binary numbers is as follows:

```
 1010
 1001
-----
10011
```

It can be seen that 1 plus 0 is 1, 0 plus 0 is 0, and 1 plus 1 is 0 with 1 carried to the left. This process can be verified by converting the numbers into decimal (10, 9) and making the addition.

The logic circuit for this process is shown in Figure 10.5, together with the truth table and the digital symbol. The unit is called a half-adder because it only handles two digits at a time. A full-adder would be able to handle three digits at a time. In order to add the four-digit numbers given above, or larger numbers, several full-adders would be connected in parallel.

Input and output units

A computer obtains its coded information from an input unit or port. The most common input device is an electric typewriter, which is electronically connected to the computer. When a key on the keyboard is pressed, the particular digit or letter is automatically translated into code and passed to the central processing unit.

The input and output ports are designed such that they can be scanned or addressed by the CPU to fetch data from or enter data to them as required by the program. A typewriter can be arranged to act

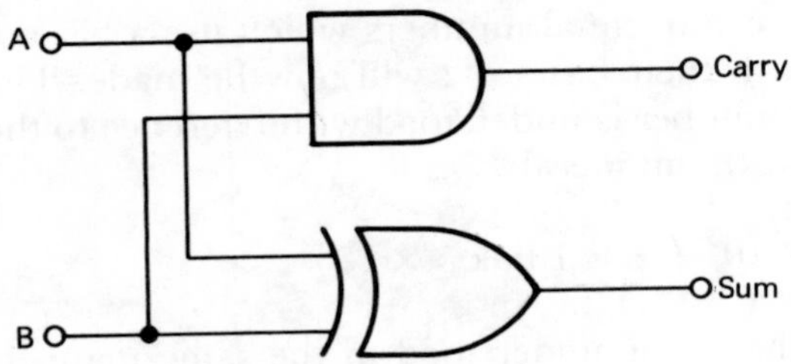

(a)

A	B	Carry	Sum
0	0	0	0
1	0	0	1
0	1	0	1
1	1	1	0

(b)

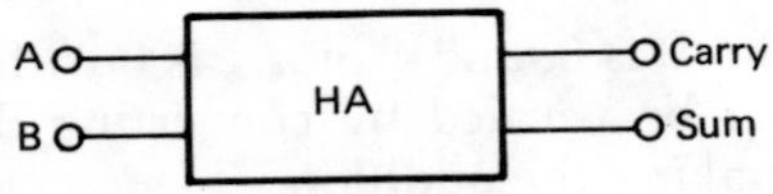

(c)

Figure 10.5 Half-adder: (a) logic circuit; (b) truth table; (c) digital symbol

as an output unit but high speed printers are more usual. These printers work at very high mechanical speeds, producing many hundreds of characters per minute and usually writing in both directions.

Hardware

A typical computer system is usually made up of a keyboard, a TV screen and a printer. The keyboard, which is similar to an electric typewriter, acts as the input device to enable programs and data to be typed in. The TV screen is usually known as a video display unit (VDU) or monitor since it displays the input program or data (and eventually, the output). The keyboard and VDU together are called a terminal. A microcomputer will usually have the CPU within the casing of the keyboard; if not, a connection is made to the CPU. A small flashing line or rectangle is displayed on the monitor screen to indicate where the next typed character will appear. It is known as a cursor. Programs or data fed into the computer are stored in the random access memory (RAM) and are then exchanged between the CPU and the RAM as the program is executed. When the power to the system is turned off all RAM data is lost. This type of storage is called *volatile* memory. The read only memory (ROM) contains programs which have been written-in during manufacture and they remain even if the power is switched off, i.e. it is *non-volatile* memory.

Program

A computer can be used over and over again, since the RAM memory can be cleared of any programs or data written in. The program is a written set of instructions telling the computer what to do. These instructions are written in a language which the computer can understand. Language in this sense means a series of strings of symbols or words which can transfer information. Programming languages are usually considered in terms of three levels. *Machine language* is a set of binary instructions that the CPU understands. *Assembly language* is a symbolic programming language that uses mnemonic (memory aid) codes for instruction. An assembler is used to translate this language into machine code or machine language. The third or *high-level* language is problem or procedure oriented in that the construction of expressions closely approaches mathematical formulation or English words. A high-level language, e.g. FOR-TRAN, will require a compiler to translate the language into machine code for the CPU. Machine code can be fed directly into a computer but the particular codes used are specific to the machine, i.e. it is machine dependent. Assembly language requires an assembler which is a unit related only to a particular computer, i.e. it is again machine dependent. High-level languages are considered as independent of a particular machine but usually some small modifications are required if a change of computer is made.

The majority of marine engineering control systems are for process control. In a process there may be many simultaneously occurring events and therefore computer programs for such control must be able to execute several different tasks at the same time. A computer, however, is a sequentially operating device. The program must therefore be written such that the computer will concentrate for a short period on each of the tasks in turn and satisfy its particular requirements. Various parts or modules of a large program are used for the various sub-systems of the computer or for frequently occurring functions. An overall executive program is then used to control and coordinate the various modules, which then seem to operate in parallel. The start-up of an engine would be an example of sequential and often simultaneous operation of various tasks.

MEASUREMENT AND MONITORING

The continuous or regular monitoring of measured values and comparison with their set limits can be readily accomplished by a microprocessor-based system. Individual functional units may be used, or a single printed circuit board may contain several of the units. A large system would use individual circuit boards containing the microprocessor, the memory, analogue-to-digital converter, etc. The various boards would be housed in a rack which would provide a 'mother board' containing plug-in sockets for the circuit boards. The plug-in sockets which form part of the mother board circuitry provide a bus for data communication between the boards and a control unit. The program for the particular process, i.e. alarm and monitoring in this case, is input to the programmable read only memories (PROM) in the memory unit. These memories together with the microprocessor form the control unit of the system. The control unit will then read input signals and supply output signals for the various process functions according to the program. A bus supervising unit will check the program execution, supply voltages and sections of the bus, and give an alarm if a fault is detected. Also the output functions will be controlled to avoid any dangerous conditions in the process.

Inputs and outputs may be digital or analogue. Digital inputs are usually contact positions indicating on or off for running machinery, etc. Digital output is provided to relays, contactors, running lamps, etc. Analogue input measured values are converted into numerical values for data processing or transmission to other parts of the system. Both multiplexers and analogue-to-digital (A/D) converters are present in this input system. A multiplexer is a selector which connects the inputs, each in turn, to a common output. The analogue output system provides signals, usually as d.c. voltages or currents, to operate instruments or regulators, etc.

Data transmission to external units is usually in serial form, one bit at a time. Transmission can then take place in one direction at a time along a two-wire system. Where a four-wire line is used, simultaneous bidirectional transmission can take place.

The central processing unit (CPU) is built up of a microprocessor and one or more memory units. The process program is usually fixed for the particular system. It is therefore stored in read only memory (ROM) or programmable read only memory (PROM). The ROM memory contents are determined during the component production. The PROM is programmed by means of special equipment. Both ROM and PROM memories are non-volatile, i.e. not lost if the supply fails. Any data which is amended during the process is stored in the random access memory (RAM).

A general layout of this system is shown in Figure 10.6. It is made up of standard modules for alarm and measurement, display, selection, bridge and other area panels, a power distribution unit and a central unit.

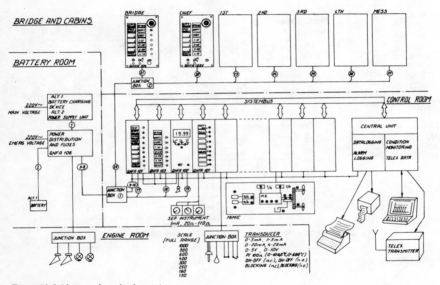

Figure 10.6 Alarm and monitoring system

The central unit contains the microprocessor which controls the various functions of data logging and alarm monitoring. Additional functions such as telex transmission, condition monitoring and trend analysis are also possible. One or more alarm monitoring modules (QHFA 101) will be used since each has space for eight analogue or on-off inputs. Each channel has an engraved plate which illuminates upon alarm and a visual alarm accept button is located alongside. The display module (QHFA 102) provides a digital display which indicates the measured value or the set limit. An audible alarm accept button is also provided. The selector module (QHFA 103) indicates the machinery space status, i.e. attended or unattended, and the engineer(s) on duty. A call button for the various engineers is also provided. Group alarms, machinery space status and call engineer are displayed on the bridge panel (QHFA 104) and the various cabin and mess panels (QHFA 105). The power supply unit (QHFA 106) provides power distribution and battery charging where this is required.

The central unit or microcomputer controls data-logging, see Figure 10.7. Measured values are printed out at regular intervals or on demand by pressing the printout button. The channels to be

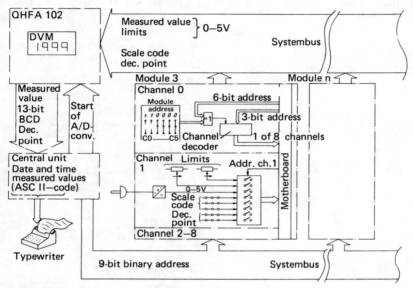

Figure 10.7 Data logging

printed out, and their sequence, is decided by the program which is based on the ship owner's particular requirements. The measuring channels are addressed using a 9-bit binary code which is transmitted along the system bus. The address is decoded in each module and one channel is addressed. The measured value is obtained as a 0-5 V signal, suitably scaled and to a selected number of decimal places. The measured value in binary code is then transmitted via the system bus to the central unit. The date, time and measured value are then printed.

Alarm monitoring follows a similar process in that the measured value is transmitted to the control unit, but in addition it is compared with the set alarm limits. This scanning process is continuous and, where an alarm condition occurs, the channel number and time will be printed out on the printer. Audible and visual alarms are simultaneously given in the machinery space and control room. Alarms are also given on the bridge and in the duty engineer's cabin when the machinery space is unattended.

The system is also capable of monitoring itself. An alarm is given if a fault develops in the system. A fault in a particular transducer or channel circuit board does not, however, affect the rest of the system. A separate alarm channel to the bridge and cabin panels indicates the presence of faults in the power supply of the system.

Condition monitoring

The conditions within a diesel engine relating to combustion pressure, indicated power, cylinder surface temperatures, condition of piston rings, etc. can be continuously monitored by the use of a microprocessor-based system. Monitoring of these parameters will result in better engine performance, reduced wear and a better overall knowledge of the general state of the engine.

A system used for the measurement of combustion conditions is shown in Figure 10.8. The combustion pressure is measured by a pressure transducer which is connected to the indicator cock of the cylinder. The transducer produces an electric signal proportional to

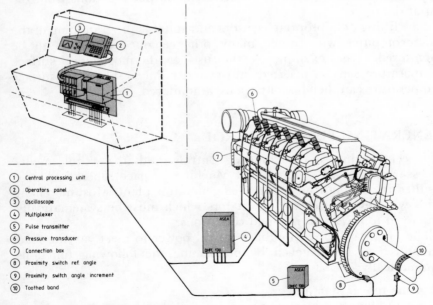

1. Central processing unit
2. Operators panel
3. Oscilloscope
4. Multiplexer
5. Pulse transmitter
6. Pressure transducer
7. Connection box
8. Proximity switch ref. angle
9. Proximity switch angle increment
10. Toothed band

Figure 10.8 Cylinder condition monitoring

the pressure applied at any particular instant. This signal is supplied to a module which provides as output the instantaneous pressure, the pressure variation with time and the maximum pressure. Digital output values are provided to a panel and analogue outputs are supplied to an oscilloscope. The crankshaft rotation angle is measured by two proximity switches. One reads the incremental angle from the flywheel teeth or a toothed band on the shaft. The other is a reference point which is the top dead centre position for the cylinder nearest to the flywheel. The pulses from the proximity switches are passed to a transmitter where they are modified and then pass to the central processing unit. The multiplexer transmits the pressure signals, cylinder by cylinder, to the central processing unit. The operator's panel communicates with the central processing unit to enable display, as digital values, of mean indicated combustion pressure, indicated power, engine speed, maximum combustion pressure, compression pressure and ignition angle. Diagrams can be displayed on the oscilloscope of pressure against crank angle and peak pressure against time. The system incorporates several test and calibration functions which enable simple operation and fault tracing. For each particular installation, parameters such as firing order, swept volume, connecting rod length and stroke length are pre-programmed into the microcomputer memory. The program will also contain the appropriate mathematics to generate the output functions from the input data.

The fitting of appropriate sensors and suitable programming of the microcomputer will enable many other engine conditions to be monitored. One example is the use of thermoelement surface temperature sensors inserted into cylinder liners. The liner surface temperature can then be continuously monitored.

GENERATING PLANT CONTROL

The centralizing of machinery controls and the requirements necessary for UMS (Unattended Machinery Space) operation have resulted in automatically controlled generating plant. Most merchant ships will have up to four alternators which must be systematically employed to meet varying load conditions.

The automatic provision of electrical power to meet varying load demands can be achieved by performing the following functions automatically:

1. prime mover start-up;
2. synchronizing of incoming machine with bus-bars;

3. load sharing between alternators;

4. safety and operational checks on power supply and equipment in operation;

5. unloading, stopping and returning to standby of surplus machines;

6. preferential tripping of non-essential loads under emergency conditions and their reinstating when acceptable.

One such system capable of all these functions is shown in Figure 10.9. Various modules are used to perform different functions and each alternator has a group of modules. A central unit and a relay unit for controlled loads complete the system. Each alternator has five

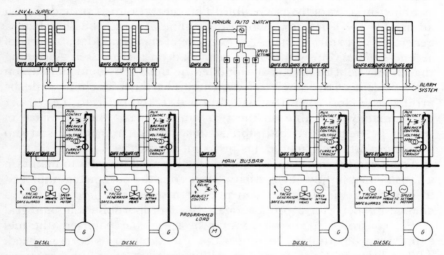

Figure 10.9 Computer controlled generating plant

modules. The basic unit (QHFG101) contains functions which provide start and stop programs, manual start and stop, start and connection in the event of black-out, and the monitoring of eight channels of external sensors or internal circuits. An additional monitoring unit (QHFG103) is used where more than eight channels are needed. The synchronizing and load sharing unit (QHFG102) operates in conjunction with the transformer unit (QHFG112) to provide automatic synchronizing, load sharing, frequency control and an overload alarm. The relay unit (QHFG111) provides additional output stages for the basic unit. One central unit (QHFG104) is used in the system to optimize the economy of operation and provide protection against overloading. Economy of operation results from the starting and stopping of alternators as loading demands. Protection against overloading is achieved by the unit simulating a heavy load, e.g. bow thruster, and ensuring the availability of power before starting the heavy load. The relay unit (QHFG113) provides additional relays for the control of heavy loads.

The start program ensures the availability of air for starting, limitation of fuel flow to the diesel engine, pre-excitation of the alternator, etc. A program is also available for automatically switching on the standby unit's prelubrication pumps for five minutes in every hour or continuously when the set is at a standstill. The stop program contains parameters for diesel alternator load relieving, idling, tripping of circuit breakers, etc.

If the bus-bar voltage disappears, i.e. black-out, an alternator is switched-in as rapidly as possible. The central unit is provided with adjustable level detectors which determine at which bus-bar load a generator will start or stop. An example of this would be a setting of second set start-up with 80 per cent load on the first set. Assuming that 20 per cent reserve is acceptable, the third set would start up on 180 per cent of the single set capacity. The third machine could be arranged to stop when the load dropped to 160 per cent, i.e. 40 per cent capacity available on the two running sets. The difference in setting between start and stop is to avoid an immediate start-up procedure after a machine has just shut down.

An alternator must run at a fixed steady speed in order to maintain a satisfactory supply of electricity. If speed is the parameter employed in governing the unit this can present problems. There must be a change in speed for a proportional (P) or proportional plus integral (P+I) controller to operate. Once the speed has changed, the fuel supply can be adjusted to return the alternator to its correct speed. The addition of derivative action will improve matters but there must still be a change in the alternator speed and therefore in the supply voltage and frequency. Where the load is electrical, as with alternators, a load sensing governor can be used to provide improved governing. The output from all three phases is monitored continuously and combined to give a total power signal. This signal, after amplification, is used to control the fuel supply. Any change in the total load will 'anticipate' the speed change and thus provide a better dynamic response for the governing system. A speed sensing governor will also be employed and would be a back-up unit should the load sensing unit fail.

INTEGRATED CONTROL

More and more sophisticated control equipment is being fitted to modern ships. The various individual systems are being integrated in order to ensure efficient ship operation and to enable reduced manning. Various countries have investigated the increased use of automation for 'Efficient Ship' or 'Future Ship' designs. All the various shipboard operational functions are being automated and integrated into one complete control system. This will include bridge systems dealing with all aspects of navigation, cargo control systems, machinery control systems and also administration and management systems. One such system will now be described.

There are four sub-systems making up the Integrated Control System.

1. Bridge Electronic System
2. Ship's Instrumentation System
3. Cargo Electronics System
4. Management Administration System.

Information can be passed between any of the operating areas by a direct connection or a local network. This enables the coordination of data for processing and decision making and also provides new forms of available data. Data is displayed on video display units at workstations which are appropriately located around the ship. All available data can be accessed and data may be input at any workstation.

Bridge system

The bridge electronic system uses a single processor, i.e. microcomputer, which can drive up to five workstations. Only one workstation will be able to control a particular set of functions at any one time. Usually two workstations are provided. These will control an automatic radar plotting aid (ARPA) display, an automatic chart table, a multi-sensor receiver (MNS 2000), an auto-pilot, and other usual bridge sensors, see Figure 10.10. The system is able to provide:

1. automatic position fixing;
2. full interaction with ARPA and the automatic chart table;
3. passage planning and monitoring;
4. auto track-keeping;
5. on-board creation of electronic charts;
6. passage economics monitoring;
7. automatic data-logging.

Where other operational areas are fitted with interfacing systems then machinery alarms and performance details, cargo and ballast information, etc. may be displayed on the bridge workstations.

Bridge system

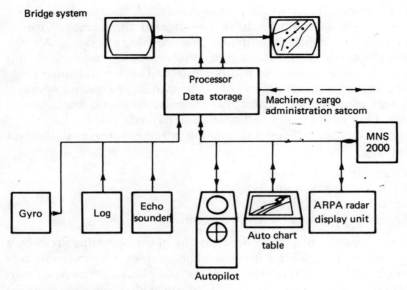

Figure 10.10 Integrated bridge electronic system

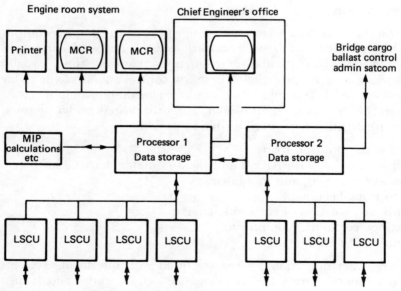

Figure 10.11 Integrated ship's instrumentation system

Machinery control system

The ship's instrumentation system will have between 100 and 3000 sensing points leading to the various items of plant. There will be a considerable number of workstations and also a certain amount of customizing, according to the particular machinery requirements. A fairly typical arrangement is shown in Figure 10.11, and provides facilities for:

1. surveillance to UMS requirements;
2. performance and condition monitoring;
3. trend analysis;
4. generator control;
5. ballast and fluids management;
6. automatic data-logging.

Inputs from sensors and control outputs are connected to Local Scanner and Control Units (LSCU) which are positioned around the machinery space near to the machinery they control. The LSCU has an inbuilt microprocessor and can function independently of the main processor, if necessary. Local control loops are completed by LSCUs for controlling outputs to valves, motors, etc. They also provide the interface for remote commands from the workstations. An error checking procedure operates on each LSCU every two seconds. Local displays are available at the LSCU of all data fed to the unit. Up to seven LSCUs can be connected to a single processor. Only one processor is required to operate the system, the second is a fully duplicated redundant unit. Each processor is used at regular intervals and inbuilt checking facilities operate continuously. A failed processor would be disconnected automatically. If both processors or the communication system between the processors and the LSCUs failed, then each LSCU would revert to the back-up mode. Each LSCU would then operate as an independent alarm and monitoring system which is wired directly to the control console in the machinery control room.

The system will carry out machinery surveillance, alarm monitoring and data-logging as required for UMS operation. The data can also be made available to many parts of the ship and an engineer may review everything in his cabin or an office in the accommodation.

Cargo system

The Cargo Electronic System uses a single processor with usually two workstations, one in the cargo control room and one in the ship's office, see Figure 10.12. Each workstation is provided with a printer.

Cargo system

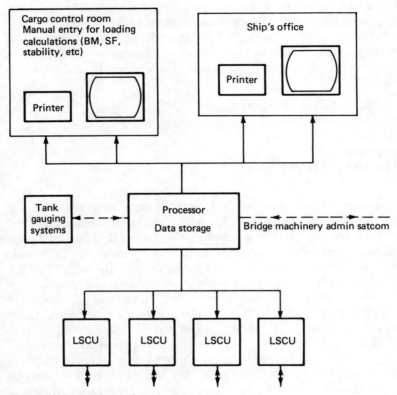

Figure 10.12 Integrated cargo electronics system

Data may be input to the system manually, e.g. for loading calculations, or directly, e.g. from tank level sensors. The system is able to provide:

1. loading calculations;
2. shear force, bending moment, stability and trim data;
3. cargo management;
4. data-logging and documentation;
5. ballast control.

The system can be interfaced with the bridge or machinery system to enable transfer of data as required.

Administration system

The Management Administration System uses a single processor and one or more workstations, each with a printer, see Figure 10.13. A

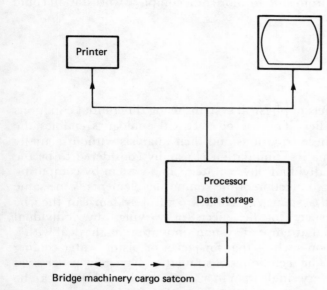

Bridge machinery cargo satcom

Figure 10.13 Integrated management administration system

number of software packages (programs) can be run to provide such facilities as:

1. Master's records;
2. wages and salaries;
3. word processing;
4. stores and maintenance planning;
5. stock control.

The processor provides large-scale data storage facilities. The many programs available can be used to reduce tedious administrative tasks, maintain up-to-date records, enable rapid access to information, etc. Appropriate security is available to prevent unauthorized access to, destruction, or corruption, of data.

Optimal control

The integration of the many forms of data available can result in improved efficiency in the operation of the ship. Trends in actual performance can be compared with design figures. Fuel consumption figures can be monitored and used to predict a suitable interval between drydocking. Conditions monitoring can lead to planned maintenance schedules to minimize repair and breakdown costs. Where INMARSAT satellite communication systems are fitted, data can be despatched from ship to shore or a complete workstation could be set up ashore.

SIMULATION

Mathematical models of physical systems using differential equations were discussed earlier. The use of electrical analogues enables the representation of these equations and their analysis without actually solving the mathematics. Simulation is usually considered to be the representation of individual physical items in a system by computing elements. The interconnection of the computing elements is the same as in the simulated system. A feedback control system can then be examined with respect to the effects of varying any individual parameter. An initial attempt at system simulation might deal with a heat exchange system such as that for jacket or piston water cooling on a diesel engine. The techniques of simulation have now progressed to the extent that every single item in a ship's machinery space can be simulated. These systems can further be made to interact with one another to produce, in every respect, the complete range of activities that may occur during an engine room watchkeeping period. The physical equipment used for the operation and control of the ship's machinery is identical to the real thing. Only the engine, its associated systems and auxiliaries are modelled. The control room therefore is life-like and realistic, even to the point of having introduced the appropriate noises.

System performance has so far been the principal consideration for simulation. The research and investigations possible with such a complex simulation are, of course, considerable. Simulators are also invaluable for operator training. 'Hands on' experience with the operating controls can be obtained with no risks involved. Normal and abnormal conditions can be simulated and the operator taught how to react and respond to any kind of fault—experience which, prior to simulators, few engineers would ever obtain even after years of on-board service. Simulator training is now recognized by the regulatory authorities and usually results in exemption from some period of sea time. A ship propulsion simulator will now be discussed in some detail.

Diesel plant simulator

A complete propulsion plant simulator comprises an engine control room, a machinery space and an instructor's room. A digital computer forms the heart of the unit and various dynamic models describe the various processes within the plant. These models can be interconnected in many ways and can be adjusted to vary the plant conditions.

The machinery control room houses the main switchboard and the control console. The main switchboard contains the generator synchronizing equipment to simulate power generation and distribution. The control console has two separate sections, which house the alarm displays and the remote control system. This console will be based upon some alarm and monitoring system as previously described. The instructor's room is separate but has a view through windows of the control room. A communicating console is provided to enable inputs to the control room equipment. The engine room is another separate space which contains panels or boxes to represent the simulated units. These panels provide indication, can be reset if the unit is considered to have a simulated failure, may be 'repaired', or provide some manual operating features. The trainee is required to visit the engine room at intervals to undertake these various tests according to the simulated condition requirements. Mimic panel displays are provided in the control room and engine room to give process details and fault indications. The complete arrangement is shown in Figure 10.14.

Computer models

A diesel engine main propulsion plant is considered, but appropriate models exist for steam propulsion units and all their associated auxiliaries. The various parts of the model are based on the physical characteristics and behaviour of the plant. They are also modular in nature to enable modifications or extensions to the simulator.

The overall plant arrangement is shown in Figure 10.15. The main features include a slow speed, large bore diesel engine with turbochargers, a fresh water cooling system provided with two central coolers, a diesel generator and a turbogenerator. The propeller may be a fixed or controllable pitch design, and either diesel or heavy fuel may be used by the main engine. An oil fired or an exhaust gas boiler will provide the steam for the turbo-alternator.

The dynamic model used for the main engine is shown schematically in Figure 10.16. A program is used to develop propeller torque from inputs of ship speed, engine speed and propeller pitch

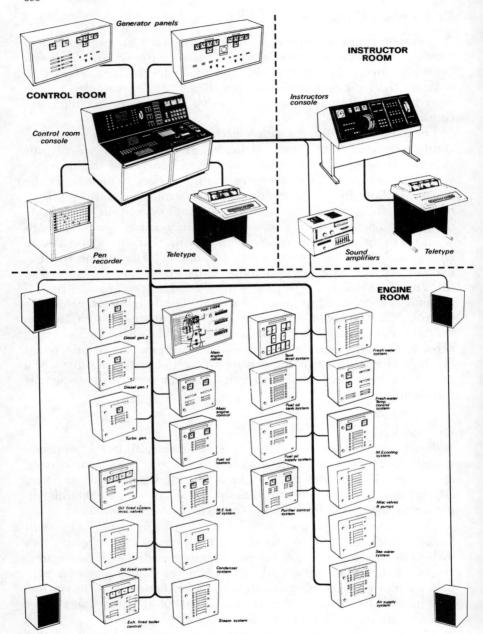

Figure 10.14 General arrangement of a simulator

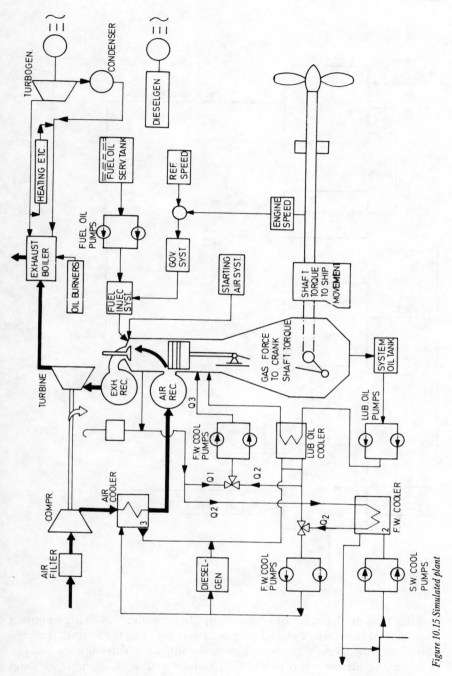

Figure 10.15 Simulated plant

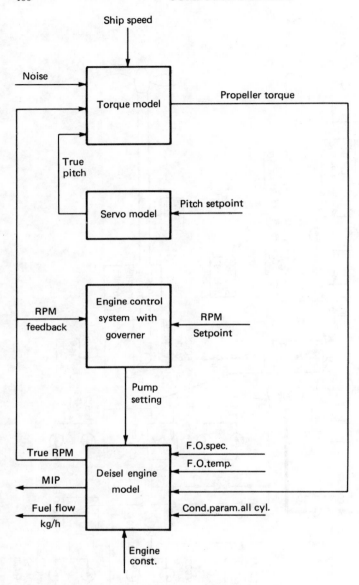

Figure 10.16 Dynamic engine model

(which may be from a controllable pitch propeller). A bridge control
unit is used to enable desired engine speed input to the system, receive
actual engine speed signals and provide output to the engine model of
a signal requiring appropriate fuel pump setting. The engine model

will calculate the output speed according to the fuel pump setting input signal. The fuel oil specification, fuel oil temperature, condition parameters for the various cylinders and engine constants are also input to the model. The model will provide output in addition to speed, of fuel flow rate and cylinder pressures.

A separate model is used for the cylinder conditions and operates in conjunction with the air intake and exhaust systems. The model uses individual inputs from all the engine cylinders and these will vary according to the engine operating conditions. All the various parameters will have dynamic responses as running conditions change. Fault conditions may be introduced into a specific cylinder and the various parameters will be realistically affected.

The boiler system model includes an exhaust gas and an oil-fired boiler. Steam separation is considered to occur in a common drum and circulation pumps move water between the two boilers. A superheater is located in the gas duct after the exhaust gas boiler. The steam drum water level is controlled by a common feed water flow control valve which is active when either boiler is in operation. The auxiliary boiler has two oil-fired burners and has a burner management system provided. A combustion control system is also modelled. A boiler safety system is included in the model to trip the auxiliary boiler when the flame is lost or an emergency low water level occurs. The feed water supply would be shut off at emergency high water level.

The steam system model comprises a turbo-generator turbine, a vacuum condenser, a steam dump system and external steam load. The turbine model includes speed control of the unit. The vacuum condenser model incorporates the effects of vacuum pump operation, sea water temperature and flow. The steam dump system is a pressure controlled valve which dumps steam to the condenser when the pressure is too high. External steam loads include accommodation heating, fuel oil heating, deck machinery steam and tank cleaning steam. The various loads can be individually set.

The pump model will calculate flow and pressure in the liquid leaving the pumps. Separate characteristics are used for different pumps and the system pressure drops are incorporated. The pump power consumption is also determined by an electrical power model. Various faults can be introduced on each pump which must be reset on the engine room panel.

The cooler model calculates the coefficient of thermal conductivity and the outlet temperatures of the two liquids. It would also determine changes in heat transfer due to changes in fluid velocity. Factors which may affect the fluid flow include the amount of liquid bypassed, any change in thermal conductivity or variations in liquid viscosity. These factors can be varied by the instructor and, once detected, must be reset in the engine room.

In order to enhance the realism of simulated conditions it is possible to provide appropriate sound simulation for the various actions undertaken.

Machinery space equipment

The machinery space in a ship's engine room is located on various flats and widely distributed. The simulate this aspect various control panels are provided in the simulator machinery room.

All the equipment shown in Figure 10.15 is provided with local panels. Also included are a temperature control panel, starting air and control air compressor panel and an indication panel. The main engine panel, for example, has a mimic diagram of the engine and 15 reset push-buttons. These buttons represent different faults and, when operated, they simulate the correction of the fault by overhaul or repair. The panel also has provision for adjustment of the fuel rack position for each cylinder.

Control room equipment

Located in the control room are the control console, a teletype and the electric switchboard.

The control console is based upon an integrated alarm and monitoring system. It will include features such as the engine room unit of the bridge control system, the pumping system and automatic electrical power generation. Condition monitoring, alarm displays, alarm and data-logging will also be provided. The operation of this type of system has been described earlier. The electrical system enables stopping, starting and synchronizing of generators from the swichboard panel. The teletype is used for logging of all alarms and any parameter changes that have been made.

Instructor's equipment

The instructor's room contains the bridge control unit and a communications system.

The bridge control unit enables the instructor to signal certain engine operating instructions to the trainee. The communications system enables the instructor to start-up the simulation model of the plant and then operate on it by changing parameters, introducing faults, etc.

Computer system

The computer model and the operating program are stored on disks and input to the computer each time a simulation is to be run. Also, the instructor is able to stop a simulation at any time and store the current system data on a disk. The simulation can then be restarted later at the point where it was stopped.

Operation

Two examples will now be described to illustrate the operation of the simulator. The instructor is able to introduce a variety of different faults which may be selected from a fault index table. The faults may be introduced individually or as a sequence.

A test on a main engine cylinder may be undertaken by first running the engine under steady-state conditions. Cylinder number 1 is selected and cylinder pressure and oil injection pressure against crank angle diagrams are obtained for reference. Fuel oil injector nozzle wear is now introduced as a fault. Since the engine speed controller may attempt to compensate by increasing the fuel supplied, the fuel link position for cylinder 1 must be locked. Only the effects on this individual cylinder are to be considered as an instructional exercise. Calm weather would also be set. The exhaust temperature will now be seen to rise and the power and mean indicated pressure (MIP) will be reduced. The cylinder and injection pressure diagrams can be obtained and compared with the reference curves. The liner and cylinder cover temperatures will be seen to rise slightly. The fresh water cooling and lubricating oil outlet temperatures will also rise very slightly and the total power output of the engine will fall. The fault is removed by resetting the push-button on the engine panel in the machinery space room.

Heavy fouling may be introduced as a fault on the sea water side of fresh water cooler number 1. The sea water side pressure drop will then decrease while the fresh water pressure drop remains normal. The sea water flow will reduce while the fresh water flow remains unaffected. The sea water side outlet temperature and the fresh water outlet temperature will rise. The fault is reset on the pump panel in the machinery space room.

In addition to its use for operator training, a simulator provides considerable scope for research and investigation into control system performance. Various items of instrumentation can be examined. Basic control loops can be investigated and, ultimately, studies on total plant performance and optimization are possible.

Appendix: Glossary of terms

For computing terms, see pages 412–415.

CONTROL TERMS

accuracy A general term describing the degree of closeness with which the indications of an instrument approach the true values of the quantities measured.

a.c. tacho generator An a.c. generator which produces an output voltage proportional to its speed.

actuator a motor providing rotary or linear motion.

adaptive control system A system in which the parameters are changed automatically in a way that will achieve the best possible performance of the system at all times.

amplification For an element or system, the ratio of the steady state amplitude of the output signal from an element or system to the amplitude of a sinusoidal input signal of a given frequency; or the ratio of the same two signal amplitudes when the input signal is of a given frequency; or the ratio of the same two signal amplitudes when the input signal has a constant unidirectional value.

amplifier A device in which an input is used to control a local source of power so as to produce an output which is greater than and bears a definite relationship to the input.

amplitude With regard to sinusoidal or oscillatory motion this is the maximum departure from the zero or rest position.

attenuation The inverse or reciprocal of gain.

automatic controller An element in an automatic controlling or regulating system which receives a signal representing the controlled condition. This is then compared with a signal representing the command signal. The output signal then operates to reduce the deviation.

404

backlash The largest distance or angle which any part of a mechanical system may be moved in a particular direction without transferring a force to the next part in the system.

bandwidth The frequency range within which certain harmonic response characteristics, such as gain and phase, are within specified limits.

calibration The means whereby the relationship between the values of the physical quantity applied to an instrument and the corresponding positions of the index are determined.

cascade control system A control system wherein one controller (the master) provides the command signal to one or more other controllers (slaves).

chart A paper sheet or surface on which a permanent record is made.

closed-loop control system A control system possessing monitoring feedback, the deviation signal formed as a result of this feedback being used to control the action of a final control element in such a way as to tend to reduce the deviation to zero.

command signal An input signal to a control system which will determine the controlled condition value.

comparing element The element which receives as input the command signal and the controlled condition and provides as an output the deviation.

constancy The ability to reproduce a continuously measured quantity over a period of time. The conditions of the test are usually specified.

continuous action Some part or a complete control system whose output is a continuous function of the input.

control action The relationship between the input and output signals of a control system.

controlled condition The physical quantity or condition of the controlled body, process or machine which the system is to control.

controlled device A body, process or machine which has a particular condition controlled by the system.

controller In a process control system this unit will combine the function of the input, comparing, amplifying, and signal processing elements.

control system   An arrangement of elements (amplifiers, converters, human operators, etc.) interconnected and interacting in such a way as to maintain, or to affect in a prescribed manner, some condition of a body, process or machine which forms part of the system.

correcting unit   In a process control system this unit combines the motor and correcting elements.

correction   An amount which must be added to or subtracted from the indicated value to obtain the true value of the measured quantity.

critically damped   This is the minimum degree of damping in an instrument or control system which will prevent oscillation after an abrupt change.

damped   An instrument or control system is damped when there is a progressive reduction in the amplitude of successive oscillations after an abrupt change.

d.c. tacho generator   A d.c. generator which provides an output voltage proportional to its speed.

dead zone   The region wherein a change of the input signal causes no change in the output signal.

derivative action   The action of a control element where the output signal is proportional to the rate of change of the input signal.

derivative action time   In a proportional plus derivative controller this is the time interval in which the proportional action signal increases by an amount equal to the derivative action signal, when the rate of change of deviation is constant.

desired value   The value of the controlled condition which the operator desires the system to maintain.

detecting element   The part of a measuring or control system which responds directly to the value of the controlled condition.

deviation   The difference between the measured value of the controlled condition and the command signal.

discontinuous action   Some part, or a complete control system, whose output is a discontinuous function of the input. Examples are on-off and bang-bang.

discrimination   The smallest change in the measured quantity which will produce an observable movement of the index.

distance/velocity lag The time period between the alteration of a signal and its unchanged arrival at another part of the system.

disturbance Any change inside or outside the control system which upsets the equilibrium.

dynamic stability A system's ability to return to a stable state after a disturbance.

feedback A signal transmitted or fed back from a later to an earlier stage.

feedforward A supplementary signal transmitted or fed along a separate path, parallel to the main forward path, from an initial to a later stage.

final controlling element The element whose action occurs directly on the controlled body, process or machine, e.g. a valve.

gain The ratio of output to input signals, which are of the same physical form, in any part of a control system.

graduation The marking or setting out of a scale.

hunting The prolonged oscillation or cycling of a controlled variable.

hysteresis The internal energy loss in an element that results in an output signal which depends not only on the input signal but whether it is increasing or decreasing in value.

index The indicator which, by its position in relation to a scale, provides a value of the measured quantity, e.g. pointer, light-spot, liquid surface, recording pen or stylus.

indicating instrument A measuring instrument in which the value of the measured quantity is visually indicated, but not recorded.

indication error The difference between the true value of the measured quantity and the indicated value.

inherent regulation A process property which results in equilibrium after a disturbance without any monitoring feedback.

input signal The signal which when received by an element results in some action.

instrument range The range of values over which an instrument is able to measure.

integral action   The action of a control element where the output signal changes at a rate proportional to its input signal.

integral action time   In a proportional plus integral controller, this is the time interval in which integral action increases by an amount equal to the proportional action signal, when the deviation is constant.

kinetic control system   A control system, the purpose of which is to control the displacement, or the velocity, or the acceleration, or any higher time-derivative of the position of the controlled device.

load   In a kinetic control system this may be the controlled device, or the properties, e.g. inertia, friction, of the controlled device that affect the operation of the system. For a process control or regulating system this is the rate at which material or energy is fed into, or removed from, the plant.

main forward path   The route from the command signal, taken by the various signals, through to the controlled device.

measuring element   This element receives the signal from the detecting element and provides a signal representative of the controlled condition.

measuring instrument   An apparatus for determining and exhibiting in some suitable manner the magnitude of a physical quantity or condition presented to it.

misalignment   The deviation present in a position control system.

motor element   The element which moves the correcting element as a result of a signal from an automatic controller.

natural frequency   A frequency at which free oscillation occurs.

observation error   The error introduced by an observer when reading an instrument.

offset   A continuing deviation usually occurring when proportional action is used alone.

on-off action   A particular case of two-step action, where one of the output signal values is zero.

open-loop control system   A control system without monitoring feedback.

output signal   The signal from one element to the next element in the loop.

overdamping An amount of damping which is greater than that required for critical damping.

overshoot The amount by which the maximum instantaneous value of the step function response exceeds the steady-state value.

plant The installation in which a process is carried out.

process The act of physically or chemically changing (including combining) matter or of converting energy.

process control system A control system, the purpose of which is to control some physical quantity or condition of a process.

proportional action The action of a control element which provides an output signal that is proportional to its input signal.

proportional band The range of values of deviation which result in the full operating range of output signal of the controlling unit as a result of proportional action only. It may be expressed as a percentage of the controller's scale range.

proportional controller A controller which provides only proportional action.

ranging Adjusting an instrument so that the index movement is in agreement with a scale at two or more positions.

ratio control system A control system in which two or more physical quantities or conditions are maintained at a predetermined ratio.

recording instrument A measuring instrument which records the values of the measured quantity on a chart.

regulating system A control system, the purpose of which is to hold constant the value of the controlled condition or to vary it in a predetermined manner.

repeatability The ability of an instrument to reproduce readings during a short duration test under fixed conditions.

resonant frequency The frequency, in a control system, at which the ratio of the amplitude of the controlled condition to the command signal is maximum.

response time With reference to a step function input signal this is the time interval between the step in the input signal and the first coincidence of the output signal with the final steady value of the output signal.

scale   A set of marks and numbers over which the index moves in order to provide a reading.

scale error   The difference between the position of a scale mark and its theoretical position on a correctly graduated scale.

scale mark   One of the marks which forms part of a scale.

scale range   The variation in the measured quantity that can be read on the scale.

self-acting controller   An automatic controller which obtains the energy required for its operation from the process it is controlling.

sensitivity   The sensitivity of an instrument at any indicated value is the relationship between the index movement and the change in the measured quantity that produces it.

servomechanism   An automatic monitored kinetic control system which includes a power amplifier in the main forward path.

servomotor   The final control element present in a servomechanism. It is the motor which receives the output from the amplifier element and drives the load.

setting   The adjustment of an instrument such that the index movement agrees with a pre-established scale at two or more points.

settling time   The time taken for the index of an instrument, or the controlled condition of a system, to reach and remain within a specified deviation from its final steady value, after an abrupt change.

set value   The command signal which is supplied to a regulating system.

signal   A physical quantity used to transmit information between one element of a control system and another.

signal processing   The manipulation of information contained in a signal by modulating, demodulating, mixing, gating, computing or filtering.

span   The input signal range that corresponds to the designed working range of the output signal.

stability   For an instrument this means that repeated readings taken over long periods, under defined conditions, give the same results. A system is considered stable if the response to an impulse input approaches zero as time approaches infinity. Also, with reference to a system, stability means that a bounded input produces a bounded output.

steady state   The final condition that a physical quantity of a system reaches when the effects of all external disturbances have ceased.

step function response   The transient response resulting from an input signal or disturbance which is a sudden occurrence or step function.

stiffness (coefficient)   When considering a kinetic control system this is the force or torque per unit deviation.

summing amplifier   An amplifier which receives two or more input voltages or currents and produces an output voltage which is proportional to their sum.

swashplate pump   A pump whose cylinders are arranged axially and whose pistons, or their connecting rods, act together on a slanting or inclined member in such a way that when relative rotation between the slanting member and the cylinder system takes place the pistons are caused to reciprocate.

synchro   An electromechanical device used for data transmission.

synchro control differential transmitter   A synchro, the rotor of which is mechanically positioned, for modifying electrical angular information received and for transmitting information corresponding to the sum or difference of the synchro and electrical angles. It is normally used to supply control transformers or other control differential transmitters.

synchro control transformer   A synchro whose primary is supplied with electrical angular information (from the connected control transmitter or control differential transmitter) and whose secondary supplies a voltage proportional to the difference between the synchro angle and the electrical angle.

synchro control transmitter   A synchro, the rotor of which is mechanically positioned, for transmitting electrical information corresponding to angular positions of the rotor. It is normally used to supply control transformers and/or control differential transmitters. On open circuit with rated voltages applied to the primary winding, the secondary supplies three single-phase voltages in phase with each other.

three-term controller   A controller which provides proportional, integral and derivative actions.

torque motor   A motor of any type, but usually a.c., which does not rotate continuously, but is arranged to exert a torque opposing, for example, that of a spring or gyroscope.

transducer   A device used for converting a signal or physical quantity of one kind into a corresponding physical quantity of another kind.

transient response   The time variation of the output signal that results when an input signal or disturbance of some specific nature is applied.

two-step action   The action of a control element when the output signal changes from one predetermined value to another as a result of the input signal changing sign.

two-step controller   A controller whose output signal changes from one predetermined value to another as a result of the deviation changing sign.

two-term controller   A controller which provides proportional action and either integral or derivative action.

undamped natural frequency   The natural frequency of oscillation of a system that would occur if damping were reduced to zero.

under damping   A degree of damping in a system which is so small that when a disturbance occurs one or more cycles of oscillation take place.

valve land   That part of the piston of a piston valve which cuts off the flow of fluid through a port by covering it.

variable stroke pump   A radial or swashplate pump in which the crank throw or swash angle respectively can be varied so that the amount of fluid delivered per revolution of the pump can be varied.

zero error   The indication given by an instrument when the measured quantity has a zero value.

COMPUTING TERMS

accumulator   A register that collects or accumulates the results of a computation

address   A binary number that specifies a particular memory location.

algorithm   A defined sequence of operations which leads to the solution of a problem.

alphanumeric   A set of characters which includes letters, numbers and some punctuation marks.

analogue computer A computer which uses data in the form of continuously variable physical quantities. The data representing, for example, a pressure or a temperature, is usually transduced into an electrical quantity which is an analogue of the data.

arithmetic and logic unit (ALU) A part of the central processing unit where arithmetic and logical operations are performed.

assemble The preparation of a machine-language program from a program written in a symbolic language such as BASIC or FORTRAN.

auxiliary storage Additional memory which is usually outside the main computer memory, e.g. floppy disk.

BASIC Beginners' All-purpose Symbolic Instruction Code. A symbolic high-level programming language.

binary number system A number system using only 0 and 1 and having a base of 2.

bit The smallest unit of data in binary notation; may be 0 or 1.

bus An electrical conductor which transmits power or data within the computer.

byte A group of adjacent bits which form a storage unit in the memory.

cathode ray tube (CRT) A display device forming part of an oscilloscope or television screen.

central processing unit (CPU) The arithmatic and logic unit and the control section of a computer considered together. The main memory may also be considered as part of this complete unit.

chip A tiny thin slice of silicon with an integrated circuit on its surface.

clock A pulse generator which provides a common timing signal to the microprocessor, the memory and the input and output devices.

compiler A program which converts high-level language into machine code.

computer A device which will accept data, perform prescribed functions on the data and then supply the results of the operations.

control unit This device enables the CPU to execute a particular task by order to units inside and outside the CPU.

digital computer A computer which uses discrete signals to represent numerical values.

disk A flat circular metal or plastic disk with magnetic surfaces on which data can be written and therefore stored.

EPROM Erasable Programmable Read Only Memory. A non-volatile memory which can be programmed and erased.

FORTRAN FORmula TRANslation. A high-level language used by scientists and engineers.

gate A logic element which operates on an applied binary signal. The gate will have a specified logical function, e.g. AND, OR, NOT.

hard copy A permanent record of computer output, usually in a printed form.

hardware The physical equipment that comprises a computer system.

hexadecimal number system A number system with a base of 16 using the numerals 0 to 9 and the letters A to F.

high-level programming language A programming language which is problem or procedure oriented, e.g. BASIC or FORTRAN.

input Data or programs which are received by a computer from an external source.

input/output device A unit which is used to transmit data to the computer or receive information from it.

instruction A set of characters which specify an operation to be performed as a unit of a program.

integrated circuit (IC) An electronic circuit formed on the surface of a tiny silicon chip.

interface A circuit whereby one part of a computer communicates with another.

machine language A set of binary instructions that can be interpreted or executed directly by a computer.

memory The data storage part of a computer.

microcomputer A digital computer comprised of a microprocessor and an electronic memory.

microprocessor A CPU located on a single silicon chip.

non-volatile memory A permanent memory whose contents remain even when power is disconnected.

output The results of computer processing of data.

peripheral A device connected to the computer.

port A physical communication point between the CPU and a peripheral.

printer A device which prints characters onto paper.

program A related set of instructions that directs and instructs the computer in accomplishing specific operations to solve a problem.

program counter A register containing the address of the next instruction.

PROM Programmable Read Only Memory. A non-volatile memory which can be programmed using special equipment.

RAM Random Access Memory. A volatile electronic memory that can be erased and modified.

read To obtain information from an input device or memory.

register A short-term memory storage unit.

ROM Read only memory. A non-volatile memory whose contents are fixed during manufacture.

software Computer programs.

store To save information in a computer memory.

terminal A computer input and/or output device.

video display unit (VDU) An output device, usually a television screen.

volatile memory A memory whose contents are lost when power is disconnected.

word The unit of information which can be transmitted, stored and operated upon at one time.

word processing The manipulation of written material, e.g. letters, reports, memos, etc.

write To transfer information into a computer memory.

non-volatile memory A type of memory that does not lose its contents when the power is disconnected.

output The result or data generated by a computer.

peripheral A device outside of the computer.

port A physical connection point used in the CPU and terminal.

program A sequence of instructions that enable a computer to carry out a task.

PROM Programmable Read Only Memory, which can be altered by the user but only once.

RAM Random Access Memory, memory that can be read from and written to.

ROM Read Only Memory, memory that can only be read and not written to.

software Computer programs.

store To save or retain data in computer memory.

terminal A combination of keyboard and video display unit (VDU), an input device and an output device.

VDU Visual Display Unit, commonly a cathode ray tube.

word A group of bits treated as a unit by the computer.

word processing A program which enables text to be manipulated.

Index